WITCH STORIES

COLLECTED BY
E. LYNN LINTON,
AUTHOR OF "AZETH THE EGYPTIAN,"
"AMYMONE," ETC.

"Thou shalt not suffer a witch to live."
—Exodus xxii. 18.

PREFACE.

In offering the following collection of witch stories to the public, I do not profess to have exhausted the subject, or to have made so complete a summary as I might have done, had I been admitted into certain private libraries, which contain, I believe, many concealed riches. But I had no means of introduction to them, and was obliged to be content with such authorities as I found in the British Museum, and the other public libraries to which I had access. I do not think that I have left much untold; but there must be, scattered about England, old MSS. and unique copies of records concerning which I can find only meagre allusions, or the mere names of the victims, without a distinctive fact to mark their special history. Should this book come to a second edition, any help from the possessors of these hitherto unpublished documents would be a gain to the public, and a privilege which I trust may be afforded me.

Neither have I attempted to enter into the philosophy of the subject. It is far too wide and deep to be discussed in a few hasty words; and to sift such evidence as is left us— to determine what was fraud, what self-deception, what actual disease, and what the exaggeration of the narrator— would have swelled my book into a far more important and bulky work than I intended or wished. As a general rule, I think we may apply all the four conditions to every case reported; in what proportion, each reader must judge for himself. Those who believe in direct and personal intercourse between the spirit-world and man, will probably accept every account with the unquestioning belief of the sixteenth and seventeenth centuries; those who have faith in the calm and uniform operations of nature, will hold chiefly to the doctrine of fraud; those who have seen much of disease and that strange condition called "mesmerism," or "sensitiveness," will allow the presence of absolute nervous derangement, mixed up with a vast amount of conscious deception, which the insane credulity and marvellous ignorance of the time rendered easy to practise; and those who have been accustomed to sift evidence and examine witnesses, will be utterly dissatisfied with the loose statements and wild distortion of every instance on record.

E. LYNN LINTON.

London, 1861.

The Witches of Scotland.

Scotland was always foremost in superstition. Her wild hills and lonely fells seemed the fit haunting-places for all mysterious powers; and long after spirits had fled, and ghosts had been laid in the level plains of the South, they were to be found lingering about the glens and glades of Scotland. Very little of graceful fancy lighted up the gloom of those popular superstitions. Even Elfame, or Faërie, was a place of dread and anguish, where the devil ruled heavy-handed and Hell claimed its yearly tithe, rather than the home of fun and beauty and petulant gaiety as with other nations: and the beautiful White Ladies, like the German Elle-women, had more of bale than bliss as their portion to scatter among the sons of men. Spirits like the goblin Gilpin Horner, full of malice and unholy cunning,—like grewsome brownies, at times unutterably terrific, at times grotesque and rude, but then more satyr-like than elfish,— like May Moulachs, lean and hairy-armed, watching over the fortunes of a family, but prophetic only of woe, not of weal,—like the cruel Kelpie, hiding behind the river sedges to rush out on unwary passers-by, and strangle them beneath the waters,—like the unsained laidly Elf, who came tempting Christian women, to their souls' eternal perdition if they yielded to the desires of their bodies,—like the fatal Banshie, harbinger of death and ruin,—were the popular forms of the Scottish spirit-world; and in none of them do we find either love or gentleness, but only fierceness and crime, enmity to man and rebellion to God. But saddest and darkest and unholiest of all was the belief in witchcraft, which infested society for centuries like a sore eating through to the very heart of humanity, and which was nowhere more bitter and destructive than among the godly children of our Northern sister. Strange that the land of the Lord should have been the favourite camping-ground of Satan, that the hill of Zion should have had its roots in the depths of Tophet!

The formulas of the faith were as gloomy as the persons. The power of the evil eye; the faculty of second sight, which always saw the hearse plumes, and never the bridal roses; the supremacy of the devil in this God-governed world of ours, and the actual and practical covenant into which men and women daily entered with him; the unlimited influence of the curse, and the sin and mischief to be wrought by charm and spell; the power of casting sickness on whomsoever one would, and the ease with which a blight could be sent on the corn, and a murrain to the beasts, by those who had not wherewithal to stay their hunger for a day, these were the chief signs of that fatal power with which Satan endowed his chosen ones—those silly, luckless chapmen who bartered away their immortal souls for no mess of pottage even, and no earthly good to breath or body, but only that they might harm their neighbours and revenge themselves on those who crossed them. Sometimes, indeed, they had no need to chaffer with the devil for such faculties: as in the matter of the evil eye; for Kirk, of Aberfoyle, tells us that "some are of so venomous a Constitution, by being radiated in Envy and Malice, that they pierce and kill (like a Cockatrice) whatever Creature they first set their Eyes on in the Morning: so was it with Walter Grahame, some Time living in the Parock wherein now I am, who killed his own Cow after commending its Fatness, and shot a Hair with his Eyes, having praised its Swiftness (such was the Infection of ane Evill Eye); albeit this was unusual, yet he saw no Object but what was obvious to other Men as well as to himselfe." And a certain woman looking over the door of a byre or cowhouse, where a neighbour sat milking, shot the calf dead and dried up and sickened the cow, "by the venomous glance of her evill eye." But perhaps she had got that venom by covenant with the devil; for this was one of the prescriptive possessions of a witch, and ever the first dole from the Satanic treasury. When Janet Irving was brought to trial (1616) for unholy dealings with the foul fiend, it was proved—for was it not sworn to? and that was quite sufficient legal proof in all witchcraft cases—that he had told her "yf schoe bure ill-will to onie bodie, to look on them with opin eyis, and pray evill for thame in his name, and schoe sould get hir hartis desyre;" and in almost every witch trial in Scotland the "evil eye" formed part of the counts of indictment against the accused. The curse was as efficacious. Did a foul-mouthed old dame give a neighbour a handful of words more forcible than courteous, and did terror, or revenge, induce, or simulate, a nervous seizure in consequence, the old dame was at once carried off to the lock-up, and but few chances of escape lay between her and the stake beyond. To be skilful in healing, too, was just as dangerous as to be powerful in sickening; and to the godly and unclean of the period all sorts of devilish cantrips lay in "south-running waters" and herb drinks, and salves made of simples; while the use of bored stones, of prayers said thrice or backwards, of "mwildis" powders, or any other more patent form of witchcraft, though it might restore the sick to health, yet was fatally sure to land the user thereof at the foot of the gallows, and the testimony of the healed friend was the strongest strand in the hangman's cord. This, indeed, was the saddest feature in the whole matter—the total want of all gratitude, reliance, trustiness, or affection between a "witch" and her friends. The dearest intimate she had gave evidence against her frankly, and without a second thought of the long years of mutual help and kindliness that had gone before; the neighbour whom she had nursed night and day with all imaginable tenderness and self-devotion, if he took a craze and dreamed of witchcraft, came forward to distort and exaggerate every remedy she had used, and every art she had employed; her very children turned against her without pity or remorse, and little lips, scarce dry from the milk of her own breasts, lisped out the glibbest lies of all. Most pitiful, most sad, was the state of these poor wretches; but instructive to us, as evidencing the strength of superstition, and the weakness of every human virtue when brought into contact and collision with it. What other gifts and powers belonged to the witches will be best gathered from the stories themselves; for varied as they are, there is a strange thread of likeness running through them all; specially is there a likeness in all of a time or district, as might be expected in a matter which belonged so much to mere imitation.

Scotland played an unenviable part in the great witch panic that swept like an epidemic over Europe during the sixteenth and seventeenth centuries. It suited with the stern, uncompromising, Puritan temper, to tear this accursed thing from the heart of the nation, and offer it, bleeding and palpitating, as a sacrifice to the Lord; and accordingly we find the witch trials of Scotland conducted with more severity than elsewhere, and with a more gloomy and savage fanaticism of faith. Those who dared question the truth of even the most unreliable witnesses and the most monstrous statements were accused of atheism and infidelity—they were Sadducees and sinners—men given over to corruption and uncleanness, with whom no righteous servant could hold any terms. And then the ministers mingled themselves in the fray; and the Kirk like the Church, the presbyter like the priest, proved to be on the side of intolerance and superstition, where, unfortunately, priests of all creeds have ever been. And when James VI. came with his narrow brain and selfish heart, to formularize the witch-lie into a distinct canon of arbitrary faith, and give it increased political significance and social power, the reign of humanity and common sense was at an end, and the autocracy of cruelty and superstition began. It is a dreary page in human history; but so long as a spark of superstition lingers in the world it will have its special and direct uses.

The first time we hear of Scottish witches was when St. Patrick offended them and the devil alike by his uncompromising rigour against them: so they tore off a piece of a rock as he was crossing the sea and hurled it after him; which rock became the fortress of Dumbarton in the days which knew not St. Patrick. Then there was the story of King Duff (968), who pined away in mortal sickness, by reason of the waxen image which had been made to destroy him; but by the fortunate discovery of a young maiden who could not bear torture silently, he was enabled to find the witches—whom he burnt at Forres in Murray, the mother of the poor maiden who could not bear torture among them: enabled, too, to save himself by breaking the wasting waxen image roasting at the "soft" fire, when almost at its last turn. Then we come to Thomas of Ercildoune, whom the Queen of Faërie loved and kept; and then to Sir Michael Scot of Balweary, that famous wizard, second to none in power; while a little further removed from those legendary times we see the dark figure of William Lord Soulis, who was boiled to death at Nine Stane Brig, in fitting punishment for his crimes. And then in 1479 twelve mean women and several wizards were burnt at Edinburgh for roasting the king in wax, and so endangering the life of the sovereign liege in a manner which no human aid could remedy; and the Earl of Mar was at their head, and very properly burnt too. And in 1480 Incubi and Succubi held the land between them, and even the young lady of Mar gave herself up to the embraces of an Incubus—a hideous monster, utterly loathsome and deadly to behold; and if the young ladies of the nobility could do such things, what might not be expected from the commonalty? But now we come out into the light of written history, and the first corpse lying on the threshold is that of the beautiful Lady Glammis (1537).

THE STORY OF LADY GLAMMIS[1]

One of the earliest, as she was one of the noblest, victims of this delusion, politics and jealousy had as much to do with her death as had superstition. Because she was "one of the Douglases," and not because she was convicted as a sorceress, did William Lyon find her so easy a victim to his hate. For it was he—the near relative of her first husband, "Cleanse the Causey" John Lyon, Lord Glammis,—who ruined her, and brought her young days to so shameful an end. And had he not cause? Did she not reject him when left a widow, young and beautiful as but few were to be found in all the Scottish land? and, rejecting him, did she not favour Archibald Campbell of Kessneath instead, and make over to him the lands and the beauties he had coveted for himself, even during the life of that puling relative of his, "Cleanse the Causey"? Matter enough for revenge in this, thought William Lyon: and the revenge he took came easy to his hand, and in fullest measure. For Lady Glammis, daughter of George, Master of Angus, and grand-daughter of that brave old savage, Archibald Bell-the-Cat, was in no great favour with a court which had disgraced her grandfather, and banished her brother; and consequently she found no protection there from the man who was seeking her ruin. Perhaps, too, she had mixed herself up with the court feuds and parties then so common, and thus had given some positive cause of offence to a government which must crush if it would not be crushed, and extirpate if it would not be destroyed. Be that as it may, William Lyon soon gathered material for an accusation, and Lady Glammis found that if she would not have his love he would have her life. She was accused on various counts; for having procured the death of her first husband by "intoxication," or unholy drugging, for a design to

---

[1] Pitcairn's 'Scottish Criminal Trials.'

poison the king, and for witchcraft generally, as a matter of daily life and open notoriety; and for these crimes she was burnt, notwithstanding her beauty and wealth and innocence and high-hearted bravery, notwithstanding her popularity—for she was beloved by all who knew her—and the honour of her stainless name. And once more, as so often, hatred conquered love, and the innocent died that the guilty might be at rest.

I must omit any lengthened notice of the trial of Janet Bowman in 1572, as also of that of a notable witch Nicneven, which name, "generally given to the Queen of the Fairies, was probably bestowed upon her on account of her crimes, and who, when 'her collore craig with stringis whairon wes mony knottis' was taken from her, gave way to despair, exclaiming, 'Now I have no hoip of myself,' saying, too, that 'she cared not whether she went to heaven or to hell.'" The Record has preserved nothing beyond the mere fact of the first, while the foregoing extract is all that I can find of the second; so that I am obliged to pass on to the pitiful tale of—

BESSIE DUNLOP AND THOM REID.[2]

Poor douce honest Bessie Dunlop, spouse to Andro Jak in Lyne, deposed, after torture, on the 8th day of November, 1576, that one day, as she was going quietly enough between her own house and Monkcastle yard, "makeand hevye sair dule with hirself," weeping bitterly for her cow that was dead, and her husband and child who were lying "sick in the land-ill," she herself still weak after gissane, or child-birth, she met "ane honest, wele, elderlie man, gray bairdit, and had ane gray coitt with Lumbart slevis of the auld fassoun; ane pair of gray brekis and quhyte schankis gartanit abone the kne; ane blak bonet on his heid, cloise behind and plane befoir, with silkin laissis drawin throw the lippis thairof; and ane quhyte wand in his hand." This was Thom Reid, who had been killed at the battle of Pinkye (1547), but was now a dweller in Elfame, or Fairy Land. Thom stopped her, saying, "Gude day, Bessie." "God speid yow, gude man," says she. "Sancta Marie," says he, "Bessie, quhy makis thow sa grit dule and sair greting for ony wardlie thing?" Bessie told him her troubles, poor woman, and the little old gray-bearded man consoled her by assuring her that though her cow and her child should die, yet her husband would recover; and Bessie, after being "sumthing fleit" at seeing him pass through a hole in the dyke too narrow for any honest mortal to pass through, yet returned home, comforted to think that the gude man would mend. After this, she and Thom foregathered several times. At the third interview he wanted her to deny her baptism, but honest Bessie said that she would rather be "revin at horis taillis" (riven at horses' tails); and on the fourth he came to her own house, and took her clean away from the presence of her husband and three tailors—they seeing nothing—to where an

---

[2] Pitcairn's 'Scottish Criminal Trials.'

assemblage of eight women and four men were waiting for her. "The men wer cled in gentilmennes clething, and the wemens had all plaidis round about them, and wer verrie semelie lyke to se." They were the "gude wychtis that wynnit (dwelt) in the court of Elfame," and they had come to persuade her to go back to fairy-land with them, where she should have meat and clothing, and be richly dowered in all things. But Bessie refused. Poor crazed Bessie had a loyal heart if but a silly head, and preferred her husband and children to all the substantial pleasures of Elfame, though Thom was angry with her for refusing, and told her "it would be worse for her."

Once, too, the queen of the fairies, a stout, comely woman, came to her, as she was "lying in gissane," and asked for a drink, which Bessie gave her. Sitting on her bed, she said that the child would die, but that the husband would recover; for Andro Jak seems to have been but an ailing body, often like to find out the Great Mysteries for himself, and Bessie was never quite easy about him. Then Thom began to teach her the art of healing. He gave her roots to make into salves and powders for kow or yow (cow or sheep), or for "ane bairne that was tane away with ane evill blast of wind or elfgrippit:" and she cured many people by the old man's fairy teaching. She healed Lady Johnstone's daughter, married to the young Laird of Stanelie, by giving her a drink brewed under Thom's auspices, namely, strong ale boiled with cloves, ginger, aniseed, liquorice, and white sugar, which warmed the "cauld blude that gaed about hir hart, that causit hir to dwam and vigous away," or, as we would say, to swoon. And she cured John Jake's bairn, and Wilson's of the town, and her gudeman's sister's cow; but old Lady Kilbowye's leg was beyond them both. It had been crooked all her life, and now Thom said it would never mend, because "the march of the bane was consumit, and the blude dosinit" (the marrow was consumed, and the blood benumbed). It was hopeless, and it would be worse for her if she asked for fairy help again. Bessie got fame too as a "monthly" of Lyne. A green silk lace, received from Thom's own hand, tacked to their "wylie coitt" and knit about their left arms, helped much in the delivery of women. She lost the lace, insinuating that Thom took it away again, but kept her fatal character for more medical skill than belonged to an ordinary canny old wife. In the recovery of stolen goods, too, she was effective, and what she could not find she could at least indicate. Thus, she told the seekers that Hugh Scott's cloak could not be returned, because it had been made into a kirtle, and that James Baird and Henry Jameson would not recover their plough irons, because James Douglas, the sheriff's officer, had accepted a bribe of three pounds not to find them. Lady Blair having "dang and wrackit" her servants on account of certain linen which had been stolen from her, learnt from Bessie, prompted by Thom, that the thief was no other than Margaret Symple, her own friend and relation, and that she had dang and wrackit innocent persons to no avail. Bessie never allowed that Thom's intercourse with her was other than honest and well conducted. Once only he took hold of her apron to drag her away to Elfame with him; but this was more in the way of persuasion than love making, and she indignantly denied the home questions put to her by the judges with but scant delicacy or feeling for an honest woman's shame. Interrogated, she said that she often saw Thom going about like other men. He would be in the streets of Edinburgh, on market days and other, handling goods like any living body, but she never spoke to him unless he spoke first to her: he had forbidden her to do so. The last time she met him before her arrest he told her of the evil that was to come, but buoyed her up with false hopes, assuring her that she would be well treated, and eventually cleared. Poor Bessie Dunlop! After being cruelly tortured, her not very strong brain was utterly disorganized, and she confessed whatever they chose to tax her with, rambling through her wild dreamy narrative with strange facility of imagination, and with more coherence and likelihood, than are to be found in those who came after her. Adjudged as "confessit and fylit," she was "convict and brynt" on the Castle Hill of Edinburgh—a mournful commentary on her elfin friend's brave words and promises.

ALISON PEARSON AND THE FAIRY FOLK.[3]

On the 28th of May, 1588, Alesoun Peirsoun, in Byrehill, was haled before a just judge and sapient jury on the charge of witchcraft, and seven years' consorting with the fairy folk. This Alesoun Peirsoun, or, as we should now write it, Alison Pearson, had a certain cousin, one William Simpson, a clever doctor, who had been educated in Egypt; taken there by a man of Egypt, "ane gyant," who, it is to be supposed, taught him many of the secrets of nature then hidden from the vulgar world. During his absence, his father, who was smith to king's majesty, died for opening of "ane preist-buik and luking vpoune it:" which showed the tendency of the family. When Mr. William came back he found Alison afflicted with many diseases, powerless in hand and foot, and otherwise evilly holden; and he cured her, being a skilful man and a kindly, and ever after obtained unlimited influence over the brain and imagination of his crazed cousin. He abused this influence by taking her with him to fairy land, and introducing her to the "gude wychtis," whose company he had affected for many years. In especial was she much linked with the Queen of Elfame, who might have helped her, had she been so minded. One day being sick in Grange Muir, she lay down there alone, when a man in green suddenly appeared to her and said that if she would be faithful he would do her good. She cried for help, and then charged him in God's name, and by the law he lived on, that if he came in God's name and for the welfare of her soul, he would tell her. He passed away on this, and soon after a lusty man, and many other men and women came to her, and she passed away with them further than she could tell; but not before she had "sanit," or blessed herself and prayed. And then she saw piping, and merriness, and good cheer, and puncheons of

---

[3] Pitcairn.

16

wine with "tassis," or cups to them. But the fairy folk were not kind to Alison. They tormented her sorely, and treated her with great harshness, knocking her about and beating her so that they took all the "poustie," or power out of her side with one of their heavy "straiks," and left her covered with bruises, blue and evil-favoured. She was never free from her questionable associates, who used to come upon her at all times and initiate her into their secrets, whether she liked it or no. They showed her how they gathered their herbs before sunrise, and she would watch them with their pans and fires making the "saws" or salves that could kill or cure all who used them, according to the witches' will; and they used to come and sit by her, and once took all the "poustie" from her for twenty weeks. Mr. William was then with them. He was a young man, not six years older than herself, and she would "feir" (be afraid) when she saw him. What with fairy teaching, and Mr. William's clinical lectures, half-crazed Alison soon got a reputation for healing powers; so great, indeed, that the Bishop of St. Andrews, a wretched hypochondriac, with as many diseases as would fill half the wards of an hospital, applied to her for some of her charms and remedies, which she had sense enough to make palateable, and such as should suit episcopal tastes: namely, spiced claret (a quart to be drunk at two draughts), and boiled capon as the internal remedies, with some fairy salve for outward application. It scarcely needed a long apprenticeship in witchcraft to prescribe claret and capon for a luxurious prelate who had brought himself into a state of chronic dyspepsia by laziness and high living; yet the jury thought the recipe of such profound wisdom that Alison got badly off on its account.

Mr. William was very careful of Alison. He used to go before the fairy folk when they set out on the whirlwinds to plague her—"for they are ever in the blowing sea-wind," said Allie—and tell her of their coming; and he was very urgent that she should not go away with them altogether,

17

since a tithe of them was yearly taken down to hell, and converts had always first chance. But many people known to her on earth were at Elfame. She said that she recognized Mr. Secretary Lethington, and the old Knight of Buccleugh, as of the party; which was equivalent to putting them out of heaven, and was a grievous libel, as the times went. Neither Mr. William's care nor fairy power could save poor Alison. After being "wirreit (strangled) at ane staik," she was "conuicta et combusta," never more to be troubled by epilepsy or the feverish dreams of madness.

THE CRIMES OF LADY FOWLIS.[4]

Nobler names come next upon the records. Katherine
Roiss, Lady Fowlis, and her stepson, Hector Munro, were
tried on the 22nd of June, 1590, for "witchcraft,
incantation, sorcery, and poisoning." Two people were in
the lady's way: Margery Campbell the young lady of
Balnagown, wife to George Roiss or Ross of Balnagown,
Lady Katherine's brother; and Robert Munro her stepson,
the present baron of Fowlis, and brother to the Hector
Munro above mentioned. If these two persons were dead,
then George Ross could marry the young Lady Fowlis, to
the pecuniary advantage of himself and the family.
Hector's quarrel was on his own account, and was with
George Munro of Obisdale, Lady Katherine's eldest son.
The charges against the Lady Katherine were, the unlawful
making of two pictures or images of clay, representing the
young lady of Balnagown and Robert Munro, which
pictures two notorious witches, Christian Ross and
Marioune M'Alester, *alias* Loskie Loncart, set up in a
chamber and shot at with elf arrows—ancient spear or
arrow-heads, found in Scotland and Ireland, and of great
account in all matters of witchcraft. But the images of clay
were not broken by the arrow-heads, for all that they shot
eight times at them, and twelve times on a subsequent trial,
and thus the spell was destroyed for the moment; but
Loskie Loncart had orders to make more, which she did
with a will. After this the lady and her two confederates
brewed a stoup or pailful of poison in the barn at
Drumnyne, which was to be sent to Robert Munro. The pail
leaked and the poison ran out, except a very small quantity
which an unfortunate page belonging to the lady tasted, and
"lay continewallie thaireftir poysonit with the liquour."
Again, another "pig" or jar of poison was prepared; this

---

[4] Pitcairn.

time of double strength—the brewer thereof that old sinner, Loskie Loncart, who had a hand in every evil pie made. This was sent to the young laird by the hands of Lady Katherine's foster-mother; but she broke the "pig" by the way, and, like the page, tasting the contents, paid the penalty of her curiosity with her life. The poison was of such a virulent nature that nor cow nor sheep would touch the grass whereon it fell; and soon the herbage withered away in fearful memorial of that deed of guilt. She was more successful in her attempts on the young Lady Balnagown. Her "dittay" sets forth that the poor girl, tasting of her sister-in-law's infernal potions, contracted an incurable disease, the pain and anguish she suffered revolting even the wretch who administered the poison, Catherine Niven, who "scunnerit (revolted) with it sae meikle, that she said it was the sairest and maist cruel sight that ever she saw." But she did not die. Youth and life were strong in her, and conquered even malice and poison— conquered even the fiendish determination of the lady, "that she would do, by all kind of means, wherever it might be had, of God in heaven, or the devil in hell, for the destruction and down-putting of Marjory Campbell." Nothing daunted, the lady sent far and wide, and now openly, for various poisons; consulting with "Egyptians" and notorious witches as to what would best "suit the complexion" of her victims, and whether the ratsbane, which was a favourite medicine with her, should be administered in eggs, broth, or cabbage. She paid many sums, too, for clay images, and elf arrows wherewith to shoot at them, and her wickedness at last grew too patent for even her exalted rank to overshadow. She was arrested and arraigned, but the private prosecutor was Hector Munro, who was soon to change his place of advocate for that of "pannel;" and the jury was composed of the Fowlis dependents. So she was acquitted; though many of her creatures had previously been convicted and burnt on the same charges as those now made against her; notably Cristiane Roiss, who, confessing to the clay image and the elf arrows, was quietly burnt for the same.

Hector Munro's trial was of a somewhat different character. His stepmother does not seem to have had much confidence in mere sorcery: she put her faith in facts rather than in incantations, and preferred drugs to charms: but Hector was more superstitious and more cowardly too. In 1588, he had communed with three notorious witches for the recovery of his elder brother, Robert; and the witches had "pollit the hair of Robert Munro, and plet the naillis of his fingeris and taes;" but Robert had died in spite of these charms, and now Hector was the chief man of his family. Parings of nails, clippings of hair, water wherein enchanted stones had been laid, black Pater-Nosters, banned plaids and cloths, were all of as much potency in his mind as the "ratoun poysoun" so dear to the lady; and the method of his intended murder rested on such means as these. They made a goodly pair between them, and embodied a fair proportion of the intelligence and morality of the time. After a small piece of preliminary sorcery, undertaken with his foster-mother, Cristiane Neill Dayzell, and Mariaoune M'Ingareach, "one of the most notorious and rank witches of the country," it was pronounced that Hector, who was sick, would not recover, unless the principal man of his blood should suffer for him. This was found to be none other than George Munro, of Obisdale, Lady Katherine's eldest son, whose life must be given that Hector's might be redeemed. George, then, must die; not by poison but by sorcery; and the first step to be taken was to secure his presence by Hector's bedside. "Sewin poistes" or messengers did the invalid impatiently send to him; and when he came at last, Hector said never a word to him, after his surly "Better now that you have come," in answer to his half-brother's unsuspecting "How's a' wi' ye?" but sat for a full hour with his left hand in George's right,

21

working the first spell in silence, according to the directions of his foster-mother and the witch. That night, an hour after midnight, the two women went to a "piece of ground lying between two manors," and there made a grave of Hector's length, near to the sea-flood. A few nights after this—and it was January, too—Hector, wrapped in blankets, was carried out of his sick bed, and laid in this grave; he, his foster-mother, and M'Ingareach all silent as death, until Cristiane should have gotten speech with their master, the devil. The sods were then laid over the laird, and the witch M'Ingareach sat down by him, while Cristiane Dayzell, with a young boy in her hand, ran the breadth of nine rigs or furrows, coming back to the grave, to ask the witch "who was her choice." M'Ingareach, prompted of course by the devil, answered that "Mr. Hector was her choice to live and his brother George to die for him." This ceremony was repeated thrice, and then they all returned silently to the house, Mr. Hector carried in his blankets as before. The strangest thing of all was that Mr. Hector was not killed by the ceremony.

Hector Munro was now convinced that everything possible had been done, and that his half-brother must perforce be his sacrifice. In his gratitude he made M'Ingareach keeper of his sheep, and so uplifted her that the common people durst not oppose her for their lives. It was the public talk that he favoured her "gif she had been his own wife;" and once he kept her out of the way "at his own charges," when she was cited to appear before the court to answer to the crime of witchcraft. But in spite of the tremendous evidence against him, Hector got clear off, as his stepmother had done before him, and we hear no more of the Fowlis follies and the Fowlis crimes. Nothing but their rank and the fear of the low people saved them. Slighter crimes than theirs, and on more slender evidence, had been sufficient cause for condemnation ere now; and Lady Katherine's poisonings, and Hector Munro's incantations, would have met with the fate the one at least deserved, save for the power and aid of clanship.

BESSIE ROY.

The month after this trial, Bessie Roy, nurreych (nurse) to the Leslies of Balquhain, was "dilatit" for sorcery generally, and specially for being "a common awa-taker of women's milk." She took away poor Bessie Steel's, when she came to ask alms, and only restored it again when she was afraid of getting into trouble for the fault. She was also accused of having, "by the space of tual yeiris syne or thairby," past to the field with other women to pluck lint, but instead of following her lawful occupation, she had made "ane compas (circle) in the eird, and ane hoill in the middis thairof;" out of which hole came, first, a great worm which crept over the boundary, then a little worm, which crept over it also, and last of all another great worm, "quhill could nocht pas owre the compas, nor cum out of the hoill, but fell doune and deit." Which enchantment or sorcery being interpreted meant, by the first worm, William King, who should live; by the second small worm, the unborn babe, of which no one yet knew the coming life; and by the third large worm the gude wyffe herself, who should die as soon as she was delivered. Notwithstanding the gravity and circumstantiality of these charges, Bessie Roy marvellously escaped the allotted doom, and was pronounced innocent. "Quhairvpoune the said Bessie askit act and instrument." Two women tried the day before, Jonet Grant and Jonet Clark, were less fortunate. Charged with laming men and women by their devilish arts—whereof was no attempt at proof—they were convicted and burnt; as also was Meg Dow, in April of the same year, for the "crewell murdreissing of twa young infant bairns," by magic.

And now we come to a very singular group of trials, opened out by that clumsy, superstitious pedant, whose name stands accursed for vice and cruel cowardice and the utmost selfishness of fear—James VI. of Scotland. If anything were wanting to complete one's abhorrence of

Carr's patron and Raleigh's murderer—one's contempt of the upholder of the divine right of kings in his own self-adoration as God's vicegerent upon earth—it would be his part in the witch delusion of the sixteenth century. Whatever of blood-stained folly belonged specially to the Scottish trials of this time—and hereafter—owed its original impulse to him; and every groan of the tortured wretches driven to their fearful doom, and every tear of the survivors left blighted and desolate to drag out their weary days in mingled grief and terror, lie on his memory with shame and condemnation ineffaceable for all time.

THE DEVIL'S SECRETARY.[5]

On the 26th of December, 1590, John Fian, *alias* Cuningham (spelt Johanne Feane, *alias* Cwninghame), master of the school at Saltpans, Lothian, and contemptuously recorded as "Secretar and Register to the Devil," was arraigned for witchcraft and high treason. There were twenty counts against him, the least of which would have been enough to have lighted up a witch-fire on that fatal Castle Hill, for the bravest and best in the land. First, he was accused of entering into a covenant with Satan, who appeared to him in white, as he lay in bed, musing and thinking ("mwsand and pansand," says the dittay in its quaint language) how he should be revenged on Thomas Trumbill, for not having whitewashed his room, according to agreement. After promising his Satanic majesty allegiance and homage, he received his mark, which later was found under his tongue, with two pins therein thrust up to their heads. Again, he was found guilty—"fylit" is the old legal term—of "feigning himself to be sick in the said Thomas Trumbill's chamber, where he was stricken in great ecstacies and trances, lying by the space of two or three hours dead, his spirit taken, and suffered himself to be carried and transported to many mountains, as he thought through all the world, according to his depositions." Note, that these depositions were made in the midst of fearful torture, and recanted the instant after. Also, he was found guilty of suffering himself to be carried to North Berwick church, where, together with many others, he did homage to Satan, as he stood in the pulpit, making doubtful speeches, saying, "Many come to the fair, and all buy not wares;" and desired him "not to fear, though he was grim, for he had many servants who should never want, or ail nothing, so long as their hair was

---

[5] Pitcairn.

on, and should never let one tear fall from their eyes so long as they served him;" and he gave them lessons, and said, "Spare not to do evil, and to eat and drink and be blithe, taking rest and ease, for he should raise them up at the latter day gloriously." But the pith of the indictment was that he, Fian, and sundry others to be spoken of hereafter, entered into a league with Satan to wreck the king on his way to Denmark, whither, in a fit of clumsy gallantry, he had set out to visit his future queen. While he was sailing to Denmark, Fian and a whole crew of witches and wizards met Satan at sea, and the master, giving an enchanted cat into Robert Grierson's hand, bade him "cast the same into the sea, holà," which was accordingly done; and a pretty capful of wind the consequence. Then, when the king was returning from Denmark, the devil promised to raise a mist which should wreck him on English ground. To perform which feat he took something like a football— it seemed to Dr. Fian like a wisp—and cast it into the sea, whereupon arose the great mist which nearly drove the cumbrous old pedant on to English ground, where our strong-fisted queen would have made him pay for his footing in a manner not quite congenial to his tastes. But, being a Man of God, none of these charms and devilries prevailed against him. A further count was, that once again he consorted with Satan and his crew, still in North Berwick church, where they paced round the church wider shins (wider scheins?), that is, contrary to the way of the sun. Fian blew into the lock—a favourite trick of his—to open the door, and blew in the lights which burned blue, and were like big black candles held in an old man's hand round about the pulpit. Here Satan as a "mekill blak man, with ane blak baird stikand out lyke ane gettis (goat's) baird; and ane hie ribbit neise, falland doun scharp lyke the beik of ane halk; with ane lang rumpill (tail); cled in ane blak tatie goune, and ane ewill favorit scull bonnett on his heid; haifand ane blak buik in his hand," preached to them, commanding them to be good servants to him, and he would be a good master to them, and never let them want. But he made them all very angry by calling Robert Grierson by his Christian name. He ought to have been called "Ro' the Comptroller, or Rob the Rower." This slip of the master's displeased them sorely, and they ran "hirdie girdie" in great excitement, for it was against all etiquette to be named by their earthly names; indeed, they always received new names when the devil gave them their infernal christening, and they made themselves over to him and denied their holy baptism. It was at this meeting that John Fian was specially accused of rifling the graves of the dead, and dismembering their bodies for charms. And many other things did this Secretar and Register to the devil. Once, at the house of David Seaton's mother, he breathed into the hand of a woman sitting by the fire, and opened a lock at the other end of the kitchen. Once he raised up four candles on his horse's two ears, and a fifth on the staff which a man riding with him carried in his hand. These magic candles gave as much light as the sun at noonday, and the man was so terrified that he fell dead on his own threshold. He sent an evil spirit, who tormented a man for twenty weeks; and he was seen to chase a cat, and in the chase to be carried so high over a hedge that he could not touch her head. The dittay says he flew through the air—a not infrequent mode of progression with such people. When asked why he hunted the cat, he said that Satan had need of her, and that he wanted all the cats he could lay hands on, to cast into the sea, and cause storms and shipwrecks. He was further accused of endeavouring to bewitch a young maiden by his devilish cantrips and horrid charms; but, by a wile of the girl's mother, up to men's arts, he practised on a heifer's hairs instead of the girl's, and the result was that a luckless young cow went lowing after him everywhere—even into his school-room— rubbing herself against him, and exhibiting all the languish and desire of a love-sick young lady. A curious old plate represents John Fian and the heifer in grotesque attitudes; the heifer with large, drooping, amorous eyes, intensely ridiculous—the schoolmaster with his magic wand drawing circles in the sand. These, with divers smaller charges, such as casting horoscopes, and wearing modewart's (mole's) feet upon him, amounting in all to twenty counts, formed the sum of the indictment against him. He was put to the torture. First, his head was "thrawed with a rope" for about an hour, but still he would not confess; then they tried fair words and coaxed him, but with no better success; and then they put him to the "most severe and cruell pains in the worlde," namely, the boots, till his legs were completely crushed, and the blood and marrow spouted out. After the third stroke he became speechless; and they, supposing it to be the devil's mark which kept him silent, searched for that mark, that by its discovery the spell might be broken. So they found it, as stated before, under his tongue, with two charmed pins stuck up to their heads therein. When they were drawn out—that is, after some further torture—he confessed anything which it pleased his tormentors to demand of him, saying how, just now, the devil had been to him all in black, but with a white wand in his hand; and how, on his, Fian's, renouncing him, he had brake his wand, and disappeared. The next day he recanted this confession. He was then somewhat restored to himself, and had mastered the weakness of his agony. Whereupon it was assumed that the devil had visited him through the night, and had marked him afresh. They searched him—pulling off every nail with a turkas, or smith's pincers, and then thrusting in needles up to their heads; but finding nothing more satanic than blood and nerves, they put him to worse tortures, as a revenge. He made no other relapse, but remained constant now to the end; bearing his grievous pains with patience and fortitude, and dying as a brave man always knows how to die, whatever the occasion. Finding that nothing more could be made of him, they mercifully came to an end. He was strangled and burnt "in the Castle Hill of Edinbrough, on a Saterdaie, in the ende of Januarie last past 1591;" ending a may be loose and not over-heroic life in a manner worthy of the most glorious martyr of history. John Fian, schoolmaster of Saltpans, with no great idea to support him, and no admiring friends to cheer him on, bore himself as nobly as any hero of them all, and vindicated the honour of manhood and natural strength in a way that exalts our common human nature into something godlike and divine.

THE GRACE WIFE OF KEITH
AND HER CUMMERS[6]

Fian was the first victim in the grand battue offered now to the royal witchfinder; others were to follow, the manner of whose discovery was singular enough. Deputy Bailie David Seaton of Tranent, had a half-crazed servant-girl, one Geillis Duncan, whose conduct in suddenly taking "in hand to helpe all such as were troubled or grieved with anie kinde of sicknes or infirmitie," excited the righteous suspicions of her master. To make sure he tortured her, without trial, judge, or jury; first, by the "pillie-winks" or thumbscrews, and then by "thrawing,"—wrenching, or binding her head with a rope—an intensely agonizing process, and one that generally comes in as part of the service of justice done to witch and wizard. Not confessing, even under these persuasions, she was "searched," and the mark was found on her throat: whereupon she at once confessed; accusing, among others, the defunct John Fian, or Cuningham, Agnes Sampson at Haddington, "the eldest witch of them all," Agnes Tompson of Edinburgh, and Euphemia Macalzean, daughter of Lord Cliftonhall, one of the senators of the College of Justice. Agnes Sampson's trial came first. She was a grave, matronlike, well-educated woman, "of a rank and comprehension above the vulgar, grave and settled in her answers, which were to some purpose," and altogether a woman of mark and character. She was commonly called the "grace wyff" or "wise wyff" of Keith; and, doubtless, her superior reputation brought on her the fateful notice of the half-crazed girl; also it procured her the doubtful honour of being carried to Holyrood, there to be examined by the king himself. At first she quietly and firmly denied all that she was charged with, but after

---

[6] Pitcairn.

having been fastened to the witches' bridle,[7] kept without sleep, her head shaved and thrawn with a rope, searched, and pricked, she, too, confessed whatever blasphemous nonsense her accusers chose to charge her with, to the wondrous edification of her kingly inquisitor. She said that she and two hundred other witches went to sea on All-Halloween, in riddles or sieves, making merry and drinking by the way: that they landed at North Berwick church, where, taking hands, they danced around, saying—

"Commer goe ye before! commer goe ye! Gif ye will not goe before, commer let me!"

Here they met the devil, like a mickle black man, as John Fian had said, and he marked her on the right knee; and this was the time when he made them all so angry by calling Robert Grierson by his right name, instead of Rob the Rower, or Ro' the Comptroller. When they rifled the graves, as Fian had said, she got two joints, a winding-sheet, and an enchanted ring for love-charms. She also said that Geillis Duncan, the informer, went before them, playing on the Jew's harp, and the dance she played was Gyllatripes; which so delighted gracious Majesty, greedy of infernal news, that he sent on the instant to Geillis, to play the same tune before him; which she did "to his great pleasure and amazement." Furthermore, Agnes Sampson confessed that, on asking Satan why he hated King James, and so greatly wished to destroy him, the foul fiend answered: "Because he is the greatest enemy I have;" adding, that he was "un homme de Dieu," and that Satan had no power against him. A pretty piece of flattery, but

---

[7] An iron instrument so constructed, that by means of a hoop which passed over the head, a piece of iron having four prongs or points, was forcibly thrust into the mouth, two of these being directed to the tongue and palate, the others pointing outwards to each cheek. This infernal machine was secured by a padlock. At the back of the collar was fixed a ring, by which to attach to a staple in the wall of her cell.—*Pitcairn's 'Scottish Criminal Trials.'*

availing the poor wise wife nothing as time went on. Her indictment was very heavy; fifty-three counts in all; for the most part relating to the curing of disease by charm and incantation, and to foreknowledge of sickness or death. Thus, she took on herself the sickness of Robert Kerse in Dalkeith, then cast it back, by mistake, on Alexander Douglas, intending it for a cat or a dog: and she put a powder containing dead men's bones under the pillow of Euphemia Macalzean, when in the pains of childbirth, and so got her safely through. As she went on, and grew more thoroughly weakened in mind and body, she owned to still more monstrous things. Item, to having a familiar, in shape of a dog by name Elva, whom she called to her by "Holà! master!" and conjured away "by the law he lived on." This dog or devil once came so near to her that she was "fleyt," but she charged him by the law he lived on to come no nearer to her, but to answer her honestly—"Should old Lady Edmistoune live?" "Her days were gane," said Elva; "and where were the daughters?" "They said they would be there," said Agnes. He answered, one of them should be in peril, and that he should have one of them. "It sould nocht be sa," cried the wise wife; so he growled and went back into the well. Another time she brought him forth out of the well to show to Lady Edmistoune's daughters, and he frightened them half to death, and would have devoured one of them had not Agnes and the rest gotten a grip of her and drawn her back. She sent a letter to Marian Leuchope, to raise a wind that should prevent the queen from coming; and she caused a ship, 'The Grace of God,' to perish—the devil going before, while she and the rest sailed over in a flat boat, entered unseen, ate of the best, and swamped the vessel afterwards. For helping her in this nefarious deed, she gave twenty shillings to Grey Meill, "ane auld, sely, pure plowman," who usually kept the door at the witches' conventions, and who had attended her in this shipwreck adventure. Then, she was one of the foremost and most active in the celebrated storm-raising for the destruction, or at least the damage of the king on his return from Denmark; giving some curious particulars in addition to what we have already had in Fian's indictment; as, that she and her sister witches baptized the cat by which they raised the storm, by putting it, with various ceremonies, thrice through the chimney crook. "Fyrst twa of thame held ane fingar, in the ane syd of the chimnay cruik, and ane vther held ane vther fingar in the vther syd, the twa nebbis of the fingaris meting togidder; than they patt the catt thryis throw the linkis of the cruik, and passit it thryis vnder the chimnay;" afterwards they knit four dead men's joints to the four feet of the cat, and cast it into the sea, ready now to work any amount of mischief that Satan might command. Then she made a "picture," or clay image, of Mr. John Moscrop, father-in-law to Euphemia Macalzean, to destroy him, at the said Euphemia's desire. She was also at all the famous North Berwick meetings, where Dr. Fian was secretary, registrar, and lock-opener; where they were baptized of the fiend, and received formally into his congregation; where he preached to them as a great black man; and where they rifled graves and meted out the dead among them. She also confessed to taking a black toad, and hanging him up by his heels, collecting all his venom in an oyster shell for three days, and she told the king that it was then she wanted his fouled linen, when she would have enchanted him to death—but she never got it. She had two Pater Nosters, the white and the black. The white ran thus:—

"White Pater Noster,
God was my Foster,
He fostered me,
Under the Book of Palm Tree.
Saint Michael was my Dame,
He was born at Bethlehem,
He was made of flesh and blood,

God send me my right food:
My right food and dyne two
That I may to yon kirk go,
To read upon yon sweet book,
Which the mighty God of Heaven shoop.
Open, open, Heaven's yaits,
Stick, stick, Hell's yaits.
All Saints be the better,
That hear the white prayer Pater Noster."

There was no harm in this doggerel, nor yet much good; little of blessing, if less of banning; nor was the Black more definite. It was shorter, which ought to have ranked as a merit:—

Black Pater Noster.
"Four newks in this house, for holy angels,
A post in the midst, that's Christ Jesus,
Lucas, Marcus, Matthew, Joannes,
God be into this house and all that belongs us."

To "sain" or charm her bed she used to say,—
"Matthew, Mark, Luke, and John
The bed be blest that I ly on."
And when the butter was slow in coming, it was enough if she chanted slowly—
"Come, butter, come!
Come, butter, come!
Peter stands at the gate.
Waiting for a buttered cake,
Come, butter, come,"

said with faith and unction, she was sure to have at once a lucky churn-full.

These queer bits of half-papistical, half-nonsensical doggerel were considered tremendous sins in those days, and the use of them was quite sufficient to bring any one to the scaffold; as their application would, for a certainty, destroy health, and gear, and life, if it were so willed. And for all these crimes—storm-raising, cat-baptizing, and the rest—Agnes Sampson, the grave, matronlike, well-educated grace wife of Keith, was bound to a stake, strangled, and burnt on the Castle Hill, with no one to seek to save her, and no one to bid her weary soul God-speed!

Barbara Napier, wife to a burgess of Edinburgh, and sister-in-law to the Laird of Carschoggill, was then seized—accused of consorting with Agnes Simpson, and consulting with Richard Grahame, a notorious necromancer, to whom she gave "3 ells of bombezie for his paynes," all that she might gain the love and gifts of Dame Jeane Lyon, Lady Angus; also of having procured the witch's help to keep the said Dame Jeane "fra wometing quhen she was in bredin of barne." She was accused of other and more malicious things; but acquitted of these: indeed the "assisa" which tried her was contumacious and humane, and pronounced no doom; whereon King James wrote a letter demanding that she be strangled, then burnt at the stake, and all her goods escheated to himself. But Barbara pleaded that she was with child; so her execution was delayed until she was delivered, when "nobody insisting in the persute of her, she was set at libertie." The contumacious majority was tried for "wilful error on assize—acquitting a witch," but got off with more luck than usual.[8]

Euphemia Macalzean,[9] or as we should say, Maclean, was even higher game. She was the daughter of Lord Cliftonhall, and wife of Patrick Moscrop, a man of wealth and standing; a firm, passionate, heroic woman, whom no

---

[8] Fountainhall says that she was convict and burnt; but is this not a mistake? Pitcairn gives the actual trial, and King James's angry letter against the contumacious assisa.

[9] Pitcairn.

tortures could weaken into confession, no threats terrify into submission. She fought her way, inch by inch, but she was "convict" at last, and condemned to be burnt alive: the severest sentence ever pronounced against a witch. In general they were "wirreit" or strangled before being burnt. There is good reason to believe that her witchcraft was made merely the pretence, while her political predilections, her friendship for the Earl of Bothwell, and her Catholic religion, were the real grounds of the king's enmity to her, and the causes of the severity with which she was treated. Her indictment contains the ordinary list of witch-crimes, diversified with the additional charge of bewitching a certain young Joseph Douglas, whose love she craved and found impossible to obtain, or rather, to retain. She was accused of giving him, for unlawful purposes, "ane craig cheinzie (neck chain), twa belt cheinzies, ane ring, ane emiraut," and other jewels; trying also to prevent his marriage with Marie Sandilands, and making Agnes Simpson get back the jewels, when her spells had failed. The young wife whom Douglas married, and the two children she bore him, also came in for part of her alleged maleficent enchantments. She "did the barnes to death," and struck the wife with deadly sickness. She was also accused of casting her own childbirth pains, once on a dog, and once on the "wantoune cat;" whereupon the poor beasts ran distractedly out of the house, as well they might, and were never seen again. She managed this marvellous piece of sleight-of-hand by getting a bored stone from Agnes Sampson, and rolling "enchanted mwildis"—earth from dead men's graves—in her hair. Another time she got her husband's shirt, and caused it to be "woumplit" (folded up) and put under her bolster, whereby she sought to throw her labour pains upon him, but without effect; as is not to be wondered at. She bewitched John M'Gillie's wife by sending her the vision of a naked man, with only a white sheet about him; and Jonett Aitcheson saw him with the sleeves of his shirt "vpoune leggis, and taile about his heid." She was also accused of endeavouring to poison her husband; and it was manifest that their union was not happy—he being for the most part away from home, and she perhaps thinking of the other husband promised her, Archibald Ruthven; which promise, broken and set aside, had made such a slander and scandal of her marriage with Patrick Moscrop. And it was proved—or what went for proof in those days—that Agnes Sampson, the wise wife, had made a clay image of John Moscrop, the father-in-law, who should thereupon have pined away and died, according to the law of these enchantments, but, failing in this obedience, lived instead, to the grief and confusion of his daughter-in-law. All these crimes, and others like unto them, were quite sufficient legal causes of death; and James could gratify his superstitious fears and political animosity at the same time, while Euphemia Maclean—the fine, brave, handsome Euphemia—writhed in agony at the stake to which she was bound when burned alive in the flames: "brunt in assis quick to the deid," says the Record—the severest sentence ever passed on a witch. This murder was done on the 25th July, 1591.

"The last of Februarie, 1592, Richard Grahame wes brant at ye Cross of Edinburghe for vitchcrafte and sorcery," says succinctly Robert Birrel, "burges of Edinburghe," in his "Diarey containing divers Passages of Staite and uthers memorable Accidents, from ye 1532 zeir of our Redemption, till ye beginning of the zeir 1605." "And in 1593, Katherine Muirhead was brunt for vitchcrafte, quha confest sundrie poynts yrof." Richard Graham was the "Rychie Graham, ane necromancer," consulted by Barbara Napier; the same who gave the Earl of Bothwell some drug to make the king's majesty "lyke weill of him," if he could but touch king's majesty on the face therewith; it was he also who raised the devil for Sir Lewis Ballantyne, in his own yard in the Canongate, whereby Sir Lewis was so terrified that he took sickness and died. Even in the presence of the king himself, Rychie boasted that "he had a familiar spirit which showed him many things;" but which somehow forgot to show him the stake and the rope and the faggot, which yet were the bold necromancer's end, little as the poor cozening wretch merited such an awful doom.

THE TWO ALISONS.

June, 1596, had nearly seen a nobler victim than those usually accorded. John Stuart, Master of Orkney, and brother of the Earl, "was dilatit of consulting with umquhile Margaret Balfour, ane wich, for the destructionne of Patrik Erll of Orkney, be poysoning." In the dittay she is called "Alysoun Balfour, ane knawin notorious wich." Alisoun, after being kept forty-eight hours in the "caschiclawis"[10]—her husband, an old man of eighty-one, her son, and her young daughter, all being in ward beside her, and tortured—was induced to confess. She could not see the old man with the Lang Irons of fifty stone weight laid upon him; her son in the boots, with fifty-seven strokes; and her little daughter, aged seven, with the thumbscrews upon her tender hands, and not seek to gain their remission by any confession that could be made. But when the torture was removed from them and her, she recanted in one of the most moving and pathetic speeches on record—availing her little then, poor soul! for she was burnt on the Castle Hill, December 16th, 1594, and her confession treasured up to be used as future evidence against John Stuart. Thomas Palpla, a servant, was also implicated; but as he had been kept eleven days and nights in the caschiclaws (or caspie-claws); twice in the day for fourteen hours "callit in the buitis;" stripped naked and scourged with "ropes in sic soirt that they left nather flesch nor hyde vpoun him;" and, as he recanted so soon as the torture was removed, his confession went for but little. So John, Master of Orkney, was let off, when perhaps he had been the only guilty one of the three.

---

[10] Dr. Jamieson conjectures the word to signify "warm hose." After encircling the leg with an iron framework, it was put into a moveable furnace or chauffer, and during the progress of heating the iron, the intended questions were successively put.—*Note in Pitcairn's 'Scottish Criminal Trials.'*

In October[11] of the same year (1596), Alesoun Jollie, spous to Robert Rae, in Fala, was "dilatit of airt and pairt" in the death of Isobell Hepburn, of Fala: and the next month, November, Christian Stewart, in Nokwalter, was strangled and burnt for the slaughter of umquhile Patrick Ruthven, by taking ane black clout from Isobell Stewart, wherewith to work her fatal charm. It does not appear that she did anything more heinous than borrow a black cloth from Isobell, which might or might not have been left in Ruthven's house; but suspicion was as good as evidence in those days, and black clouts were dangerous things to deal with when women had the reputation of witches. So poor Christian Stewart was strangled and burnt, and her soul released from its troubles by a rougher road, and a shorter, than what Nature would have taken if left to herself. "Strange that while all these dismal affairs were going on at Edinburgh, Shakspeare was beginning to write his plays, and Bacon to prepare his essays. Ramus had by this time shaken the Aristotelian philosophy, and Luther had broken the papal tyranny."[12] Truly humanity walks by slow marches, and by painful stumbling through thorny places!

---

[11] Pitcairn's 'Scottish Criminal Trials.'
[12] Chambers' 'Domestic Annals of Scotland.'

THE TROUBLES OF ABERDEEN.[13]

Aberdeen was not behind her elder sister. One man and twenty-three women were burned in one year alone for the crime of witchcraft and magic; and the Records of the Dean of Guild faithfully detail the expenses which the town was put to in the process. On the 23rd of February, 1597, Thomas Leyis cost them two pounds thirteen shillings and fourpence, for "peattis, tar barrelis, fir, and coallis, to burn the said Thomas, and to Jon Justice for his fie in executing him;" but Jonet Wischart (his mother), and Isobel Cocker, cost eleven pounds ten shillings for their joint cremation; with ten shillings added to the account for "trailling of Monteithe (another witch of the same gang) through the streits of the town in ane cart, quha hangit herself in prison, and eirding (burying) her." The dittay against these several persons set forth various crimes. Janet Wischart, who was an old woman notorious for her evil eye, was convicted, amongst other things, of having "in the moneth of Aprile or thairby, in anno nyntie ane yeiris, being the first moneth in the raith (the first quarter) at the greiking" (breaking) of the day, cast her cantrips in Alexander Thomson's way, so that one half of the day his body was "rossin" (burned or roasted) as if in an oven, with an extreme burning drought, and the other half melting away with a cold sweat. Upon Andrew Wobster—who had put a linen towel round her throat, half choking her, and to whom she said angrily, "Quhat wirreys thow me? thow salt lie: I sall give breid to my bairnis this towmound, and thou sall nocht byd ane moneth with thin, to gif tham breid"—she had laid such sore cantrips, that he died as she predicted: which was a cruel and foul murder in the eyes of the law, forbye the sin of witchcraft. But she had other victims as well. James

---

[13] 'Antiquarian Researches of Aberdeen, by Gavin Turriff: Spalding Club Miscellany. Chambers' 'Domestic Annals,' to the end of the Aberdeen trials.

Low, a stabler, refused to lend her his kiln and barn, so he took a "dwining" illness in consequence, "melting away like ane burning candle till he died." His wife and only son died too, and his "haill geir, surmounting three thousand pounds, are altogether wrackit and away." Beside this evidence there was his own testimony availing; for he had often said on his death-bed, that if he had lent Jonet what she had demanded, he would never have suffered loss. She had also once brought down a dozen fowls off a roost, dead at her feet; and had ruined a woman and her husband, by bidding them take nine grains or ears of wheat, and a bit of rowan tree, and put them in the four corners of the house— for all the mischance that followed after was due to this unholy charm; and once she raised a serviceable wind in a dead calm, by putting a piece of live coal at two doors, whereby she was enabled to winnow some wheat for herself, when all the neighbours were standing idle for want of wind; and she bewitched cows, so that they gave poison instead of milk; and oxen, so that they became furious under the touch of any one but herself; and she sent cats to sit on honest folks' breasts, and give them evil dreams and the horrors; and furthermore, she was said to have gone to the gallows in the Links, and to have dismembered the dead body hanging there, for charms; and twenty-two years ago she was proved to have been found sitting in a field of corn before sunrising, peeling blades, and finding that it would be "ane dear year," for the blade grew widershins, and it was only when it grew sungates (from east to west) that it would be a full harvest and cheap bread for the poor; and once her daughter-in-law had found her, and another hag, sitting stark by her fireside, the one mounted on the shoulders of the other, working charms for her health and well-being. So she cost the town of Aberdeen the half of eleven pounds odd shillings, for the most effectual manner of carrying out her sentence, which was, that she "be brint to the deid."

43

Her son Thomas Leyis was not so fortunate as her husband and daughters: "qwik gangand devills" were these; for they escaped the flames this time, and were banished instead. But Thomas was less lucky. He was dilatit of being a common witch and sorcerer, and the partner of all his mother's evil deeds. One of his worst crimes was having danced round the market-cross of Aberdeen, he and a number of witches and sorcerers—the devil leading; "in the quhilk dans, thow, Thomas, was foremost, and led the ring, and dang the said Katherine Mitchell (another of the accused) because scho spillit your dans, and ran nocht so fast about as the rest." Thomas had a lover too, faithless Elspet Reid, and she, turning against him, as has been the manner of lovers through all time, gave tremendous evidence in his disfavour. She said that he had once offered to take her to Murrayland, and there marry her; a man at the foot of a certain mountain being sure to rise at his bidding, and supply them with all they wanted; and when he was confined in the church-house, she came and whispered to him through the window, and the man in charge of Thomas swore that she said she had been meeting with the devil according to his orders, and that when she sained herself he had "vaniest away with ane rwmleng (rumbling)." In the morning, too, before the old mother's conviction, "ane ewill spreit in lyiknes of ane pyit (magpie)," went and struck the youngest sister in her face, and would have picked out her eyes, but that the neighbours to the fore dang the foul thief out of the room; and again, on the day after conviction, and before execution, the devil came again as ane kae (crow), and would have destroyed the youngest sister entirely had he not been prevented: which two visitations were somehow hinged on to Thomas, and included in the list of crimes for which he was adjudged worthy of death.

Helen Fraser, of the same "coven," was a most dangerous witch. She had the power to make men transfer their affections, no matter how good and wholesome the wife deserted:—and she never spared her power. By her charms she caused Andrew Tullideff to leave off loving his lawful wife and take to Margaret Neilson instead: so that "he could never be reconceillit with his wife, or remove his affection frae the said harlot;" and she made Robert Merchant fall away from the duty owing to his wife, Christian White, and transfer himself and his love to a certain widow, Isobel Bruce, for whom he once went to sow corn, and fell so madly in love that he could never quit the house or the widow's side again; "whilk thing the country supposed to be brought about by the unlawful travelling of the said Helen; "and was further *testified by Robert himself*," says Chambers significantly. Helen Fraser was therefore burnt; and it is to be hoped that the men returned to their lawful mates.

Isobel Cockie, who was burnt in company with Thomas Lee's mother, old Jonet, meddled chiefly with cows and butter. She could forespeak them so that they should give poison instead of milk, and the cream she had once overlooked was never fit for the "yirning." Her landlord once offended her by mending the roof of her house while she was from home, and Isobel, who did not choose that her things should be pulled about in her absence, and perhaps some of her cantrips discovered, "glowrit up at him, and said, 'I sall gar thee forthink it that thow hast tirrit my hows, I being frae hame.'" Whereupon Alexander Anderson went home sick and speechless, and gat no relief until Isobel gave him "droggis," when his speech and health returned as of old. Isobel had been the dancer immediately after Thomas Lees at the Fish Cross, "and because the dewill playit not so melodiously and well as thow cravit, thow took his instrument out of his mouth, then tuik him on the chafts (chops) therewith, and playit thyself theiron to the haill company." What further evidence could possibly be required to prove that Isobel

Cockie was a witch, and one that "might not be suffered to live"?

Other trials did Aberdeen entertain that year on this same wise and Christian count. There was that of Andrew Man, a poor old fellow specially patronized by the Queen of Fairy who sixty years ago had come to his mother's house, where she was delivered of a bairn just like an ordinary woman, and no devil or Queen of Elfin at all. Andrew was then but a boy, but he remembered it all well, and how he carried water for her, and was promised by her that he should know all things, and should be able to cure all sorts of sickness except the "stand deid;" and that he should be "well entertainit," but should seek his meat ere he died, as Thomas Rhymer had done in years long past. Twenty-eight years after this the queen came again, and caused one of his cattle to die on a hillock called the Elf-hillock, but promised to do him good afterwards; and it was then that their guilty albeit poetic and loving intercourse began. Andrew was told in his dittay that he could cure "the falling sickness, the bairn-bed, and all other sorts of sickness that ever fell to man or beast, except the *stand-deid*, by baptizing them, reabling them in the auld corunschbald,[14] and striking of the gudis on the face, with ane foot in thy hand, and by saying their words, 'Gif thou wilt live, live; and gif thow wilt die, die,' with sundry other orisons, sic as Sanct John and the three silly brethren, whilk thow canst say when thow please, and by giving of black wool and salt as a remeid for all diseases, and for causing a man prosper, so that his blude should never be drawn." Once, Andrew Man, by putting a patient nine times through a hasp of unwatered yarn, and a cat as many times backwards through the same hasp, cured the patient by killing the cat. This was logical, and quite easy to be understood. Andrew's devil whom he affirmed to be an

---

[14] Apparently untranslateable.

angel, and whose name was Christsonday, was raised by saying Benedicite, and laid again by putting a dog under his arm, then casting it into the devil's mouth with the awful word "Maikpeblis!" "The Queen of Elphen has a grip of all the craft," says the dittay, "but Christsonday is the gudeman, and has all power under God; and thow kens sundry deid men in their company, and the king that died at Flodden, and Thomas Rhymer is there." And as the queen had been seen in Andrew's company in a rather beautiful and poetic manner, the whole affair was settled, and no man's mind was left in doubt of the old creature's guilt. For, Andrew was told, "Upon Rood-day in harvest, in this present year, whilk fell on a Wednesday, thow saw Christsonday come out of the snaw in the likeness of a staig (young male horse), and the Queen of Elphen was there, and others with her, riding upon white hackneys." "The elves have shapes and claithes like men, and will have fair covered tables, and they are but shadows, but are starker (stronger) nor men, and they have playing and dancing when they please; the queen is very pleasant, and will be auld and young when she pleases; she makes any king whom she pleases.... The elves will make thee appear to be in a fair chalmer, and yet thow wilt find thyself in a moss on the moor. They will appear to have candles, and licht, and swords, whilk will be nothing else but dead grass and straes." So Andrew's doom was sealed, for all that he denied his guilt, and he was convicted and burnt like the rest.

Marjory Mutch came to her end because, having a deadly hatred against William Smith, she bewitched his oxen, as they were ploughing, so that they all ran "wood" or mad that instant, broke the plough, and two of them plunged up over the hills to Deer, and two ran up Ithan side, and could never be taken or apprehended again. She was notorious for bewitching cattle; and that she was a witch, and good for nothing but burning, a gentleman proved to the satisfaction of all present, for he found a soft spot on her which he pricked without causing any pain; a test that ought to have been eminently satisfactory and conclusive—but was not; for she was "clenged"—cleansed, or acquitted.

Ellen Gray, convicted of many of the ordinary crimes of witchcraft, did away with all chance of mercy for herself when, on being taken, she looked over her shoulder, saying, "Is there no mon following me?" and Agnes Wobster was a witch because in a great snow she took fire out of a "cauld frosty dyke," and carried the same to her house. They were both burnt, as they merited. Jonet Leisk cast sickness and disease on all she knew, and made whole flocks run "wode" and furious; geese too; but she was "clenged," or cleared; so was Gilbert Fidlar; but Isobell Richie, Margaret Og, Helen Rogie, and others, were burnt, for the satisfaction of offended justice.

Margaret Clark, too, came to no good end, because being sent for by the wife of Nicol Ross, when in child-bed, she gave her ease by casting her pains upon Andrew Harper, who fell into such a fury and madness during her time of travail, that he could not be holden, and only recovered when the gentlewoman was delivered. And what did Violet Leys do, but bewitch William Finlay's ship so that she never made one good voyage again, all because her husband had been discharged therefrom, and Violet the witch was most mightily angered? And Isobell Straquhan, too, had she not powers banned even in the blessing? She went one day to "Elspet Murray in Woodheid, she being a widow, and asked of her if she had a penny to lend her, and the said Elspet gave her the penny; and the said Isobell took the penny and bowit (bent) it, and took a clout and a piece of red wax, and sewed the clout with a thread, the wax and the penny being within the clout, and gave it to the said Elspet Murray, commanding her to use the said clout to hang about her craig (neck), and when she saw the man she loved best, take the clout, with the penny and wax, and stroke her face with it, and she so doing, would attain into the marriage of that man whom she loved." She also made Walter Ronaldson leave off beating his wife, by sewing certain pieces of paper thick with threads of divers colours, and putting them in the barn among the corn, since which time Walter left off dinging his poor spouse, and was "subdued entirely to her love." So Isobell Straquhan made one of the tale of twenty-two unfortunate wretches who were executed in Aberdeen that year, for the various crimes of witchcraft and sorcery.

No evidence was too meagre for the witch-hunters; no accusation too absurd; no subterfuge or enormity sufficiently transparent to show the truth behind. When Margaret Aiken, "the great witch of Balwery,"[15] went about the country dilating honest women for witches, "by the mark between their eyes," it was evident to all but the heated and credulous, such as John Cowper, the minister of Glasgow, and others, that she used this as a mere means to save time, she herself having been tortured into confession, and now seeing no way of safety but by complicity and witch-finding. She told of one convention held on a hill in Atholl, where there were twenty-three hundred witches, and the devil among them. "She said she knew them all well enough, and what mark the devil had given severally to every one of them. There was many of them tried by swimming in the water, by binding of their two thumbs and their great toes together, for being thus casten in the water, they floated ay aboon." It was not only the malevolent witch that suffered in this wild raid made against reason and humanity. The doom dealt out to the witch who slew was equally allotted to the witch who saved. Yet the witchologists made a difference between the two.

---

[15] Patrick Anderson's MS. history of Scotland, quoted by Robert Chambers, in his 'Domestic Annals of Scotland.'

"Of witches there be two sorts," says Thomas Pickering, in his 'Discovrse of the damned Art of Witchcraft,' printed 1610, "*the bad witch* and *the good witch*; for so they are commonly called. The *bad witch* is he or she that hath consulted in league with the Deuill; to vse his helpe for the doing of hurte onely, so as to strike and annoy the bodies of men, women, children, and cattell, with diseases and with death itselfe; so likewise to raise tempests by sea and by land, &c. This is commonly called *the binding* witch.

"The *good witch* is he or she that by consent in a league with the Deuill doth vse his helpe for the doing of good onely. This cannot hurt, torment, curse, or kill, but onely heale and cure the hurt inflicted vpone men or cattell by badde witches. For as they can doe no good but onely hurt; so this can doe no hurt but good onely. And this is that order which the Deuill hath set in his kingdome, appointing to severall persons their severall offices and charges. And the Good Witch is commonly called the Vnbinding Witch."

But the good witch, as Pickering calls her, was no better off than the bad. Indeed she was held in even greater dread, for the black witch hurt only the body and estate, while the white witch hurt the soul when she healed the body; the healed part never being able to say "God healed me." Wherefore it was severed from the salvation of the rest, and the wholeness of the redemption destroyed. In consequence of this belief we find as severe punishments accorded to the blessing as to the banning witches; and no movement of gratitude was dreamt of towards those who had healed the most oppressive diseases, or shown the most humane feeling and kindness, if there was a suspicion that the power had been got uncannily, or that the drugs had more virtue than common.

WHITE WITCHES.[16]

Thus on November the 12th, 1597, Janet Stewart in the Canongate, Christian Levingstone in Leith, Bessie Aiken, also of Leith, and Christian Sadler of Blackhouse, were brought to trial for no worse crimes than healing and helping sundry of their neighbours. Christian Levingstone was "fylit and convict" for abusing (deceiving) Thomas Gothray, who went to her complaining that his gear went from him, and that he was bewitched; which she said was true; promising to help him, and "let him see where the witchcraft was laid." So she took him down his own stair, and dug a hole with her knife, and took out a little bag of black plaid, wherein were some grains of wheat, worsted threads of many colours, some hair, and nails of men's fingers, affirming that he was bewitched by these means, and bidding his wife catch them in her apron. If this bag had not been found, said Christian, he would have been wrackit both in mind and body; which was a clear case of "abusing," if you will. This "scho deponit in presens of my Lord Justice vpoun the tent day of Julij last past to be of veritie." She also said that her daughter had been taken away by fairy folk, and that she had learnt all her wise-wife knowledge from her, and as a proof of this knowledge, she prophesied that Gothray's wife, then "being with barne," should bear a man child; which proved to be true, to the sad strengthening of the accusations against her. Another time she and Christian Sadler were prayed by Robert Bailie, mason in Haddington, to go and cure his wife. Christian Sadler recommended her to take three pints of sweet wort, and boil it with a quantity of fresh butter; which she did, and drank it too, but with no good effects of healing, as we may suppose. Again, shortly before her accusation, she was sent for by Christian Sadler, on some other devil's deed;

---

[16] Pitcairn.

and together they made Andrew Pennycuik a cake baked with the blood of a red cock; but he could not eat it. Then they took his shirt and dipped it in the well at the back of his house, and brought it to him and put it on him, dripping as it was, "quhairthrow he maist haif sownit amang their hands," giving him to understand that now he would be mended, "albeit that it was onlie plane abusione, as the event declarit." Not finding the cake of red cock's blood or the dripping shirt of great efficacy, Andrew went then to Janet Stewart, craving his health at her hands "for God's sake;" but we are not told the result.

Janet Stewart was fylit for going to Bessie Inglis in the Kowgate, Bessie being deidlie sick; when Janet took off her "mutche and sark" (cap and shift), washed them in south-running water, and put them on her again at midnight, wet as they were, saying three times, "In the name of the Father, the Son, and the Holy Ghost." She also "fyrit," or put a hot iron into water, and burnt straw at the four corners of the bed, as Michael Clarke, smith, had learnt her; and she healed women of the mysterious child-bed disorder called wedonymph, by taking a garland of woodbine and putting them through it, afterwards cutting it into nine pieces, which she threw into the fire. This charm she said she had learnt from Mr. John Damiet, an Italian, and a notorious enchanter. And she cured sundry persons of the falling-evil by hanging a stone about their necks for five nights, which stone she said she got from Lady Crawford.

Christian Sadler was "fylit and convict" for taking in hand to heal the young Laird of Bargany, with a salve made of quicksilver, which she rubbed into the patient, alleging that she learnt it of her father; but she did the same by "unlessum" (unwholesome) means, said the dittay, she having no such knowledge as would enable her to cure leprosy, which the most expert men in medicine are not able to do. Robert Hunter, too, since deceased, having a flaw in his face, she undertook to cure with a mixture of quicksilver in a drink. She said the flaw was leprosy, but it was nothing of the kind; and "God knows how the drink was composed," but the gentleman died twelve hours after, "as was notourlie confessit of hirself, and can nocht be denyit, quhairby scho was giltie of his death be hir craft; ministering to him vnlessum things, quhairof he deit suddenlie." So the four women were convicted and condemned, sentenced to be strangled at a stake, then burnt, and all their goods forfeit to the crown. Only Bessie Aiken got off by reason of her pregnancy; and after having suffered "lang puneischment be famine and imprisonment," was finally banished the kingdom for life.

In July, 1602, James Reid suffered for the same kind of offences—taking three pennies and a piece of "creisch" (grease) from the bag of his master the devill, whom he met on Bynnie-crags, and learning from him the art of healing by means of silk laces, south-running waters, charms, incantations, and other "unlessum" means. He cured Sarah Borthwick by his sorcery and devilry, bringing her south-running water from the "Schriff-breyis-well," and casting a certain quantity of salt and wheat about her bed: and he consulted with certain for the destruction of David Libbertoune, baxter and burges of Edinburgh, his spouse, their corn, and goods, by taking a piece of raw flesh, and making nine nicks in it, then putting part under the mill door and part under the stable door; while, to ruin the land, he enchanted stones and cast them on the fields. He cured John Crystie of a swelling, by putting three silk laces round his leg for ten weeks; and his deeds becoming notorious and his character lost, he was adjudged worthy of death, and judicially murdered accordingly.

Who was safe, if a half-fed scrofulous woman had fancies and the megrims? The first person on whom her wild imagination chose to cast the grim shadow of witchcraft was surely doomed, however slight the evidence, or whatever the manifest quality of the disease. There was poor Patrick Lowrie, fylit July 23, 1605—what had he done? Why, he and Jonet Hunter, "ane notorious wich," bewitched Bessie Saweris' (Sawyer's) her corn, and took all her fisnowne (fushion, foison, pith, strength, flavour) from her; and then he fell foul of certain "ky," so that they gave no milk; and he had cured the horse of Margaret Guffok, the witch of Barnewell, twenty years ago; and struck Janet Lowrie blind; and, as a climax, uncannily helped Elizabeth Crawford's bairn in Glasgow, which had been strangely sick for the last eight or nine years. And the way in which he helped her was thus. He took a cloth off the said bairn's face, "saining" it, and crossing the face with his hand; he kept the cloth for eight days, then came back and covered her face again with it; whereupon the child slept without moving for two days, and at the end of that time Patrick Lowrie wakened her, and her eye, which "had been tynt throw disease, was restored to her, and in five days she was cured and mended." He was also fylit of having met the devil on the common waste at Sandhills, in Kyle, when a number of men and women were there; and for having entertained him under the form of a woman, one Helen M'Brune (this was a succubus); also of having received from him a hair belt, at one end of which was the similitude of "four fingeris and ane thumbe, nocht far different from the clawis of the devill;" which belt Jonet Hunter had, and it was burnt at her trial; also of having dug up dead bodies, to dismember them for his deadly charms; and also for being "ane cowmone and notorious sorcerer, warlok, and abuser of the peopill, be all vnlawfull charms and devillische incantationes, vset be him this xxiiij yeir begane." To which terrific array was added the testimony of Mr. David Mill, who said how, in his own place, he was "brutit and commonlie called Pait ye Witch, and that he gat his father's malison," and had been spoken of as sure to make an ill end. So he did, poor fellow; for the Lord Advocate threatened to prosecute the assize if they acquitted him, which insured his effectual condemnation, and Pate the Witch was burnt with his fellows.

THE MISDEEDS OF ISOBEL GRIERSON.[17]

Two years afterwards, on March the 10th, 1607, Isobel Grierson, "spous to John Bull," came into court with anything but clean hands. She was accused of having visited Adam Clarke and his wife—they lying decently in bed, their servant being in the other bed beside them—not as an honest woman, but in the form of a cat, being accompanied by other cats which made a great and fearful noise. Whereat Adam Clarke, his wife, and servant were so affrighted they were almost mad. At the same time arrived the devil in the shape of a black man, and came to the servant girl then standing on the floor, and drew her up and down the house in a fearful manner, first taking the curtche (cap) off her head and casting it into the fire, whereby the poor woman had a sickness which lasted six weeks. Isobel killed William Burnet by casting a cutting of plaid in at his door, after which the devil, for the space of half a year, perpetually appeared to him as a naked child, holding an enchanted picture in his hand, and standing before the fire; but sometimes he appeared as Isobel herself, who, when William Burnet called to her by name, would vanish away. So she haunted and harried him till he pined away and died. She bewitched Mr. Brown, of Prestonpans, by throwing an enchanted "tailzie" (cut or piece) of beef at his door, sending the devil to distress him for half a year, appearing to him herself in the form of an infant bairn, and so hardly treating him, that Brown died as Burnet had done. Then she bewitched Robert Peddan, who got no good from any remedy, and knew not what ailed him, until he suddenly remembered that he and Isobel had had a quarrel about nine shillings which he owed her and would not pay; so he went to her and paid her, asking humbly for his health again; which came. Robert Peddan deposed, too, that, being once

---

[17] Pitcairn and Chambers.

56

at his house, she wanted her cat, whereupon she opened his window, put out her hand, and drew the cat in: at which time was working a brewing of good sound ale, which all turned to "gutter dirt." Another time she or her spirit went at night to his house and drew Margaret Donaldson, his wife, out of her bed, and flung her violently against the floor; whereat the wife was very ill and sore troubled, and cried out on her. Isobel, hearing of this, went to the neighbours, and said they were to bring her and Margaret together again; which they did; and Margaret had her health for nine or ten days. But Meg, not leaving off calling out against her, Isobel went to her, "and spak to hir mony devillisch and horribill words," saying, "The faggot of hell lycht on thé, and hell's cauldron may thow seith in!" So Meg was sick again after this; and as a poor beggarwoman coming to the door to ask meat told her she was bewitched, for that she had the right stamp of it, the case grew serious, and Margaret cried out more loudly than before. Then Isobel went again to her house with a creil on her back, and said passionately, "Away, theiff! I sall haif thy hairt for bruitting of me sae falslie;" which so frightened Meg that she took to her bed, and Isobel was arrested, tried, convicted, and burnt.

BARTIE PATERSON'S CHARM.[18]

That same year James Brown was ill. Bartie Paterson went to him, and gave him drinks and salves made of green herbs, and bade him "sitt doun on his kneis thre seuerall nychtis, and everie nycht, thryse nyne tymes, ask his helth at all living wichtis, aboue and vnder the earth in the name of Jesus." He gave Alexander Clarke a drink of Dow-Loch water—poor Alexander Clarke was fond of consulting witches—causing him each time he lifted the mug to say, "I lift this watter in the name of the Father, Sone, and Holy Ghaist, to do guid for their helth for quhom it is liftit." And he was able to cast a spell over cattle by saying—

"I charme thé for arrow-schot,
For dor-schot, for wondo-schot,
For ey-schot, for tung-schot,
For lever-schot, for lung-schot,
For hert-schot, all the maist,
In the name of the Father, the Sone, and Haly Ghaist.
To wend out of fleisch and bane,
Into stek and stane,
In the name of the Father, the Sone, and Haly Ghaist.
Amen."

So the law put a stop to his incantations, and he was strangled and burnt, and all his goods escheit to the crown. But the crown did not get a very full haul, for poor Bartie was scarce removed from beggary.

---

[18] Pitcairn.

BEIGIS TOD AND HER COMPEERS.[19]

In 1608, on May the 27th, Beigis Tod in Lang Nydrie came to her fate. She had long been a frequenter of Sabbaths, and once was reproved by the devil for being late, when she answered respectfully, "Sir, I could wyn na soner!" Immediately thereafter she passed to her own house, took a cat, and put it nine times through the chimney work, and then sped to Seaton Thorne "be north the yet," where the devil called Cristiane Tod, her younger sister, and brought her out. But Cristiane took a great fright and said, "Lord, what wilt thou do with me?" to whom he answered, "Tak na feir, for ye sall gang to your sister Beigis, to ye rest of hir cumpanie quha are stayand vpoun your cuming at the Thorne." Cristiane Tod, John Graymeill, Ersche (Irish), Marion, and Margaret Dwn, who were of that company that night, had all been burnt, so now Beigis had her turn. She fell out with Alexander Fairlie, and made his son vanish away by continual sweating and burning at his heart, during which time Beigis appeared to him nightly in her own person, but during the day in the similitude of a dog, and put him almost out of his wits. Alexander went to her to be reconciled, and asked her to take the sickness off his son, which at first she refused, but afterwards consenting, she went and healed the youth, a short time before she was arrested—to be burnt. Two years after this Grissel Gairdner was burnt for casting sickness upon people; and in 1613 Robert Erskine and his three sisters were executed—he was beheaded—for poisoning and treasonable murder against his two nephews. But before this, in 1608, the Earl of Mar brought word to the Privy Council that some women taken at Broughton or Breichin, accused of witchcraft, and being put to "ane assize and convict albeit they persevered constant in their

---

[19] Pitcairn.

deniall to the end, yet they wes burnet *quick* after sic ane crewell maner that sum of thame deit in dispair, renunceand and blasphemand, and vtheris, half brunt, brak out of the fyre and wes cassin *quick* into it againe, quhill they war brunt to the deid." Even this horrible scene does not seem to have had any effect in humanizing men's hearts, or opening their eyes to the infamy into which their superstition dragged them; for still the witch trials went on, and the young and the old, and the beautiful and the unlovely, and the loved and the loveless, were equally victims, cast without pity or remorse to their frightful doom.

Sixteen hundred and sixteen was a fruitful year for the witch-finders. There was Jonka Dyneis of Shetland,[20] who, offended with one Olave, fell out in most vile cursings and blasphemous exclamations, saying that within a few days his bones should be "raiking" about the banks: and as she predicted so did it turn out—Olave perishing by her sorcery and enchantments. And not content with this, she cursed the other son of the poor widowed mother, and in fourteen days he also died, to Jonka's own undoing when the Shetlanders would bear her iniquities no longer. And there was Katherine Jonesdochter, also of Shetland, who cruelly transferred her husband's natural infirmities to a stranger: and Elspeth Reoch of Orkney, who pulled the herb called melefowr (millfoil?) betwixt her finger and thumb, saying, "In Nomine Patris, Filii, et Spiritûs Sancti," thus curing men's distempers in a devilish and unwholesome manner: and Agnes Scottie, who refused to speak word to living man before passing "the boundis of hir ground, and their sat down, plaiting her feit betwixt the merchis," that a certain woman might have a good childbirth; who was also convicted "of washing the inner nuke of her plaid and aprone," for some wicked and sinister purpose; for what

---

[20] Dalyell's 'Darker Superstitions of Scotland.'

sane Scottish woman would wash her clothes more than was absolutely necessary? and who could curse as well as cure, and transfer as well as give the sickness she could heal: and Marable Couper who threw a "wall piet" at a man who spoke ill of her, and made his face bleed, so that he went mad, and could only be recovered by her laying her hands on him, whereby he received his senses and his health again: and Agnes Yullock, who went to the guid wyfe of Langskaill, and by touching her gave her back her health: and William Gude, who had power over all inanimate things, and by his touch could give them back the virtue they had lost. These are only a few, very few, of the cases to be found in the various judiciary records of the year 1616—a year no worse than others, and no better, where all were bad and blood-stained alike.

In 1618 one of the saddest stories of all was to be read in the tears of a few sorrowful relatives, and in the exultation of those fanatics who rejoiced when the accursed thing plucked out from them was of more goodly savour and of a fairer form than usual, and thus was a meeter sacrifice for the Lord. Of all the heartrending histories to be found in the records of witchcraft, the history of Margaret Barclay and her "accomplices" is saddest, most sorrowful, most heartrending.

THE PITIFUL FATE OF MARGARET BARCLAY.[21]

Margaret was a young, beautiful, high-spirited woman, wife of Archibald Dein, burgess of Irvine, and not on the best of terms with John Dein, her husband's brother. Indeed, she had had him and his wife before the Kirk session for slander, and things had not gone quite smoothly with them ever since. When, therefore, the ship, The Grace of God, in which John Dein was sailing, sank in sight of land, drowning him and all his men, the old quarrel was remembered, and Margaret, together with Isobel Insh and John Stewart, a wandering "spaeman," was accused of having sunk the vessel by charms and enchantments. Margaret disdainfully denied the charge from beginning to end: Isobel said she had never seen the spaeman in her life before; but Stewart "clearly and pounktallie confessit" all the charges brought against him, and also said that the women had applied to him to be taught his magic arts, and that once he had found them both modelling ships and figures in clay for the destruction of the men and vessel aforesaid. And as it was proved that Stewart had spoken of the wreck before he could have known it by ordinary means, suspicion of sorcery fell upon him, and he was taken: and made his confession. He said that he had visited Margaret to help her to her will, when a black dog, breathing fire from his nostrils, had formed part of the conclave; and Isobel's own child, a little girl of eight, added to this, a black man as well. Isobel, after denying all and sundry of the charges brought against her, under torture admitted their truth. In the night time she found means to escape from her prison, bruised and maimed with the torture as she was; but in scrambling over the roof she fell to the ground, and was so much injured that she died five days afterwards. Margaret was then tortured: the spaeman

---

[21] Scott's 'Demonology and Witchcraft.'

had strangled himself, which was the best thing he could do, only it was a pity he did not do it before; and poor Margaret was the last of the trio. The torture they used, said the Lords Commissioners, was "safe and gentle." They put her bare legs into a pair of stocks, and laid on them iron bars, augmenting their weight one by one, till Margaret, unable to bear the pain, cried out to be released, promising to confess the truth as they wished to have it. But when released she only denied the charges with fresh passion; so they had recourse to the iron bars again. After a time, pain and weakness overcame her again, and she shrieked aloud, "Tak off! tak off! and befoir God I will show ye the whole form!" She then confessed—whatever they chose to ask her; but unfortunately, in her ravings, included one Isobel Crawford, who when arrested—as she was on the instant— attempted no defence, but, paralyzed and stupefied, admitted everything with which she was charged. Margaret's trial proceeded: sullen and despairing, she assented to the most monstrous counts: she knew there was no hope, and she seemed to take a bitter pride in suffering her tormentors to befool themselves to the utmost. In the midst of her anguish her husband, Alexander Dein, entered the court, accompanied by a lawyer. And then her despair passed, and she thought she saw a glimmer of life and salvation. She asked to be defended. "All that I have confessed," she said, "was in an agony of torture; and before God all that I have spoken is false and untrue. But," she added pathetically, turning to her husband, "ye have been owre lang in coming!" Her defence did her no good; she was condemned, and at the stake entreated that no harm might befall Isobel Crawford, who was utterly and entirely innocent. To whom did she make this prayer? to hearts turned wild and wolfish by superstition; to hearts made fiendish by fear; to men with nothing of humanity save its form—with nothing of religion save its terrors. She might as well have prayed to the fierce winds blowing round the court-house, or the rough waves lashing the barren shore! She was taken to the stake, there strangled and burnt: bearing herself bravely to the last. Poor, brave, beautiful, young Margaret! we, at this long lapse of time, cannot even read of her fate without tears; it needed all the savageness of superstition to harden the hearts of the living against the actual presence of her beauty, her courage, and her despair!

Isobel Crawford was now tried; "after the assistant minister, Mr. David Dickson, had made earnest prayer to God for opening her obdurate and closed heart, she was subjected to the torture of the iron bars laid upon her bare shins, her feet being in the stocks, as in the case of Margaret Barclay." She endured this torture "admirably," without any kind of din or exclamation, suffering above thirty stone of iron to be laid on her legs, never shrinking thereat in any sort, but remaining steady and constant. But when they shifted the iron bars, and removed them to another part of her legs, her constancy gave way, as Margaret's had done, and she too broke out into horrible cries of "Tak off! tak off!" She then confessed—anything—everything—and was sentenced: but on the way to her execution she denied all that she had admitted, interrupted the minister in his prayer, and refused to pardon the executioner, according to form. Her brain had given way, and they fastened to the stake a bewildered, raving maniac. God rest their weary souls!

MARGARET WALLACE
AND HER DEAR BURD. [22]

Margaret Wallace (1622), spous to John Dynning, merchant and citizen of Glasgow, hated Cuthbert Greg. She had sent Cristiane Grahame to him, wanting his dog; but he would not give it, saying, "I rather ye and my hussie (cummer, gossip) baith was brunt or ye get my dog." Margaret, coming to the knowledge of this speech, went to him angrily, and said, "Ffals land-loupper loun that thow art, sayis thow that Cristiane Grahame and I sall be brunt for witches? I vow to God I sall doe ye ane evill turne." So she did, by means of a cake of bread, casting on him the most strange, unnatural, and unknown disease, such as none could mend or understand. Suspecting that he was bewitched, his friends got her to come and undo the mischief she had done: so she went into the house, took him by the "schaikill bane" (shoulder-blade) with one hand, and laid the other on his breast, but spoke no word, only moved her lips; then passed from him on the instant. The next day she went again to his house, and took him up out of bed, leading him to the kitchen and three or four times across the floor, though he had been bedridden for fifteen days, unable to put his foot to the ground. And if all that was not done by devilish art and craft, how was it done? asked the judges and the jury. Another time she went to the house of one Alexander Vallange, where she was taken with a sudden "brasch" of sickness, and was so hardly holden that they thought she would have "ryved" herself to fits. She cried out piteously for her "dear burd," and the bystanders thought she meant her husband: but it turned out to be the witch Cristiane Grahame that she wanted—whom they immediately sent for. Cristiane came at once, and took Margaret tenderly in her arms, saying "no one should hurt

---

[22] Pitcairn.

her dear burd, no one;" then carried her down stairs into the kitchen, and so home to her own house. The little daughter of the house ran after them; on the threshold, she was seized with a sudden pain, and falling down cried and screamed most sorely. Her mother went to lift her up crossly, but she called out, "Mother, mother, ding me nocht, for there is ane preyne (pin) raschet throw my fute." She "grat" all the night, and was very ill; her parents watching by her through the long hours: but when Margaret wanted the mother to let her be cured by Cristiane's aid, she said sternly, no, "scho wad commit her bairne to God, and nocht mell with the devill or ony of his instrumentis." However, Margaret Wallace healed the little one unbidden; by leaping over some bits of green cloth scattered in the midst of the floor, and then taking her out of bed and laying her in Cristiane Grahame's lap—which double sorcery cured her instantly. Cristiane Grahame had been burnt for a witch some time before this trial; and now Margaret Wallace, in this year of our Lord 1622, was doomed to the same fate: bound to a stake, strangled, burnt, her ashes cast to the wind, and all her worldly gear forfeit to king's majesty, because she was a tender-hearted, loving woman, with a strong will and large mesmeric power, and did her best for the sick folk about her.

THOM REID AGAIN.[23]

Isobell Haldane confessed before the Session of Perth, May 15, 1623, that she had cured Andro Duncan's bairn by washing it and its sark in water brought from the Turret Port, then casting the water into a burn; but in the going "scho skaillit (spilt) swm quhilk scho rewis ane evill rew, becaus that if onye had gone ower it they had gottyn the ill." She confessed, too, that about ten years since, she, lying in her bed, was taken forth, whether by God or the devil she knows not, and carried to a hill: the hill-side opened, and she went in and stayed there from Thursday to Sunday at eleven o'clock, when an old man with a gray beard brought her forth. The old man with the gray beard, who seems to have been poor Bessie Dunlop's old acquaintance, told her many things after this visit. He told her that John Roch, who came to the wright's shop for a cradle, need not be so hasty, for his wife would not be lighter for five weeks, and then the bairn should never lie in the cradle, but would die when baptized: as it proved, and as John Roch deposed on her trial. Also, he told her that Margaret Buchanan, then in good health, should prepare herself for death before Fastings Even, which was a few days hence; and Margaret died as she predicted. And Patrick Ruthven deposed that he, being sick—bewitched by one Margaret Hornscleugh— Isobell came to see him, and stretched herself upon him, her head to his head, her hands on his, and so forth, mumbling some words, he knew not what. And Stephen Ray deposed that three years since he had detected Isobell in a theft, whereon she clapped him on the back, and said, "Go thy way; thow sall nocht win thyself ane bannok of breid for yeir and ane day;" and so it proved. He pined away, heavily diseased, and did not do a stroke of work for just three hundred and sixty-six days, of

---

[23] Pitcairn and Chambers.

the full four-and-twenty hours' count. But Isobell said that her sole words were, "He that delyueret me frome the ffairy ffolk sall tak amends on thé:" and that she had never meaned to harm him, nor even to answer him ungently. But she confessed to various charms; such as a cake made of small handsful of meal, gotten from nine several women who had been married, virgins—through a hole in which sick children were to be passed, to their decided cure; and she confessed to getting water, silently going, and silently returning, from the well of Ruthven, in which to bathe John Gow's child; and to having made a drink of focksterrie[24] leaves for Dan Morris's child, who "wes ane scharge" (changeling or fairy child), which focksterrie drink she made it swallow; when it died soon after. So Isobell Haldane shook hands with life, and went back to Thom Reid and the fairy folk on the hill, helped thither by the hangman.

---

[24] Star-grass, queries Pitcairn; but is it not rather fox-tree—fox-glove?

BESSIE SMITH.

In the July of this same year Bessie Smith of Lesmahago also confessed to sundry unlawful doings. When people who were ill of the heart fevers went to her for advice, instead of employing honest drugs such as every Christian understood and nauseated, she bade them kneel and ask their health "for God's sake, for Sanct Spirit, for Sanct Aikit, for the nine maidens that died in the boor-tree in the Ladywell Bank. This charm to be buik and beil to me, God grant that sae be." This charm, with the "wayburn" leaf to be eaten for nine mornings, was sufficient to prove Bessie Smith of Lesmahago a necromancer; and the presbytery of Lanark did quite righteously, according to its lights, when they made her come before them and confess her crimes, humbly. Fortunately, they did not burn her.

THOMAS GRIEVE'S ENCHANTMENTS (1623).[25]

Thomas Grieve was a notorious enchanter, according to the Session, which prided itself on being "ripely advised." He put a woman's sickness on a cow, which ran mad, and died in consequence; and he cured William Kirk's bairn by stroking its hair back from its face and wrapping it in an enchanted cloth, whereby it slept, and woke healed. He cured cattle of "the heastie," or any other bovine disease untranslateable, by sprinkling the byre with enchanted water; and he cured sick people by putting them through a hank of yarn, which then he cut up and threw into the fire, where it burned blue. He healed one woman by "fyring"— putting a hot iron, which was supposed to burn the obsessing witch—into some magic water brought from Holywell, Hill-side, and making her drink it; and he cured another woman by burning a poor hen alive, first making her carry it, when half roasted, under her arm; and he took in hand to heal Elspeth, sister of John Thomson, of Corachie—passing with her two brothers in the night season from Corachie towards Burley, enjoining them not to speak a word all the way, and whatever they heard or saw, not to be anywise "effrayed," saying "it micht be that thai would heir grit rumbling and sie vncouth feirfull apparitiones, but nothing suld annoy thame." Arrived at the ford at the east of Birley he washed her sark; and during the time of this washing there was a great noise made by fowls in the hill, beasts that arose and fluttered in the water— "beistes that arrais and flichtered" in the water; and when he put her sark upon her again, Elspeth mended and was healed. And of another patient he propounded this wise opinion, come to by the examination of his sark: "Allace, the withcraft appointit for ane vther hes lichtit vpoune him," but it had not yet reached his heart. And further than

---

[25] Chambers, Dalyell, Pitcairn.

all this, which was bad enough, he made signs and crosses, and muttered uncouth words, and believed in himself and the devil: so he was strangled and burnt, and an end come to of him: for which the neighbours all were glad, even those he had benefited, and the ministers were quite satisfied that they had given glory to God in the holiest manner open to them.

KATHERINE GRANT AND HER STOUP.[26]

Katherine Grant, in the November of the year 1623, was dilatit for that she had gone to Henry Janies' house, with "a stoup in hir hand, with the boddome foremost, and sat down ryght fornent the said Henrie, and gantit thryce on him: and going furth he followit hir; and beiyan the brigstane, scho lukit over her shoulder, and turned up the quhyt of her eye, quhair by her divilrie, their fell ane great weght upoun him that he was forcit to set his bak to the wall, and when he came in, he thoucht the hous ran about with him, and theirefter lay seik ane lang tyme." Katherine Grant was not likely to overcome the impression of such testimony as this: that she should have gone to any man's house and yawned thrice, and added to this devilry the further crime of looking over her shoulder, was quite enough evidence of guilt for any sane man or woman in Orkney. Can we wonder, then, that she was not suffered to vex the sunlight longer by carrying pails bottom upwards, or yawning thrice in the faces of decent folk, and that she was taken forth to be strangled, burnt, and her ashes cast to the four winds of the merciful heaven?

---

[26] Dalyell, quoting the judiciary records of Orkney.

THE MISDEEDS OF MARION RICHART.[27]

"Mareoune" Richart, *alias* Langland, dwelt on one of the wild Orkney islands, not far from where mad Elspeth Sandisome kept the whole country in fear lest she should do something terrible to herself or to others. Marion was invited to go the house, and try her skill at curing her, for she was known to be an awful witch, and able to do whatever she had a mind in the way of healing or killing. So she went, and set herself to her charm. She took some "remedie water"—which she made into "remedy water," by carrying it in a round bowl to the byre where she cast into it something like "great salt," taken from her purse, spitting thrice into the bowl, and blowing in her breath—and with this magic "remedie watter forspeking," she bade Elspeth's woman-servant wash her feet and hands, and she would be as well as ever she had been before. This was bad enough; but worse than this, she came to Stronsey on a day, asking alms of "Andro Coupar, skipper of ane bark," to whom said Andrew rudely, "Away witch, carling; devils ane farthing ye will fall!" whereupon went Marion away "verie offendit; and incontinentlie he going to sea, the bark being vnder saill, he ran wode, and wald half luppen ourboord; and his sone seing him gat him in his armes, and held him; quhairvpon the sicknes immediatelie left him, and his sone ran made; and Thomas Paiterson, seeing him tak his madnes, and the father to turn weill, ane dog being in the bark, took the dog and bladdit him vpon the twa schoulderis, and thaireftir flang the said dogg in the sea, quhairby those in the bark were saiffed." So Marion Richart, *alias* Langland, learnt the hangman's way to the grave in the year of grace 1629; and her corpse was burned, when the hangman's rope had done its work.

---

[27] Hibbert, quoting the Orkney Records.

LADY LEE'S PENNY AND THE WITCHES OF 1629.[28]

Isobel Young, spous to George Smith, was burnt, in 1629, for curing cattle, as well as for the other crimes belonging to a witch. She had sought to borrow Lady Lee's Penny—a precious stone or amulet, like to a piece of amber, set in a silver penny, which one of the old Lee family had gotten from a Saracen in the Crusades—and which Lee Penny was to help her in her incantations, for curing "the bestiall of the routting evill," whatever that might have been. But Lady Lee let her have only a flagon of water in which the amulet had been steeped, which did quite as well, and helped to set the stake as quickly as anything else would have done. Various other mischancy things did Isobel Young. She stopped a certain mill, and made it incapable of grinding for eleven days: she forespoke a certain boat, and though all the rest returned to Dunbar full and richly laden, this came back empty, whereby the owner was ruined: she bewitched milk that it would give no cream, and churns, so that no butter would come: she twice crossed the mill water on a wild and stormy night, when the milne horses could not ride it out, and where there was no bridge of stone or wood; but Isobel the witch crossed and recrossed those raging waters under the stormy sky, and came out at the end as dry as if from a kiln. And was not this as unholy as taking off her "curch" at William Meslet's barn-door, and running "thrice about the barn widdershins," whereby the cattle were caused to fall dead in "great suddainty?" Then, as further iniquity, she had dealings with Christian Grinton, another witch, who one night came out of a hole in the roof in the likeness of a cat; and she cast a sickness from off her husband, and laid it on his brother's son, who, knowing full well that he

---

[28] Pitcairn. Sharpe's Introduction to Law's 'Memorials.'

was bewitched, came to the house, and there saw the "firlott"—a certain measure of wheat—running about, and the stuff poppling on the floor, which was the manner of the charm. Drawing his sword, this husband's brother's son ran on the pannel (the accused) to kill her, but was witch-disabled, and only struck the lintel of the door instead; so he went home and died, and Isobel Young was the cause of his death by the cantrip wrought in the locomotive firlott and the poppling grain. Forbye all this, she was seen riding on "ane mare"—at least her apparition was seen so riding—and by her sorcery and devilish handling the mare was made to cast its foal, and since died. So Isobel Young was of no more value to the world or its inheritors, and died by the cord and the faggot, decently, as a convicted witch should. And Margaret Maxwell and her daughter Jane were haled before the Lords of Secret Council for having procured the death of Edward Thomson, Jane's husband, "by the devilish and detestable practice of witchcraft;" and Janet Boyd was tried for "the foul and detestable crime" of receiving the devil's mark, besides being otherwise dishonestly intimate with him; but this was in 1628, and we are now in 1629: and then the Lords of the Privy Council published a thundering edict, forbidding all persons to have recourse to holy words, or to make pilgrimages to chapels, and requiring of its Commissioners to make diligent search in all parts for persons guilty of this superstitious practice, and to have up and put in ward all such as were known to be specially devoted thereto. The meaning of the decree was to plague the Catholics, and Hibbert quotes part of this "Commission against Jesuits, Priests, or Communicants and Papists, going in pilgrimage." But whatever the political significance of the edict, the social effect was to make the search after the White Witches, or Black, hotter and more bitter than ever.

ELSPETH CURSETTER AND HER FRIENDS.[29]

Elspeth Cursetter was tried, May 29 (still in 1629), for all sorts of bad actions. She bade one of her victims "get the bones of ane tequhyt (linnet), and carry thame in your claithes"; and she gave herself out as knowing evil, and able to do it too, when and to whomsoever she would; and she sat down before the house of a man who refused her admittance—for she was an ill-famed old witch, and every one dreaded her—saying, "Ill might they all thrive, and ill may they speed," whereby in fourteen days' time the man's horse fell just where she had sat, and was killed most lamentably. But she cured a neighbour's cow by drawing a cog of water out of the burn that ran before William Anderson's door, coming back and taking three straws— one for William Anderson's wife, and one for William Coitts' wife, and one for William Bichen's wife—which she threw into the pail with the water, then put the same on the cow's back; by which charm the three straws danced in the water, and the water bubbled as if it had been boiling. Then Elspeth took a little quantity of this charmed water, and thrust her arm up to the elbow into the cow's throat, and on the instant the cow rose up as well as she had ever been; but William Anderson's ox, which was on the hill, dropped down dead. Likewise she worked unholy cantrips for a sick friend with a paddock (toad), in the mouth of a pail of water, which toad was too large to get down the mouth, and when it was cast forth another man sickened and died immediately: and she spake dangerous words to a child, saying, "Wally fall that quhyt head of thine, but the pox will tak the away frae thy mother." As it proved, for the little white head was laid low a short time after, when the small-pox raged through the land. "Thow can tell eneugh yf thow lyke," said the mother to her afterwards,

---

[29] Dalyell.

76

"that could tell that my bairne wold die so long befoir the tyme." "I can tell eneugh if I durst," replied Elspeth, over proud for her safety. But in spite of all this testimony, Elspeth got off with "arbitrary punishment," which did not include burning or strangling, so was luckier than her neighbours. Luckier than poor Jonet Rendall was, who, on the 11th of November (1629), was proved a witch by the bleeding of the corpse of the poor wretch whom she had "enchanted" to his death. For "as soon as she came in the corpse having lain a good space, and not having bled any, immediately bled much blood, as a sure token that she was the author of his death." And had she not said, too, when a certain man refused her a Christmas lodging, "that it wald be weill if the gude man of that hous sould make ane other yule banket" (Christmas banquet); by which curse had he not died in fifteen days after? Wherefore was she a proved murderess as well as witch, and received the doom appointed to both alike. Alexander Drummond was a warlock who cured all kinds of horrid diseases, the very names of which are enough to make one ill; and he had a familiar, which had attended him for "neir this fifty yeiris:" so he was convicted and burnt.

Then came Jonet Forsyth, great in her art. She could cast sickness on any one at sea, and cure him again by a salt-water bath; she could transfer any disease from man to beast, so that when the beast died and was opened, nothing could be found where its heart should have been but "a blob of water;" she knew how to charm and sain all kinds of cattle by taking three drops of a beastie's blood on All Hallow E'en, and sprinkling the same in the fire within the innermost chamber; she went at seed time and bewitched a stack of barley belonging to Michael Reid, so that for many years he could never make it into wholesome malt; and this she did for the gain of Robert Reid, changing the "profit" of the grain backwards and forwards between the two, according as they challenged or displeased her. All this did

Jonet Forsyth of Birsay, to the terror of her neighbours and the ultimate ruin of herself, both in soul and body. Then came Catherine Oswald,[30] spouse to Robert Aitcheson, in Niddrie, who was brought to trial for being "habite and repute" a witch—defamed by Elizabeth Toppock herself a witch and, as is so often the case, a dear friend of Katie's. Elizabeth need not have been so eager to get rid of her dear friend and gossip, for she was burnt afterwards for the same crimes as those for which poor Catherine suffered the halter and the stake. It seems that Katie was bad for her enemies. She was offended at Adam Fairbairn and his wife, so she made their "twa kye run mad and rammish to died," and also made a gentleman's bairn that they had a-fostering run wood (mad) and die. And she fired William Heriot's kiln, full of grain; and burnt all his goods before his eyes; and made his wife, in a "frantick humour," drown herself; and she cursed John Clark's ground, so that for four years after "by hir sorceries, naether kaill, lint, hempe, nor any other graine" would grow thereon, though doubly "laboured and sowen." She bewitched Thomas Scott by telling him that he looked as well as when Bessie Dobie was living, whereby he immediately fell so deadly sick that he could not proceed further, but was carried on a horse to Newbiggin, where he lay until the morrow, when "a wife" came in and told him he was forespoken. And other things as mischievous—and as true—did Catherine Oswald, as the Record testifies. She was well defended, and might have got off, but that a witness deposed to having seen Mr. John Aird the minister, and a most zealous witch-finder, prick her in the shoulder with a prin, and that no blood followed thereafter, nor did she shrink as with pain or feeling. And as there was no gainsaying the evidence of the witch-mark, Satan and Mr. John Aird claimed their own. Was Catherine's brand like a "blew spot, or a little tate, or reid

<hr />

[30] Law's 'Memorials,' (Sharpe's Introduction,) and Dalyell.

spots, like flea-biting?" or with "the flesh sunk in and hallow?" according to the description of such places, published by Mr. John Bell, minister of the gospel in Gladsmuir. We are seldom told of what precise character the marks were, only that they were found, pricked, and tested, and the witch hung or burnt on their testimony.

SANDIE AND THE DEVIL.[31]

Soon after Catherine Oswald's execution, one of her crew or covin, who had been with her on the great storm in "the borrowing days (in anno 1625), on the Brae of the Saltpans," a noted warlock, by name Alexander Hunter, or Hamilton, *alias* Hatteraick, which last name he had gotten from the devil, was brought to execution on the Castle Hill. It was in 1629 that he was taken. It was proved that on Kingston hills he had met with the devil as a black man, or, as Sinclair says, as a mediciner; and often afterwards he would meet him riding on a black horse, or he would appear as a corbie, cat, or dog. When Alexander wanted him he would beat the ground with a fir stick lustily, crying, "Rise up, foul thief!" for the master got but hard names at times from his servants. This fir stick, and four shillings sterling, the devil gave to him when the compact was first made between them; and he confessed, moreover, that when raised in this manner he could only be got rid of by sacrificing to him a cat or dog, or such like, "quick." Also he set on fire Provost Cockburn's mill of corn, by taking three stalks from his stacks, and burning them on Garleton Hills; and he owned to a deadly hatred against Lady Ormiston, because she once refused him "ane almous," and called him "ane custroune carle." So, to punish her, he and some witches raised the devil in Salton Wood, where he appeared like a man in gray clothes, and gave him the bottom of a blue clew, telling him to lay it at the lady's door: "which he and the women having done, 'the lady and her daughter were soon thereafter bereft of their naturall lyfe.'" But Sinclair's account is the most graphic. I will give it in his own words:—

"Anent Hattaraick, an old Warlock.

---

[31] Chambers, Sinclair, Dalyell.

"This man's name was Sandie Hunter, who called himself Sandie Hamilton, and it seems so called Hattaraik by the devil, and so by others as a Nickname. He was first a Neatherd in East Lothian, to a gentleman there. He was much given to charming and cureing of men and Beasts, by words and spels. His charms sometimes succeeded and sometimes not. On a day, herding his kine upon a Hill side in the summer time, the Devil came to him in form of a Mediciner, and said, 'Sandie, you have too long followed my trade, and never acknowledged me for your master. You must now take on with me, and I will make you more perfect in your calling.' Whereupon the man gave up himself to the devil, and received his Mark with this new name. After this he grew very famous throw the countrey for his charming and cureing of diseases in men and beasts, and turned a vagrant fellow like a Jockie, gaining Meat, Flesh, and Money by his Charms, such was the ignorance of many at that time.

"Whatever House he came to, none durst refuse Hattaraik an alms, rather for his ill than his good. One day he came to the yait of Samuelstown, when some Friends after dinner were going to Horse. A young Gentleman, Brother to the Lady, seeing him, switcht him about the ears, saying, 'You Warlok Cairle, what have you to do here?' whereupon the Fellow goes away grumbling, and was overheard to say, 'You shall dear buy this, ere it be long.' This was *Damnum Minatum*. The young Gentleman conveyed his Friends a far way off, and came home that way again, where he slept. After supper, taking his horse and crossing Tine-water to go home, he rides throw a shadowy piece of a Haugh, commonly called the Allers, and the evening being somewhat dark he met with some Persons there that begat a dreadful consternation in him, which for the most part he would never reveal. This was *malum secutum*. When he came home, the Servants observed terror and fear in his countenance. The next day he became distracted, and was bound for several days. His sister, the Lady Samuelstoun, hearing of it, was heard to say, 'Surely that knave Hattaraik is the cause of his Trouble. Call for him in all haste.' When he had come to her, 'Sandie,' says she, 'what is this you have done to my brother William?' 'I told him,' says he, 'I should make him repent his striking of me at the Yait lately.' She gave the Rogue fair words, and promising him his Pock full of Meal with Beef and Cheese, persuaded the Fellow to cure him again. He undertook the business; 'but I must first,' says he, 'have one of his Sarks,' which was soon gotten. What pranks he plaid with it cannot be known. But within a short while the gentleman recovered his health. When Hatteraik came to receive his wadges, he told the Lady, 'Your Brother William shal quickly goe off the Countrey but shall never return.' She, knowing the Fellow's prophecies to hold true, caused her Brother to make a Disposition to her of all his patrimony, to the defrauding of his younger brother George. After that this Warlock had abused the Countrey for a long time, he was at last apprehended at Dunbar, and brought into Edinburgh, and burnt upon the Castle Hill." But not until he had delated several others of hitherto good repute, so that for the next few months the witch-finder's hands were full.

THE MIDWIFE'S DOUBLE SIN.

Notably was arrested about this time, Alie Nisbet, midwife; and three others. Alie was accused of witchcraft; and of a softer, but as heinous a crime as witchcraft. This she confessed to; but the breaking of the seventh commandment in Christian Scotland, in the year 1632, was a far more dangerous thing than we can imagine possible in our laxer day; and Alie was on the horns of a dilemma, either of which could land her in ruin, death, and perdition. She was accused, among other things, of having taken her labour pains from off a certain woman, using "charmes and horrible words, amongs which thir ware some, *the bones to the fire and the soull to the devill*;" but this Alie denied, strenuously, though she admitted that she might have bathed the woman's legs in warm water, which she had bewitched for good, by putting her fingers into it and running thrice round the bed, widershins; but the spoken charm as given she would have none of. The labour pains, however, left the woman, and were foully and unnaturally cast upon another who had no concern therewith, so that she died in four-and-twenty hours from that time, and Alie was the murderess by all the laws of sorcery. She was accused, also, of having poured some enchanted water on a threshold over which a servant girl, against whom she had a spite, must pass, and the servant girl died therefrom. Alie was wirriet and burnt and troubled the world no more.

KATHERINE GRIEVE AND JOHN SINCLAIR.[32]

Katherine Grieve, too (1633), was brought to judgment and sentenced to be "taken to the mercat crose and brunt in the cheick, in example of others," with the future prospect, that if she haunted suspected places, or used charms "scho sould be brunt in asches to the dead without dome or law, and that willinglie, of hir owne consent." For Katherine's curses had wronged both man and beast, which evil thing she had brought to pass by the power of the devil her master. However, she was forced to undo her evil, and by laying on of hands cure the sore she had made: so she got off with this smaller punishment of branding, and a rebuke. And there was John Sinclair tried that same year; a cruel villain to others, if loving to his own. For under silence and cloud of night he took his distempered sister, sitting backward on the horse, and carried her from where she lay to the Kirk of Hoy. Then a voice came to him, saying "Seven is too many, but four might do;" and in the morning a boat with five men in it struck on the rocks, and four perished, but one was saved; by which fiendish and unholy sacrifice John Sinclair's sister was cured. He was proved to be their murderer, for when the dead men were found, and he was "forcit to lay his handis vpoun thame, they guishit out with bluid and watter at the mouth and noise." John Sinclair's thread of life needed no more waxing to make it run smoothly and easily. The hangman knew where the knot lay; and cut it to the perfect satisfaction of all the country.

---

[32] Dalyell's 'Darker Superstitions.'

BESSIE BATHGATE'S NIPS.[33]

A year after this Bessie Bathgate, spouse to Alexander Rae, fell into trouble and the hands of the police. George Sprot, wobster, had some cloth of Bessie's, which he kept too long for her thinking. She went and took it violently away, and nipped his child in the thigh till it skirled, "and of which nip it never convalesced, but dwamed thereof and died by hir sorcerie." Also, said Sprot's wife, giving her child an egg that came out of Bessie's house there struck out a lump as big as a goose egg upon the child, which continued on her till her death, which was occasioned by nothing else than this "enchanted egg." Furthermore she threatened Sprot that "he should never get his Sunday's meat to the fore by his work;" and he forthwith fell into extreme poverty, by which her words came true. To William Donaldson she said—he outrunning her as she chased him to beat him for calling her a witch—"Weill, sir, the devill be in your feit," and he fell lame and impotent straightways, and so continued ever since. Other things of the same kind did she, bewitching Margaret Horne's cow that it died, "and that night it died there was women seen dancing on the rigging of the byre;" also she was seen by "two young men at 12 howers at even (when all persons are in their beds) standing barelegged and in hir sark valicot, at the back of hir yard, conferring with the devill, who was in gray cloaths;" which, with other offences of the same nature, were, we should have thought, heavy enough to have lost a world. But Elizabeth Bathgate, spouse to Alexander Rae, was acquitted; though how the verdict came about no one can possibly understand.

It was not that any fit of mercy or humanity had come over the people. More than twenty poor wretches suffered about this time, Sir George Home of Manderston, being

---

[33] Pitcairn. Law's 'Memorials.' Chambers.

one of the chief of the prosecutors: for Sir George and his wife did not live very lovingly together, and she was given to witches and warlocks—or they said she was—to see if she could not get rid of him by enchantments and sorceries: so Sir George had a pleasant mixture of spite and self-defence in his onslaught, and the whole country-side was in a stir. About this time too, John Balfour, of Corhouse, took on himself the office of witch-finder and pricker by thrusting "preens" into the marks; but he was not accepted quite blindly, and measures were taken for examining his pretensions to this special branch of knowledge. In general the pricker was the master of the situation, and brought all the rest to his feet.

BESSIE SKEBISTER.[34]

All the honest men of the isle knew Bessie Skebister. She was the shrewdest witch in the whole country, and it was a usual thing with them when they thought their boats in danger to send to her to know the truth; and, "Giff Bessie say it is weill, it is weill" was a common proverb in the Orkney Islands. She did other things besides foreknowing the fall of storms, for she took James Sandieson when in a strange distemper and tormented him greatly. "In his sleip, and oftymes waking," says the dittay, "he was tormented with yow, Bessie, and vther two with yow, quhom he knew not, cairying him to the sea, and to the fyre, to Norroway, Yetland, and to the south—that ye had ridden all this wayes, with ane brydle in his mouth." Moreover, Bessie was a "dreamer of dreams," as well as a rider of sick men's souls; so she was strangled and burnt.

---

[34] Dalyell.

THE TRIAL OF SPIRITS.[35]

The trial of Katherine Craigie (1640), had a certain dash of poetry and romance in it, not often found in these woeful stories. Friend Robbie—now friend, now foe—lay a-dying, and Katherine must needs go see him with the rest. The wild waves were beating round that rugged Orkney Isle, when Katherine went over the heather to Robbie's house. "What now, Robbie! ye are going to die!" she said. "I grant that I prayed ill for yow, and now I see that prayer hath taken effect. Jonet," quoth she, turning to the wife, "if I durst trust in yow, I sould knaw quhat lyeth on your guidman and holdis him downe. I sould tell whether it was ane hill spirit, ane kirk spirit, or ane water spirit that so troubles him." Jonet was too anxious not to promise secrecy or help, or anything else that Katherine wished; so the next morning, before daylight, Katherine brought three stones to Robbie's house, and put them into the fire, where they remained until after sunset. While the night was passing, they were taken from the fire, and put under the threshold of the door, then, in the early morning, thrown, one after the other, into a pail of water, where Jonet heard one of them "chirle and chirme." Upon which Katherine said that it was a kirk spirit that troubled the guidman Robbie, and he must be washed with the water in which the stones had "chirled and chirmed." This ceremony was repeated thrice, and at the third time Katherine herself washed Robbie, on whom this unusual cleansing had most powerful and beneficial effects. When one thinks of the normal state of filth in which these honest people lived, it is not surprising if any form of ablution proved of a most supernatural benefit. But Katherine Craigie got into the trouble from which there was no escape; and friend Robbie

---

[35] Chambers.

went back to his dirt, persuaded of the Satanic agency of a bath.

Quite as full of poetic feeling was James Knarstoun's manner of charming with stones, when he took one stone for the ebb, another for the hill, and the third for the kirkyard, listening carefully as to what stone should make the "bullering" noise that would betray the tormenting spirit, and enable the magician to send him home again: a process through which Katherine Carey went (1617) when she found that her patient was troubled with the spirit of the sea, which would not let him bide in peace and quiet. Such touches as these redeem the subject from the sad monotony of sorrow and death which else pervades it from end to end, and lift it from the domain of the devil into the brighter and lovelier world of the Spirits of Nature.

SIXTEEN HUNDRED AND FORTY-THREE.

In 1643 there was a fierce onslaught against the poor persecuted servants of the devil. Thirty women suffered at once in Fife alone; and the more zealous of the ministers hounded on the people to terrible cruelties. There was one John Brugh,[36] "a notorious warlock in the parachin of Fossoquhy, by the space of 36 yearis," who was wirreit at a stake and burnt; and Janet Barker and Margaret Lauder, "indwellers and servans in Edinburgh," who came to confession boldly, and showed that they had read the story of Europa to some purpose, though to a great deal of confusion. They accused Janet Cranstoun of seducing them, by promising them that if they gave themselves over to her and the devil, they should be "as trimlie clad as the best servans in Edinburgh." Coupled with the fact that they had witch-marks, their confession was accepted as undeniable, and their fate inevitably sealed.

And there was Marion Cumlaquoy,[37] in Birsay, who bewitched David Cumlaquoy's corn seed, and made it run out too soon. She had been very anxious to know when David would sow, and when she was told, she went and stood "just to his face" all the time he was casting, and that year his seed failed him, so that he could only sow a third of his land; though he had as much grain as heretofore, and it had never run out too soon all the years he had farmed that land. And she went to Robert Carstairs' house by sunrise one day, bringing milk to his good mother, though not used to show such attention; and as she left she turned herself three several times "withershins" about the fire, and that year Robert Carstairs' "bear (barley) was blew and rottin," and his oats gave no proper meal, but made all who ate thereof heart-sick, albeit both bear and oats were good

---

[36] Chambers.
[37] Dalyell.

and fresh when he put them in the yard. And if all this was not proof against Marion Cumlaquoy, what would the Orkney courts hold as proof? As the past, so the present; and Marion Cumlaquoy must learn in prison and at the stake the evils that honest folk found in her power of "enchanting" corn and crops. There were many others in this same year, to catalogue whom would become at least wearisome and monotonous: they must be passed by unmentioned, and left to the silence and oblivion which is the privilege of the unfortunate dead.

But among the victims was one Agnes Finnie,[38] a bitter-tongued, evil-tempered old hag, who had a curse and a threat for every one who offended her; who killed young Fairlie with a terrible disorder, because he called her "Winnie Annie;" and laid so frightful a disease on Beatrix Nisbet, for some other trifling offence, that she lost the use of her tongue; who made a "grit jist" (great joist) fall down on the leg of Euphame Kincaid's daughter, because Euphame called her a witch on being called by her a drunkard; and appeared to John Cockburn in the night—the doors and windows being fast closed—terrifying him by her hideous old apparition in his sleep, because he had disagreed with her daughter; and who did all other wicked and uncanny things, like a raving, unprincipled, old hag as she was. She even forespoke Alexander Johnstone's bairne, so that it was eleven years old before it could walk, and all because she was not made godmother, or "had not gotten its name;" and she made Margaret Williamson sick and blind, by saying most outrageously, "The devill blaw thé blinde!" And she was a bad mother and evil exemplar to her daughter, bringing her up to be as vile as herself, at least in the way of quarrelling and fighting with her neighbours, and then backing her with an unfair amount of her own supernatural powers. Thus, one day, Margaret

---

[38] Chambers and Law; Sharpe's Introduction.

Robinson, the daughter in question, was using high words with Mawse Gourlay, spouse of Andrew Wilson, and Mawse, in a rage, called her "ane witche's get," which was about the worst thing that could be said in those days between a couple of scolds. "Gif I be ane witche's get," cried Margaret, in extremest fury, "the devill ryve the saull out of ye befoir I come again!" After which cruel and devilish imprecation, helped on by Winnie Annie's horrible art used at Margaret's instigation, Andrew Wilson became "frenatik" and stark mad: his eyes starting out of his head in the most terrible and frightful manner as he went about, ever pronouncing these words as his ordinary and continual speech—the perpetual raving of his madness—"The devill ryve the saull out o' me!" For all which crimes—though she was ably defended—though, when her house was searched, "there was neither picture, toad, nor any such thing found therein, which ever any witch in the world was used to practize,"—yet the evidence was held to be too strong, and Winnie Annie Finnie was ordained to be "brunt to the deid," and her ashes cast out to the winds of heaven.

Janet Brown[39] was another of those who got into hot quarters. She confessed that she had charmed James Hutton and Janet Scott with these words:—

"Our Lord forth did raide,
His foal's foot slade;
Our Lord down lighted,
His foal's foot righted;
Saying flesh to flesh, blood to blood, and stane to stane,
In our Lord his name."

She said this was a charm that had been learnt her by a nameless man from Strathmiglo; but Margaret Fisher,[40] in

---

[39] Hibbert's 'Description of the Shetland Islands.'
[40] Dalyell. Evidently the same thing with a different reading:—*red*, rode; *sool-soot*, stirrup; *sled*, slipped; *shinew*, sinew.

Weardie, spoke it somewhat differently. She had for her spell:—

"Our Lord to hunting red,
His sool-soot sled,
Down he lighted,
His sool-soot righted;
Blod to blod,
Shinew to shinew,
To the other sent in God's name,
In the name of the Father, Sone, and Holy Ghost."

Either version was equally efficacious as a cure to the sick and a curse to the whole; and equally deadly as a crime in those who used it. And there was Margaret Young, "ane honest young woman of good reputation, without any scandal or blot," who lay miserably in prison for ten weeks, without trial or release; but she got off at last on her husband's becoming her surety. And Jonet Thomeson, who bewitched Andrew Burwick's corn, so that when carried to the mill it leapt up into his wife's face like mites, and as it were "nipped" her face until it swelled; and when it was made into "meat," neither he nor his wife could abide the smell of it; and when they did manage to eat it, it tasted like pins ("went owre lyke prinsis"), and could not be quenched for thirst: and the dogs would not eat of it, and the neighbours would not buy it; so poor Andrew Burwick's gear was destroyed, and his means most sorely diminished. For all which deadly sorcery and malice Jonet Thomeson, *alias* Greibok, was made to smart severely.

Marion Peebles[41] came to an untimely end, not unreasonably, according to the witch-haters. She was "a wicked, devilish, fearful, and abominable curser," and the world could not be too soon rid of her; for had she not

---

[41] Hibbert, &c.

changed herself into the likeness of an unchristian beast, a mere shapeless monster, a huge and ugly "pellack-quhaill" (porpoise), and in this form wrecked the boat of Edward Halcro, to whom she and her husband had "ane deadlie and veneficial malice?" Halcro and four other men were in the boat, and public suspicion pointed at once to Marion, and affirmed this wreck to be caused by her wicked deed. So when two of the dead bodies were brought to land, she and her husband had to undergo the *bahr-recht*—the ordeal by touch of the dead—to prove themselves innocent or guilty. When they came where they lay the "said umquhile Edward bled at the collar-bane or craig-bane;" the other in the hand and fingers, "gushing out bluid thairat, to the great admiration of the beholders, and judgment of the Almytie." Many and heavy were Marion's misdeeds. She cursed Janet Robinson, and "accordingly showers of pains and fits fell upon the victim." She looked upon a cow, and it "crappit togidder till no lyfe was leukit for her." She took away the profit of Edward Halcro's brewing, and destroyed the milk of Andrew Erasmusson's kye for thirteen days. Indeed, her character was so well known that when Swene, her husband, was working in a peat moss where a sickly fellow was one of the gang, his fellows would ask him seriously "if he could not make his wife go to her pobe (foster-father) the devil, and bid him loose a knot, so that the man might get back his health?" Once she cast a sickness on a woman, then took it from her and flung it on a calf, which went mad and died; and she crippled a man, then cured him under compulsion, by putting her fingers first to his leg and then to the ground, which she did twice, muttering to herself; but the report of this getting about, she was angry and banned the man once more, yet once more was forced to cure him;—this time by means of a bannock prepared with her own hands, whereby she cast his malady on a cow. Poor cowey died of her strange sickness, and poor Marion died of a worse disease—the rope and the faggot: and then the neighbourhood slept in peace.

SINCLAIR'S STORIES.[42]

On a certain day in a certain month, A.D. 1644, a woman went to the house of another woman in Borrowstonness. She went early, and instantly fell to mauling and pulling her, crying, "Thou traitour thief, thou thought to destroy my son this morning, but it was not in thy power!" And then she pulled her mutch from off her head, and mauled and maltreated her anew. Now the meaning of the row was, that this woman had a son out at sea, whom she, so cruelly assaulted, had sought to destroy by means of a sudden storm raised by magic means this very day. The storm was actually raised, and many of the crew suffered; but the son of the woman at Borrowstonness was washed overboard by one wave, and washed on board again by another wave, which so filled all the mariners with amaze that they came ashore. The dispute between the two women becoming noised abroad, and the thing being as the one had said, it was found that they were both in equal fault—that the one had done, and the other known, too much; wherefore they were burnt as witches, and the world had the satisfaction of hearing them confess before they died.

Another woman, "about thirty and two, or three and thirty years of age, a most beautiful and comely person as was in the country about," wife to one Goodaile, a cooper, in Carrin, was fyled for a witch and put in prison. She was the devil's favourite and dear delight; and at their meetings she was the person whom "he did most court and embrace, calling her constantly my dear mistress, setting her always at his right hand, to the great discontent of his old haggs, whom, as they now conceived, he slighted;" but her time came at last, and the law caught hold of her in place of the devil, and gave her a yet more stringent embrace. James

---

[42] Sinclair's 'Invisible World Discovered.'

Fleming, a sea-captain, and a man of great personal courage and physical strength, was set to watch her, for the magistrates feared lest the devil should attempt her rescue, since he loved her so well; and to him she said, that if she got no deliverance by one o'clock in the morning, she would lay her breast open to him and confess freely. James Fleming, a little alarmed at this, and not liking to encounter the devil single-handed, took down fourteen of his ship's company with him, "not forgetting the reading of Scripture and earnest prayer to God." Sure enough the foul fiend came: for on a sudden at midnight a tremendous hurricane arose, which unroofed the house where they all were, and threatened to bring the whole place about their ears, and a voice was heard calling to her by a strange name to come away: "at which time she made three several loups upward, increasing gradually till her feet were as high as his breast." But though James Fleming's hair was standing widershins on his head, and though his heart failed him for dread and fear, and he "beteached" himself to God "with great amazement," yet his muscles continued as serviceable as ever, and at last got the better even of the Prince of Darkness. He held this beautiful and comely person in his powerful arms, and kept her there, through all her struggles to get free; and at last succeeded in throwing her down upon the ground, where for some time she grovelled and foamed like one in the falling sickness, and then sank into a deep sleep. When she awaked she complained bitterly of the devil, saying how that he had promised to release her and carry her over to Ireland, touching at Paisley by the way, where she had a sister living; but now she saw through all his treachery and perfidiousness, and understood how she had been made his dupe. She was burnt in all penitence and good conduct, as was also another woman about the same time, who, putting up her arm to swear that she was not a witch, had it suddenly withered and stiffened so that she could not bring it back again; nor was she able to do so, until a minister who was there, had intreated God in her behalf; for the ministers were always men of mighty power on such occasions, and either made or marred at their pleasure. If they chose to accept a case as possession, they prayed and exorcised; but if it seemed good to them to call it witchcraft, then the poor wretch's life was doomed, and no man might hope to save. It was very seldom they cared so much for humanity as to choose the more merciful of the two absurdities. Sometimes, though, the devil was as good as his word, and made at least an attempt, if a clumsy one, to release his servants: as when he took Helen Eliot from the steeple of Culross where she was confined, and carried her in his arms through the air. He might have landed her in safety somewhere—who knows?—had she not cried out, "O God! whither are you taking me?" At which words he let her fall "at the distance from the steeple of about the breadth of the street of Edinburgh, whereby she broke her legs and otherwise seriously injured herself." Many thousand people flocked to see the dimple which her heels had made, and over which no grass would grow again. So at last they built a stone dyke round it, and kept the impression safe.

In 1649 Lady Pittathrow was delated of witchcraft. She was put in prison waiting for her trial; but one morning she was found dead, having strangled herself, or been strangled by the devil—the world might determine which according to its pleasure. Shortly after, Bessie Grahame was apprehended for a few drunken words said against John Rankin's wife, who had since died. During a confinement of thirteen weeks she was visited by the minister, who found her obdurate in confession, and was much inclined to find her innocent of crime. But Alexander Bogue, a pricker, came to examine her, and discovered the mark, into which he thrust a pin, which neither pained nor drew blood. Still she was held to be innocent, until one day Mr. James Fergusson, the minister, heard her talking to the devil as soon as she was alone. He knew it was the devil, for his voice was hollow and ghoustie, and the servant, Alexander Sympson, was like to have fallen back for fear. Still Bessie would never confess anything beyond general unworthiness and the usual tale of vague misdeeds, owning, indeed, to a special horror of him, the minister, and how she was not "let to love him," as indeed was no special miracle; and then she fell to railing at him bitterly, which was less a miracle than all else. So she was burnt, dying obdurate and unconfessed; and thus another murder reeked up to heaven, crying aloud for vengeance, because John Rankin's wife died suddenly, and an intemperate old woman swore in her cups and had a habit of speaking to herself.

Agnes Gourlay was accused of charming milk. She told Anna Simpson to throw a small quantity of the milk into the "grupe" or sewer of the byre, saying, "God betak us to! May be they are under the earth that have as much need of it as they that are above the earth!" After which bread and salt were to be put into the cows' ears, and milk would come. Agnes got off by penance and confession: which was more than Janet Couts did, or Archibald Watt, *alias* "Sole the Paitlet;" though eleven other poor creatures delated escaped their doom, partly because the burgh of Lanark disliked having so many mouths to feed in prison pending their trial.

At Lauder, in 1649, Hob Grieve was accused of witchcraft. Twenty years agone his wife, who had been burnt for a witch, told Hob that he might get rich if he would follow her counsel and go along with her. So he went with her to a haugh on Gallow-water, to meet, as she said, a gentleman there; but he saw only a large mastiff dog, "which amazed him." At last came the devil as a black man, telling him that if he would take suit and service with him he should be made rich. He was to be officer at the meetings, and hold the door at the sabbaths. Hob consented, and for eighteen years held that office; but it does not seem that the foul fiend kept his part of the condition, for Hob had enough to do to find salt for his porridge. He was always poor, and remained poor to the end, with all the kicks and none of the halfpence; and for his eighteen years of servitude got only suspicion and ill-will, without fat or fry to comfort him. When taken, he "delated" many, who, for the most part, confessed. After he had filled the prison, so that it could hold no more, he accused another still, a woman of Lauder. The magistrate kept the secret, wishing to wait until some of the accused were "emptied out," having nowhere to put her; but the devil, always at mischief, went to her in the night time, and told her what Hob Grieve had said. Next day she arose and came to the prison, railing at Hob, calling him warlock and slave to the devil, and what not. She was told to go home, but she sat down on the Tolbooth stairs, and said she would never stir until she and that slave of Satan had been confronted. The bailie himself came to her, and told her to go home; but that was too mild a proceeding. "No," she cried, "I must be set face to face with that rascal who has delated me, an honest woman, for a witch." She was set face to face with him, and she fell down on her bare knees, and cursed him. Says she, "Thou common thief, how dare thou for thy soul say that ever before this time thou saw me or I saw thee, or ever was in thy company, either alone or with others?" Hob listened to her railings patiently, till commanded by the bailie to speak, when says he, "How came she then to know that I had called her a witch? Surely none but the devil, thy old master and mine, has told thee so much." "The devil and thou perish together, for he is not my master though he be thine. I defy the devil and all his works!" said the woman. Then Hob reminded her of the many times and places where they had met while in the same service; whereat she cried, "Now I perceive that the devil is a lyar and a murderer from the beginning, for this night he came to me, and told me to come and abuse thee; and never come away till I was confronted with thee, and he assured me that thou would deny all and say, thou false tongue, thou lyest!" She then confessed all with which she was charged, and was executed. Hob was a very penitent sinner: being now a mere lunatic, he was easy to manage, and exceeding confidential in his confessions. He said that once in Musselburgh water the devil had tried to drown him when he had a heavy creil on his back; and even since he had been in prison he had come to cast him into the fire. But though there was a very crowd "fylit" by this poor maniac, he was innocent of the death of a certain woman who was hanged a short time after. The magistrates, glutted to satiety with victims, wanted to save her; but she would accept no chance offered to her. She had been fyled as a witch, she said, and as a witch she would die. And had not the devil once, when she was a young lassie, kissed her, and given her a new name? Reason enough why she should die, if even nothing worse lay behind. At last the day of her execution came, and she was taken out to be burnt with the rest. On her way to the scaffold she made this lamentable speech:—"Now all you that see me this day, know that I am now to die a witch by my own confession; and I free all men, especially the ministers and magistrates, of the guilt of my blood. I take it wholly on myself. My blood be upon my own head; and as I must make answer to the God of heaven presently, I declare I am as free of witchcraft as any child; but being delated by a malicious woman, and put in prison under the name of a witch, disowned by my husband and friends, and seeing no ground of hope of my coming out of prison or ever coming in credit again, through a temptation of the devil, I made up that confession on purpose to destroy my own life, being weary of it, and choosing rather to die than to live." How many poor wretches had been like this unhappy creature—disowned by husband and friends, seeing no ground of hope of ever coming in credit again, and therefore in despair choosing rather to die than to live! In this special case even the magistrates, usually so passionately determined that all the accused should be found guilty and suffer death, even they seem to have sought her release, and to have refused the evidence of her confession as long as they could; but the times were not sufficiently enlightened for them to refuse it altogether; and so she gained the fiery goal whither her anguish and despair impelled her.

MANIE HALIBURTON.[43]

In 1649, John Kinnaird, the witch-finder, made deposition that he had "pricked" Patrik Watson, of West Fenton, and Manie Haliburton, his spouse, and that he had found the devil's mark on Patrik's back a little under the point of his left shoulder, and on Manie's neck a little above her left shoulder; of which marks they were not sensible (had no feeling in them), neither came there any blood when pricked. So Manie, seeing that the scent was hot and the game up, made confession, and saved further trouble. She said that eighteen years ago, the devil had come to her in likeness of a man, calling himself a physician, saying that he had good salves, and specially oylispek (oil of spike or spikenard), wherewith he would cure her daughter, then sick. So she bought some of his salves, and gave him two English shillings for her bargain, forbye bread and milk and a pint of ale. In eight days' time he came again, and stayed all night; and the next morning, Patrik being "forth" and Manie yet in bed, she became more intimately acquainted with the devil than an honest woman should. We do not read that Manie was tortured, and, considering that it was not an unusual thing to keep suspected witches twenty-eight days and nights on bread and water, they being stripped stark naked, with only a haircloth over them, and laid on a cold stone, or to put them into hair-shirts steeped in vinegar, so that the skin might be pulled from off them, we feel that poor Manie got off pretty well with only cremation as the result of her mad confessions.

But one of the most extraordinary things of all was that wonderful bit of knavery and credulity called

---

[43] Pitcairn.

THE DEVIL OF GLENLUCE,[44]

When Master Tom Campbell set the whole country in a flame, and brought no end of notice and sympathy upon his house and family. In 1654 one Gilbert Campbell was a weaver in Glenluce, a small village not far from Newton Stewart. Tom, his eldest son, and the most important personage in the drama, was a student at Glasgow College; and there was a certain old blaspheming beggar, called Andrew Agnew—afterwards hanged at Dumfries for his atheism, having said, in the hearing of credible witnesses, that "there was no God but salt, meal, and water"—who every now and then came to Glenluce to ask alms. One day old Andrew visited the Campbells as usual, but got nothing; at which he cursed and swore roundly, and forthwith sent a devil to haunt the house, for it was soon after this refusal that the stirs began, and the connection was too apparent to be denied. For what could they be but the malice of the devil sent by old Andrew in revenge? Young Tom Campbell was the worst beset of all, the demon perpetually whistling and rioting about him, and playing him all sorts of diabolical and malevolent tricks. Once, too, Jennet, the young daughter, going to the well, heard a whistling behind her like that produced by "the small slender glass whistles of children," and a voice like the damsel's, saying, "I'll cast thee, Jennet, into the well! I'll cast thee, Jennet, into the well!" About the middle of November, when the days were dark and the nights long, things got very bad. The foul fiend threw stones in at the doors and windows, and down the chimney head; cut the warp and threads of Campbell's loom; slit the family coats and bonnets and hose and shoon into ribbons; pulled off the bed-clothes from the sleeping children, and left them cold and naked, besides administering sounding slaps on those parts of their little

---

[44] Sinclair.

104

round rosy persons usually held sacred to the sacrifices of the rod; opened chests and trunks, and strewed the contents over the floor; knocked everything about, and ill-treated bairn and brother; and, in fact, persecuted the whole family in the most merciless manner. The weaver sent his children away, thinking their lives but barely safe, and *in their absence there were no assaults whatever*—a thing to be specially noted. But on the minister's representing to him that he had done a grievous sin in thus withdrawing them from God's punishments, they were brought back again in contrition. Only Tom was left behind, and nothing ensued until Tom appeared; but unlucky Tom brought back the devil with him, and then there was no more peace to be had.

On the Sunday following Master Tom's return, the house was set on fire—the devil's doing: but the neighbours put the flames out again before much damage had ensued. Monday was spent in prayer; but on Tuesday the place was again set on fire, to be again saved by the neighbours' help. The weaver, in much trouble, went to the minister, and besought him to take back that unlucky Tom, whom the devil so cruelly followed and molested; which request he, after a time, "condescended to," though assuring the weaver that he would find himself deceived if he thought that the devil would quit with the boy. And so it proved; for Tom, having now indoctrinated some of his juniors with the same amount of mechanics and legerdemain as he himself possessed, managed that they should be still sore troubled—the demon cutting their clothes, throwing peats down the chimney, pulling off turf and "feal" from the roof and walls, stealing their coats, pricking their poor bodies with pins, and raising such a clamour that there was no peace or rest to be had.

The case was becoming serious. Glenluce objected to be made the head-quarters of the devil; and the ministers convened a solemn meeting for fast and humiliation; the upshot of which was that weaver Campbell was led to take back his unlucky Tom, with the devil or without him. For this was the point at issue in the beginning; the motive of which is not hard to be discovered. Whereupon Tom returned; but as he crossed the threshold he heard a voice "forbidding him to enter that house, or any other place where his father's calling was exercised." Was Tom, the Glasgow student, afraid of being made a weaver, consent or none demanded? In spite of the warning voice he valiantly entered, and his persecutions began at once. Of course they did. They were tremendous, unheard of, barbarous; in fact, so bad that he was forced to return once more for a time to the minister's house; but his imitator or disciple left behind carried on business in his absence. On Monday, the 12th day of February, the demon began to speak to the family, who, nothing afraid, answered quite cheerily: so they and the devil had long confidential chats together, to the great improvement of mind and morals. The ministers, hearing of this, convened again, and met at weaver Campbell's, to see what they could do. As soon as they entered, Satan began: "Quum literatum is good Latin," quoth he. These were the first words of the Latin rudiments, as taught in the grammar-school. Tom's classical knowledge was coming into play.

After a while he cried out, "A dog! a dog!" The minister, thinking he was alluded to, answered, "He thought it no evil to be reviled of him;" to which Satan replied civilly, "It was not you, sir, I spoke to: I meant the dog there;" for there was a dog standing behind backs. They then went to prayer, during which time Tom—or the devil—remained reverently silent; his education being not yet carried out to the point of scoffing. Immediately after prayer was ended, a counterfeit voice cried out, "Would you know the witches of Glenluce? I will tell of them," naming four or five persons of indifferent repute, but one of whom was dead. The weaver told the devil this, thinking to have caught him tripping; but the foul fiend answered promptly, "It is true she is dead long ago, but her spirit is living with us in the world."

The minister replied, saying, "Though it was not convenient to speak to such an excommunicated and intercommuned person, 'the Lord rebuke thee, Satan, and put thee to silence. We are not to receive information from thee, whatsoever fame any person goes under. Thou art seeking but to seduce this family, for Satan's kingdom is not divided against itself.'" After which little sparring there was prayer again; so Tom did not take much by this move.

All the while the young Glasgow student was very hardly holden, so that there was more prayer on his special behalf. The devil then said, on their rising, "Give me a spade and a shovel, and depart from the house for seven days, and I will make a grave and lie down in it, and shall trouble you no more."

The good man Campbell answered, "Not so much as a straw shall be given thee, through God's assistance, even though that would do it. God shall remove thee in due time." Satan cried out, impudently, "I shall not remove for you. I have my commission from Christ to tarry and vex this family." Says the minister, coming to the weaver's assistance, "A permission thou hast, indeed; but God will stop it in due time." Says the demon, respectfully, "I have, sir, a commission which perhaps will last longer than yours." And the minister died in the December of that year, says Sinclair. Furthermore, the demon said he had given Tom his commission to keep. Interrogated, that young gentleman replied in an off-hand way, that "he had had something put into his pocket, but it did not tarry." They then began to search about for the foul fiend, and one gentleman said, "We think this voice speaks out of the children." The foul fiend, very angry at this—or Master Tom frightened—cries out, "You lie! God shall judge you for your lying; and I and my father will come and fetch you to hell with warlock thieves." So the devil discharged (forbade) the gentleman to speak anything, saying, "Let him that hath a commission speak (meaning the minister), for he is the servant of God." The minister then had a little religious controversy with the devil, who answered at last, simply, "I knew not these scriptures till my father taught me them." Nothing of all this disturbing the easy faith of the audience, they, through the minister, whom alone he would obey, conjured him to tell them who he was; whereupon he said that he was an evil spirit come from the bottomless pit of hell, to vex this house, and that Satan was his father. And then there appeared a naked hand, and an arm from the elbow downward, beating on the floor till the house did shake again, and a loud and fearful crying, "Come up, father! come up, father! I will send my father among ye! See! there he is behind your backs!"

Says the minister, "I saw, indeed, a hand and an arm, when the stroke was given and heard."

Says the devil, "Saw ye that? It was not my hand, it was my father's; my hand is more black in the loof."

"Oh!" said Gilbert Campbell, in an ecstacy, "that I might see thee as well as I hear thee!"

"Would ye see me?" says the foul thief. "Put out the candle, and I shall come but[45] the house among you like fire-balls; I shall let ye see me indeed."

Alexander Bailie of Dunraget said to the minister, "Let us go ben,[46] and see if there is any hand to be seen." But the demon exclaimed, "No! let him (the minister) come ben alone: he is a good honest man: his single word may be believed." He then abused Mr. Robert Hay, a very honest gentleman, very ill with his tongue, calling him witch and warlock: and a little while after, cried out, "A witch! a witch! there's a witch sitting upon the ruist! take her

---

[45] To the outer room.
[46] To the inner room.

away." He meant that there was a hen sitting on one of the rafters. They then went to prayer again, and, when ended, the devil cried out, "If the good man's son's prayers at the College of Glasgow did not prevail with God, my father and I had wrought a mischief here ere now." Ah, Master Tom, did you then know so much of prayer and the inclining of the counsels of God?

Alexander Bailie said, "Well, I see you acknowledge a God, and that prayer prevails with him, and therefore we must pray to God, and commit the event to him." To whom the devil replied, having an evident spite against Alexander Bailie, "Yea, sir, you speak of prayer, with your broad-lipped hat" (for the gentleman had lately gotten a hat in the fashion with broad lips); "I'll bring a pair of shears from my father's which shall clip the lips of it a little." And Alexander Bailie presently heard a pair of shears go clipping round his hat, "which he lifted, to see if the foul thief had meddled with it."

Then the fiend fell to prophesying. "Tom was to be a merchant, Bob a smith, John a minister, and Hugh a lawyer," all of which came to pass. Turning to Jennet, the good man's daughter, he cried, "Jennet Campbell, Jennet Campbell, wilt thou cast me thy belt?"

Quoth she, "What a widdy would thou do with my belt?"

"I would fain," says he, "fasten my loose bones together."

A younger daughter was sitting "busking her puppies" (dressing her puppets, dolls), as young girls are used to do. He threatens to "ding out her harns," that is, to brain her; but says she quietly, "No, if God be to the fore," and so falls to her work again. The good wife having brought out some bread, was breaking it, so that every one of the company should have a piece. Cries he, "Grissel Wyllie! Grissel Wyllie! give me a piece of that haver bread. I have gotten nothing this day but a bit from Marritt," that is, as they speak in the country, Margaret. The minister said to them all, "Beware of that! for it is sacrificing to the devil!" Marritt was then called, and inquired if she had given the foul fiend any of her haver bread. "No," says she; "but when I was eating my due piece this morning, something came and clicked it out of my hands."

The evening had now come, and the company prepared to depart; the minister, and the minister's wife, Alexander Bailie of Dunraget, with his broad-lipped hat, and the rest. But the devil cried out in a kind of agony—

"Let not the minister go! I shall burn the house if he goes." Weaver Campbell, desperately frightened, besought the minister to stay; and he, not willing to see them come to mischief, at last consented. As he turned back into the house, the devil gave a great gaff of laughing, saying, "Now, sir! you have done my bidding!" which was unhandsome of Tom—very.

"Not thine, but in obedience to God, have I returned to bear this man company whom thou dost afflict," says the minister, nowise discomposed, and not disdaining to argue matters clearly with the devil.

Then the minister "discharged" all from speaking to the demon, saying, "that when it spoke to them they must only kneel and pray to God." This did not suit the demon at all. He roared mightily, and cried, "What! will ye not speak to me? I shall strike the bairns, and do all manner of mischief!" No answer was returned; and again the children were slapped and beaten on their rosy parts—where children are accustomed to be whipped. After a while this ended too, and then the fiend called out to the good-wife, "Grissel, put out the candle!"

"Shall I do it?" says she to the minister's wife.

"No," says that discreet person, "for then you shall obey the devil."

Upon which the devil shouted, with a louder voice, "Put out the candle!" No one obeyed, and the candle continued burning. "Put out the candle, I say!" cries he, more terribly than before. Grissel, not caring to continue the uproar, put it out. "And now," says he, "I will trouble you no more this night." For by this time I should suppose that Master Tom was sleepy, and tired, and hoarse.

Once again the ministers and gentlemen met for prayer and exorcism; when it is to be presumed that Tom was not with them, for everything was quiet; but soon after the stirs began again, and Tom and the rest were sore molested. Gilbert Campbell made an appeal to the Synod of Presbyters, a committee of whom appointed a special day of humiliation in February, 1656, for the freeing of the weaver's house from this affliction. In consequence whereof, from April to August, the devil was perfectly quiet, and the family lived together in peace. But after this the mischief broke out again afresh. Perhaps Tom had come home from college, or his father had renewed his talk of settling him firmly to his own trade: whatever the cause, the effect was certain, the devil had come back to Glenluce.

One day, as the good-wife was standing by the fire, making the porridge for the children, the demon came and snatched the "tree-plate," on which was the oatmeal, out of her hand, and spilt all the meal. "Let me have the tree-plate again," says Grissel Wyllie, very humbly; and it came flying back to her. "It is like if she had sought the meal too she might have got it, such is his civility when he is intreated," says Sinclair. But this would have been rather beyond even Master Tom's power of legerdemain. Things after this went very ill. The children were daily thrashed with heavy staves, and every one in the family underwent much personal damage; until, as a climax, on the eighteenth of September, the demon said he would burn the house down, and did, in fact, set it on fire. But it was put out again, before much damage was done.

After a time—probably by Tom's going away, or becoming afraid of being found out—the devil was quieted and laid for ever; and Master Tom employed his intellect and energies in other ways than terrifying his father's family to death, and making stirs which went by the name of demoniac.

This account is taken almost verbatim from an article of mine in "All the Year Round;" and if a larger space has been given to this than to many other stories, it is because there was more colouring, and more distinctness in the drawing, than in anything else that I have read. Though scarcely belonging to a book on witches, there is yet a hook and eye, if a very slender one, in the fact that the old beggar, Andrew Agnew, was hanged; and we may be sure that it was not only his atheism, but also his naughty tricks with Satan, and his connection with the devil of Glenluce, that helped to fit the hangman's rope round his neck. There are many other stories of haunted houses, notably, Mr. Monpesson's at Tedworth caused by the Demon Drummer, and the Woodstock Devil who harried the Parliamentary Commissioners to within an inch of their lives, and others to the full as interesting; but there is no hook and eye with them—nothing by which they can be hung on to the sad string of witches, or witchcraft murders. Baxter has two or three such stories; and the curious in such matters will find a large amount of interesting matter in the various works referred to at the foot of the pages; matter which could not be introduced here, because of its not belonging strictly to the subject in hand. I do not think that any candid or unprejudiced person will fail in seeing the dark shadow of fraud and deceit flung over every such account remaining. The importance of which, to me, is the evident and distinct likeness between these stories and the marvels going on now in modern society.

JONET WATSON AND THE DEVIL IN GREEN.

Steadily went on these appalling judicial crimes. In February, 1658, two women and a man were in the Tolbooth at Edinburgh, imprisoned on the charge of witchcraft. One of the women died in prison, the other, Jonet Anderson,[47] confessed that before her marriage, which had been only three months ago, she had given herself up body and soul to the devil, and that when she was married she had seen him standing by the pulpit. She was kept only so long as was necessary to prove her not pregnant, and then was executed, fully repentant. In August four women, "ane of them a maiden," were burnt on the Castle Hill in ghastly company; and soon after five more from Dunbar; and then again nine from Tranent, all confessing. These seemed to have stayed the appetite of the magistrates for a time, as we come across no more until 1661, when a painful collection of lies, slanders, and confessions again harrow up every feeling, and outrage every reasoning faculty.

Jonet Watson was one of the first to make her confession. She said that in April last, bypast or thereby, she being at the burial of Lady Dalhousie, a rix dollar was given to Jean Bughane, to be divided among a certain number of poor folk, whereof she was one. But Jean ran away with the money, so poor Jonet got none of it: whereat being very grieved and angry, when she came to her own house she wished to be revenged on Jean, and at the wish appeared the devil in the likeness of a pretty boy in green clothes, and asked: "what ailed her, and what revenge would she have?" He then gave her his mark and left her under the form of a black dog, and for three days after she had a gnat constantly with her, and one morning when she was changing her linen it sat down upon her shoulder,

---

[47] Chambers.

where she had one of her marks. Also about the time of last Baal-fyre night (the beginning of May) she was at a meeting in Newton-dein, where was the devil dressed in green clothes, with a black hat on his head. And here she denied Christ, and took upon herself to be his servant, he laying his hand on her head, and receiving from her "all that was under his hand," when he gave her the name of "weill-dancing Jonet," and she and a few more danced like Tam o' Shanter's hags, and probably tired the devil out.

Beatrice Leslie[48] was a witch too, and Agnes, wife of William Young, gave her some wholesome advice and honest reproof on the matter, whereby Beatrice was offended, and gave her a terrible look; and that very night William Young awakened out of his sleep all in terror and dismay, crying out that Beatrice, with a number of cats, was devouring him. Beatrice had a cat which two coal-heaving damsels killed by letting some coals fall on it, afterwards adding to their offence by throwing away her coal-basket. So Beatrice cursed them, and told them "they should see an ill sight before eight days were past:" as it fell out, for according to her threatening they were both killed in the coal-pit, though no one else was hurt; and when she was brought to see and touch the corpses, the one bled at the nose and the other at the ear, thus proving her guilt beyond the possibility of denial. Also she helped Alexander Wilson's wife in child-bed, by cantrips and unholy sleights; sticking a bare knife betwixt the bed and the straw, sprinkling salt about the bed, and saying, "Lord, let never ane worse wight waken thee, nor hes laid thee downe," with other villanies, unwholesome to honest folk; so Beatrice Leslie saw the sun for the last time between the cord and the flames.

---

[48] Chambers.

THE LANTHORNE AND THE BAHR-RECHT.[49]

Christian Wilson, *alias* the Lanthorne, which name she had gotten from the devil at the time of her baptism, was too famous in her generation. She lived near her brother Alexander, and there was notorious ill blood between them, perhaps because of her notorious evil proceedings. One evening Alexander was found dead in his own house, naked, with his face torn and cut, but without a spot of blood anywhere. Yet a "greate lumpe of fleisch" had been cut out of his cheek more cleanly than any ordinary razor could have cut either flesh or cheese. Christian bore herself strangely. She expressed no sorrow, perhaps because she felt none, and absolutely refused to see or touch the corpse according to the fashion of the honest and the orthodox of the time. This refusal did her much harm in men's minds, for was it not very evident that she was afraid of the bier-law, or bahr-recht, which, in 1661, when all this took place, was such a useful agent of the police, and helped so powerfully to the discovery of murder? The bailies and ministers heard the rumours affecting her, and commanded her to be brought into the house to touch the corpse, as the rest had done. "She came trembling all the way to the house, but she refused to come nigh the corpse, or to touch it, saying that 'she never touched a dead corpse in her life.'" The neighbours did not allow of her plea, and dragged her to the murdered man, that she might touch it softly. She went forward to do so. "But before shoe did it, the Sone being shyning in at the howse, shoe exprest herselfe thus, humbly desyring that, 'as the Lord made the Sone to shine and give light into that howse, that also he would give light to discovering of that murder!' And with these words shoe tuitching the wound of the dead man verie

---

[49] Pitcairn and Sinclair.

115

softlie, it being whyte and cleane, without any spot of blood or the lyke, yet immediately, while her fingers was upon it, the blood rushed owt of it, to the greate admiratioune of all the behoulders, who tooke it for discoverie of the murder according to her own prayers." Another charge, no less grave than that of murder, was, that William Richardson, having felled one of her hens with a stone, she frowned on him threateningly, and said he should never throw another stone. And he never did; for immediately he fell into ane "franicie" and madness, took to his bed, and died in a few days, all the time of his sickness crying out against Cristiane Wilson, who, he said, was tormenting him in the likeness of a grey cat. After his death his nephew teased the witch by calling her "The Lanthorne," which every one knew to be her devil-name; but Cristiane threatened him, and said that "if he did not hold his peace she would make him die by the same death as his uncle," which was proof sufficient of the truth of the grey cat and her guilty sorcery. This was the same Cristiane Wilson who, when she was being carried off to Nidrie, there to be confronted with another witch, was suddenly lifted off the pillion by a furious blast of wind, which she got the devil to raise in the hope of her rescue. But though she was blown into the stream, she swam lightly as a witch should and as only a witch could, and her jailers fished her out again, to secure her better for the future. As the sky was cloudless when the blast arose, and as no storm followed after, there was no possibility of doubting the Satanic origin of that mighty puff of wind. Besides, did not Jennot Cock, another confessing witch, say to John Stevin, when he told her that Cristiane was to be carried to Nidrie to-morrow, "Will not yow think it a sport, if the deivill raise a whirrell of wind, and tak her away from among yow by the gette (way) to-morrow?" This and that together made the thing certain; and the fall of the poor wretch was included in the dittay as one of the counts against her, proving her witchcraft.

Witch-finding now increased rapidly in Scotland. No fewer than fourteen special commissions were issued for the sole purpose of trying witches for the sederunt of November the 7th, 1661; and on the 23rd of January, 1662, fourteen more were made out. It was the popular amusement of the day, and no one or two men then living could have turned the tide in favour of these poor persecuted creatures. Even Sir George Mackenzie, that "noble wit of Scotland," failed to make any reasonable impression on the besotted public, though his pleadings and writings got him into immense disfavour with the religious part of the community, and caused him to be ranked as an atheist and Sadducee, and classed with the Pilates and Judases of history. Though it had been the Bull of Pope Innocent VIII. in 1484, which had first stirred up the zeal of the godly against witchcraft, and written that terrible text, "Thou shalt not suffer a witch to live," in still more terrible characters of blood and suffering, yet Calvinistic Scotland soon outstripped even the superstitious Papacy in her frantic piety, and poured out a sea of innocent blood which will stain her pages with an ineffaceable stain, for ever and for ever. Yet she was nearly a hundred years behind Rome in her zeal, for it was not till June, 1563, that she made the subject matter for legislation at all, and then the Estates[50] enacted "that 'nae person take upon hand to use any manner of witchcrafts, sorcery, or necromancy, nor give themselves furth to have ony sic craft or knowledge thereof therethrough abusing the people;' also, that 'nae person seek ony help, response, or consultation, at ony sic users or abusers of witchcrafts ... under pain of death.' This is the statute under which all the subsequent witch trials took place." But bad as it was under the Presbyterians and the Elders, it is true that under the Restoration the witch persecutions in Scotland were even more excessive than

---

[50] Chambers' 'Domestic Annals.'

117

during the reign of the Covenanters, and that the return of Charles II. brought satisfaction and pleasure to the younger women only of his dominions, but nothing save torture to the old, the poor, and the despised. Ray says that about a hundred and twenty witches suffered in the year 1661, the year after the Restoration had brought joy and gladness to all loyal hearts; so that it mattered little whether Puritan or Cavalier, Presbyterian or Episcopalian, had the upper hand. Superstition was the greatest lord of all, and a slavish adherence to a few words fettered men down hopelessly to ignorance and wickedness.

At this time (1661) John Kincaid and John Dick were the most notorious prickers; and they let no one escape whom they had the chance of hurting. One John Hay, an old man of sixty, and of untarnished reputation, fell into Dick's hands, accused of sorcery by "a distracted woman," whose words were not worth the wind that wafted them. But Dick shaved him, and pricked him, and tortured him in all allowable ways, then sent him off to Edinburgh, two hundred miles away, to be locked up in the Tolbooth, pending further proceedings. The case against him was too slight for even those times to entertain, and he was liberated on his own petition, and a few testimonials: but John Dick was not reproved, nor was his zeal thought extreme or passionate.

MISCELLANEOUS.

Margaret Bryson[51] quarrelled with her husband about the selling of a cow; she went to the house-door, "and there did imprecate that God or the devil might take her from her husband;" which naturally ended in the devil's appearing and forcing her into the covenant with him that had its final expression at the stake.

Margaret Hutchison was a witch, too. She laid on Henry Balfour the pains of a child-bed woman, and caused such a universal swelling of his body that he died thereof; and she threatened John Boost for calling her a witch, and threw a piece of raw flesh against his house, which the very dogs and cats would not eat; and she sent a plague of cats to John Bell's house, and tormented him and his wife by appearing at their hearth-side at night, combing her hair: so Margaret Hutchison was no better than she should be, and the world was well rid of her.

Isabel Ramsey for her part was convicted of taking sixpence from the devil, and entering into a long chat with him upon sundry local matters; and, indeed, she herself confessed that he gave her a dollar, which turned into a sklaitt stane: for nothing that the devil did for these witches ever turned to good, so that one is more surprised at their stupidity than offended by their guilt.

Jennet Cock[52] had an ill name, past all forbearance or overlooking. She was never easy unless she was after some evil, and the world must positively be quit of her. She bewitched William Scott's bonny bay horse, worth pounds and pounds of money, and made him mad; and she told a brute who beat her that he should live to be hanged, which not very unlikely prediction was fulfilled; and she kept company with the devil on terms that no honest woman

---

[51] Law—Sharp's Introduction.
[52] Dalyell.

should endure; and she and Jean Dickson, another witch, cured a neighbour's child by cutting off a dog's head, with which they played some devilish cantrip that healed the bairn; and she it was who made that speech concerning Christiane Wilson and the gaff of wind; so Jennet Cock was adjudged dangerous to be at large, and was put into prison, there to await her trial. And she was tried, but, strange to say, acquitted of the charges brought against her; she was not let loose though, but kept still in durance till a fresh case could be completed against her. Jennet Cock was rather notorious for her evil eye and power of overlooking, and in her dittay is thus charged:—"There being an outcast betwixt yow and Jeane Forrest, because schoe had called yow a witch, yow came to the said Jeane, her landlord's house, where she was with some nyghboures, desyreing to make aggriement betwixt yow. Ye malitiouslie and bitterlie girneing and gnashing your teeth, and beating your hands upon your knies, said, 'O them that called me a witch! O them that called me a witch!' And at that tyme, the said Jeane Forrest, her chylde being in good health, on the morne the chylde, by your sorceries and witchcraft dyed; and the mother, at the chylde's departour, called out with a loud voyce upone her nighbours, saying, 'Alace! that ever I had adoe with that witch Janet Cock, for shoe has been at my bed syd all this night standing, and I could not get red of her: and behold the fruit of it—my chylde is dead!'" This deposition was made September 10, 1661, and surely Jennet Cock never escaped the consequences of such a cantrip as this!

Marion Grinlaw[53] and Jean Howison, "the survivors of ten women and a man who had been imprisoned at Musselburgh," petitioned the Council for their release. "Some of the rest died of cold and hunger. They themselves had lain in durance *forty weeks*, and were now in a state of

---

[53] Chambers.

extreme misery, *although nothing could be brought against them*. Margaret Carvie and Barbara Horniman, of Falkland, had in like manner been imprisoned at the instance of the magistrates and parish minister, had lain six weeks in jail, subjected to a great deal of torture by one who takes upon him the trial of witches by pricking; and so great was their sufferings that life was become a burden to them, notwithstanding that they declared their innocence, and nothing to the contrary had been shown. The Council ordered all these women to be liberated:" which was a marvellous outstep of humanity, and one for which its previous acts could hardly have prepared us. The next year it seems to have had a small side-blow of rationality. It had become sensible of the vile inhumanity of John Kincaid, and threw the wretch into prison, then issued a proclamation repudiating the seizure of suspected persons, which had been made illegally, unauthorizedly, and out of only envy and covetousness. Nevertheless, it took care to issue twelve fresh commissions for trying witches, immediately after; being chiefly anxious to keep all the business in its own hands, and shut the door against any outside free lances. John Kincaid lay for nine weeks in jail, then was liberated only on condition that he would prick no more without warrant. He sent up a whining petition, setting forth that he was an old man, and if confined longer might be brought to mortal sickness; so to avert this terrible catastrophe, the old sinner had his liberty given to him again: he ought to have had instead the doom of the murderer for blood-money!

CLOWTS AND THE SERPENT.[54]

In the parish of Innerkip, on March 4, 1662, Marie Lamont, a "young Woman of the adge of Eighteen Yeares," offered herself for voluntary confession. She said that five years ago Kattrein Scot taught her to take kyes' milk. She told her to go out in misty mornings with a hair rope (harrie tedder), which she was to draw over the mouth of a mug, saying, "In God's name, God send us milk, God sent it, and mickle of it." By which means she and Kattrein got much of their neighbours' milk which they made into butter and cheese. Also she said, that two years and a half since, the devil came to them at Kattrein Scot's house, where many of them were present, and gave them all wine to drink and wheat bread to eat, and they danced and were very merry, the devil shaking hands with them, and she delivering herself over to him in baptism. And at her baptism she was given the name of "Clowts," and bid to call the devil "Serpent." Further, "Shee confessed that at that sam tym the devil nipit her upon the right syd, qlk was very painful for a tym, but yairefter he straikit it with his hand, and healed it; this she confesses to be his mark." At a certain meeting which she spoke of, when she and the rest went to raise storms to hinder the Killing fishery, the devil came to them in the likeness of a brown dog, but she and Kattrein were as cats, and in this form they ran into Allan Orr's house and took a bite of a herring lying in a barrel. They then put it back again, and Allan Orr's wife, afterwards finishing the herring, took heavy disease, and died. The reason of this malicious act was, that Allan Orr had put Margaret Holm (one of the cats) out of her house, and this was the manner in which she chose to be revenged— "threitening in wrath, that he and his wife sould not be long together." Many other things did she confess: one of which

---

[54] Law's 'Memorials'—Sharp's Introductory Notice.

was how the devil once "convoyed her home in the dawing; and when shee was com near the house wherein she was a servant, her master saw a waff of him as he went away from her." Another time she and some other witches met at the back gate of Ardgowand, where his Cloutieship appeared in the likeness of a black man with cloven feet, directing them to take white sand and cast it about the gates of Ardgowand, and about the minister's house; and while they were about the business he turned them into the likeness of cats, by shaking his hands above them. And at another time they went to cast the longston into the sea, to cause storms and shipwrecks, and the devil kissed them as they went away, apparently better pleased than ordinarily with his Clowts and Kats. All these things did poor Marie Lamont, aged eighteen, confess to the minister and Laird of Innerkip; and they, not knowing the virtue of purgatives and port wine, nor understanding the value of rest and silence, took the poor young soul at her word, and found her guilty of all the crimes and follies with which a diseased body, and a mind overset and charged, had prompted her to accuse herself.

And now we come to

THE WITCHES OF AULDEARNE:[55]

And Isobell Gowdie's marvellous confessions: still in A.D. 1662. Isobell was neither pricked nor tortured before she entered on her singular history of circumstantial lies. She was probably a mere lunatic, whose ravings ran in the popular groove, and who was not so much deceiving, as self-deceived by insanity. The assize which tried her was composed of highly respectable people, and she seems to have been only encouraged to rave, not forced to lie. She began by stating that one day, fifteen years ago, as she was going between "the towns" or farmsteads of Drumdewin and the Heads, she met the devil, who spoke to her and invited her to meet him that night at the parish church of Auldearne. She promised that she would, and accordingly she went, and he baptized her by the name of "Janet," and accepted her service. Margaret Brodie held her while she denied her Christian baptism; and then the devil marked her on the shoulder, sucking out the blood which he "spouted" into his hand, then sprinkled it on her head, saying, "I baptize thee, Janet, in my own name!" But first he had put one hand on the crown of her head, and the other on the soles of her feet, while she made over to him all that lay betwixt, giving herself body and soul into his keeping. He was in the Reader's desk while all this took place, appearing as a "mickle, black, hairy man" reading out of a black book; so Isobell was henceforth Janet in the witch world, and was one of the most devoted of her covin; for they were divided into covins or bands, she said, and placed under the leadership of proper officers. John Young was the officer of her covin, and the number composing it was thirteen. She and others of her band took Breadley's corn from off his land. They took an unchristened child which they had raised out of its grave, parings of their nails, ears

---

[55] Pitcairn.

of all sorts of grain, and cole-wort leaves, all chopped very fine and small, and mixed up well together; and this charm they buried on his land, whereby they got all the strength of his corn and goods to themselves, and parted them among the covin. Another time they yoked a plough of paddocks (toads). The devil held it, and John Young drove it: it was drawn by toads instead of oxen, the traces were of quickens (dog-grass), the coulter was a riglen's horn (ram's horn), so was the sock; and they went two several times about the field, all the covin following and praying to the devil to give them the fruit of that land, and that only thistles and briars might grow on it for the master's use. So Breadley had trouble enough to work his land, and when it was worked he got no good out of it, but only weeds and thorns, while the covin made their bread of his labour.

When asked how she and her sister witches managed to leave their husbands o' nights, she said that, when it was their Sabbath nights, they used to put besoms or three-legged stools in bed beside their husbands; so that if these deluded men should wake before their return, they might believe they had their wives safe as usual. The besoms and three-legged stools took the right form of the women, and prevented a too early discovery. To go to these Sabbaths they put a straw between their feet, crying "Horse and Hattock in the Devil's name!" and then they would fly away, just as straws in the wind. Any kind of straw would do, and they who saw them floating about in the whirlwind, and did not sanctify themselves, could be shot dead at the witches' pleasure, and their bodies remained with them as horses, and small as straws.

These night meetings always ended with a supper; the Maiden of the Covin being placed next to the devil, as he was partial to young, plump, blooming witches, and did not care much for the "rigwoodie hags," save to beat and belabour them. And after they had gotten their meat they would say as a grace—

"We eat this meat in the devil's name,
With sorrow and *sich* (sighs) and mickle shame;
We shall destroy both house and hald;
Both sheep and nolt intil the fauld,
Little good shall come to the fore,
Of all the rest of the little store."

And when supper was done, each witch would look steadily upon their "grisly" president and say, bowing low, "We thank thee, our Lord, for this!" But it was not much to thank him for in general; for the old adage seems to have been pretty nearly kept to, and the cooks, at least, not to speak of the meat, to be of the very lowest description. The poor witches never got more from the devil than what they might have had at home; which was one more added to the many proofs that the mind cannot travel beyond its own sphere of knowledge, and that even hallucinations are bounded by experience, and clairvoyance by the past actual vision.

Then Isobell went to the Downie Hills, to see the gude wichtis who had wrought Bessie Dunlop and Alesoun Peirsoun such sad mishap. The hill side opened and she went in. Here she got meat more than she could eat, which was a rare thing for her to do in those days, and seemed to her one of the most noticeable things of the visit. The Queen of Faerie was bravely clothed in white linen, and white and brown clothes, but she was nothing like the glorious creature who bewitched Thomas of Ercildoun with her winsom looks and golden hair; and the king was a braw man, well favoured and broad faced; just an ordinary man and woman of the better classes, buxom, brave, and comely, as Isobell Gowdie and her like would naturally take to be the ultimate perfection of humanity. But it was not all sunshine and delight even in the hill of Faerie, for there were "elf bullis rowting and skoylling" up and down, which frightened poor Isobell, as well as her auditory: for here she was interrupted and bidden on another track. She then went on to say that when they took away any cow's milk they did so by twining and platting a rope the wrong way and in the devil's name, drawing the tether in between the cow's hinder feet, and out between her fore feet. The only way to get back the milk was to cut the rope. When they took away the strength of any one's ale in favour of themselves or others, they used to take a little quantity out of each barrel, in the devil's name (they never forgot this formula), and then put it into the ale they wished to strengthen; and no one had power to keep their ale from them, save those who had well sanctified the brewing. Also she and others made a clay picture of a little child, which was to represent all the male children of the Laird of Parkis. John Taylor brought home the clay in his "plaid newk" (corner), his wife brake it very small like meal, and sifted it, and poured water in among it in the devil's name, and worked it about like rye porridge ("vrought it werie sore, lyk rye-bowt") and made it into a picture of the Laird of Parkis' son. "It haid all the pairtis and merkis of a child, such as heid, eyes, nose, handis, foot, mowth, and little lippes. It wanted no mark of a child; and the handis of it folded down by its sydes." This precious image, which was like a lump of dough or a skinned sucking pig, was put to the fire till it shrivelled and became red as a coal; they put it to the fire every other day, and by the wicked power enclosed in this charm all the male children of the Laird of Parkis would suffer, unless it were broken up. She and the rest went in and out their neighbours' houses, sometimes as jackdaws, sometimes as hares, cats, &c., and ate and drank of the best; and they took away the virtue of all things left "unsained;" and each had their own powers. "Bot," said Isobell, sorrowfully, "now I haw no power at all." In another confession she told all about her Covin. There were thirteen in each, and every person had a nickname, and a spirit to wait on her. She could not remember the names of all, but she gave what she could. Swein clothed in grass green waited on Margaret Wilson, called Pickle-nearest-the-wind: Rorie in yellow waited on Bessie Wilson, or Throw-the-corn-yard: the Roaring Lion in seagreen waited on Isobell Nichol, or Bessie Rule: Mak Hector, a young-like devil, clothed in grass green, was appropriated by Jean Martin, daughter to Margaret Wilson (Pickle-nearest-the-wind), the Maiden of the Covin and called Over-the-Dyke-with-it; this name given to her because the devil always takes the maiden in his hand next him, and when he would leap they both cry out, "Over the dyke with it!" Robert the Rule in sad dun, a commander of the spirits, waited on Margaret Brodie, Thief-of-hell-wait-upon-herself: he waited also on Bessie Wilson, otherwise Throw-the-corn-yard: Isobell's own spirit was the Red Riever, and he was ever clothed in black: the eighth spirit was Robert the Jakes, aged, and clothed in dun, "ane glaiked gowked spirit," and he waited on Bessie Hay, otherwise Able-and-Stout: the ninth was Laing, serving Elspet Nishie, re-named Bessie Bauld; the tenth was Thomas, a faerie:—but there Isobell's questioners stopped her, afraid to hear aught of the "guide wychtis," who might be then among them, injuring those who offended them to death. So no more information was given of the spirits of the Covin. She then told them that to raise a wind they took a rag of cloth which they wetted, then knocked on a stone with a beetle (a flat piece of wood) saying thrice—

"I knok this ragg wpon this stane,
To raise the wind in the Divelle's name;
It sall not lye, vntil I please againe!"

When the wind was to be laid, they dried the rag, and said thrice—

"We lay the wind in the divellis name,
It sall not rise quhill we lyk to raise it again!"

And if the wind would not cease the instant after they said this, they called to their spirit: "Thieffe! thieffe! conjure the wind and caws it to lye!" As for elf-arrow heads, the devil shapes them with his own hand, and then delivers them to elf boys who sharpen and trim them with a thing like a packing-needle: and when Isobell was in elf-land she saw the boys sharpening and trimming them. Those who trimmed them, she said, are little ones, hollow and hump-backed, and speak gruffly like. When the devil gave the arrows to the witches he used to say—

"Shoot these in my name,
And they sall not goe heall hame."

And when the witches shoot them, which they do by "spanging" them from their thumb nails, they say—

"I shoot yon man in the devillis name,
He sall nott win heall hame!
And this salbe alswa trw,
Thair sall not be an bitt of him on liew."[56]

Isobell had great talent for rhymes. She told the court how, when the witches wanted to transform themselves into the shape of hare or cat, they said thrice over—always thrice—

"I sall goe intill ane haire,
With sorrow, and sych, and mickle caire;
And I sall goe in the divellis name,
Ay whill I com hom againe."

---

[56] On life: alive.

Once Isobell said this rhyme, when Patrik Papley's servants were going to labour. They had their dogs with them, and the dogs hunted her—she in the form of a hare. Very hard pressed, and weary, she had just time to run to her own house, get behind the chest, and repeat—

"Hair, hair, God send thé caire,
I am in a hairis likeness now,
But I sall be a woman ewin now;
Hair, hair, God send thé caire!"

Else the dogs would have worried her, and posterity have lost her confessions. Many other doggrels did Isobell teach her judges; but they were all of the same character as those already given: scanty rhymes in the devil's name, when they were not actual paraphrases of the mass book. Some were for healing and some for striking; some in the name of God and all the saints, others in the devil's name, boldly and nakedly used; but both equally damnable in the eyes of the judges, and equally worthy of death. The elf-arrows spoken of before were of great use. The devil gave them to his covin and they shot men and women dead, right and left. Sometimes they missed, as when Isobell shot at the Laird of Park as he was crossing the burn, and missed, for which Bessie Hay gave her a great cuff: also Margaret Brodie, when she shot at Mr. Harie Forbes, the minister at Auldearne, he being by the standing stanes; whereupon she asked if she should shoot again, but the devil answered, "Not! for we wold nocht get his lyf at that tym." Finding the elf-arrows useless against Mr. Harie Forbes, they tried charms and incantations once when he was sick. They made a bag, into which they put the flesh, entrails, and gall of a toad, a hare's liver, barley grains, nail pairings, and bits of rag, steeping all in water, while Satan stood over them, saying—and they repeating after him—

"He is lying in his bed, and he is seik and sair,
Let him lye in till that bedd monthes two and dayes thrie mair!
He sall lye in till his bed, he salbe seik and sair,
He sall lye in till his bedd, monthes two and dayes thrie mair!"

When they said these words they were all on their knees with their hair about their shoulders and eyes, holding up their hands to the devil, beseeching him to destroy Mr. Harry; and then it was decided to go into his chamber and swing the bag over him. Bessie Hay—Able-and-Stout—undertook this office, and she went to his room, being intimate with him, the bag in her hands and her mind set on slaying him by its means; but there were some worthy persons with him at the time, so Bessie did no harm, only swung a few drops on him which did not kill him. They had a hard taskmaster in the devil—Black Johnnie, as they used to call him among themselves. But he used to overhear them, and would suddenly appear in the midst of them, saying, "I ken weill anewgh what ye wer saying of me," and then would beat and buffet them sore. He was always beating them, specially if they were absent from any of the meetings, or if they forgot anything he had told them to do. Alexander Elder was being continually thrashed. He was very soft and could never defend himself in the least, but would cry and scream when the devil scourged him. The women had more pluck. Margaret Wilson—Pickle-nearest-the-wind—would defend herself finely, throwing up her hands to keep the strokes from her; and Bessie Wilson—Throw-the-corn-yard—"would speak crusty with her tongue and would be belling against him soundly." He used to beat them all up and down with scourges and sharp cords, they like naked ghosts crying, "Pity! pity! mercy! mercy, our Lord!" But he would have neither pity nor mercy, but would grin at them like a dog, and as if he would swallow them up. He would give them most beautiful money, at least to look at; but in four-and-twenty hours it would be all gone, or changed to mere dirt and rubbish. The devil wore sometimes boots and sometimes shoes, but ever his feet were cloven, and ever his colour black. This, with some small variations, was the sum of what Isobell Gowdie confessed in her four depositions taken between the 13th of April and 27th of May in the year of grace 1662.

Janet Braidhead, spous to John Taylor, followed next. Her first confession, made on the 14th of April, set forth how that she had known nothing of witchcraft until her husband and his mother, Elspeth Nishie, had taught her; her first lesson from them being the making of some "drugs" which were to charm away the fruit and corn, and kill the cattle, of one John Hay in the Mure. After that, she was taken to the kirk at Auldearne, where her husband presented her for the devil's baptism and marking, which were done in the usual manner. She also gave evidence of the clay picture which was to destroy all the male children of the Laird of Park; and she gave a long list of the frequenters of the Sabbaths, including some of the most respectable inhabitants of the place; and in many other things she confirmed Isobell Gowdie's depositions, specially in all regarding the devil and the unequivocal nature of their connection with him, which was put into plain and unmistakable language enough.

We are not told the ultimate fate of Isobell Gowdie and Janet Braidhead, but they had confessed enough to burn half Scotland, and it is not likely that they escaped the doom assigned to their order.

THE SECRET SINS OF MAJOR WEIR.[57]

On the 4th of April, 1670, one Major Thomas Weir, an old man of seventy, expiated his crimes on the Gallowlie of Edinburgh. A bad man, surely; a canting, loose-lived hypocrite, who made his puritanism the cloak for his secret crimes, serving sin with his body in daily and most detestable service, while his lips spoke only of zeal to God and the soul's devoutest exercise. Still, it was a terrible fate for nothing more heinous than an unclean life; a purification by fire in truth, but not for the sanctification of souls. Perhaps he would have got off altogether, had he not been charged with witchcraft. Incest and the foulest vices were bad enough, but witchcraft was worse. Yet no intelligible charge of sorcery was brought against this man save the fact that he got the love of all manner of women, poor and old though he was; and the testimony of a frightened woman who gave a rambling account of shapes, and lights, and women, all gathered down in Stinking-close, near to where the major lived; all of which were, of course, phantoms, spectres, or devils, conjured up by his magical and devilish arts. This, and the frantic saying of his poor old sister, when she heard of his death, that if they had burnt his staff they had destroyed his power, formed about the sum of the witchcraft evidence against him. He was arrested on his own confession. Unable to bear the weight of his secret vices, he gave himself up to the authorities, who at first were disposed to think him mad, but who afterwards, reporting him sane and collected enough, set him on his trial. After he had once spoken he would say no more, would make no defence and no further confession: he would not pray, he would not appeal to God. Like a beast he had lived, like a beast he would die, and "since he was going to the devil," he said, "he did not wish to anger him."

---

[57] Chambers. Sinclair. Various tracts.

He would have no paltering with an outraged God by the way; so the fire and the faggot came as the culmination of a life which in its mildest phase was infamous, but which belonged to no lawful tribunal of man to punish.

If he died sullenly and in mute and dumb despair, his sister's anguish found wild and desperate expression. She told her judges all about her horrible life with him, and how he had been long given up to sorcery and magic, as well as to things not now to be mentioned; and how his power lay in that staff of his which had been burnt along with him. That thornwood staff, with its crooked head and carved figures like satyrs running through, seems to have heavily burdened the poor creature's mind, for she told her judges that when she wished to plague her brother she would hide it, and give it back to him only when he threatened to reveal her nameless infamy if she did not restore it. On the morning of her execution she said that she would expiate the most shameful life that had ever been lived by dying the most shameful death; but no one knew exactly what she meant. When she came to the place of execution—she was mercifully hung—she began to talk wildly of the Broken Covenant, and exhort the people back to their old faith, and then she attempted to throw off all her clothes that she might die "naked and ashamed." This was the lowest depth of degradation of which her crazed old brain could conceive, and was what she meant in the morning when alluding to the manner of her death. The executioner had to struggle mightily with her before he was able to overmaster her, she smiting him on the cheek the while; but at last he flung her "open-faced" on the ground, and threw some linen cloths over her; but "her hands not being tyed when she was throwen over, she laboured to recover hirselfe, and put in her head betwixt two of the steps of the leather, and keiped that powster for a tyme, till she was put from itt." It is curious to mark the little bit of sanity in all this mournful lunacy, when the familiar things of life were spoken of. She

134

had always been a great spinner, and the fame now went abroad that the devil had helped her in this. Asked if it was not so, she at the first denied disdainfully; use only and industry, she said, had made her so deft at her work, and the devil had done nothing for her; but afterwards she maundered off into some nonsense about her yarn, and how her distaff was often found full when she had left it empty; and how the weaver could never weave the thread spun from this yarn, which, of course, was "devil's dust" of the true kind. She was mad enough, the wretched being, and could not fail to trip if stones were laid in her path. But her first instincts respecting her every-day occupation were right, and are singularly illustrative of some of the phenomena of madness, and of how intimately with one's life is interwoven common sense, even in the fibres of a diseased brain. She said further that she was persuaded "her mother was a witch, for the secretest thing that either I myself or any of the family could do, when once a mark appeared upon her brow, she could tell it them, though done at a great distance! Being demanded what sort of a mark it was, she answered, 'I have some such like mark myself when I please, on my forehead.' Whereupon she offered to uncover her head for visible satisfaction; the minister refusing to behold it, and forbidding any discovery, was earnestly requested by some spectators to allow the freedom: he yielded. She put back her head-dress, and, seeming to frown, there was an exact horse-shoe, shaped for nails, in her wrinkles—terrible enough, I assure you, to the stoutest beholder." Her further confessions were curious, involving, as they did, a visit from a tall woman who had one child at her back and one or two at her feet; and who came to her, wanting her to speak to the Queen of Fairy, and to strike and do battle with the said queen on her behalf. The next day came "ane little woman," with a piece of a tree, or the root of some herb, and she told her that so long as she kept the same she should do well, and should attain all she might desire. So she spun at her yarn, and found more yarn on the "pirn" than she thought to find; which frightened her. This took place when she "keeped a school at Dalkeith, and teached childering." She also rambled on about a fiery chariot in which she and her brother had paid visits, and of his mysterious visitors and his thornwood staff; and when nothing more was to be got out of her she was hung, and the world was all the cleaner for the loss of so much folly and wickedness from out the general mass.

THE DUMB GIRL OF POLLOK.[58]

On the 14th of October, Sir George Maxwell, of Pollok, and his household were much agitated and disturbed. He had been taken suddenly and dangerously ill, with pains which read like the pains of pleurisy; and though he got partially well, had still some awkward symptoms remaining. A young deaf and dumb girl, of unknown origin, signified that "there is a woman whose son has broke his fruit yeard that did prick him in the side." This was found to mean that Jennet Mathie, relict of John Stewart, under-miller in Schaw Mill, had formed a wax picture with pins in its side, which "Dumby" said was to be found in her house in a hole behind the fire, and which she further offered to bring to them at Pollok, provided certain two of the men servants might accompany her to protect her. The young daughters of Sir George did not believe the story, but the two servants, Laurence Pollok and Andrew Martine, professed themselves converts, and insisted on seeing the thing to an end. So they went to Jennet's house, and into the kitchen, all standing on the floor near the fire; "when little Dumby comes quickly by, slips her hand into a hole behind the fire, and puts into Andrew Martine's hand, beneath his cloak, a wax picture with two pins in it," that in the right side very long, and that in the left shorter: which corresponded with the severity of the laird's pains. The picture was brought to Sir George; so was Jennet Mathie, who was apprehended on the spot and whom Sir George then sent to prison. When questioned, she denied all knowledge of the picture or the pins, and said it was the work of the dumb girl; but on its being shown that her son Hugh had once robbed Sir George's orchard—which was what Dumby meant by "broke his fruit yeard"—and that Sir George, when told that he was no longer in Pollokland,

[58] Chambers. Dickie. Tracts.

but had gone to Darnlie, had said, "I hope my fingers may be long enough to reach him in Darnlie"—these circumstances were held quite sufficient evidence that the Stewart family would do the laird all the mischief they could. The prosecution wanted no stronger proof, and the affair went on.

Jennet was obstinate, and would confess nothing; upon which they searched her and found the devil's mark. After this, Sir George got better for a short space, but soon the pains returned, and then the dumb girl said that John Stewart, Jennet's eldest son, had made another clay image, four days since, and that it was now in his house beneath the bolster among the bed straw. So she and the servants went there again, and sure enough they found it; but as it was only lately made, it was soft and broke in their hands. John said simply he did not know who had put it there; but he and his young sister Annabel were apprehended: and the next day Annabel confessed.

She said, that on the 4th of January last past, while the clay picture was being formed, a black gentleman had come into her mother's house, accompanied by Bessie Weir, Marjorie Craig, Margaret Jackson, and her own brother John. When confronted with John she wavered, but John was no nearer release for that. He was searched, and many marks were found on him; and when found the spell of silence was broken, and he confessed his paction with the devil as openly as his sister, giving up as their accomplices the same women as those she had named. Of these, Margaret Jackson, aged fourscore or so, was the only one to confess; but as she had many witch marks she could not hope for mercy, so might as well make a clean breast of it at once. On the 17th of January a portion of clay was found under Jennet Mathie's bolster, in her prison at Paisley. This time it was a woman's portrait, for Sir George had recovered by now, and the witches were against the whole family equally. On the 27th Annabel made a fuller deposition. She said that last harvest the devil, as a black man, had come to her mother's house, and required her, the deponent, to give herself to him; promising that she should want for nothing good if she did. She, being enticed by her mother and Bessie Weir, did as was desired—putting one hand on the crown of her head, and another on the soles of her feet, and giving over to him all that lay between; whereupon her mother promised her a new coat, and the devil made her officer at their several meetings. He gave her, too, such a nip on the arm that she was sore for half an hour after, and gave her a new name—Annippy, or an Ape according to Law. Her mother's devil-name was Landslady; Bessie Weir was called Sopha; Marjorie Craig was Rigeru; Margaret Jackson Locas; John Stewart, Jonas; and they were all present at the making of the clay image which was to doom Sir George to death. They made it of clay, then bound it on a spit and turned it before the fire, "Sopha" crying "Sir George Maxwell! Sir George Maxwell!" which was repeated by them all. Another time, she said, there was a meeting, when the devil was dressed in "black cloathes and a blew band, and white hand cuffs, with hoggers on his feet, and that his feet were cloven." The black man stuck the pins into the picture, and his name was Ejoall, or J. Jewell. For the devil delighted in giving himself various names, as when he caused himself to be called Peter Drysdale, by Catherine Sands and Laurie Moir, and Peter Saleway by others.

John now followed suit. He confessed to his own baptism; to the hoggers on the black man's legs, who had no shoes, and spoke in a voice hollow and ghousty; to the making the clay image; and to his new name of Jonas. On the 15th of February, 1677, John Stewart, Annabel Stewart, and Margaret Jackson all adhered to these depositions, but Jennet and Bessie and Margerie denied them. Jennet's feet were fixed in stocks, so that she might not do violence to her own life: and one day her gaoler declared that he had found her bolster, which the night before was laid at least six yards from the stocks, now placed beneath her; the stocks being so heavy that two of the strongest men in the country could hardly have carried them six yards. He asked her "how she had win to the bolster," and she answered that she had crept along the floor of the room, dragging the stocks with her. Before the court she said that she had got one foot out of the hole, and had drawn the stocks with her, "a thing altogether impossible." Then John and Annabel exhorted their mother to confess, reminding her of all the meetings which she had had with the devil in her own house, and that "a summer's day would not be sufficient to relate what passages had been between the devil and her." But Jennet Mathie was a stern, brave, high-hearted Scotch woman, and would not seal her sorrow with a lie. "Nothing could prevail with her obdured and hardened heart," so she and all, save young Annabel, were burnt; and when she was bound to the stake, the spectators saw after a while a black, pitchy ball foam out of her mouth, which, after the fire was kindled, grew to the size of a walnut, and flew out into sparks like squibs. This was the devil leaving her. As for Bessie Weir, or Sopha, the devil left her when she was executed, in the form of a raven; for so he owned and dishonoured his chosen ones.

"The dumbe girl, Jennet Douglas, now speaks well, and knows Latine, which she never learned, and discovers things past!" says Sinclair. But she still followed her old trade. She had mesmeric visions, and was evidently a "sensitive;" and some of the people believed in her, as inspired and divine, and some came, perhaps mockingly, to test her. But they generally got the worst off, and were glad to leave her alone again. One woman came and asked her "'how she came to the knowledge of so many things,' but the young wench shifted her, by asking the woman's name. She told her name. Says the other, 'Are there any other in Glasgow of that name?' 'No!' sayes the woman. 'Then,' said the girle, 'you are a witch!' Says the other, 'Then are you a devil!' The girl answers 'The devil doth not reveal witches; but I know you to be one, and I know your practices too.' On which the poor woman ran away in great confusion;" as, indeed, she might—such an accusation as this being quite sufficient to sign her death-warrant. To another woman who came to see and question her, she said the same thing; taking her arm, and showing the landlord a secret mark which she told him the woman had got from the devil. "The poor woman much ashamed ran home, and a little while after she came out and told her neighbours that what Jennet Douglas had said of her was true, and earnestly entreated that they might show so much to the magistrates, that she might be apprehended, otherwise the devil says she will make me kill myself." The neighbours were wise enough to think her mad, as she was, and took her home; but the next day she was found drowned in the Clyde; fear and despair had killed her before the stake-wood had had time to root and ripen. The dumb girl herself was afterwards carried before the great council at Edinburgh, imprisoned, scourged through the town, and then banished to "some forraigne Plantation," whence she reappears no more to vex her generation. God forgive her! She has passed long years ago to her account, and may her guilty soul be saved, and all its burning blood-stains cleansed and assoilzed!

LIZZIE MUDIE AND HER VICTIMS.[59]

The year after Sir George Maxwell's affair there was another case at Haddington which gave full employment to the authorities. Margaret Kirkwood, a woman of some means, hanged herself one Sunday morning during church time. Her servant, Lizzie Mudie, who was at kirk like a good Christian, suddenly called out, to the great disturbance of the congregation. She began repeating all the numbers—one, two, three, four, &c.—till she came to fifty-nine; then she stopped and cried, "The turn is done!" When it was afterwards found that Margaret Kirkwood had hung herself just about that moment, and that her age was fifty-nine, Lizzie Mudie was taken up and searched. She was found a witch by her marks, and soon after confessed, delating five women and one man as her accomplices. But the five women and the one man were obstinate, and would not say that they were guilty, though they were pricked and searched and marks found on them. Lord Fountainhall was present at the searching of the man, and he gives an account of it: "I did see the man's body searched and pricked in two sundry places, one at the ribs and the other at his shoulder. He seemed to find no pain, but no blood followed. The marks were blewish, very small, and had no protuberancy above the skin. The pricker said there were three sorts of witches' marks: the horn mark, it was very hard; the breiff mark, it was very little; and the feeling mark, in which they had sense and pain." "I remained very dissatisfied with this way of trial," says my Lord farther on, "as most fallacious; and the fellow could give me no account of the principles of his art, but seemed to be a drunken, foolish rogue." One of Lizzie Mudie's five victims was an old woman of eighty, named Marion Phinn, who had always borne a good character, "never being

---

[59] Law's 'Memorials.'

stained with the least ignominy, far less with the abominable crime of witchcraft." But though she petitioned the council to free her on her own caution, she was kept hand-fast and foot-bound in gaol, being far too dangerous in the helplessness and feebleness of her eighty years to be let out with the chance of bewitching mankind to death. This she could do, and work all other miracles; but she could not help herself to sunlight and liberty.

BRAVE OLD KATHERINE LIDDELL.[60]

In 1678 two old women of Prestonpans were burnt. They made a voluntary confession, and accused a few more of their craft. These in their turn accusing others, in a very short time seventeen unhappy creatures were collected together, all charged with the sin of witchcraft, intercommuning with the devil, voluntary transformation into ravens, cats, crows, &c., with all the other stock pieces of the hallucination. The judges seemed inclined to favour them, and Sir John Clerk of Pennycuik, when desired to sit on the commission appointed to try the seven given up by the parish of Loanhead, declined, "alleging drily that he did not feel himself warlock (that is, conjuror) enough to be judge upon such an inquisition." These poor creatures had deep sleeps, during which no pinching would awake them; but though the judges saw them when in these sleeps, and heard their confessions as to where they had been and what they had been doing during the time, they were regarded as diabolical trances, and dealt with accordingly. Nine of the East Lothian women were burnt, and the "seven of Loanhead were reserved for future procedure." Among the accused was one Katherine Liddell, a strong-minded, stout-hearted, old widow, who feared no man, spoke her mind freely, and had a body with nerves like cart ropes and muscles of iron. The bailie of Prestonpans, John Rutherford, had caused her to be seized in the late panic, and, though there was nothing against her, he had her pricked in various parts of her body "to the great effusion of her blood, and whereby her skin is raised and her body highly swelled, and she is in danger of life." A drummer, two salt-makers, and others, assisted him in this torture; for John Kincaid had found zealous followers: and any man with a peculiar temperament, and a heart hardened by

---

[60] Chambers.

144

superstition against suffering, might take on himself the office of pricker to his own soul's satisfaction, and the torture and murder of his fellow-creatures. Katherine Liddell, besides being actively tortured, was kept without sleep for six days and nights, but the stout old woman would confess nothing. On the contrary, she presented a petition to the Council, charging John Rutherford and the rest with "defamation, false imprisonment, and open and manifest oppression," and demanded vengeance and restitution in loud and vigorous terms. The Council, unaccustomed to this sort of thing, and used only to victims as tame as they were considered powerful, soon released her, dropping her like hot iron, and condemning Rutherford and his associates as too hasty and ill-advised: then, somewhat further redeemed themselves by an unusual act of justice and common sense, in sentencing David Cowan, "pricker"—the one who had been the most active of her tormentors—to be confined during pleasure in the Tolbooth.

Katherine Liddell did not do much good to her afflicted sisterhood, though she had helped herself: for that same year, in August,[61] "the devil had a great meeting of witches in Loudian, where, among others, was a warlock who formerly had been admitted to the ministrie in the Presbyterian tymes, and when the bishops came in conformed with them." This warlock minister was Mr. Gideon Penman, minister of Crighton, and a man of notoriously loose life; but whether he carried his defiance of good so far as to dance with the hags at the Sabbath, and "beat up those that were slow," and preach damnable doctrines and blasphemous travesties of the Christian faith in the devil's services, or whether he was only an immoral man—better out of the ministry than in it—remains for each reader's private judgment to determine. Ten of the

---

[61] Law's 'Memorials.'

accused stoutly affirmed that Mr. Gideon Penman was their devil's parson; but as he as stoutly denied it, he was liberated on his own security, while nine out of the ten were condemned to be strangled and burnt, which was done accordingly. They gave some curious details, as, that, when they renounced their baptism and gave themselves over to Satan by laying one hand on their head and the other on their feet he kissed them, and that he was cold to the touch, and his breath like a damp air; that he scourged them oft, and was a most "wicked and barbarous master;" and that when he administered the sacrament to them the bread was like wafers, and the drink like blood or black moss-water: that he transformed them to the likeness of bees, and crows, and ravens, when they flew about from place to place as he ordered.

THE DEVIL IN HIS CUPS.[62]

On December 19, 1679, the parish of Borrowstonness was again in an uproar concerning the evil doings of witches and wizards, the chief of whom was Annaple Thomson, once a widow, but now a wife. She was charged with having one day met the devil on her way between Linlithgow and Borrowstonness, when he "in the lyknes of ane black man told yow that yow wis ane poore puddled bodie, and had ane evill lyiff, and difficultie to win throw the warld; and promised that iff ye wald followe him, and go alongst with him, yow should never want, but have ane better lyiff; and abowt fyve wekes therafter, the Devill appeired to yow, when yow wis goeing to the coal-hill, about sevin o'clock in the morning. Having renewed his former tentatiowne yow did condescend thereto, and declared yowrselff content to follow him, and becwm his servant;"—which was bad of Annaple Thomson, and sure to bring her to ineffectual grief. Then some others, men and women both, were further informed of their misdeeds. They were told that "ye, and each person of yow, wis at several mettings with the Devill in the linkes of Borrowstownes, and in the howse of yow, Bessie Vickar, and ye did eatt and drinke with the Devill, and with on another, and with witches in hir howss in the nycht tyme; and the Devill and the said William Craw browght the ale which ye drank, extending to about sevin gallons, from the howss of Elisabeth Hamilton." So did the rest. Margaret Pringle, whose right wrist the devil had grievously pained, "but having it twitched of new againe, it immediatelie becam haill;" Margaret Hamilton, with whom the devil had at sundry times "drank several choppens of ale with yow," when they met at the town-well at Borrowstonness and talked together like two old gossips; also, another Margaret

---

[62] Scots' Magazine.

Hamilton, relict of James Pullwart, with whom the devil conversed in the likeness of a black man, but afterwards removed from her as a dog—they all committed abominable sins with the devil, and entertained him familiarly like any other cummer. And were they not all at the meeting with the "Devill and other witches at the croce of Murestaine," above Kinneil, upon "the threttin of October last, where yow all danced, and the Devill acted the pyiper, and where yow endevored to have destroyed Andrew Mitchell, sone to John Mitchell, elder in Dean of Kinneil?" The case was considered clear enough for all rational men in Borrowstonness; so Annabel Thomson, Margaret Pringle, the two Margaret Hamiltons, William Craw, and Bessie Vickar, were "found guiltie be ane assyse of the abominable cryme of Witchcraft," and were ordered to be taken to the west end of Borrowstonness, "the ordinar place of execution," betwixt two and four in the afternoon, and "there be wirried at a steack till they be dead, and thereafter to have their bodies burnt to ashes."

THE GHOST OF THE BLACK-BROWED MAID.[63]

If bodies were safe after death, characters were not. Isabel Heriot was maid of all work to the minister at Preston. "She was of a low Stature, small and slender of Body, of a Black Complexion. Her Head stood somewhat awry upon her Neck. She was of a droll and jeering Humour, and would have spoken to Persons of Honour with great Confidence." After some short time of service, her master the minister began to dislike her, because she was not eager in her religious duties; so he discharged her: and in 1680 she died—and "about the time of her death her face became extreamly black." Two or three nights after her burial, one Isabel Murray saw her, in her white grave-clothes, walk from the chapel to the minister's louping-on stone (horse-block). Here she halted, leaning her elbow on the stone, then went in at the back gate, and so towards the stable. A few nights after this stones were flung at the minister's house, over the roof, and in at the doors and windows; but they fell softly for the most part, and did no especial damage. Yet one night, just as the minister was coming in at the hall door, a great stone was flung after him, which hit the door very smartly and marked it. Isabel Murray was also hit with stones, and the serving-man who looked to the horses was gripped at the heel by something which made him cry out lustily. So it went on. Stones and clods, and lighted coals, and even an old horse-comb long since lost, were perpetually flying about, and only by severe prayer was the minister able to lay the devil who molested them.

Soon Isabel Murray reappeared with a fresh set of circumstances concerning the ghost of her namesake Isabel Heriot, the maid of all work. She said that as she was coming from church between sermons, to visit her house

---

[63] Sinclair's 'Invisible World.'

and kailyard for fear some vagrant cows might have got over the dyke—which were very likely of the true Maclarty type—on going down her own yard, which was next to the minister's, she saw again the apparition of Isabel Heriot, as she was when laid in her coffin. "Never was an egg liker to another than this Apparition was like to her, as to her Face, her Stature, her Motion, her Tongue, and Behaviour; her face was black like the mouten soot, the very colour which her face had when she died." The ghost was walking under the fruit-trees, and over the beds where the seeds had been sown, bending her body downwards, as if she had been seeking somewhat off the ground, and saying, "A stane! a stane!" Her lap was full of stones; as some people supposed the stones she cast in the night-time; and these stones she threw down, as if to harbour them, at a bush-root in the garden. Isobel Murray, nothing daunted, goes up to her.

"Wow!" says she, "what's thou doing here, Isabel Heriot? I charge thee by the law thou lives on to tell me."

Says the ghost, "I am come again because I wronged my master when I was his servant. For it was I that stealed his Shekel (this was a Jewish shekel of gold which, with some other things, had been stolen from him several years before), which I hid under the Hearthstone in the Kitching, and then when I flited took it into the Cannongate, and did offer to sell it to a French Woman who lodged where I served, who askt where I got it. I told her I found it between Leith and Edinburgh." Then she went on to make further confession. Having fyled herself for a thief she went on to show how she had been also a witch. "One night," says the ghost, "I was riding home late from the Town, and near the Head of Fanside Brae, the Horse stumbled, and I said, The Devil raise thee; whereupon the Foul Thief appeared presently to me, and threatened me, if I would not grant to destroy my Master the Minister, he would throw me into a deep hole (which I suppose is yet remaining); or if I could not get power over my master, I should strive to destroy the Shoolmaster."

"It was very remarkable," says George Sinclair, as a kind of commentary, "that one of the minister's servant-women had given to the schoolmaster's servant-woman some Linnings to make clean, among which there was a Cross cloth of strong Linning, which could never be found, though diligent search was made for it, till one morning the Master awakening found it bound round about his Night Cap, which bred admiration both to himself and his Wife. No more skaith was the Devil or the Witches able to do him. What way this was done, or for what end it cannot be well known: but it is somewhat probable that they designed to strangle and destroy him in the night time, which is their usual time in working and doing of mischief. This happened about the time (I suppose) that the Devil had charged Isabel Heriot to destroy this honest man. Yet within two days a young child of his, of a year old, fell sick, which was quickly pulled away by death, none knowing the cause or nature of the disease."

Isabel Murray went on to say, that furthermore the ghost confessed to her, that she, Isabel Heriot, when in life, had met the devil a second time at Elfiston Mill, near to Ormiston: and she told what foulness the devil did to her. Also, one night as she was coming home from Haddington Market with some horse-corn, she met the devil at Knock-hills, and he bade her destroy Thomas Anderson, who was riding with her. When she refused he threw all the horse-corn off the horse. "This Thomas Anderson was a Christian man," and when Murray told her tale "well remembered that Isabel had got up the next morning timeously," and brought home her oats which had lain in the road all the night. She said too that she had cheated her master whenever she went to the market to buy oats, charging him more than they cost—not an unusual practice with servants at market anywhere; and she told Isabel Murray that the stone cast at her was not for herself but for her goodman, who had once flung her, the ghost, into the jawhole, and abused her. At this point Murray said she began to be frightened, and ran home in all haste. So Isabel Heriot's character was settled for ever, and her neighbours only thought the judgment came too late.

THE SUCCUBUS[64]

William Barton, a loose-lived man of notoriously strong passions, was apprehended for witchcraft. His confession included the not very frequent Scottish element of a Succubus—a demon under the form of a beautiful woman who beguiled him, and to whom he made himself over for love and gold. She baptized him under the name of John Baptist, gave him her mark, and fifteen pounds Scots in good gold as Tocher-money; and then they parted. When he had gone but a little way she called him back and gave him a mark to spend at the Ferry, desiring him to keep the fifteen pounds safe and unbroken. At this point in his confession the poor wretch was weary, and asked leave to go to sleep; which, for a wonderful stretch of humanity, the judges granted. Suddenly he awakened with a loud laugh. The magistrates asked why he laughed?—and he said that during his sleep the devil had come to him, very angry at his confession, and bidding him deny all when he awoke, "for he should be his Warrand." After this he became "obdured," and would never confess anything again; the devil persuading him that no man should take his life. And even when they told him that the stake was set up and the fire built round, he only answered, "he cared not for all that, for," said he, "I shal not die this day." How should he if no man was to kill him? Upon this the executioner came into the prison, but fell stone dead as he crossed the threshold. Hastily the magistrates offered a reward to the executioner's wife if she would undertake her husband's office, and strangle the poor mad fellow before he was burnt; which she agreed to do, for all that she was in great pain and grief, clapping her hands and crying, "Dool for this parting my dear burd Andrew Martin!" When the warlock heard that a woman was to put him to death, he fell

---

[64] Sinclair.

into a passion of crying, saying that the devil had deceived him, and "let no man ever trust his promises again!"

Barton's wife was imprisoned with him. On her side she declared that she had never known her husband to be a warlock; he on his that he had never known her to be a witch: but presently the mask fell off, and she confessed. She said that malice against one of her neighbours had driven her to give herself over to the devil, that he had baptized her by the name of Margaratus, and taken her to be very near to him; a great deal too near for even a virtuous woman's thoughts. When asked if she had found pleasure in his society, she answered, "Never much." But one night, going to a witches' dance upon Pentland Hills, he went before them all in the likeness of a rough tanny dog, playing on a pair of pipes. The spring he played, said she, was "The silly bit chicken, gar cast it a pickle, and it will grow mickle;" and coming down the hill they had the best sport of all: the devil carried the candle and his tail went, "ey wig wag, wig wag!" Margaratus was burnt with her husband.

THE ISLAND WITCHES.

The Orkney and Shetland islanders were rich in witchcraft superstitions. They had all the Norwegian beliefs in fullest, ripest quality, and held to everything that had been handed down to them from Harald Harfagre and his followers. Kelpies and trows, and brownies and trolls, which somehow or other went out with taxation and agriculture, peopled every stream and every meadow, and witches were as many as there were men who loved nature, or women who had a faculty for healing and the instinct of making pets. Somewhere about the middle of the seventeenth century a woman was adjudged a witch because she was seen going from Hilswick to Brecon with a couple of familiars in the form of black crows or corbies, which hopped on each side of her, all the way. Which thing, not being in the honest nature of these fowls to do, she was strangled and burnt. But most frequently the imp took the form of a cat or dog; sometimes of a respectable human being; as was the case about seventy years ago, when it was notorious that the devil, as a good braw countryman, helped a warlock's wife to delve while her husband was engaged at the Haaf. According to the same authority too,[65] not longer ago than this time, when the devil dug like any navvy, a woman of the parish of Dunrossness was known to have a deadly enmity against a boat's crew that had set off from the Haaf. The day was cloudless, but the woman was a witch, and storms were as easy for her to raise as to blow a kiss from the hand. She took a wooden basin, called a *cap*, and set it afloat in a tub of water; then, as if to disarm suspicion, went about her household work, chanting softly to herself an old Norse ditty. After she had sung a verse or two she sent her little child to look at the tub, and see whether the cap was

---

[65] Hibbert's 'Shetland Islands.'

whummilled (turned upside down) or no. The child said the water was stirring but the bowl was afloat. The woman went on singing a little louder; and presently sent the child again to see how matters stood. This time the child said there was a strange swell in the water, but the cap still floated. The woman then sang more loud and fierce; and again she sent. The child came back saying the waters were strangely troubled, and the cap was whummilled. Then she cried out, "The turn is done!" and left off singing. On the same day came word that a fishing yawl had been lost in the Roust, and all on board drowned. The same story is told of some women in the island of Fetlar, who, when a boat's crew had perished in the Bay of Funzie, were found sitting round a well, muttering mysterious words over a wooden bowl supernaturally agitated. The whole thing, as Hibbert says, forcibly reminds one of the old Norse superstition of the Quern Song.

It was no unusual thing for men and women of otherwise peaceable and cleanly life to tamper with the elements in those dim and distant days. Even seventy years ago a man named John Sutherland of Papa Stour was in the habit of getting a fair wind for weather-bound vessels: and the Knoll of Kibister, in the island of Bressay, now called Luggie's Knowe,[66] testifies by its name to the skill and sorrowful fate of a well-known wizard of the seventeenth century. There on that steep hill used Luggie to live, and in the stormiest weather managed somehow always to have his bit of fresh fish: angling with the most perfect success, even when the boats could not come into the bay. When out at sea Luggie had nothing to do but cast out his lines to have as plentiful a dinner as he could desire. "He would out of Neptune's lowest kitchen, bring cleverly up fish well-boiled and roasted;" but strange and mischancy as the art was, his companions got accustomed to it, "and would by a

---

[66] Hibbert and Sinclair.

natural courage make a merry meal thereof, not doubting who was cook." But Luggie's cleverness proved fatal to him. Men were not even adept fishers in those days without danger, and jealousy and fear helped to swell the reputation of his natural skill into supernatural power: so he was tried for a sorcerer, and burnt at a stake at Scalloway. We need hardly wonder at the fate of poor Luggie, considering the times. If it were possible to hang two women on the 26th of January, 1681— actually to hang them in the sight of God and this loving pitiful human world, "for calling kings and bishops perjured bloody men,"[67] we need not wonder to what lengths superstition in any of its other forms was carried. We have made a stride since then, with seven-leagued boots winged at the heels.

A family of bright young sons[68] lived on one of the Shetland islands. A certain Norwegian lady had reason to think herself slighted by one of them, and she swore she would have her revenge. The sons were about to cross a voe or ferry; but one was to take his shelty, while the rest were to go by the boat. Mysteriously the shelty was found to have been loosed from its tether, and was gone; so all the heirs male of the race were under the necessity of going by the boat across the voe. It was the close of day—a mild windless evening: not a ripple was on the water, not a cloud in the sky; and no one on either bank heard a cry or saw the waters stir. But the youths never returned home. When they were searched for the next day they could nowhere be found: only the boat drifting to the shore, unharmed and unsteered. When the deed was done the shelty was brought back to its tether as mysteriously as it had been taken away.

Trials and executions still went on; some at Dumfries, and some at Coldingham[69] where Margaret Polwart was publicly rebuked for using charms and incantations to

---

[67] Fountainhall.
[68] Hibbert.
[69] Chambers.

recover her sick child whom "that thief Christian Happer had wronged." But as a neighbour told her very wisely, "They that chant cannot charm, or they that lay on cannot take off the disease, or they that do wrong to any one, cannot recover them," so what was the good of all her notorious cantrips with Jean Hart and Alison Nisbet—the last of such evil fame that she had lately been scratched for a witch—that is, had blood drawn above her breath? Margaret Polwart might be thankful that she got off with only a rebuke for using charms in place of drugs, and consorting with witches to undo witches' work. In 1696, Janet Widdrow and Isobel Cochrane were brought to trial, but not burnt for the present; but two poor creatures, M'Rorie and M'Quicken, did not escape: nor some others, of no special dramatic interest.

And now we come to that marvellous piece of disease and imposture combined, the notorious case of "Bargarran's Daughter."

THE RENFREWSHIRE WITCHES.[70]

Christian Shaw, Bargarran's daughter, was a little girl of about eleven years of age, "of a lively character and well inclined." On the 17th of August, 1696, she saw the woman servant, Katherine Campbell, steal a drink of milk from the can, whereupon she threatened to tell her mother; but Campbell, "being a young woman of a proud and revengeful temper, and much addicted to cursing and swearing upon any light occasion," turned against her vehemently, wishing "that the Devil might harle her soul through hell," and cursing her with violent imprecations. Five days after this, Agnes Naismith, an old woman of bad fame, came into the courtyard, and asked Christian how old she was, and how she did, inquiring also after the health of other members of the family. Christian gave her a pert answer, and there the matter ended; but the next night the young girl was taken with fits, and the first act of the long and mournful tragedy began. In her fits she cried out against Katherine Campbell and Agnes Naismith, saying they were cutting her side and otherwise tormenting her; then she struggled as with an unseen enemy, and her body was, now bowed stiff and rigid, resting in an arch on her head and her heels alone, and now shaken with such a strange motion of rising and falling, as it had been a pair of bellows; her tongue was drawn into her throat, and even the great Dr. Brisbane of Glasgow himself was puzzled by what name to call her passion, for she began to vomit strange things, which she said the witches, her tormentors, forced upon her—such as crooked pins, small fowl bones, sticks of candle fir, filthy hay, gravel stones, lumps of candle-grease, and egg-shells. And still she cried out against Katherine Campbell and Agnes Naismith; holding long conversations with the former, whom she affirmed to

---

[70] Watson's Tract, printed 1698. Chambers, Dickie, and various other sources.

be sitting close by when she was perhaps many miles away, and arguing with her out of the Bible: exhorting her to repent of her sins with more unction than logical clearness of reasoning. Agnes Naismith she took somewhat into favour again; for the poor old woman, having been brought by the parents into the chamber where she lay, and having prayed for her a little simple prayer very heartily, the afflicted damsel condescended to exempt her from further persecution for the moment, saying that she was now her defender and did protect her from the fury of the rest. For the crafty child had seen too well how her first venture had sped not to venture on a broader cast. One day being in her fits she made a grip with her hands as if to catch something, then exclaimed that J. P. was then tormenting her, and that she had got a grip of his jerkin which was "duddie" (tattered) at the elbows; and immediately her mother and aunt heard the tearing of cloth, and the girl showed them in her hands two pieces of red cloth newly torn, where never a bit of red cloth had been before. Then she went off into a swoon or "swerf," and lay as if dead a considerable time. These fits continued with more or less severity far into the winter of the next year, and with ever new victims claimed by her as her tormentors. Now it was Elizabeth Anderson; now James and Thomas Lindsay—the latter a young lad of eleven, "the gley'd or squint-eyed elf," as she called him; now "the scabbed-faced lass," who came to the door to ask alms; and now the weary old Highland body, begging for a night's lodging; then Alexander Anderson, father of Elizabeth; and Jean Fulton, the grandmother; and then Margaret Lang—Pincht Margaret as she was called—"a Name given her by the Devil, from a Pincht Cross cloath, ordinarily worn on her Brow;" and her daughter, Martha Semple. Of the twenty-one people accused by this wicked girl, Margaret Lang and her daughter were the most remarkable—the one for her courage, her fine character and powerful mind, the other for her youth, her beauty, and child-like innocence of nature. When she heard that she was accused, Margaret—who had been advised to get out of the way for a time, but who had answered disdainfully, "Let them quake that dread and fear that need, but I will not gang"—went up straight to Bargarran house, and passing into the chamber where Christian lay, put her arms round her and spoke to her soothingly, saying, "The Lord bless thee and ding the devil frae thee!" She then asked her pointedly if she had ever seen her among her tormentors?—to which the girl said. "No, but she had seen her daughter Martha." Afterwards she retracted this admission and said that Margaret had really afflicted her, but that she was under a spell when asked and could not confess. Martha could not take things so gently. "She was as well-Favoured and Gentill a Lass as you'l look on, and about 17 or 18 years of Age," says an old authority in an anonymous letter written to a couple of initials. Poor Martha! her youth and beauty and passionate distress moved even the bigoted wretches who condemned her; but their compassion led to nothing pitiful or merciful, and the poor, bright, beautiful girl passed into the awful doom of the rest. Then the authorities "questioned" the witches; they were pricked, according to custom and the national law; and "There was not any of them, save Margaret Fulton, but marks were found on them, which were altogether insensible. That a Needle of 3 Inches length was frequently put in without their knowledge, nor would any Blood come from these places." Elizabeth Anderson, a girl of seventeen, a beggar, James Lindsay, of fourteen, and gley'd Thomas, his brother, not yet twelve—who for a halfpenny would turn himself widershins and stop a plough at a word—were found willing and able to confess. Elizabeth Anderson was especially determined that things should not be lost for the want of finding. She said that about twenty days ago her father had told her to go with him to Bargarran's yard, somewhere about noon, where they met a black man with a bonnet on his head, and a band round his neck, whom her father and Agnes Naismith, then present, told her was the devil: that certain people, named, were also in their company; that their discourse was all of Christian Shaw, then lying sick, "whose Life they all promis'd to take away by the stopping of her Breath;" that they all danced in the yard; that her father "Discharged her to tell anything she saw, or she would be Torn in Pieces: and that she was more Affraied of the forsaid persons than she was of the Devil." This confession was made on the 5th of February, 1697. A few days later her imagination was more lively. About seven years ago, she said, as she was playing round the door of her grandmother, Jean Fulton's, house, she saw "ane black grim man" go into the house to her grandmother, where he abode for a while talking. Jean bade her take the gentleman by the hand, and he would give her "ane Bony Black, new Coat; which accordingly she did." But his hand was cold and she was afeard: and then he vanished away. The same thing happened once again, when the black gentleman and her grandmother fell a-talking together by "rounding in other's ears," but the girl understood not what they said. This time she would not touch his hand for all his promises of bran new clothes; so "the gentleman went away in a flight," and she saw him no more for long after. The next time was when her father "desired her to go with him through the Country and seek their Meat; to which she replyed she need not seek her Meat, seeing she might have Work:" but her father prevailed, and took her to a moor where above twenty people were assembled; whose names she gives in a formidable muster. Now the devil tempted her anew with meat and clothes, but she would not consent; so he and her father stepped aside and conferred together. Their meeting this day was for the destruction of a certain minister's child, which they were to effect by means of a wax picture and pins. Another time it was for the destruction of another

162

minister's child by the same means, and she heard Margaret Rodger say, "Stay a little, till I stop ane Pin in the Heart of it:" which accordingly she did. This time her father took her on his back over the water to Kilpatrick in a Flight, saying Mount and Fly. She was with the witch crew when they drowned Brighouse by upsetting his boat, and when they strangled a child with a sea napkin: after which they all danced with the devil "in ane black Coat, ane Blew Bonnet, ane Blew Band," who played the pipes for them, and gave them each a piece of an unchristened bairn's liver to eat, so that they should never confess if apprehended. With other abominations too foul to be repeated.

The same day, February 18th, James Lindsay, the elder of the two brothers, confessed. Jean Fulton was his grandmother too, and he said that one day, when she met him, she took his little round hat and plack from him. Being loath to part with the same, he ran after her crying for them: which she refusing, he called her an old witch, and ran away. Whereupon she threatened him. Eight days after this, as he was begging through the country near Inchannan where she lived, he met her again; and this time she had with her "ane black grim man with black cloaths, ane black Hat and blew Band," who offered his hand, which James took and which he found cold as it gript him straitly. The gentleman asked if he would serve him for a Bonny black coat and a black hat, and several other things, to which he replied "Yes, I'll do't." He then went to all the meetings, and saw all the people and did all the things that Elizabeth had spoken of; even to strangling Montgomerie's bairn with a sea napkin at twelve o'clock at night, while the servant girl was watching by the cradle. Young Thomas the gley'd followed next, confessing to just the same things, even to the liver of the "uncrissened bairn," which all eat save Elizabeth and their two selves: a slip-by that accounted for their confessions. And now justice had a good handful to begin with, so the work of accusation went briskly forward. Bargarran's daughter still continued bringing out crooked pins and stones and all sorts of unmentionable filth from her mouth, and still went on quarrelling with the devil whom she called an old sow, and holding conversations with the apparitions of her tormentors, still mixed up fraud with epilepsy, and lies and craft and wicked guile with hysteria, till the witch-fires were fairly lighted, and seven of the poor wretches "done to death." Among whom brave Margaret and her beautiful child held the most prominent place. Never for a moment did Margaret Lang lose her courage or self-possession. Seeing a farmer whom she knew, among the crowd assembled round the gallows, she called out to him bitterly, "that he would now thrive like a green bay-tree, for there would be no innocent blood shed that day;" but what she meant for irony the people took for confession. When she was burned, the answer of a spectator to one who asked if the execution was over, showed what feeling they had about her: "There's ane o' the witches in hell, an' the rest 'ill shune follow!" said he contentedly. Another man, whose stick was taken to push back the legs of the poor wretches as they were thrust out of the flames, when it was returned to him, flung it into the flames, saying, "I'll tak nae stick hame wi' me to nay hous that has touched a witch." When all was over and the sacrifice was complete, Bargarran's daughter declared herself satisfied and cured; no more "bumbees" came to pinch her—no more charms of balls of hair or waxen eggs were laid beneath her bed—no more apparitions thronged to vex her, nor had she fits or tossings, foamings or strange swellings as of old; the devil left off tempting her with promises of a fine gentleman for a husband; the witches no longer allured her by phantom aprons filled with phantom almonds; the Lord "helped the poor daft child," as Mrs. M. had prayed, though she was scarce worth the helping, and the world was oppressed with her lies no more. But the blood of the murdered innocent

164

lay red on the ground, and cried aloud to heaven for vengeance against the murderers. The case of Bargarran's daughter has been always accepted as one of the most puzzling on record; but when may not mankind be puzzled if they have but sufficient credulity? Subtract from this account the possible and the certain—the possible frauds and the certain lies—and what is left? A diseased girl, hysterical and epileptic, full of hallucinations and pretended fancies, with a certain quickness of hand which the tremendous gullibility of her auditory rendered yet more facile—unscrupulous, mendacious; the only thing surprising in the whole matter was that there was not one man of sufficient coolness of judgment, or quickness of perception, to see through the imposture and set his grip on it ere it passed. Dickie and Mitchell, who a few years back visited the house where all this took place, found a slit or hole in the wooden partition between her bedroom and the room next it; a slit, evidently made purposely, and not a natural defect in the wood, and so placed that when the bed was made up (the bed of richly-carved oak yet stands or stood there) it could not be seen by any one in the room. This little fact seems to speak volumes, and to help materially towards establishing the questions of fraud and connivance. The remote sequel is the only consoling feature in the case. From being the most notorious impostor and the most cruel, false, and deadly persecutor of her time, Bargarran's daughter, as Mrs. Miller, became one of the best and most famous spinners of fine and delicate thread. She caused certain machinery to be brought from Holland, and wrought at her spinning wheel with all the intelligence and zeal that, earlier, had been so miserably employed to the ruin and destruction of her fellow-creatures. It is to be hoped that the coolness and reflection of maturity gave her grace to repent of the sins of her girlhood, and that after-penitence wiped out the terrible stains of youthful lying and murder.

MISCELLANEOUS.

That same year also Sir John Maxwell, of Pollok, and some other gentlemen, were commissioned to try two poor women, Mary Millar and Elspeth M'Ewen, and if guilty adjudge them to death; which they were found to be, and adjudged accordingly; and a few months after, Margaret Laird—still in Renfrewshire—was reputed to have been "under ane extraordinary and most lamentable trouble, falling into strange and horrible fits, judged by all who have seen her to be preternatural, arising from the devil and his instruments." The suspected witches who were accused of troubling her, were seized and put upon their trial. So was Mary Morrison, spouse of Francis Duncan; but her husband petitioned so earnestly for her release for sake of her "numerous poor family" starving in neglect at home, and there being no kind of proof against her, she was at length released and set at liberty. "The Lord-Advocate soon after reported to the Privy Council a letter he had received from the Sheriff of Renfrewshire, stating that 'the persons imprisoned in that county as witches are in a starving condition, and that those who informed against them are passing from them, and the sheriff says he will send them in prisoners to Edinburgh Tolbooth, unless they be quickly tried.' His lordship was recommended to ask the sheriff to support the prisoners till November next, when they would probably be tried, and the charges would be disbursed by the treasury. A distinct allowance of a groat a day was ordered on the 12th of January, 1699, for each of the Renfrewshire witches."[71]

In July of the same year, Ross-shire contributed a famous quota. Twelve luckless creatures were reported at once as being guilty of the "diabolical crimes and charms of witchcraft," and by the 2nd of January, 1700, two of

---

[71] Chambers.

166

them had confessed, and were sentenced to such arbitrary punishment as the committee might think proper. "This is the first appearance of an inclination in the central authorities to take mild views of witchcraft," says Chambers; but we have not seen the last of capital punishments, for on the 20th of November, 1702, Margaret Myles was hanged at Edinburgh. That she was a witch was proved not only by her own confession, but by her inability to say the Lord's Prayer, even when the minister, Mr. George Andrews, tried to teach her. When he desired her to pray "her heart was so obdured that she answered she could not; for, as she confessed, she was in covenant with the devil, who had made her renounce her baptism." He then wished her to say the Lord's Prayer after him, and she began, but she would say nothing but "Our Father which wart in heaven," and could not by any means be got to say the right word. He then reproached her, saying, "How could she bid him pray for her, since she could not pray for herself?" and, singing two verses of the 51st Psalm, he made her show a little penitence. Then he essayed her again, trying to make her repeat after him, "I renounce the devil," but she would only say, "I unce the devil;" "for by no means would she say distinctly that she renounced the devil, and adhered unto her baptism, but that she unced the devil, and hered unto her baptism. The only sign of repentance she gave was after the napkin had covered her face, for then she said, 'Lord, take me out of the devil's hands, and put me in God's.'"

The next year, "The Rigwoodie Witch," lean Marion Lillie of Spott, was had before the Kirk Session to account for her dealings in the village. She was a passionate-tongued old dame, who had handled roughly one of her neighbours while in the condition that looked forward to Mrs. Gamp and the caudle-cup; so roughly, indeed, that Mrs. Gamp and the caudle-cup were forestalled, and the poor woman was brought to an unpleasant pass; so the

Rigwoodie witch got something not so pleasant as a month's nursing, and was put out of the way of handling pregnant women roughly for the future.

THE STIRK'S FOOT.[72]

Jean Neilson lived in Torryburn, a village in the west of Fife, and she and Lillias Adie, a woman of more than equivocal reputation, were not on the best of terms. Jean Neilson was but a poor sickly body, full of fancies and uncatalogued ailments; and because she had no scientific name to give them, she gave Lillias the credit of having created them by her magic. She swore that she was bewitched, and that old Lillias was the bewitcher. Upon which the ministers and elders of the kirk in Torryburn met in solemn conclave on the 29th of July, and called Lillias before them to give an account of her bad practices. Lillias had no mind that they should lose their trouble. She confessed herself a witch without further ado; said how that she had met the devil by the side of a "stook" in the harvest field, where she had renounced her baptism and accepted him on the instant as her lord and lover; how he had embraced her, when she found his skin cold, and saw his feet cloven like a "stirk's." Since then she had joined in dances with him and others whom she named; for Lillias, like all the rest, seemed to think there was safety in a multitude, and delated several of the parish, to bear her company in her uncomfortable position; and she told how, at the back of Patrick Sands' house in Vellyfield, they were lighted by a mysterious light, just sufficient to let them see each other's faces, and to show the devil with a cap covering his ears and neck. The minister and elders had now rich game in view, and they held meeting after meeting to examine those whom Lillias accused, and feed their ears with all the wild and monstrous tales they chose to pour into them. But what became of them eventually no one now knows: only of a surety Lillias Adie was burned "within the sea mark," and Jean Neilson might now bear

---

[72] Chambers.

her uncatalogued ailments in peace. The minister of Torryburn at that time was one Allen Logan—the Reverend Allen Logan—notorious for his skill in detecting witches, and his zeal in hunting them down. When administering the communion he would flash his eye through the congregation and say harshly, as by knowledge, "You witch-wife, get up from the table of the Lord," casting a ball for the conscience-stricken to kick at; when, ten to one, some poor old trembling wretch would totter up, and so go mumbling through the doors, "thus exposing herself to the hazard of a regular accusation afterwards." He was always "dinging" against witchcraft; and one day a woman called Helen Kay took up her stool and went out of the church. She said she thought he was "daft" "to be always dinging against witches thae' gait;" but the elders thought differently, and Helen Kay was convicted of profanity, and ordained to sit before the congregation and be openly rebuked.

THE HORRIBLE MURDER
OF JANET CORNFOOT.[73]

While Lillias Adie was being burned in the west of Fife, Beatrix Laing, at Pittenweem in the east, was put to sore trouble. Patrick Morton, a youth of sixteen "free from any known vice," sent up a petition to the Privy Council (June 13, 1704), stating, that being employed by his father to make some nails for a ship lying off Pittenweem, Beatrix Laing, spouse to William Brown, tailor, and late treasurer of the burgh, came and demanded some nails. He "modestly" refused her, saying that he was engaged in another job, and could not therefore work for her; whereupon she went away, "threatening to be revenged, which did somewhat frighten him, because he knew she was under a bad fame and reputed for a witch." The next day, on passing Beatrix's door, "he observed a timber vessel with some water and fire coal in it at the door, which made him apprehend that it was a charm laid for him, and the effect of her threatening; and immediately he was seized with such a weakness in his limbs that he could hardly stand or walk." For many weeks this strange kind of lingering disease and discomfort went on, he "still growing worse, having no appetite, and his body strangely emaciated," all because of Beatrix having "slockened" fire coals in a vessel as a malevolent charm for him; till about May the disease ripened, and the symptoms of hysteria and epilepsy presented themselves. He swelled prodigiously; his breathing was like the blowing of a pair of bellows; his body was rigid and inflexible; his tongue was drawn into his mouth; and he cried out vehemently against Beatrix Laing and others—for these accusations never came alone; professing to know his tormentors by their touch if brought to him, although his eyes were blinded, and the bystanders

---

73 Chambers; Sinclair; and an anonymous tract.

held their peace. In short, he played the same antics here in the east as Bargarran's daughter had played in the west. Beatrix and the rest were flung into prison, and every effort was made to induce them to confess. Beatrix was pricked, and kept without sleep for five days and nights; but she held out manfully. She would not consent to accept the modest youth's interpretation of his illness, and denied strongly all hand in it, and all trafficking with witch charms or unholy arts. At last she was conquered. Sleeplessness and torture did their appointed work, and she made a rambling statement of baptismal renunciation, and the like, delating Janet Cornfort and others, which confession she recanted as soon as she had got a little strength; and specially that part where she had spoken of her fine packs of wool which she had sold so well at the market, coming home afterwards on a big black horse, which she gave into her husband's hands. Her husband, she had said, was embarrassed with this big black horse, and asked what he should do with it? to which she had answered, "Cast his bridle on his neck and you will be quit of him." So the horse flew off overhead with a great noise, and Beatrix Laing's startled husband for the first time understood its real character.

In revenge at her obduracy the magistrates "put her in the stocks, and then carried her to the Thieves' Hole, and from that transported her to a dark dungeon, where she was allowed no manner of light, or human converse; and in this condition she lay for five months." All this while the magistrates of the burgh were pressing on the Privy Council the absolute need of trying her; but the Earl of Balcarres and Lord Anstruther, two members of the council connected with the district, interposed their influence, and got the poor creature set at liberty;—"brought her off as a dreamer," says the anonymous pamphlet angrily. But she was forced to turn her face from Pittenweem, and "wandered about in strange places, in the extremity of

172

hunger and cold, though she had a competency at home, but dared not come near her own house," for fear of the fury and rage of the people: dying at last "undesired" in her bed at St. Andrews.

Beatrix was wandering about in strange places, safe if sorrowful, but Alexander Macgregor clinched her muttered charge against Janet Cornfoot by accusing her of perpetually haunting him—she and two other witches, and his Cloutieship along with them. They tormented him chiefly in the night time, while he was sleeping in his bed. Janet, under torture confessed; but retracted immediately after, saying that the minister himself had beaten her with his staff to make her speak out: and there being considerable doubt of her guilt in the minds of the gentry of the district, even of the chastising minister himself, she was allowed to escape, by connivance. But another minister of the neighbourhood, with more zeal than humanity and more grace than knowledge, stopped her in her flight, and sent her back to Pittenweem. There the mob got hold of her. They had been fearfully excited by Beatrix Laing's acquittal and Janet's escape, and they were not disposed to let this unexpected glut to their vengeance go. They seized poor Janet Cornfoot, tied her up hard in a rope, beat her unmercifully, then dragged her by the heels through the streets and along the shore. "The appearance of a bailie for a brief space dispersed the crowd, but only to show how easily the authorities might have protected their victim if they had chosen." Resuming their horrible work, the rabble tied Janet to a rope stretching between a vessel in the harbour and the shore, swinging her to and fro, and amusing themselves by pelting her with stones. Tiring at length of this sport, they let her down with a sharp fall upon the beach, beat her again unmercifully, and finally covering her with a door, pressed her to death (Jan. 30, 1705). Janet's daughter was in the town, and knew what was taking place down by that blood-stained shore, but she dared not interfere; and during all the time this hideous murder was going on—lasting for nearly three hours—neither magistrate nor minister came forward to protect or interpose. Are verily and in truth "the powers that be ordained of God," or has not the devil sometimes something to do with the laying on of hands?—so much of the devil, at least, as is represented by ignorance, inhumanity, superstition, and cowardice, always conspicuous qualities of the more zealous of every denomination.

About this time,[74] Thomas Brown, another of the accused, died of "hunger and hardship" in prison; and at the close of the year, two Inverness men, George and Lachlan Rattray, were executed, being found "guilty of the horrid crimes of mischievous charms, by witchcraft and malefice, sorcery or necromancy." And many witches were also burnt on the top of Spott Loan.

---

[74] Chambers.

THE SPELL OF THE SLAP.[75]

In 1708, William Stensgar, of Southside, in Orkney, had rheumatism. He sent to an old beggar-woman, called Catherine Taylor—a cripple herself, but none the less qualified to heal others by her magic arts. She came to him about an hour before sunrise and took the case in hand, bidding him follow her till they came to a certain kind of gate or stile, called a slap or grind; William's wife accompanying them with a stoup of water. At this slap Catherine touched his knee, saying, "As I was going by the way I met the Lord Jesus Christ in the likeness of another man; he asked me what tidings I had to tell? I said I had no tidings to tell, but I am full of pain, and can neither gang nor stand. Thou shalt go to the holy kirk, and thou shalt gang round about, and then sit down upon thy knees, and say thy prayers to the Lord, and then thou shalt be as heal as the hour when Christ was born." After this precious charm, which the old cripple said had been taught her when a child, she repeated the 23rd Psalm; and then the evil spirit which had caused the rheumatism was assumed to be "telled out" into the stoup of water; at all events William Stensgar would have no more of it. Then the water was emptied out over the slap or gate so that the next person passing by the stile might get it instead of William. One man who had watched this devilry from the beginning, evaded the foul fiend by pushing his way through the hedge higher up; but another unfortunate wretch, not so lucky or not so early a riser, coming blundering over the stile as usual, got laid hold of by the fiend which William Stensgar had shaken off, and was holden by it hardly.

---

[75] Hibbert.

THE PLAGUE OF CATS.[76]

Year by year witches became scarcer, none of any special note presenting themselves till we come to the case of Margaret Nin-Gilbert, of Caithness, which happened in the year 1718; the same year as that in which the minister of Redcastle lost his life by witchcraft, and Mr. M'Gill's house at Kinross (he was minister there) was so egregiously troubled by a spirit which nipped the sheets and stuck pins into eggs and meat, and clipt away the laps of a gentlewoman's hood and a servant maid's gown tail, and flung stones down the chimney, which "wambled a space" on the floor, and then took a flight out of the window, and threw the minister's bible into the fire, and spoilt the baking, and played all sorts of mad pranks to disquiet the family and defy God. If such things as these could be done in the light of the sun, why, should not Margaret Nin-Gilbert have supernatural power? Nin-Gilbert had a friend, one Margaret Olson, a woman of it is said wicked behaviour, whom Mr. Frazer put out of her house, taking as his tenant instead one William Montgomerie. Upon this Margaret Olson went to her friend Nin-Gilbert, the notorious witch, and besought her to harm Mr. Frazer; but Mr. Frazer being a gentleman of rank and fortune was defended from the witches, and Nin-Gilbert confessed she had no power or inclination to hurt him. However, one night as he was crossing a bridge, they attempted him, but succeeded not; and he, on being questioned, said he perfectly remembered "his horse making a great adoe at that place, but that by the Lord's goodness he escaped." Also he had a great sickness at the time these women were taken, but he had common sense enough to refuse to ascribe it to them. Finding that they could not prevail against Mr. Frazer, they turned their attention to

---

[76] Law's 'Memorials;' and Chambers.

Montgomerie, "mason, in Burnside of Scrabster," who was also under the ban for having accepted the tenancy of which Margaret Olson had been dispossessed. Suddenly his house became so infested with cats that it was no longer safe for his family to remain there. He himself was away, but his wife sent to him five times, threatening that if he did not return home to protect them, she would flit to Thurso; and his servant left them suddenly, and in mid term, because five of these cats came one night to the fireside where she was alone, and began speaking among themselves with human and intelligible voices. So William Montgomerie, mason at Scrabster, returned home to do battle with the enemy. The cats came in their old way and in their old numbers; and William prepared his best. On Friday night, the 28th of November, one of the cats got into a chest with a hole in it, and when she put her head out of the hole, William made a lunge at her with his sword, which "cutt hir," but for all that he could not hold her. He then opened the chest, and his servant, William Geddes, stuck his dirk into her hind quarters and pinned her to the chest. After which, Montgomerie beat her with his sword and cast her out for dead; but the next morning she was gone; so there was no doubt as to her true character. Four or five nights after this, his servant, being in bed, "cryed out that Some of these catts had come in on him." Montgomerie ran to his aid, wrapt his plaid about the cat and thrust his dirk through her body, then smashed her head with the back of an axe, and cast her out like the first. The next morning she too was gone, and there was proof positive for another case. So as none of these cats belonged to the neighbourhood, and there were eight of them assembled together in one night, "this looking like witchcraft, it being threatened that none should thrive in my said house," William Montgomerie made petition to the Sherrif-Deput of Caithness, to visit "some person of bad fame," who was reported to have fallen sick immediately on this encounter, and search out if she had any wounds on her body or not. "This representation seeming all the time to be very incredulous and fabulous, the sheriff had no manner of regard yrto." But when, on the 12th of February, Margaret Nin-Gilbert was seen by one of her neighbours "to drop at her own door one of her leggs from the midle, and she, being under bad fame for witchcraft, the legg, black and putrified, was brought before the Sheriff-depute" (not the sheriff himself, the Earl of Caithness, who might have had a little more common sense)—then the said Sheriff-depute ordered Nin-Gilbert to be seized and examined. Margaret made short work of it. Being interrogated the 8th of February, 1719, she confessed that she was under compact with the devil, whom she had met in the likeness of a black man as she was travelling some long time byegone in ane evening; confessed also that he sometimes appeared to her as a great black horse, and other times as if riding on a black horse, and sometimes as a black cloud, and sometimes as a black hen. Confessed also that she was at William Montgomerie's house that evening, when he attacked her as a cat, and that he broke her leg with the dirk or axe, which since had fallen off from the rest of her body: also, that Margaret Olson was there with her, who, being stronger than she did cast her on the dirk when her leg was broken. She then delated four other women, one of whom, Helen Andrew, had been so crushed and maimed by Montgomerie, "that she dyed that same night of her wounds or few days yrafter:" and another, M'Huistan, "cast herself a few days afterwards from the rocks of Borrowstoun into the sea, since which time she was never seen; while a third, Jannet Pyper, she identified as having a red petticoat on her. Asked how they managed not to be discovered said, the devil raised a fog or mist to conceal them." When her confession was ended, her accomplices were apprehended; but she herself died in prison in a fortnight's time. Margaret Olson was then examined. She was "tryed in the shoulders" (for witches' marks), "where there were several small spots, some read, some blewish; after a needle was driven in with great force almost to the eye she felt it not. Mr. Innes, Mr. Oswald, minister, and several honest women, and Bailzie Forbes, were witnesses to this. And further, that while the needle was in her shoulder, as aforesaid, she said, 'Am not I ane honest woman now?'" So this instance of human wickedness and folly ended by the usual method of the cord and the stake.

THE YOUNG HONOURABLE'S DECEITS.

January, 1720, saw distress and confusion at Calder in Mid Lothian. Lord Torphichen's third son, the Honourable Patrick Sandilands, was bewitched, and the whole country was in excitement. If the devil could touch a Lord's son, who was safe? There was no doubt of the fact, let who would deny it. Lord Torphichen's son though he was, the Honourable Patrick Sandilands was worse holden than the meanest hind on the estate. He was buffeted about the room; flung down in trances, from which no horsewhippings—and it is to be hoped he had plenty of them, and well laid on—could revive him; he pronounced prophecies; was lifted up in the air; taken off long journeys between the space of two flashes of light; had the gift of clairvoyance; and put out all the candles by his very presence—his powers depending, as such powers generally do, on darkness and confusion for their perfect development. Lord Torphichen soon left off the use of the horsewhip, and he and all the family came to the conclusion that the Honourable Patrick was bewitched. So they got hold of the witch, a brutish, ignorant, half-witted woman living in the village of Calder, and put her in prison, waiting her confession. As for that, it was not difficult to get at. Yes, she was a witch; had been a witch for many years; had once given the devil her own dead child to make a roast of; had made an image of the young laird; and had three associates, two women and a man. Mad William Mitchell, the Tinklarian Doctor,[77] as he was called, went on foot in ill weather without food from the West Bow to Lord Torphichen's house at Calder, to see what he could do towards discovering the devil in the witches. This was on the 14th of January—the day of the

---

[77] A crazy old Illuminatus, who had a "call," and wrote the Tinkler's Testament.

solemn fast, which was all the help that the awakening reason of the times would allow the Honourable Patrick Sandilands. True, the witch and her confederates were in prison, but there was no gallows planted, and no fire set: only the ministers, and elders, and saints, and people, convened in solemn and sacred prayer, to beseech God to drive out the devil from a lying, mischievous, hysterical lad. But crazy William Mitchell took very little by this move, Lord Torphichen not favouring his pretensions to special and private illumination. The sermon was preached in the Calder Kirk by the Rev. Mr. John Wilkie, minister of Uphall, the sorcerers being present, and was found so powerful that the devil was fairly exorcised, and the boy soon after wholly recovered. In time he went to sea, rose to the command of an East Indiaman, but perished in a storm, leaving a meritorious name singularly stained with boyish sins. "It brings us strangely near to this wild-looking affair," says Chambers, "that the present Lord Torphichen (1860) is only *nephew* to the witch-boy of Calder."

THE LAST OF THE WITCHES.

And now we draw near to the close of this fatal superstition. In 1726, Woodrow notes "some pretty odd accounts of witches," had from a couple of Ross-shire men, but fails to give us very accurate details, save only that one of them at her death "confessed that they had, by sorcery, taken away the sight of one of the eyes of an Episcopal minister, who lost the sight of his eye upon a sudden, and could give no reason for it." And early in the year of 1727[78] the last witch-fire was kindled with which the air of bonnie Scotland was polluted. Two poor Highland women, a mother and daughter, were brought before Captain David Ross of Littledean, deputy-sheriff of Sutherland, charged with witchcraft and consorting with the devil. The mother was accused of having used her daughter as her "horse and hattock," causing her to be shod by the devil, so that she was ever after lame in both hands and feet; and the fact being satisfactorily proved, and Captain David Ross being well assured of the same, the poor old woman was put into a tar-barrel and burned at Dornoch in the bright month of June. "And it is said that after being brought out to execution, the weather proving very severe, she sat composedly warming herself by the fire prepared to consume her, while the other instruments of death were getting ready." The daughter escaped: afterwards she married and had a son who was as lame as herself; and lame in the same manner too; though it does not seem that he was ever shod by the devil and witch-ridden. "And this son," says Sir Walter Scott, in 1830, "was living so lately as to receive the charity of the present Marchioness of Stafford, Countess of Sutherland in her own right."

This, then, is the last execution for witchcraft in Scotland; and in June, 1736, the Acts Anentis Witchcraft

---

[78] Scott. Dickie. Chambers, &c.

were formally repealed. Henceforth, to the dread of the timid, and the anger of the pious, the English Parliament distinctly opposed the express letter of the Law of God, "Thou shalt not suffer a witch to live;" and declared the text upon which so much critical absurdity had been talked, and in support of which so much innocent blood had been shed, vain, superstitious, impossible, and contrary to that human reason which is the highest law of God hitherto revealed unto men. But if Parliament could stay executions it could not remove beliefs, nor give rationality in place of folly. Not more than sixty years ago an old woman named Elizabeth M'Whirter[79] was "scratched" by one Eaglesham, in the parish of Colmonel, Ayrshire, because his son had fallen sick, and the neighbours said he was bewitched. Poor old Bessie M'Whirter was forced over the hills to the young man's house, a distance of three miles, and there made to kneel by his bedside and repeat the Lord's Prayer. When she had finished, the youth's father took a rusty nail and scratched the poor old creature's brow in the form of a cross; scratched it so effectually that it was many weeks in healing, and the scar remained to the last day of her life. If Elizabeth M'Whirter had lived a generation earlier, she might have run a race with death and a tar barrel, and been defeated at the end, like the poor old wretch at Dornoch.

But still the old faith lingers in those beautiful vales, and hides in the fastnesses of the mountain glens; still brownies haunt the ruined places, and witches send forth blight and bale at their will; still the elfin people ride on the whirlwind and dance in the moonlight; and the hill and the flood and the brae and the streamlet have their attendant spirits which vie with the churchyard ghost in impotent malevolence to men. And the gift of second sight, though dying out because of these degenerate times of utilitarianism and power-loom weaving, is yet to be found

---

[79] Dickie's 'Philosophy of Magic.'

where the old blood runs thickest, and the old ideas are least disturbed; and still the whole nation clings with spasmodic force to its gloomy creed of the Predestined and the Elect, and holds by the early faith from whose narrow bounds others have emerged into a brighter and a wider path. No more witch-fires are now lighted on the Castle Hill; no more grave and reverend divines give themselves up, like Mr. John Aird, to discovering the devil's mark stamped visibly on human flesh; yet the heart of the people has not abandoned its ancient God, and though the altars may be dressed with the flowers of another season, and the name upon the plinth be carved in other characters, yet is the indwelling idol the same. The God which Calvinistic Scotland yet worships is the same God as that to which the witches and wizards of old were sacrificed; he is the God of Superstition, the God of Condemnation, in whose temple Nature has no place, and Humanity no rights.

The Witches of England.

"Every old woman with a wrinkled face, a furr'd brow, a hairy lip, a gobber tooth, a squint eye, a squeaking voice, or a scolding tongue, having a ragged coate on her back, a skull-cap on her head, a spindle in her hand, and a Dog or Cat by her side, is not only suspected but pronounced for a witch," says John Gaule;[80] while Reginald Scot[81] puts forth as his experience:—"One sort of such as are said to be witches, are women which be commonly old, lame, bleareyed, pale, fowle, and full of wrinckles; poor, sullen, superstitious, and Papists; or such as know no religion; in whose drousie minds the devill hath gotten a fine seat; so as, what mischief, mischance, calamity or slaughter is brought to passe, they are easily perswaded the same is done by themselves; imprinting in their minds an earnest and constant imagination thereof. They are leane and deformed, showing melancholy in their faces, to the horror of all that see them. They are doting, scolds, mad, devilish; and not much differing from them that are thought to be possessed with spirits, so firm and steadfast in their opinions, as whosoever shall only have respect to the constancy of their words uttered, would easily believe they were true indeed." Dr. Harsnet, in his "Declaration of Popish Impostures," gives the subject a masterly touch of common sense and satire:—"These things," saith he, "are raked together out of old doating Heathen Histriographers, Wizzardizing Augurs, Imposturizing Soothsayers, Dreaming Poets, Chimerical Conceiters, and Coiners of Fables, &c. Out of these is shap'd the true Idea of a *Witch*, an old weather-beaten Crone, having her Chin and Knees

---

[80] 'Select Cases of Conscience.'
[81] 'Discoverie of Witchcraft.'

meeting for Age, walking like a Bow leaning on a Staff, Hollow-Ey'd, Untooth'd, Furrow'd on her Face, having her Lips trembling with the Palsy, going mumbling in the Streets: One that hath forgotten her Pater Noster, and yet hath a shrewd Tongue to call a Drab a Drab. If she hath learn'd of an old Wife in a Chimney End Pax, Max, Fax, for a Spell; or can say Sir John Grantham's Curse for the Miller's Eels, All ye that have stolen the Miller's Eels, laudate Dominum de Cœlis: And all they that have consented thereto, Benedicamus Domino: Why then beware, look about you, my Neighbours. If any of you have a Sheep sick of the Giddies, or a Stag of the Mumps, or a Horse of the Staggers, or a Knavish Boy of the School, or an idle Girl of the Wheel, or a young Drab of the Sullens, and hath not Fat enough for her Porrage, or Butter enough for her Bread, and she hath a little Help of the Epilepsy or Cramp, to teach her to roll her Eyes, wry her Mouth, gnash her Teeth, startle with her Body, hold her Arms and Hands stiff, &c. And then with an old Mother Nobs hath by Chance call'd her Idle young Housewife, or bid the Devil scratch her; then no doubt but Mother Nobs is the Witch, and the young Girl is Owl-blasted, &c." Then he goes on to say, with more force and right judgment than one could have expected from one of his generation:—"They that have their Brains baited, and their Fancies distemper'd with the Imaginations, and Apprehensions of Witches, Conjurers, and Fairies, and all that Lymphatical Chimæra, I find to be marshall'd in one of these five Ranks: Children, Fools, Women, Cowards, sick or black melancholick discompos'd Wits."

These then are the sentiments of three somewhat wise and sane men, who lived in a time of universal madness, and gave their minds to the task of stemming the raging torrent. For the whole world was overrun with witches. From every town came crowds of these lost and damned souls; from every hovel peered out the cursing witch, or

186

cried aloud for help the stricken victims. These poor and old and wretched beings, upon whose heads lighted the wrath of a world, and against whom every idle lad had a curse and a stone to fling at his will, were held capable of all but omnipotence. They could destroy the babe in the womb and make the "mother of many children childless among women;" they could kill with a look and disable with a curse; bring storms or sunshine as they listed; by their "witch-ropes," artfully woven, draw to themselves all the profit of their neighbours' barns and breweries; yet ever remained poor and miserable, glad to beg a mouthful of meat, or a can of sour milk from the hands of those whom they could ruin by half a dozen muttered words; they could take on themselves what shapes they would, and transport themselves whither they would: no bolt or bar kept them out, no distance by land or sea was too great for them to accomplish; a straw—a broomstick—the serviceable imp ever at hand—was enough for them; and with a pot of magic ointment, and a charm of spoken gibberish, they might visit the king on his throne, or the lady in her bower, to do what ill was in their hearts against them, or to gather to themselves what gain and store they would. Yet with all this power the superstitious world of the time saw nothing doubtful or illogical in the fact of their exceeding poverty, and never stayed to think that if they could transport themselves through the air to any distance they chose, they would be but slippery holding in prison, and not very likely to remain there for the pleasure of being tortured and burnt at the end. But neither reason nor logic had anything to do with the matter. The whole thing rested on fear, and that practical atheism of fear, which denies the power of God and the wholesome beauty of Nature, to exalt in their stead the supremacy of the Devil. This belief in the Devil's material presence and power over men was the dark chain that bound them all. Even the boldest opponent of the Witchcraft Delusion dared not fling it off; not the bravest man or freest thinker could shake his mind clear of this terrible trammel, this bugbear, this mere phantasm of human fear and ignorance, this ghastly lie and morbid delusion, or abandon the slavish worship of Satan for the glad freedom of God and Nature. It was much when such men as Scot,[82] and Giffard,[83] and Gaule of Staughton,[84] Sir Robert Filmer,[85] Ady,[86] Wagstaffe,[87] Webster,[88] Hutchinson,[89] and half a dozen more shining lights could bring themselves to deny the supernatural power of a few half-crazed old beggar-women, and plead for humanity and mercy towards them, instead of cruelty and condemnation; but not one dare take the wider step beyond, and deny the existence of that phantom fiend, belief in whom wrought all this misery and despair. Even the very best of the time gave in to this delusion, and discussed gravely the properties and proportions of what we know now were mere lies.

"We find the illustrious author of the 'Novum Organum' sacrificing to courtly suppleness his philosophic truth, and gravely prescribing the ingredients for a witch's ointment;—Selden maintaining that crimes of the imagination may be punished with death;—The detector of Vulgar Errors, and the most humane of physicians giving the casting vote to the vacillating bigotry of Sir Matthew Hale;—Hobbes, ever sceptical, penetrating, and sagacious, yet here paralyzed and shrinking from the subject, as if afraid to touch it;—The adventurous explorer, who sounded the depths and channels of the 'Intellectual System' along

---

[82] 'Discoverie of Witchcraft,' 1584.
[83] 'Dialogue concerning Witches,' 1603.
[84] 'Select Cases of Conscience touching Witches and Witchcraft,' 1646.
[85] 'Advertisement to the Jurymen of England,' 1653.
[86] 'A Candle in the Dark,' 1656.
[87] 'Question of Witchcraft debated,' 1669. "Wagstaffe was a little crooked man, of a despicable presence. He was laughed at by the boys of Oxford because they said he himself looked like a wizard."
[88] 'Displaying of Witchcraft,' 1677.
[89] 'Historical Essay concerning Witchcraft,' 1720.

all the 'wide-watered' shores of antiquity, running after witches to hear them recite the Common Prayer and the Creed, as a rational test of guilt or innocence;—The gentle spirit of Dr. Henry More, girding on the armour of persecution, and rousing itself from a Platonic reverie on the Divine Life to assume the hood and cloak of a familiar of the Inquisition;—and the patient and inquiring Boyle, putting aside for a while his searches for the grand Magisterium, and listening, as if spell-bound, with gratified attention to stories of witches at Oxford and devils at Mascon."[90] In the Church and amongst the more notoriously "religious" men of the time it was worse. In Archbishop Cranmer's 'Articles of Visitation' (1549) is this clause:—"You shall enquire whether you know of any that use Charms, Sorcery, Enchantments, Soothsaying, or any like Craft invented by the Devil;" and Bishop Jewel, preaching before Queen Elizabeth (1558), informed her how that "witches and sorcerers within these last few years are marvellously increased in your Grace's realm. Your Grace's subjects pine away even unto their death, their colour fadeth, their flesh rotteth, their speech is benumbed, their senses are bereft; I pray God they never practise further than upon the subject.... These eyes have seen most evident and manifest marks of their wickedness." At the next Parliament the new Bill against the detestable sin of witchcraft was passed, and Strype says, partly on account of the Lord Bishop's earnest objurgation. Dalton's[91]

---

[90] Introduction to Potts's 'Discovery of Witches,' edited by James Crossley, Esq. Chetham Society. 1845.

[91] Conjuration or invocation of any evil spirit was felony without benefit of clergy; so also to consult, covenant with, entertain, feed, or reward any evil spirit, or to take up any dead body for charms or spells; to use or practise witchcrafts, enchantment, charm, or sorcery, so that any one was lamed, killed, or pined, was felony without benefit of clergy, to be followed up by burning. Then 'The Country Justice' goes on to give the legal signs of a witch, and those on which a magistrate might safely act, as legal "discoveries." She was to be found and proved by insensible marks; by teats; by imps in various shapes, such

189

'Country Justice' (1655) shows to what a pass, a century later, witchcraft had come in credulous England. Truly Scot was right when he said that his greatest adversaries were "young ignorance and old customs." They have always been the greatest adversaries of all truth. Of late, thank God, the march of humanity has been steadily, if slowly, towards the daylight; but at present you and I, my reader, have to do with the most debasing superstition that ever afflicted history, in the matter of those poor wretched servants of the devil—those witches and wizards, who somehow managed to lose on all sides—to suffer in time and be ruined for eternity, and to get only ill-will and ill-usage from man and fiend alike.

THE WITCH OF BERKELEY.

One of our earliest English witches, so early indeed that she becomes mythical and misty and out of all possible proportion, was the celebrated Witch of Berkeley,[92] who got the reward of her sins in the middle of the ninth century, leaving behind her a tremendous lesson, by which, however, after generations did not much profit. The witch had been rich and the witch had been gay, but the moment of reckoning had to come in the morning; the feast had been noble and well enjoyed, but the terrible account had to be paid when all was over; and the poor witch found her ruddy-cheeked apple, now that the rind was off and eaten, filled with nothing but dust and ashes—which she must

---

as toads, mice, flies, spiders, cats, dogs, &c.; by pictures of wax or clay; by the accusations of the afflicted; by her apparition seen by the afflicted as coming to torment them; by her own sudden or frequent inquiries at the house of the sick; by common report; by the accusations of the dying; and the bleeding of the corpse at her touch; by the testimony of children; by the afflicted vomiting pins, needles, straw, &c.; in short, by all the foolery, gravely formularized, to be found in the lies and deceptions hereafter related.

[92] Thomas Wright's 'Narrative of Sorcery and Magic.' Southey's Ballad.

digest as best she may. As the moment of her death approached, she called for the monks and the nuns of the neighbouring monasteries, and sent for her children to hear her confession; and then she told them of the compact she had made, and how the Devil was to come for her body as well as her soul. "But," said she, "sew me in the hide of a stag, then place me in a stone coffin, and fasten in the covering lead and iron. Upon this place another stone, and chain the whole down with heavy chains of iron. Let fifty psalms be sung each night, and fifty masses be said by day, to break the power of the demons. If you can thus keep my body for three nights safe, on the fourth day you may bury it—the Devil will have sought and not found." The monks and the nuns did as they were desired; and, on the first night, though the demons kept up a loud howling and wailing outside the church, the priests conquered, and the old witch slept undisturbed. On the second night the demons were more fierce and clamorous, and the monks and the nuns told their beads faster and faster; but the fiends were getting more powerful as time went on, and at last broke open the gates of the monastery, in spite of prayer and bolt and bar; and two chains of the coffin burst asunder, but the middle one held firm. On the third night the fiends raged sore and wild. The monastery was shaken to its foundations, and the monks and the nuns almost forgot their paters and their aves in the uproar that drowned their voices and quailed their hearts; but they still went on, until, with an awful crash, and a yell from all the smaller demons about, a Devil, larger and more terrible than any that had come yet, stalked into the church and up to the foot of the altar, where the old woman and her coffin lay. Here he stopped, and bade the witch rise and follow him. Piteously she answered that she could not—she was kept down by the chain in the middle: but the Devil soon settled that difficulty; for he put his foot to the coffin, and broke the iron chain like a bit of burnt thread. Then off flew the covering of lead and iron, and there lay the witch, pale and horrible to see. Slowly she uprose, blue, dead, stark, as she was; and then the Devil took her by the hand, and led her to the door where stood a gigantic black horse, whose back was all studded with iron spikes, and whose nostrils, breathing fire, told of his infernal manger below. The Devil vaulted into the saddle, flung the witch on before him, and off and away they rode—the yells of the clamouring demons, and the shrieks of the tortured soul, sounding for hours, far and wide, in the ears of the monks and the nuns. So here too, in this legend, as in all the rest, the Devil is greater than God, and prayer and penitence inefficacious to redeem iniquity.

EARLY HISTORIC TRIALS.

Coming out from these purely legendary times, we find ourselves on the more solid ground of an actual legal record—the 'Abbreviatio Placitorum;'[93] which informs us that in the tenth year of King John's reign, "Agnes, the wife of Odo the merchant, accused Gideon of sorcery (de sorceria), and she was acquitted by the judgment of the (hot) iron." This is the earliest historic trial to be found in any legal document in England. Nothing more appears until 1324, when two Coventry men,[94] specially appointed out of twenty-seven implicated, undertook the slaying of the King, Edward II., the two Dispensers his favourites, the Prior of Coventry, his caterer and his steward, because they had oppressed the town, and dealt unrighteously with its inhabitants. These two men went to a famous necromancer then living in Coventry, called Master John of Nottingham, whom, with his servant Robert Marshall of Leicester, they engaged to perform the work required. But Robert Marshall proved faithless, and betrayed his master to the authorities; telling them how they had received a sum of money for the work in hand, with which sum of money they had bought seven pounds of wax and two yards of canvas, to make seven images—six for the six already enumerated, the seventh for one Richard de Lowe, who had done no one any harm, but on whom they wished to try the effect of the spell, as a modern anatomist would try his experiments on cats, or dogs, or rabbits. He told them how he and Master John of Nottingham had been to a ruined house under Shorteley Park, about half a league from Coventry, where they remained at work from the Monday after the Feast of Saint Nicholas to the Saturday after the Feast of Ascension, making these images of wax and canvas by which they

---

[93] Thomas Wright's 'Narrative of Sorcery and Magic,' and 'Trial of Dame Alice Kyteler.'
[94] Idem.

were to bewitch their noble enemies to death. And first, to try the potency of the charm, Master John took a long leaden pin, and struck it two inches deep into the forehead of the image representing Richard de Lowe, upon which Richard was found writhing and in great pain, screaming "harrow!" and having no knowledge of any man; and so he languished for some days. Then Master John drew out the leaden pin from the brow, and struck it into the heart of the image, when immediately Richard de Lowe died, as any number of witnesses could testify. The necromancer and his man, and the twenty-seven Coventry men implicated in this bit of sorcery, were tried at common law, and acquitted for want of evidence.

That same year, too, occurred one of the most picturesque trials for witchcraft known: the trial of Dame Alice Kyteler, which Mr. Wright, with so much industry and learning, has exhumed from the dusty old records where it was buried, and set out into the light of present knowledge and apprehension. But Dame Alice was an Irishwoman, and so does not rightly come into a book on English witches; else it would be a pleasant, if sad, labour to tell how she was arrested on the charge of holding nightly conferences with her spirit or familiar, Artisson, who was sometimes a cat, and sometimes a black shaggy dog, and sometimes a black man with two tall black companions, each carrying an iron rod in his hand—to which fiendish Proteus she had sacrificed, in the highway, nine red cocks, and nine peacocks' eyes; and also for having, between complines and twilight, raked all the filth of Kilkenny streets to the doors of her son-in-law William Outlawe, murmuring to herself—

"To the house of William, my sonne, Hie all the wealth of Kilkennie towne."

Of how, too, she blasphemously travestied the holy sacrament, having a wafer with the Devil's name stamped on it instead of Christ's; and how she had a pipe of ointment wherewith she greased a staff "upon which she ambolled and gallopped thorough thicke and thin, when and what manner she listed." But it does not belong to my present subject: nor to tell how one of her accomplices, poor weak Petronilla de Meath, was burnt at Kilkenny, not having strength or courage to resist the monstrous confession forced upon her; but how the other, Basil, escaped, according to the natural law by which the strongest always come off the best. Perhaps the fact that Dame Alice took refuge in England may give her a slight claim to a place in these pages; but the question is doubtful, so we must let her go—as also her son-in-law, William Outlawe, whose strict imprisonment of nine weeks led to no bad result, and, let us hope, cooled his blood, which was a trifle too near to boiling point.

Then we stumble over the threshold of the chamber where Friars Bacon and Bungay are sleeping, while stupid Miles is watching the Brazen Head whose brief solemn words were spoken in vain; going forward just a few paces until we come to the death-beds of Bungay and Vandermast, and Friar Bacon's clever cheating of the Devil at last. But we are still on the outskirts of legendary land, and must go on to the middle of the fourteenth century before we get a firm hold. About this time the subject of witchcraft occupied much of the attention and thought of the Church, but the priests had not yet quite closed their fingers round it; for in 1371 a man was arrested for sorcery, and "brought before the justices of the King's Bench, by whom he was acquitted for want of evidence, which shows that it was still looked upon merely as an offence against common law."[95] It was only when it became the superstition which some men are pleased to call "religion" that it got stained with its deepest dyes. Early in 1406

---

[95] 'Introduction to the Narrative of the Proceedings against Dame Alice Kyteler.' By Thomas Wright. 1843.

Henry IV. gave instructions to the Bishop of Norwich to search for the sorcerers, witches, and necromancers reported to be rather rife in that respectable diocese, and if he could not convert them from the evil of their ways, he was to bring them to speedy punishment; and in 1432 the Privy Council ordered to be seized and examined a Franciscan friar of Worcester, by name Thomas Northfield; another friar, John Ashwell; John Virley "a clerk;" and Margery Jourdemaine—the same Margery generally called the Witch of Eye, who, nine years later, was burnt at Smithfield for her complicity in the treasonable practices of Dame Eleanor of Gloucester. In 1441 Dame Eleanor herself was arrested, and "put in holt, for she was suspecte of treason;" and with her the Witch of Eye, who was burnt; and Roger, a clerk "longing to her," who was placed on a high scaffold against St. Paul's Cross on the Sunday, and there "arraied like as he should never thrive in his garnementys;" while heaped up round about were all his instruments taken with him, to be showed among the people, and create a proper fear and horror in their mind. The end of poor Roger the clerk was, that he was dragged from the Tower to Tyburn, there hanged, beheaded, and quartered; his head set on London Bridge, and his four quarters sent—one to Hereford, and one to Oxenford, another to York, and the fourth to Cambrigge. As for Dame Eleanor, that proud, dark, unscrupulous heroine of romance, every one knows the story of her disgrace and shame; how she came from London to Westminster, and walked through the streets of the city barefooted and bareheaded, carrying the waxen taper of two pounds' weight, and doing penance before all the crowd of citizens assembled to see her "on her foot and hoodles;" and how she offered up her taper on the high altar of "Poules;" and when all was done, was sent to Chester prison, "there to byde while she lyveth."

After her, in 1478, comes "the high and noble princesse Jaquet," Duchess of Bedford, charged with having, by the aid of "an image of lede, made lyke a man of arms, conteyning the length of a mannes fynger, and broken in the myddes, and made fast with a wyre," turned the love of King Edward IV. from one Dame Elianor Butteler daughter of the old Earl of Shrewsbury, to whom he was affianced, unto her own child, Elizabeth Grey, sometime wife to Sir John Grey, knight; and in 1483 poor Jane Shore was bound to do penance, walking bareheaded and barefooted, clad only in her kirtle, carrying a wax taper, and acknowledging her sins, because Richard of Gloucester had a withered arm, and wanted to put a few enemies out of the way of that arm and its desires. He employed the same accusation against many of those enemies, but so patently for political motives and without even the semblance of reason, that these attainders can scarcely be set down in any manner to the charge of witchcraft. Then in 1484 came the bull of Innocent VIII., which gave authority to the inquisitors to "convict, imprison, and punish" the unfortunate servants of the Devil, who thus found themselves a mark for every one's shaft.

In Henry the Eighth's time treasure-seeking was the most fashionable phase of necromancy. There was Neville of Wolsey's household, who consulted Wood—gentleman, magician, and treasure-seeker extraordinary—but only for a charm or magic ring which should bring him into favour with his prince, saying that his master the Cardinal had such an one, and he would fain participate; and he did at last get Wood to make him one that would bring him the love of women. Wood could find treasures wherever hidden, and was sure of the philosopher's stone; nay, he would "chebard" (jeopard) his life but that he could make gold as he listed, and offered to remain in prison till he had accomplished it, "twelve months on silver and twelve and a half on gold." In this same reign, too, was arrested

William Stapleton for sorcery. William[96] was a monk of St. Benet in the Holm, Norfolk, and William loved not his monkish life; so he got out, seeking money to buy his dispensation. And not having the money at hand himself, nor knowing how to get it, he took to treasure-seeking as the easiest manner open to him of making a fortune. But his conjurations and his magic staff only led him to some Roman remains, and nothing more; so he borrowed of a friend instead, then settled in Norfolk, and turned to treasure-seeking again, uselessly; got into intrigues that did him no good; and had three spirits, Andrea Malchus, Inchubus, and Oberion—the last a dumb devil who would not speak, being in the service of my Lord Cardinal.

In 1521 the Duke of Buckingham died on the scaffold, led into some imprudent actions by the predictions of his familiar magician, one friar Hopkins; and Hopkins, to make amends, died broken-hearted shortly after. And there was the Maid of Kent (1534), Elizabeth Barton, who had trances and gave revelations, and was on intimate terms with Mary Magdalen and the Virgin, and who was probably a "sensitive" made use of by the Catholics to try and frighten the King from his marriage with the "gospel eyes;" but poor Elizabeth Barton came to a sad pass with her revelations and trances; and Mary Magdalen, who had given her a letter written in heaven and all of gold, forgot to forewarn or shield her from her cruel and shameful end at Tyburn that cloudy fitful day of April, with the gallows standing out against the flecked sky, and the poor raving nun, half-enthusiast half-impostor, praying bareheaded at its foot—she and her accomplices waiting for the moment to die.

In 1541 we find a nobler name on the scaffold—Lord Hungerford—"beheaded for procuring certain persons to conspire that they might know how long Henry VIII. would

---

[96] Wright's 'Narrative of Sorcery and Magic.' 1851.

live;" and that same year an Act was passed against false prophecies, and another against conjurations, witchcraft, and sorcery, making it felony without benefit of clergy. But six years later Edward VI. abrogated that statute; not for any tenderness to witches, but because with it was bound up a prohibition against pulling down crosses. In 1549 Ket's rebellion was troublesome; its vigour due partly to the old prophecy repeated through the plains of Norfolk—

"Hob, Dic, and Hic, with Clubs and clouted Shoon, Shall fill up Duffin-dale with slaughtered Bodies soon."

And then we come to nothing more until 1559, when Elizabeth "renewed the same article of inquiry for sorcerers," but punishing the first conviction only with the pillory. The following year eight men were taken up for conjurations and sorcery, and tried at Westminster, where they had to purge themselves by confession, penitence, and a repudiating oath. In 1562 the Earl and Countess of Lennox, Anthony Pool, Anthony Fortescue, and some others, were condemned for treason and meddling with sorcerers; though, indeed, Elizabeth herself was not free from either the superstition or its practice; for did she not patronize Dr. Dee and his "skryer" John Kelly, with his ranting about Madimi in her gown of "changeable sey," and all the other spirits who came in and out of the "show-stone," and talked just the same kind of rubbish as spirits talk now in modern circles? But the poor "figure-flinger, with his tin pictures," was a sorcerer not to be protected, so got tried and condemned—poor figure-flinger!

In 1562, the year of Lady Lennox's business, a new Act against witchcraft was passed; and in 1589 one Mrs. Deir practised conjuration against the Queen, for which she was tried, but acquitted for want of evidence; but the Queen had excessive anguish in her teeth that year, by night and by day. When Ferdinand Earl of Derby died, about this time, of perpetual and unceasing sickness, a waxen image was found in his chamber stuffed with hair the exact colour of his; which sufficiently accounted for his illness and the mysterious manner of his death, though a Sadducee and sceptic might have whispered of poison, or a physician have spoken of cholera; from which disease indeed, by the minute symptoms so carefully detailed, the poor earl's death seems to have been—if not from poison, which might have produced the same effects. Still, the accusation of sorcery was so convenient—such a cloak for viler sins! The latter half of Elizabeth's reign was disgraced by many witch persecutions, for the subject was beginning to attract painful notice now; and, though it was not till James I. had set the smouldering fragments all a-blaze that the worst of the evils were done, still enough was doing now for the philosopher to deplore and the humanitarian to lament. In 1575 many were hanged at Barking; in 1579 three were executed at Chelmsford, four at Abingdon, and two at Cambridge. In 1582 thirteen at St. Osith's, the evidence against one being that she had been heard to talk to something when alone in her house; while of the other, a woman swore that she looked through her window one day, when she was out, and there "espied a spirite to looke out of a potcharde from under a clothe, the nose thereof being browne like unto a ferret." In 1585 one was hanged at Tyburn and one at Stanmore; 1589 saw three sent into eternity at Chelmsford; in 1593 we have the witches of Warbois; and two years later (1595) three at Barnet and Brainford; in 1597 several at Derby and Stafford; so that by degrees the thing came to be a notorious matter of social life; and the poor and the aged and the disliked lived in fear and peril, daily increasing. At this time, too, possessions were many and ghosts walked abroad without let or hindrance. Richard Lee saw one at Canterbury (1575), and Master Gaymore and others saw another at Rye two years after. "But," says Reginald Scot, "certainely some one knave in a white sheet hath cosened and abused many thousands that way, specially when Robin Goodfellow kept

200

such a coile in the Country. For you shall understand that these bugs specially are spied and feared of sicke folke, children, women, and cowards, which, through weaknesse of minde and body, are shaken with vain dreames and continuall fear. The Scythians, being a stout and a warlike nation, as divers writers report, never see any vaine sights, or spirits. It is a common saying, a Lion feareth no bugs. But in our childhood our mothers' maids have so terrified us with an ugly devil having hornes on his head, fire in his mouth, and a taile at his back, eyes like a bason, fanges like a dog, clawes like a beare, a skinne like a Niger, and a voice roring like a Lion, whereby we start and are afraid when we hear one cry Bough; they have so fraied us with bullbeggars, spirits, urchens, elves, hags, fairies, satyrs, pans, fauns, sylens (syrens?), kit with the cansticke, tritons, centaures, dwarfes, giants, imps, calcats, conjurors, nymphes, changelings, incubus, Robin Goodfellow, the spoorn, the mare, the man in the oke, the hell-waine, the firedrake, the puckle, Tom thombe, hob-gobbin, Tom tumbler, boneles, and such other bugs, that we are afraid of our own shadowes; insomuch as some never fear the devil, but in a dark night; and then a polled sheep is a perillous beast, and many times is taken for our father's soul, specially in a churchyard, where a right hardy man heretofore scant durst passe by night, but his haire would stand upright. For right grave writers report, that spirits most often and specially take the shape of women, appearing to monks, &c., and of beasts, dogs, swine, horses, goats, cats, haires, of fowles, as crowes, night owles and shreek owles; but they delight most in the likenesse of snakes and dragons." All of which "wretched and cowardly infidelity" was rampant in England when good Queen Bess ruled the land—rampant doubly, so that there was no holding in of this furious madness after James I. had got his foot in the stirrup, and was riding a race neck and neck with the Devil. But I must turn back a few years, and tell of

THE AFFLICTIONS OF ALEXANDER NYNDGE,

A precious babe of grace snatched from destruction. They are to be found in 'A Booke declaring the fearfull vexation of one Alexander Nyndge, Beynge moste Horriblye tormented wyth an euyll spirit, the xx. daie of Januarie. In the yere of our Lorde 1573, at Lyeringswell in Suffolke;' and this book sets forth the details of the various fits which Alexander Nyndge indulged in, for the purpose, as it seems, of enabling his brother Edward to prove his power of exorcism. His first fit began one evening at seven—his father, mother, brothers, and the residue of the household being present; his chest and body swelled, his eyes stared wildly as if starting from their sockets, his back bent inward: the household was disturbed and sore affrighted, but brother Edward had courage enough to say that it was an evil spirit, and undertook to exorcise it. So he charged the foul fiend to come out of him, and the countenance of his brother became more sad and fearful than it was before. Edward was not dismayed but returned to the conflict full of confidence, not giving in even when Alexander and the devil had a wrestle together; or rather when the devil within him seemed as if he would have torn him to pieces, so great was his rage and malice. After some time of this kind of work, Edward got the devil to confess to one or two little matters. In the first place his name was Aubon, and he came last from Ireland; he had come for Alexander's soul, which his brother was not disposed to give up; and by a strange slip of the tongue he called Christ *his* Redeemer: but Edward rebuked him, as became a learned M.A., reminding him that He was Alexander's Redeemer in truth, but not his, the foul fiend's. Even this palpable blunder did not enlighten the Nyndge household as to whose was really the "hollow ghostly" voice proceeding out of Alexander's chest. At last, when Edward had tired him very much, and powerfully shaken him, he said, gruffly, "Bawe wawe, bawe wawe!" and Alexander was transformed, "much like a picture in a play," while a terrible roaring voice sounded "Hellsownd." Then they opened the windows to allow the foul spirit to escape; and in two minutes Alexander leaped up joyfully, crying, "He is gone! he is gone!" After this he had a second, and then a third, attack; but his brother, praying in his right ear, comforted him and finally cured him, for he was never after tormented. Luckily he had not fixed upon any unhappy old woman as the cause of his disorder, so it passed for a case of simple "possession," which prayer and supplication had overcome.

ADE DAVIE'S MOURNING.[97]

Ade Davie, wife of Simon Davie husbandman, had a wiser man for her husband, simple and unlearned as he was, than had many a wretched creature for her judge. Ade suddenly became sad and pensive as she never had been in times past. Her husband did his best to cheer her, but Ade still continued sorrowful; when, at last her burden grew heavier than she could bear, falling down at Simon's feet she besought him to forgive her, for that she had grievously offended both God and him. "Her poor husband being abashed at this her behaviour, comforted her as he could; asking her the cause of her trouble and greefe; who told him that she had, contrary to God's law, and to the offence of all good Christians, to the injury of him, and specially to the losse of her own soul, bargained and given her soul to the devill, to be delivered unto him within short space. Whereunto her husband answered, saying, 'Wife, be of good cheer, this thy bargain is void and of none effect; for thou hast sold that which is none of thine to sell: sith it belongeth to Christ, who hath bought it, and dearly paid for it, even with his blood, which he shed upon the crosse; so as the devil hath no interest in thee.' After this, with like submission, teares, and penitence, she said unto him, 'Oh, husband, I have yet committed another fault, and done you more injury; for I have bewitched you and four children.' 'Be content,' quoth he, 'by the grace of God, Jesus Christ can unwitch us; for none evill can happen to them that fear God.'"

This fresh and pure idyl comes to us with a sweet and wholesome savour, in the midst of the foul quagmires of superstition where it stands; and that poor husbandman's simple faith in God's goodness and his wife's virtue is more touching than many a grand heroic deed which has

---

[97] Reginald Scot.

the suffrages of all history to float it through the life of the world. Simon Davie was an unlettered man, but he was strong-hearted and believing, and, thinking that earnest prayer might comfort his wife, when the time approached for the Devil to come and close his bargain, knelt down by her and prayed, she joining with him fervently. Then they heard a low rumbling noise below which made the windows shake, and which convinced the poor wife that it was the Devil trying to take possession of her soul, but barred out from the chamber by the fervent prayers aforesaid. In the morning it was found that the noise came from a dog which had devoured a sheep that was newly flayed and hung against the wall; and in due time, Ade Davie recovering her reason—for she was crazed, and took every fire to be the fire lighted to burn her for witchcraft—came to the knowledge that she had never sold her soul to the Devil at all, and had never bewitched husband or children, but had always been a faithful wife and fond mother—afflicted with a light brain and nervous imagination.

THE POSSESSION OF MILDRED NORRINGTON.[98]

Mildred, the "base daughter" of Alice Norrington, being seventeen years of age, was likewise possessed of the Devil, in much the same way as Alexander Nyndge had been. She lived as servant with William Spooner of Westwell, in the county of Kent, and her case attracted great attention. All the divines of the neighbourhood assembled at Spooner's house on the 13th of October, 1574, to endeavour to cast out the Devil by such means of prayer and exorcism as they had at their command. Powerfully did they pray; mightily roared the Devil; "And tho' we did command him many times, in the Name of God, and of his Son Jesus Christ, and in his mighty Power to speak, yet he would not, until he had gone through all his Delays, as roaring, crying, striving, and gnashing of teeth, and otherwise, with mowing and other terrible Countenances, and was so strong in the Maid that four men could scarce hold her down." This continued for about two hours, and then he spoke out, but very strangely, crying, "He comes, he comes," and "He goes, he goes." When charged to tell the exorcists who had sent him, he said, "I lay in her way like a Log, and I made her run like Fire; but I could not hurt her." "And why so?" said we. "Because God kept her," said he. When asked when he came to her, he said, "At night, in her bed." And when charged to tell them his name, he said, "The Devil, the Devil." But being still more powerfully exhorted, he roared and cried as before, and spake terrible words: "I will kill her; I will kill her; I will tear her in pieces; I will kill you all!" Asked again, and conjured so that he could not escape, he was forced to confess that his name was Satan, and Little Devil, and Partner, and that old Alice had sent him—old Alice in

[98] Reginald Scot. Dr. Hutchinson.

Westwell Street, with whom he had lived these twenty years shut up in two bottles. "Where be they?" said we. "In the back side of her house," said he. "In what place?" said we. "Under the wall," said he. The other was at Kennington, in the ground. Then we asked him what old Alice had given him. He said, "Her will, her will." "What did she bid thee do?" said we. "Kill her maid," he said, because she did not love her. He then said that he had been to the vicarage loft in the likeness of two birds, and that old Alice had sent him and his servant (another devil) to kill those whom she loved not. "How many hast thou killed for her?" said we. "Three," said he. "Who are they?" said we. "A man and his child," said he. "What were their names?" said we. "The child's name was Edward," said he. "What more than Edward?" said we. "Edward Ager," said he. "What more?" said we. "Richard Ager," said he. "Where dwelt the man and the child?" said we. "At Dig, at Dig," said he. This Richard Ager was a gentleman of forty pounds' land by the year; a very honest man, but would often say he was bewitched, and languished long ere he died. The Devil—or Mildred for him—said that he had also killed Wotton's wife, and that he used to fetch old Alice meat and drink and corn, and that he had been at many houses (named) doing her wicked will. Then he was adjured so that he could not resist, when he cried out that he would go, he would go, and so he departed. Then said the maid, "He is gone. Lord have mercy on me! for he would have killed me!" So those ministers and neighbours present all kneeled down and thanked God for Mildred's deliverance; and she kept her countenance, and did not betray herself. But a short time after, the "bruit of her divinity and miraculous trances" spreading far and wide, Mr. Thomas Wotton, "a man of great Worship and Wisdom, and for deciding and ordering of Matters, of rare and singular Dexterity," got to the true understanding of the case, when "the Fraud was found, and the cozenage confessed, and she received condign Punishment." After her trial, and when she knew the worst, she "showed her Feats, Illusions, and Trances, with the Residue of all her miraculous Works in the Presence of divers Gentlemen of great Worship and Credit at Boston-Malherb, in the House of the said Mr. Wotton." "Now compare this wench with the witch of Endor, and you shall see that both the cozenages may be done by one art," says Reginald Scot.

MISCELLANEOUS.

It was in this same year that Agnes Brigs and Rachel Pindar had to do penance at St. Paul's Cross, in London,[99] having been convicted of cheat and imposture in pretending to vomit pins and straws and old "clouts," and other such impossibilities; and for counterfeiting possession by the Devil, which the philosophers of the time thought was no subject to trifle with, or affect in any manner whatsoever. And then, a few years later, a young Dutchman living at Maidstone was dispossessed of ten devils, and the mayor of the town got to subscribe his name to the account, which turned out afterwards to be nothing but fraud and lies. In 1579[100] four witches were hung up together, the chief accusation against one of them, Mother Still, being, "that she did kill one Saddocke with a touch on the shoulder, for not keeping promise with her for an old cloak, to make her a safeguard; and that she was hanged for her labour:" and another, Ellein Smith, was executed at Maldon,[101] on the testimony of her little son of eight, who accused her of having three spirits—Great Dick in a wicker bottle, Little Dick in a leathern bottle, and Willet kept in a woolpack. Upon which the house was commanded to be searched, and "the bottles and packe were found, but the spirites were banished awaie."

---

[99] Stow.

[100] Scot, quoting a little pamphlet, without a title, which I cannot find.

[101] From an extremely rare black-letter book, entitled 'A Detection of damnable driftes, practized by three Witches arraigned at Chelmsforde, in Essex, at the laste Assizes there holden, whiche were executed in Aprill 1579. Set forthe to discouer the Ambushementes of Sathan, whereby he would surprise us lulled in securitie, and hardened with contempte of God's vengeance threatened for our offences. Imprinted at London, for Edward White, at the little North-dore of Paules.'

At the Rochester assizes, held 1591, Margaret Simons,[102] the wife of John Simons, of Brenchley in Kent, was arraigned for witchcraft, on the charge of bewitching the son of John Ferrall the vicar. An ill-conditioned young cub was he, and prentice to Robert Scotchford, clothier; and the father himself seems to have been little better than his son—making a bad pair between them for the teacher and "pattern child" of Brenchley. There had long been ill blood between Mr. John Ferrall, vicar, and Margaret Simons; and one day it came somewhat to a head; for, when the boy was passing Margaret's house on his way home, her little dog jumped out at him and barked. "Which thing the boy taking in evil part," says Reginald Scot, in his quaint, blunt, incisive way, "drew his knife, and pursued him therewith even to her door; whom she rebuked with some such words as the boy disclaimed, and yet neverthelesse would not be perswaded to depart in a long time." The consequence of the fray was, that the boy in five or six days' time fell dangerously ill. Then the vicar, "who thought himself so privileged as he little mistrusted that God would visit his children with sicknesse," declared that his son was bewitched by Margaret Simons, who also had done the like evil to himself; for whenever he wished to read the service with special emphasis and care his voice always failed him, so that his congregation could scarce hear him at all. Margaret made answer that his voice was always hoarse and low, and particularly when he strained himself to speak loudest then it ever failed him: but there was no witchcraft in the case, for all that Mr. Ferrall had procured the health of his son at the hands of another witch, who had taken off the charm and effected a perfect cure. Margaret had a very narrow escape for her life. The whole of the jury, save one man, were against her, but she had in her favour the fact that the vicar was very unpopular, and,

---

[102] Scot.

justly or unjustly, lay under some odious charges; so, what with the sane juryman's exertions in her favour, and Mr. Ferrall's small hold on the interest and affections of his parishioners, she was brought in Not Guilty, and the hangman's cord fell slack from his greedy grasp.

It must have been somewhere about this time that the execution mentioned by Dr. More in his 'Antidote to Atheism' took place, when a mother and daughter were hanged at Cambridge for witchcraft and service to the Devil. When the mother was called on to renounce and forsake her old master, she refused to do so, saying that he had been faithful to her for fourscore years, and she would not be faithless now to him. And in that obstinacy she died, with a courage and constancy worthy a better cause. The daughter was of a contrary mind. She avowed her misdeeds, and asked for pardon and grace, was penitent, and faithful, and earnest in prayer. All of which the Devil took, as may be imagined, very heinously; and showed his displeasure by sending, in the midst of a dead calm, so sudden and violent a blast of wind, that the mother's body was driven sharply against the ladder, and was like to have overturned it, while the gallows shook with such force that the men standing round were fain to hold the posts, for fear of all being flung to the ground. It was somewhat before this, that at Town Malling, in Kent, one of Queen Mary's Justices, "on the complaint of many wise men, and a few foolish boyes, laid an archer by the heels because he shot so near the white at buts. For he was informed and perswaded that the poor man played with a fly, otherwise called a devill or familiar. And because he was certified that the archer aforesaid shot better than the common shooting, which he before had heard of or seen, he conceived it could not be in God's name, but by inchantment, whereby the archer (as he supposed, by abusing the Queen's liege people) gained some one day two or three shillings, to the detriment of the commonwealth, and to his owne inriching.

And therefore the archer was severely punished, to the great encouragement of archers, and to the wise example of justice, but specially to the overthrow of witchcraft." Which quaint little anecdote of Scot's is worth a whole handful of jewels more richly set.

We are coming now to one of the most curious of the older trials, that of—

THE WITCHES OF S. OSEES,

held before Brian Darcey. It is contained in a rare and beautiful little black-letter book,[103] and is spoken of by Scot in his 'Discovery' without much sparing of ridicule. It opens thus: "If there hath bin at anytime (Right Honorable) any meanes used to appease the wrath of God, to obtaine his blessing, to terrifie secreete offenders by open transgressors punishments, to withdraw honest natures from the corruption of euill company, to diminish the great multitude of wicked people, to increase the small number of virtuous persons, and to reforme all the detestable abuses which the peruerse witte and will of man doth dayly devise, this doubtlesse is no lesse necessarye than the best, that Sorcerers, Wizzardes, or rather Dizzardes, Witches, Wise women (for so they will be named), are rygorously punished. Rygorously? sayd I; why it is too milde and gentle a tearme for such a mercilesse generation: I should rather have sayd most cruelly execueted; for that no punishment can be thought vpon, be it in neuer so high a degree of torment, which may be deemed sufficient for such a deuilishe and damnable practise." These were the sentiments of W. W., as propounded to his patron "the right

---

[103] 'A true and just Recorde of the Information, Examination, and Confession of all the Witches, taken at S. Osees in the countie of Essex; whereof some were executed, and other some entreated according to the determination of lawe. Wherein all men may see what a pestilent people Witches are, and how vnworthy to lyve in a Christian Commonwealth. Written orderly, as the cases were tryed by euidence by W. W. Imprinted in London at the three Cranes, in the Vinetree, by Thomas Dawson. 1582.' 'A true and just Recorde of the Information, Examination, and Confession of all the Witches, taken at S. Osees in the countie of Essex; whereof some were executed, and other some entreated according to the determination of lawe. Wherein all men may see what a pestilent people Witches are, and how vnworthy to lyve in a Christian Commonwealth. Written orderly, as the cases were tryed by euidence by W. W. Imprinted in London at the three Cranes, in the Vinetree, by Thomas Dawson. 1582.'

honourable and his singular good lorde, the Lord Darcey," to whom he inscribes his little book. For Brian Darcy, evidently a relation, had lately put in practice the views and opinions of a worthy citizen and zealous Christian touching witches, at the great holocaust offered up at "S. Osees" (St. Osyth), in the 23rd year of Queen Elizabeth's reign (1582): and witch hatred therefore ran in the blood.

The first complainant in this process was Grace Thurlowe, wife of John Thurlowe, who came to make her moan about the evil practices of her neighbour, Ursley Kempe, alias Grey. About twelve months since, said Grace, her son Davy was strangely taken and greatly tormented. Ursley came, like the rest of the neighbours, to see him; but, unlike the rest, she thrice took the child by the hand, saying each time, "A good childe, howe are thou loden:" going out of the house and returning between each phrase, which was evidently a charm, and no holy way of pitying a sick child. After this she said to Grace, "I warrant thee, I, thy childe shall doe well enough;" and sure it was so, for that night the child slept well, and after another such cantrip visit from Ursula, mended entirely. This was not much to complain to the magistrates about, but Grace had another and more grievous count. After this evident cure of her son she was delivered of a woman child, and, ungratefully enough, asked not Ursley to be her nurse; whereat sprang up a quarrel, and the child in consequence fell out of the cradle and brake its neck; not because it was clumsily laid, or carelessly rocked, but because Ursley was a witch and had a grievance against Grace. And to this mischance, when she heard of it, all that the old dame said, was, "It maketh no matter; for she might have suffered me to have the keeping and nursing of it." Then a trouble and a "fratch" ensued, and Ursley threatened Grace with lameness, whereat Grace answered, "Take heed, Ursley, thou hast a naughtie name;" but in spite of her warning the old witch did her work, so that Grace was taken with such lameness that she had to go upon her hands and knees. And thus it continued; whenever she began to amend her child fell ill, and when her child was well she was cast down lame and helpless.

Then Annis Letherdall had her word. Annis and Ursley had a little matter of commerce between them, but Annis failed the suspected woman, "knowing her to be a naughtie beast." So Ursley in revenge bewitched Annis's child, and that so severely that Mother Ratcliffe, a skilful woman, doubted if she could do it any good; yet for all that she ministered unto it kindly. And, as a proof that it was Ursley, and only Ursley, who had so harmed the babe, and that its sad state came in no wise from bad food, bad nursing, and filthy habits, the little creature of only one year old, when it was carried past her house, cried "wo, wo," and pointed with its finger windowwards. What evidence could be stronger? So then, to clinch the matter and strike fairly home, the magistrate examined Thomas Rabbet, Ursley's "base son," a child of barely eight years of age, and got his version of the mother's life. The little fellow's testimony went chiefly on the imps at home. His mother had four, he said—Tyffin, like a white lamb; Titty, a little grey cat; Pygine, a black toad; and Jacke, a black cat; and she fed them, at times with wholesome milk and bread, and at times they sucked blood from her body. He further said that his mother had bewitched Johnson and his wife to death, and that she had given her imps to Godmother Newman, who put them into an earthen pot which she hid under her apron, and so carried them away. One Laurence then said that she had bewitched his wife, so that when "she lay a drawing home, and continued so a day and a night, all the partes of her body were colde like a dead creatures, and yet at her mouth did appeare her breath to goe and come." Thus she lingered, said her husband, until Ursley came in unbidden, turned down the bedclothes, and took her by the arm, when immediately she gasped and died. Ursley at first would confess nothing beyond having had, ten or eleven years ago, a lameness in her bones, for the cure of which she went to Cook's wife of Wesley, who told her that she was bewitched, and taught her a charm by which she might unwitch herself and cure her bones; which charm quite answered its purpose, and had never failed her with her neighbours; all else she denied. But upon Brian Darcy[104] "promising to the saide Ursley that if she would deale plainely and confesse the truth that she should have fauour, so by giving her faire speeche she confessed as followeth." "Bursting out with weeping" and falling on her knees, she said, yes, she had the four imps her son had told of, and that two of them, Titty and Jack, were "hees," whose office was to punish and kill unto death; and two, Tiffin and Piggin, were "shees," who punished with lameness and bodily harm only, and destroyed goods and cattle. And she confessed that she had killed all the folk charged against her; her brother-in-law's wife, and Grace Thurlowe's cradled child, making it to fall out of its cradle and break its neck solely by her enchantments; and that she had bewitched that little babe of Annis Letherdall's, and Laurence's wife, and, in fact, that she had done all the mischief with which she was charged. Then, not liking to be alone, she said that Mother Bennet had two imps; the one a black dog, called Suckin, the other red like a lion, Lyerd: and that Hunt's wife had a spirit too, for one evening she peeped in at her window when she was from home, and saw it look out from a potcharde from under a bundle of cloth, and that it had a brown nose like a ferret. And she told other lies of her neighbours, saying that her spirit Tiffin informed her of all these things; and Brian Darcy sat there, gloating over these maniacal revelations. But in spite of his soft words and fair

---

[104] This was his manner of dealing with the accused, and its falsehood, iniquity, and injustice need no comment.

promises, Ursley Kempe was condemned, and executed when her turn came.

Joan Pechey, widow, was then brought forward; and Ales Hunt, herself an accused witch, deposed against her that she was angry because, at a distribution of bread made by the said Brian Darcy, she had gotten a loaf which was too hard baked for her; whereat in a pet she said it might have been given to some one younger, and not to her, with no teeth to eat through the crust. And then Ales watched her home, and saw her go in alone to her own house where no human soul was; but there she heard her say, as to some one, "Yea, are you so sawsie; are yee so bolde; you were not best to bee so bolde with mee: For if you will not bee ruled, you shall have Symonds sawse; yea, saide the saide Joan, I perceive if I doe give you an inch you will take an ell." All of which talk Ales Hunt found was to no Christian creature, but to her foul and wicked imps. The which testimony her sister, Margerie Sammon, confirmed, saying that old Joan was as clever as their own mother (a noted witch, one Mother Barnes), or any one else in S. Osees skilled in sorcery and magic. Another examinate then came forward with a story of a bewitched cow unbewitched by a fire lighted around it: which, however, does not apparently touch any of the accused. And then the accuser, Ales Hunt, was made to take the place of the accused, and listen to the catalogue of her own sins. The chief witness against her was her little daughter-in-law (step-child?) Febey, of the age of eight or thereabouts, who deposed to her having two little things like horses, the one white the other black, which she kept by her bedside in a little low earthern pot with wool, colour white and black, and which she fed with milk out of a black "trening" dish. When the Commissioners went to search the place they found indeed the board which Phœbe said was used to cover them, and she pointed out the trening dish whence they were fed; but the little things like horses were gone; when Phœbe said

217

they had been sent to Hayward of Frowicke. After a time Alice Hunt was brought to confess not only to two, but four, imps; two like colts, black and white, called Jack and Robbin; and two like toads, Tom and Robbyn. Mother Barnes, her mother, gave them to her, she said, when she died; and she gave her sister, Margerie Sammon, two also. When Margerie was confronted with Alice and heard what she had deposed, she got very angry and denied the whole tale, saying: "I defie thee, though thou art my sister," saying that she had never any imps given to her on her mother's death-bed, or at any other time. But Alice took her aside and whispered something in her ear; after which Margerie, "with great submission" and many tears, confessed that she had in truth these two imps, given to her by her mother as her sister had said, and that she had carried them away that same evening in a wicker basket filled with black and white wool. Her mother had said that if she did not like to keep them old Joan Pechey would be glad of them; but she did not part with them just then; and that she was to feed them on bread and milk, otherwise they would suck her blood. Their names were Tom and Robbin, and last evening she took them away—being perhaps afraid to keep them longer, now that the scent was warm—and went into Read's ground, where she bade them "go." Immediately they skipped out of the wicker basket toward a barred gate going into Howe Lane, to Mother Peachey's house, whereat she, Margerie, said, "All evill goe with you, and the Lorde in heaven blesse mee from yee."

All of which Mother Peachy, who seems to have been an upright, high-spirited old dame, stoutly denied. She was threescore year and upwards, she said, and had lived forty years in S. Osees in honour and good repute. She knew Mother Barnes, yet knew her for no witch, nor ever heard her to be so accompted, or to have skill in any witchery; nor was she at her death-bed; nor knew she of her imps. For her own part she denied that she had any "puppettes, spyrites, or maumettes;" or had had any spirits conveyed to her by Margery Sammon, or since Mother Barnes's death. She denied all that Ales Hunt had said, as, "Yea, art thou so bolde," &c., she denied that she had had any hand in Johnson's death, as she had been accused of, but when he died said only he was a very honest man: she also denied some very shocking passages with her son, which he, however, had been brought to confess; and when questioned more closely concerning her imps, said that she had only a kitten and a dog at home. When asked of what colour were they? she answered tartly, "Ye may goe and see."

Ales Newman was also condemned and executed; being obstinate to the last; denying the four counts with which she was charged, viz. her imps, the slaughter of her own husband, of John Johnson, and of his wife. But William Hoke deposed that on his death-bed her husband had been perpetually crying out against her, saying, "Dost thou not see—dost thou not see?" meaning the imp with which she tormented him, and which he strove vainly to beat away. Seeing her obstinacy, Brian Darcy told her that he would sever her and her spirits asunder; to which she answered quickly, "Nay," sayth shee, "that shal ye not, for I will carry them with mee." Then seeing that they took note of her words, she added, "if I have any." The admission was enough, and she was hanged.

Elizabeth Bennet denied that she had had any hand in the bewitching to death Johnson or his wife, saying that the aforesaid Ales had done it all. But William Bonner had his stone ready for her on the other side, accusing her of bewitching his wife, for "shee, being sickely and sore troubled, the said Elizabeth vsed speeches vnto her, saying, a goode woman howe art thou loden, and then clasped her in her armes and kissed her. Wherevpon presently after her vpper Lippe swelled and was very bigge, and her eyes much sunked into her head, and shee hath lain sithence in a very strange case." Yet these two women were familiar friends, and "did accompanie much together;" which shows that friendship was as dangerous as enmity in those mad times when the swelling of a lip, or the familiarity of a house pet, could bring the best of a district to the gallows. And then Ursley Kemp's testimony was remembered against Elizabeth, and the mysteries of Suckin and Liard sought to be fathomed. Elizabeth at the first was obdurate and would confess to nothing beyond that she had certainly a pot, but no wool therein, and no imps to lay on it; but at last she too was persuaded by Brian Darcy's fine false words; so falling on her knees, "distilling tears," she made her public moan. William Byet and she dwelt as neighbours together, she said, living as neighbours should, well and easily; but latterly they had fallen out, because William called her "old Trot" and "old witch," and "did ban and curse her and her cattle." So she replied with calling him "knave," saying, "Wind it vp Byet, for it will light vpon yourself." And Byet's beast died forthwith. Then Byet's wife beat her swine with great "gybels," and made them sick; and once she ran a pitchfork through the side of one so that it was dead, and when the butcher who bought it came to dress and cut it up, it proved "a messel," so she had no money for it, for the butcher would not keep it and she was forced to take it back again. So far was only the ordinary quarrelling of ill-tempered country folk, and nothing very damaging to confess to; but now Brian Darcy's fair words drew from her all about her imp Suckin, a he and like a black dog, and Lierd, a she and like a hare or a lion, and red. Suckin had first come to her a long time ago, as she was returning home from the mill; he held her by the coats, she being amazed, but vanished when she prayed. Again, when nigh hand at home, he tugged at her coats as before, yet vanished when she prayed. The next day he came with Lierd, and asked "why she was so snappish yesterday?" and thus they were for ever troubling and visiting her, till at last she yielded to their solicitations, and set them to the work she was accused of. This was the second instance in which Brian Darcy found that old Ursley and her imp Tiffin had spoken the truth.

Ales Manfielde bewitched John Sayer's cart, keeping it standing stock still for above an hour, because she was offended that he would not let his thatcher cover in an oven for her; and she lamed all Joan Chester's cattle, because Joan refused her some curds. So Ales Manfielde was condemned and executed; but not before she made her confession. She said that Margaret Greuell (Greville), twelve years since, gave her four imps—Robin, Jack, William, and Puppet or Mamet: they were like black cats, two shes and two hes, and were put into a box with some wool, and placed on a shelf by her bed. But Margaret denied it all, even when Ales was confronted with her; denied too that queer tale of how she had bewitched John Carter's two brewings, so that half a seame had to go to the swill tub, all because he would not give her Godesgood. The brewing was only unbewitched when John's son, a tall lusty man of thirty-six, managed to stick his arrow in the brewing-vat. He had shot twice before, but missed, though he was a good shot and stood close to the vat—which was evident sorcery, somehow. Margaret denied also that she had bewitched Nicholas Strickland's wife so that she could make no butter, because Nicholas, who was a butcher, refused her a neck of mutton. But in spite of all her denials, she, the hale woman of fifty-four, was condemned to remain in prison, heaven knows for how long; escaping the gallows by a greater miracle than any recorded of herself.

Elizabeth Ewstace, a year younger than Margaret Greville, was told that she had bewitched Robert Sanneuer, drawing his mouth all awry so that it could be got into its place again only with a sharp blow; and that she had killed his brother Crosse, three years ago, and bewitched his wife when with child and quite lusty and well, so that she had a most strange sickness, and the child died soon after its birth; that she made his cows give blood instead of milk; and caused his hogs "to skip and leap about the yarde in a straunge sorte," because of the small bickerings to which S. Osees seemed specially subject. And she hurt all Felice Okey's geese, and in particular her favourite goose, because she, Felice, had turned hers out of her yard; all of which Elizabeth Eustace denied to the face of Alice Mansfield and her other accusers. And as, on being searched, she was found to have no "bigges" or witch marks, she was mercifully kept in prison—for the time. And Annis Glascocke, wife of John the sawyer, got into the trouble that had its end only in the hangman's cord, because Mychel the shoemaker charged her with being a "naughtie woman," and because Ursley Kemp, informed by Tiffin, accused her of sundry things about as true as all the rest of the story. Being found well supplied with witch marks, her denial was not allowed to go for much; whereupon she abused Ursley, and said she had bewitched her and made her like to herself, she, Annis Glascocke, all the time ignorant and innocent of her devilish arts.

Then came the sad story of Henry Celles (Selles) and his wife Cysley. They were said to have killed Richard Ross's horses, because Richard had refused Cicely a bushel of malt which she had come for, bringing a poke to put it in. And to make the accusation stronger, little Henry their son, only nine years old, affirmed that at Candlemas last past about midnight there came to his brother John a spirit, which took him by the left leg and also by the little toe, and which was like his little sister, only that it was black. At which his brother cried out, "'Father, father, come helpe me; there is a black thing that hath me by the legge as big as my sister;' whereat his father saide to his mother, 'Why thou ——, cannot you keepe your imps from my children?' Whereat she presently called it away from her sonne, saying, 'Come away, come away.' At which speeche it did

222

depart." He further said that his mother fed her imps daily with milk out of a black dish; that their names were Hercules, Sotheons, or Jacke which was black and a he, and Mercurie, white and a she; that their eyes were like goose eyes; and that they lay on some wool under a stack of broom at the old crab-tree root. And also that his mother had sent Hercules to Ross for revenge; at which his father, when he heard of it, said, "She was a trim fool." As she very likely was; but for other things than sending imps to her neighbours. John, a little fellow of six and three-quarters, confirmed his brother's deposition, adding to it that "the imps had eyes as big as himself," and that his mother fed them with thin milk out of a spoon. He gave the names of other people whom his mother had bewitched, and he showed his scarred leg, and the nail of the little toe still imperfect. And Joan Smith deposed that one day, as she was making ready to go to church, holding her babe in her arms, her mother, one Redworth's wife, and Cicely were all at her door, ready to draw the latch as she came out, "whereat the grandmother to the childe tooke it by the hand, and shoke it, saying, 'A mother pugs, art thou coming to church?' and Redworth's wife, looking on it, said, 'Here is a iolie and likely childe—God blesse it.' After which speeches, Selles his wife saide, 'shee hath neuer the more children for that, but a little babe to play withall for a time.' And she saith within a short time after her said childe sickened and died. 'But,' she saith"—her womanly heart carrying it over her superstition—"'that her conscience will not serve her to charge the said Cysley or her husband to be the causers of any suche matter, but prayeth God to forgive if they haue dealt in any such sorte.'" Then Thomas Death accused Cicely Selles and one Barker's wife of bewitching George Battell's wife and his own daughter Mary, who got such good of the witches by a wise man's ministering that she saw her tormentor standing in bodily shape before her; and Ales Baxter was pricked to the heart by a white imp like a cat which then vanished into the bushes close by, and so badly holden that she could neither go nor stand nor speak, and did not know her own master when he came by, but was forced to be taken home in a chair by two men. All of which Henry Selles and his wife Cicely denied; specially the story of the imp and the children, who, if there were imps at all in the matter, were the only imps afloat. But denial did them no good, for Cicely had witch marks, so was condemned, and the two little lying varlets made themselves orphans and homeless.

A very crowd of witnesses came to testify against Annis Herd. Of some she had bewitched the cream, of others the milk; of some the cows or pigs or wives; but all this was mere floating accusation until the Commissioners got hold of her little "base" daughter of seven, who gave them plenty of information. Asked if her mother had imps, she said "Yes;" in one box she had six "auices," or blackbirds, and in another box six like cows as big as rats, with short horns, lying in the boxes on white or black wool. And she said that her mother gave her one of the cow imps, a black and white one, called Crowe; and to her little brother one, red and white, called Donne; and that she fed the avices or blackbirds with wheat and barley and oats and bread and cheese; giving to the cows wheat straw, bean straw, oat straw, or hay, with water or beer to drink. When her brother sees these blackbird imps come a "tuitting and tetling" about him, added the little base daughter, he takes and puts them in the boxes. Some of them sucked on her mother's hands, and some on her brother's legs, and when they showed her the marks she pointed them out one by one, saying, "Here sucked aves and here blackbird." She was sharp enough though to shield herself, young as she was; for when asked why one of her hands had the same kind of mark, she said it was burnt. Anis Herd was kept in prison, but not hanged just then, for she could not, luckily for her, be got to confess to anything very damaging. She said that she was certainly angry with the churl Cartwright for taking away a bough which she had laid over a flow in the highway, but she had not bewitched him or his; and that she had, truly, kept Lane's wife's dish fourteen days or more, as Lane's wife had said, and that Lane's wife had sent for the twopence which she, Anis, owed her, and that she had grumbled with her—also with this neighbour and that neighbour, according to the habits of S. Osees—but that she had bewitched none of them. And she denied the avices and the blackbirds and all and sundry of the stories of Crow or Dun; which, indeed, with some others spoken of by the children, seem to have been, *if existing at all*, toys or treasures kept hoarded from them, to which they added these magical and absurd conditions as their imaginations taught them or their examiners prompted.

Joan Robinson, another S. Osees witch, was to blame for various acts of sorcery and witchcraft—hurting one woman's brood goose, and another's litter of pigs, drowning cows, laming ambling mares, and the rest of the witch's playful practices; all of which she, too, denied strenuously, but nevertheless formed one of the thirteen victims whom the offended justice of the times found necessary to condemn and execute. So this sad trial came to an end, and Brian Darcy covered his name with infamy so long as W. W. has a black letter copy extant.

The following singular table is drawn up at the end of the book:—

"The names of XIII Witches and those that have been bewitched by them.

The Names of those persons that have beene bewitched and thereof haue dyed, and by whome, and of them that haue receyved bodyly harme, &c. As appeareth vpon sundrye Enformations, Examinations, and Confessions taken by the worshipfull Bryan Darcey, Esquire; and by him certified at large vnto the Queene's Maiestie's Justices of Assise of the Countie of Essex, the XXIX of Marche, 1582.

S. Osythes.	The Witches.		
	1. Ursley Kempe, alias Gray	} bewitched to death	{ Kempes wife, Thorlowes Childe, and Strettons wife.
	2. Ales Newman and Ursley Kempe	} bewitched to death	{ Letherdalles childe, and Strettons wife.
Confessed by Ursley and Elizabeth.	The said Ales and Ursley Kempe	} bewitched	{ Strattons Childe, Grace Thorlowe, whereof they did languish.
	3. Elizabeth Bennet	} bewitched to death	{ William Byet, and Joan his wife, and iii of his beasts. The wife of William Willes, and William Wittingalle.
	Elizabeth Bennet	} bewitched	{ William Bonners Wife, John Butler, Fortunes Childe; whereof they did languish.
	Ales Newman	} bewitched to death	{ John Johnson and his Wife, and her own Husband, as it is thought.
Confessed the cattell.	4. Ales Hunt	} bewitched to death	{ Rebecca Durrant and vi beasts of one Haywardes.
	5. Cysley Celles	} bewitched to death	{ Thomas Deaths Childe.

226

Little Clapton.	Cysley Celles	} bewitched {	Rosses Mayde, Mary Death, whereof they did languish.
Thorpe. 6.	Cysley Celles and Ales Manfielde	}	bewitched Richard Rosses horse and beasts and caused their Impes to burne a barne with much corne.
Confessed by Ales Manfield.	7. Ales Manfielde and Margaret Greuell	} bewitched to death {	Robert Chesson, and Greuell husband to Margaret.
	Ales Manfielde and Margaret Greuell	}	bewitched the widdow Chesson, and her husband, v beasts and one bullocke, and seuerall brewinges of beere, and batches of bread.
Thorpe. 8.	Elizabeth Ewstace	} bewitched to death {	Robert Stannevettes Childe, and Thomas Crosse.
	Elizabeth Ewstace	}	bewitched Robert Stanneuet, vii milch beasts, w^h gaue blood in steede of milke, and seuerall of his Swine dyed.
Little Okley. 9.	Annys Herd	} bewitched to death {	Richard Harrisons wife, and two wives of William Dowsinge, as it is supposed.
	Annys Herd	}	bewitched Cartwright two beasts, made, sheepe, and lambes xx; West swine, and pigs; Diborne, a brewing of beere, and seuerall other losses of milke and creame.

| Walton. | 10. | Joan
Robinson | } | bewitched beasts, horses, swine, and pigs, of seuerall men. |

"The sayd Ursley Kemp had foure spyrites, viz., their names Tettey a hee like a gray Cat, Jack a hee like a black Cat, Pygin a she like a black Toad, and Tyffin a she like a white Lambe. The hees were to plague to death, and the shees to punish with bodily harme, and to destroy cattell.

"Tyffyn, Ursley's white Spirit, did tell her alwayes (when she asked) what the other witches had done: and by her the most part were appelled, which spirit telled her alwayes true. As is well approved by the other Witches confession.

"The sayd Ales Newman had the sayd Ursley Kemps spirits to vse at her pleasure. Elizabeth Bennet had two spirits, viz., their names Suckyn, a hee like a blacke Dog: and Lyard, red lyke a Lyon or Hare.

"Ales Hunt had two spirits lyke Colts, the one blacke, the other white.

"11. Margery Sammon had two spirits lyke Toads, their Names Tom and Robyn.

"Cysley Celles had two spirits by seuerall names, viz., Sotheons, Hercules, Jack, or Mercury.

"Ales Manfield and Margaret Greuell had in common by agreement, iiii Spirits, viz., their names Robin, Jack, Will, Puppet, alias Mamet, whereof two were hees, and two were shees, lyke vnto black Cats.

"Elizabeth Ewstace had iii Impes or Spirits of colour white, grey, and black.

"Annis Herd had vi Impes or Spirites, like auises and black byrdes, and vi other like Kine, of the bygnes of Rats, with short hornes; the Auises shee fed with wheat, barley, otes, and bread, the Kine with straw and hay.

| Annys
Glascocke. | } | These have not confessed any thing touching the hauing of spirits. |

12. Joan Pechey.

13. Joan Robinson.

Annis Glascocke } bewitched { Mychell Steuens Childe.

to death   The base Childe at Pages.

William Pages Childe.

Thus did W. W. and Bryan Darcey finish their respective works, in which, perhaps, this formal tabular statement, this pretence at scientific arrangement and accuracy, is the strangest and most revolting element.[105]

Another rare and curious[106] black-letter pamphlet gives a marvellous account of a woman's possession, as it happened in Somersetshire; which perchance we of the light-minded and sceptical nineteenth century might interpret differently to what the believing sixteenth held likely.

---

[105] The names of the imps which haunted various persons was curious. A Dutch boy had Pretty Betty, Cuckow, Longtail; and Bernard gives us his list:— "Mephistophiles, Lucifer, Little Lord, Fimodes, David, Jude, Little Robin, Smack, Litefoote, Nonesuch, Lunch, Makeshift, Swash, Pluck, Blue, Catch, White, Collins, Hardname, Tibb, Hiff, Ball, Puss, Rutterkin, Dickie, Prettie, Grissel, and Jacke;" together with "Pippin, Philpot, Modu, Soforce, Hilco, Smolkin, Hillio, Hiaclito, Lustie, Huffe, Cap, Killico, Hob, Fratello, Fliberdigibbet, Hoberdidance, Tocobatto, and Lustie Jollie Jenkin." We have seen some of these already, and those who read farther will find a few more, and some quite as quaint and odd not set down in this list.

[106] 'A true and most dreadfull discourse of a Woman possessed with the Deuill; who, in the likenesse of a headlesse Beare, fetched her oute of her Bedde, in the presence of seven persons, most straungely roulled her thorow three Chambers, and downe a high paire of stairres on the fower and twentie of May last, 1584. At Ditchet, in Somersetshire. A matter as miraculous as ever was seen in our time. Imprinted at London for Thomas Nelson.'

THE WOMAN AND THE BEAR.

One Stephen Cooper, of Ditchet, a yeoman of honest reputation, good wealth, and well beloved by his neighbours, being sick and weak, sent his wife Margaret to a farm of his at Rockington, Gloucestershire, where she remained a few days—not finding all to her liking, she said. When she returned she found her husband somewhat better, but she herself was strange and wild, using much idle talk to him concerning an old groat which her little son had found and which she wanted to see, and raving about the farm in Gloucestershire, as if she had been bewitched, and knew not what she said. Then she began to change in very face, and to look on her husband with "a sad and staring countenance;" and, one night, things came to a climax, for she got very wild and bad, and shook so frightfully that they could scarce keep her down in the bed; and then she began talking of a headless bear, which, she said, she had been into the town to beat away during the time of her fit, and which had followed her from Rockington: as the sequel proved was true. Her friends and husband exhorted her to prayer and patience, but she still continued marvellously holden, the Devil getting quite the better of her until Sunday night, when she seemed to come to her worst. Suddenly the candle, which they had not been noticing, went out, and she set up a lamentable cry; they lighted another, but it burnt so dim it was almost useless, and the friends and neighbours themselves began to be disquieted. Wildly and hurriedly cried Margaret, "Look! do you not see the Devil?" herself all terrified and disturbed. They bade her be still and pray. Then said Margaret, "Well, if you see nothing now, you shall see something by and bye;" and "forthwith they heard a noise in the streete, as it had been the coming of two or three carts, and presently they in the chamber cried out, 'Lord helpe us, what manner of thing is this that commeth here!'" For up to the bedside where the woman lay with heaving breasts and dilated eyes, came a thing like a bear, only that it had no head and no tail; a thing "half a yard in height and half a yard in length" (no bigger, Margaret? not so big as a well-trussed man on all-fours?) which, when her husband saw, he took a joyn'd stool, and "stroke" at it, and the blow sounded as though it had fallen on a feather bed. But the creature took no notice of the man: it wanted only Margaret. Slowly it paddled round the bed, then smote her thrice on the feet, took her out of bed, and rolled her to and fro in the chamber, round about the floor and under the bed; the husband and friends, sore amazed and affrighted, only calling on God to assist them, not daring to lift a hand for themselves or her. And all the while the candle grew dimmer and dimmer, so that they could scarce see each other: which was what Margaret and the headless bear, no doubt, desired. Then the creature took her in its arms, thrust her head between her legs so that he made her into a round ball, and "so roulled her in a rounde compasse like an Hoope through three other Chambers, downe an highe paire of staires, in the Hall, where he kept her for the space of a quarter of an hour." The people above durst not come down, but remained above, weeping pitifully and praying with loud and fervent prayer. And there was such a terrible stench in the hall, and such fiery flames darting hither and thither, that they were fain to stop their noses with clothes and napkins, expecting every moment to find that hell was opening beneath their feet, and that they would be no longer able to keep out of harm's way and the Devil's. Then Margaret cried out, "He is gone. Now he is gone!" and her husband joyfully bade her come up to him again; which she did, but so quickly that they greatly marvelled at it, and thought to be sure the Devil had helped her. Yet she proved to be none the worse for the encounter: which was singular, as times went. They then put her in bed, and four of them kept down the clothes, praying fervently. Suddenly the woman was got out of bed:

she did not move herself by nerves, muscles, or will, of course; but she was carried out by a supernatural power, and taken to the window at the head of the bed. But whether the devil or she opened the window, the pamphlet does not determine. Then her legs were thrust out of the window, and the people heard a thing knock at her feet as if it had been upon a tub; and they saw a great fire, and they smelt a grievous smell; and then, by the help of their prayers, they pulled Margaret into the room again, and set her upon her feet. After a few moments she cried out, "O Lord, methinks I see a little childe!" But they paid no heed to her. Twice or thrice she said this, and ever more earnestly; and at last they all looked out at the window, for they thought to be sure she must have some meaning for her raving. And "loe, they espied a thing like unto a little child, with a bright shining countenaunce casting a greate light in the chamber." And then the candle, which had hitherto burnt blue and dim, gave out its natural light so that they could all see each other. Whereupon they fell to joyful prayer, and gave thanks to God for the deliverance. And Margaret Cooper was laid in her bed again, calm, smiling, and collected, never more to be troubled by a Headless Bear which rolled her about like a ball, or by a bright shining child looking out from the chinks of a rude magic lantern. As for the bear, I confess I think he was nearer akin to man than devil; that he was known about Rockington in Gloucestershire; and that Margaret Cooper understood the conduct of the plot from first to last. But then this is the sceptical nineteenth century, wherein the wiles of human cunning are more believed in than the power of the devil, or the miracles of supernaturalism. Yet this was a case which, in spite of all its fraud and folly so patently displayed, was cited as one of the most notorious and striking instances of the power of Satan over the bodies as well as the souls of those who gave themselves up to the things of the world.

THE WITCHES OF WARBOIS.[107]

In 1589, Robert Throckmorton, Esquire, lived at Warbois, in Huntingdonshire. He had five daughters, the eldest of whom, Miss Joan, was fifteen, while the rest came down in steps, two years or so between each, in the ordinary manner. On the tenth of November, Mistress Jane, being then near ten years of age, was suddenly seized with a kind of fit. She "screeked" loud and often, lay as if in a trance for half an hour or more, shook one leg or one arm and no other, "as if the Palsie had been in it," made her body so stiff and rigid that no man could bend her, and went through the usual forms of a young girl's hysteria. A neighbour, one Alice Samuel, who lived next door to the Throckmortons, went in to see the afflicted child; for all the neighbours were flocking in to see her as a kind of curiosity; and, stepping up into the chimney-side, sat hard down by her, she being held in another woman's arms by the fire. Suddenly the child cried out, "Did you ever see one more like a Witch than she is?" pointing to Mother Samuel; "take off her black-thrumb'd cap, for I cannot abide to look at her."

Nothing was thought of her words at the time, the mother merely chiding her for her lightness of speech; but "the old woman hearing her, sat still, without saying a word, yet looked very dismally, as those that saw her remembered very well." And as well she might, poor old soul; for she must have known that Mrs. Jane's light speech would in all probability be heavy enough to bring her down to the grave.

Doctoring did the child no good. Dr. Barrow of Cambridge, the most noted man of the district, gave the distemper no satisfactory name, and his remedies were

---

[107] 'A compleat History of Magick, Sorcery, and Witchcraft.' By Richard Boulton. 1715.

powerless to remove it; Mr. Butler, another skilful man, was equally at fault; and when, about a month after Mrs. Jane had been attacked, two other daughters were driven to the like extremity, and "cry'd out upon Mother Samuel, 'Take her away, look where she standeth there before us in a black thrumb'd Cap (which she commonly wore, though not then); it's she that hath bewitched us, and she will kill us if you don't take her away,'" the parents were moved to believe the whole thing supernatural, and that Mother Samuel had indeed bewitched them as they said. About a month after the affliction of these two, a younger child, not quite nine years old, was taken like the rest; and soon after Mrs. Joan, of fifteen, went the same way—only more severely handled than them all. Mrs. Joan had a specialty in her fits. She was not only hysterical like her sisters, but she had a Spirit, and this Spirit sounded in her ears information of things to come: as, that the servants as well as the five children should be bewitched—which they were, but did not become so notorious as the little impostors of better blood; all recovering so soon as they left the house for other situations, and nothing more being heard of them. Things went on then in this manner, the children being perpetually tormented with fits, and for ever crying out against old dame Samuel, when, in February of the next year (1590), it was resolved to bring her to the house that the children might "scratch" her, and so relieve themselves somewhat. Whereupon she, her young daughter Agnes, and one Cicely Burder—both of whom were accused of the same malpractices as herself—were haled to Mr. Throckmorton's, there to undergo their preliminary ordeal. Every care was taken to prevent the mother from holding any communication with her daughter Agnes; but at the entry she managed to lean over and whisper to her. Mr. Pickering, the children's uncle, who had undertaken to conduct this Scratching, was ready to swear that she said, "I charge thee do not confess anything;" but Mother Samuel

234

swore, in her turn, that she had only charged her to hasten home to get her father his dinner; for that same father was a terrible old Turk, and not likely to wait patiently for his dinner or aught else.

When the women went into the house the children were standing by the fire, perfectly well; but the instant they saw Mother Samuel, they fell down in their fits, leaping and springing about like fishes newly taken out of the water, drawing their heads and heels backwards, and throwing out their arms with great groans that were terrible and troublesome to those that beheld them. They screamed and struggled to get at the old woman, scratching at the bed-clothes, or the maids' aprons, or anything they could touch, crying out, "O! that I had her! O! that I had her!" And when Mr. Pickering forced Mother Samuel's hand within theirs, they scratched at it with so much vehemence that one of them splintered her nails "with her eager desire of revenge;" doing the same by Cicely Burder, who thus, we are not told how or why, found herself in a dangerous and equivocal position, but seems to have got well out of it in time. Or perhaps she died between whiles, happily for herself.

For the next few months it was Mrs. Elizabeth Throckmorton who kept up the ball. Mr. Pickering took her away with him to his own house, where she fooled them all to the top of their bent, crying out to Mother Samuel to take away her mouse, for she would have none of it, and exclaiming in piteous tones that Mother Samuel was trying to force a cat, or a frog, or sometimes a toad, into her mouth; hopping about on one leg, pretending to be utterly incapable of putting the other to the ground; sometimes going for two steps at a time, when "she would halt and give a beck with her head as low as her knees;" asking if no one heard the spirit within her lapping the milk she had just taken; playing at cards with her eyes shut, or seemingly so; and falling into drowsy fits which took her even in the midst of meals, or any while else specially untimely. Her bewitchment took a certain controversial turn too, and witnessed for the Pope and the Devil; for "on the Eleventh, one asked her if she loved the Word of God; whereupon she was much troubled and tormented. When they asked, Love you Witchcraft? she was content. Love you the Bible? it shaked her. Love you Papistry? the Devil within her was quiet. Love you Prayer? it raged. Love you the Mass? it was still. Love you the Gospel? it heaved up her Belly; so that every good thing it disliked; but whatever concerned Popish Idolatry it was pleased with." Mr. Pickering kept this sectarian young lady from March to September, and then it pleased Mistress Elizabeth to require change of air and scene, and she demanded to be taken back to her father's house at Warbois. There she played off her tricks with new vigour, when Lady Cromwell, wife of Sir Henry Cromwell, Knt., hearing of these heavy afflictions came to visit the children and comfort the parents. The children of course went off into their customary state; it was not their game to disappoint my Lady; "and were so grievously Tormented that it moved the good Lady's Heart with Pity, so that she could not forbear Tears, and caused old Mother Samuel to be sent for, who durst not deny to come, because her Husband was Tenant to Sir Henry Cromwell." As soon as she came in, the children were so much worse that the Lady, transported beyond herself, and exceedingly angry that Mother Samuel would not confess to her crime, seized hold of her as she was struggling to get free of their hands and slip out of the room, pulled off her kircher, and cut off a lock of her hair, which she gave privately to Mrs. Throckmorton together with the old dame's hairlace; bidding her burn them. The old woman turning against the Lady, said, half sorrowfully, "Madam, why do you use me thus? I never did you any harm as yet:" words to be remembered and treasured up against her, when the hour came. That very night Lady Cromwell had bad dreams concerning Mother Samuel and her cat, which she said came to strip all the flesh from her—and awakened, crying mightily and much distressed. From that time she had fits, and continued very hardly holden till her dying day, which was one year and a quarter after the visit to Warbois. So Mother Samuel's words were held to have been witch's threats, and the whole country was convinced that Lady Cromwell had died by her magic arts, and bewitched. As she was, poor lady, with nervous fear and superstition and ignorance.

The next year, in the winter of 1591, Mr. Henry Pickering, a young student at Cambridge, tried to make Dame Samuel confess, but she would not suffer him or his companions to speak, and when they desired her to speak softlier, answered: "She was born in a Mill, begot in a Kiln, and must have her Will, and could speak no softlier." Then Mr. Henry began to question her on her faith, but got only tart answers; so, losing patience, he said that if she did not repent and confess to having worked that wickedness on the children, he hoped one day to see her burn at the stake, and that he would bring wood and faggots and the children should blow the coals. To which old Dame Samuel replied that she "would rather see him doused over head in the pond;" and so went away home, to be beaten for gossiping and staying late, by that terrible old Turk of hers.

And now the children would be well only when the dame was with them; so the parents sought to engage her to live with them, but the old Turk would not give his consent, and beat her severely with a cudgel on the slightest pretext. The whole thing angered him, and his dame could not do right let her do what she would. However, he was prevailed on to spare her for eight or nine days, during which time the lying little girls professed themselves cured of all their haunting spirits—dun chickens, naked babes, and the like; to the old woman's extreme consternation and passionate assurances of innocence. Then the children turned against

Agnes Samuel, the daughter, declaring that she had bewitched them equally with the mother: whereupon the father, Mr. Throckmorton, went to bring her to the house; when she hid herself in an attic or loft, barricading herself in by sacks of wool piled up on the trapdoor. She was forced to come down at last, and her fear was made the chief evidence against her. The hour had come round for her on Time's cruel dial, and she could not escape the inevitable decree that had gone forth. All this while the old mother was forcibly detained at Mr. Throckmorton's house; the children pretending that they could be well only in her presence, and absolutely refusing to let her go, though she was sick and fearful and weary, and cried to get home again to her daughter and husband. That uncompromising oaken cudgel of his was less terrible than the awful suspicion under which she was living here; and the harassing uncertainty of her life—never knowing what new lie the children might frame against her, nor how much nearer they might bring her to the gallows by some wicked fancy or delusion—was infinitely worse than all the oaths and ill-usage of home, of which she knew at least the extent and end. She seems to have been a gentle-spirited old creature in spite of her crusty tongue; and at the beck of every one who chose to knock her about and require from her service and submission. When Mr. Throckmorton had teased and threatened and exhorted her, till she was completely "dazed and mazed" with all she heard—and when the children had acted their fits with such power and accuracy that they simulated nature to the life, and had impressed even her with all the wicked things which their Spirits told them of her and of her daughter—her mind, enfeebled by suffering and terror, gave way, and she was deluded into a confession of sin and penitence; after which she obtained leave to go home. As her husband gave her but a harsh welcome, angry with her for her weakness in confessing, she recanted as of course; when Mr. Throckmorton, getting hold of her by an open window beneath which his friends were stationed, bullied and deluded her once more into making a confession which they might hear; and on the strength of which he carried off both dame and daughter, to be examined by the Bishop of Lincoln.

The Bishop found her easy. Yes, she had an imp; a dun chicken which sucked on her chin, and which she had sent to torment the Throckmorton girls. The dun chicken and the rest of the spirits were now at the bottom of her stomach, and made her so full and heavy that she could not lace her coat, nor was the horse on which she rode able to carry her all the way: she had three spirits, all like dun chickens— Pluck, Catch, and White, which had been given her by an "upright man," extremely hard, of the name of Langland, of no particular dwelling and now gone beyond seas; and she had sent all three to the children and had plagued them sorely. This she said at various times, at each clause conjuring the devil and her spirits to inform her of the facts required by the Right Reverend Father in God. After her examination she and her daughter were committed to gaol; but Mr. Throckmorton got Agnes out on bail that he might take her home to the children, and see what they would say of her. This seemed to him the best way to complete the evidences of guiltiness against her, which at present were very slight and worthless. So the net closed tighter and tighter round this hapless family, and soon the deep black waves, rolling onward, dashed over their devoted heads.

When they heard that Agnes was brought back to Warbois, the children fell into their fits again, each saying, "I am glad, I am glad; none so glad as I." They knew the cruel sport preparing for them, and were in no hurry to abandon the pleasant excitement of their Possession, during which they were made so many centres of public interest, petted and commiserated and looked at and talked about and made of more consequence than the finest lady in the land. When the game was over they must sink down into the humdrum lives of good little girls in a country town, of no possible interest to living being outside their own house door. Surely an event to be deferred to the latest moment possible! For the first three or four days after Agnes' arrival they condescended to be well, but, being by that time tired of their new companion, they fell back into their former state, and cried out against her more bitterly than they had ever done against her mother. She was more helpless, too, than the mother, and more entirely in their power; so that the sport was greater, and the fear of opposition or detection less. Specially did Mistress Joan, the eldest girl, torment her; who, being at this time seventeen, had other ideas of spirits than dun chickens, mice, or frogs, which were all very well in the days of her infancy but quite uninteresting to her now. The manner in which she introduced her Spirits was singular. One day, just after her nose had bled, and she had said "it would be a good thing to throw her handkerchief into the fire, and burn the young witch," she suddenly looked about her smiling, and said, "What is this in God's Name that comes tumbling to me? It tumbles like a Foot-bal, it looks like a puppit-player, and appears much like its Dame's old thrumb Cap. 'What is your Name, I pray you?' said she. The Thing answered, his Name was Blew. To which she answered, 'Mr. Blew you are welcome, I never saw you before; I thought my Nose bled not for nothing, what News have you brought? What,' says she, 'dost thou say I shall be worse handled than ever I was? Ha! what dost thou say? that I shall now have my Fits, when I shall both hear and see and know every Body? that's a new Trick indeed. I think never any of my Sisters were so used, but I care not for you: do your worst, and when you have done, you will make an end.'" Then she cried out that Agnes Samuel had too much liberty, and must be more strictly looked to; for that Mr. Blew had told her she should have no peace till she and the old dame were hanged.

Mrs. Joan had opened a most prolific and amusing vein. Her imagination stopped at nothing, and she showed herself no mean hand at romance. She was very consecutive too, and kept up the likeness well. In the evening Mr. Blew appeared again, chiefly for the purpose of telling her that young Nan Samuel was his Dame, and to ask when the Spirit Smack, of whom he was jealous, had been with her. Mrs. Joan said she knew of no Smack. "You do," says the Thing, "and it is he that tells you all these things, but I will curse him for it." "Do your worst to me or him, I care not for you," says she. "Farewel," says the Thing. "Do you bid me farewel?" says she; "farewel, and be hanged; and come again when you are sent for." So then she came out of her fit. The next day a strange gentleman coming, Mrs. Elizabeth passed off into one of her wild states, and Mr. Throckmorton, "to show the gentleman a wonder," sent for young Agnes, and made her say after him, "I charge thee, thou Devil, as I love thee, and have Authority over thee, and am a Witch, and guilty of this matter, that thou suffer this Child to be well at this present." Upon which Mrs. Elizabeth wiped her eyes, and was perfectly well; and the wretched young girl was by so many steps nearer to her doom. The next day was a grand field-day for Mrs. Joan. Her spirits were in admirable disorder. Mr. Smack came from fighting with Pluck about her, for they were both in love with her, and had fought with great cowl staves last night in old dame's back yard, and Smack had broken Pluck's head, for which Mrs. Joan was not at all thankful, but, when he looked for a little loving word of gratitude, answered, scornfully, that she wished Pluck had broke his neck also, and so bid him go and be hanged for she would have nought to do with him. Presently in came Mr. Pluck, hanging down his broken head and looking very sheepish, but jealous and angry with Smack who seemed to have the best chance of them all with the young lady. Another day it was Catch who came in limping, with a broken leg got from the redoubtable Smack; but when Mrs. Joan tried to break his other leg with a stick she had in her hand—for she was a very scornful young lady to them—she could not; for ever as she struck at him he leaped over the stick, "just like a Jack-an-apes," as she said. Mr. Blew's turn came next. He appeared before her at supper with his arm in a sling: Smack had broken it. So Smack broke Pluck's head, Catch's leg, and Blew's arm, and then came himself to tell her that he would beat them all again, with the help of his cousin another Smack, and one Hardname, whose "Name standeth upon eight Letters, and every Letter standeth for a Word, but what his Name is otherwise we know not." Then Smack and she conversed about the propriety of "scratching" Agnes Samuel; and it was agreed between them that she should not scratch her then, because her face would be healed by the Assizes, but just before that time when all the world might see the marks.

And now began a scene of painful brutality. Whenever the children fell into their fits, they would only consent to be got out of them by Agnes' repeating a form of conjuration, in which she acknowledged herself to be a witch and guilty of their disease, commanding the devil, whom she had sent into them, to leave them. Then they came round, and were well until strangers called, when they invariably went off into their fits—which we can quite well understand—or until they got tired of the monotony of health. The most terrible threats were held out against Nan Samuel; and each child talked to its particular spirit with passion and fury of scratching her. It came at last: the little diabolical tempers which rose higher and higher with each fresh indulgence, getting weary of only fits and muttered communications with spirits and the thirst for blood grew into a frenzy. One of the younger children, Mrs. Mary, one day fell into a "very troublesome Fit," which held her half an hour, and at the last, growing better, she said, "Is it true?

Do you say this is the day I must scratch the young Witch? I am glad of it; I will pay her home both for myself and Sisters." The young Pickering men who were standing by, hearing this, sent for Agnes to come into the room; when she came in the child cried out, "Art thou come, thou young Witch, who hath done all this mischief?" At which Agnes seemed surprised, this being the first time Mrs. Mary had abused her. Then one of the company told her to take Mary in her arms, and carry her down stairs; but she had no sooner got hold of her than the child fell to scratching her head and face with eager fierceness; the poor girl standing still and holding down her head, not defending herself but only crying out pitifully, while the child scratched on her face a broad and bleeding wound. When she was out of breath and thus forced to leave off, she cried and said "she was sorry for her cruelty, but the Thing made her do it, so that she could not help herself." Another day it was another of them who fell upon the maid, she not defending herself or resenting, but "crying out sadly, desiring the Lord to pitty her." Then they abused her, saying, "Thy Mother is a Witch, thy Father is a Witch, and thou art a Witch, and the worst of all;" and then they clamoured for the father, the old Turk, and would have him in to scratch him too. Just at that moment old Samuel chanced to come in to see his daughter—for he knew what kind of treatment she had to undergo—when a great hubbub arose. The children cried out against him, and—wretched young hypocrites!— exhorted him in the godliest terms to confess and repent; called him witch and naughty man and all the rest of the injuries then current; while he retorted fiercely and rudely, and told one of the little baggages she lied—as she did. But Mr. Throckmorton got angry, and would not let him go till he had pronounced the same conjuration as that by which his poor daughter was forced to "fyle" herself; and when he had said the words, the child came out of her fit, and acted amazement and shame to the life. So it went on: the children having their fits, being visited by their spirits, of whom there were nine now afloat—three Smacks, Pluck, Blew, Catch, White, Callicot, and Hardname—and every day or so scratching poor Nan till her face and back and hands were one mass of scars and wounds. And then the Assize time came, and the three Samuels—father, mother, and daughter—were put upon their trial for bewitching Lady Cromwell to death, and tormenting Mrs. Joan Throckmorton and her sisters. There could be no mistake about it now, for not only had they all three convicted themselves by their own confessions in the conjuration which they had been obliged to repeat, but even before the judge, Mrs. Jane played off the like trick, falling into a terrible fit which only old Samuel could get her out of by repeating the charm. At first he was obstinate and sturdily refused to say the words; but on the judge telling him that he should be brought in guilty if he did not, he consented, and had no sooner said—"As I am a witch, and did consent to the death of the Lady Cromwell, so I charge thee, Devil, to suffer Mrs. Jane to come out of her Fit at this present"— than Mrs. Jane wiped her eyes, looked round her, and said, "O Lord father where am I?" pretending to be quite amazed at her position. No hand is wanting when there is stoning to be done. Now that the Samuels were fairly convicted of witchcraft in one instance, witnesses came forward to prove them guilty of the like in others. It was remembered how certain persons had died who had offended the old dame; how others had lost their cows and whole farm stock in consequence of giving her rough language; how, even since she had been in gaol, she had bewitched to his death one of the turnkeys who had chained her to a bedpost, and had cruelly afflicted the gaoler's own son, so that he could not be recovered but by "scratching" her; with the further proof that when the grand jury returned a true bill, "billa vera," against them, old father Samuel burst out passionately to her with, "A plague of God light on thee, for thou art she that has brought us all to this, and we may thank thee for it." So the judge, "after good divine counsel given to them, proceeded to Judgment, which was to death." But the poor old woman set up a plea of being with child, though she was near fourscore years of age; at which all the court laughed, and she herself most of all, thinking it might save her. Some one standing near to Agnes counselled her to try the like plea; but the brave young girl, who had something of her father's spirit in her, indignantly refused. "No," said Agnes, with the gallows straight before her, and this desperate plea perhaps able to save her—"no; it shall never be said that I was both Witch and ——." She died with the same haughty courage maintained to the last: but old mother Samuel maundered through a vast number of confessions—implicated her husband—confessed to her spirits—but with one affecting touch of nature, through all her drivel and imbecility steadily refused to criminate her daughter. No, her Nan was no witch; she was clear and pure before God and towards man; and neither force nor cajolery could make her forswear that bit of loving truth.

When those three helpless wretches were fairly dead, the children, upon whose young souls lay the ineffaceable stain of Murder, and whose first steps in life had been through innocent blood, gave up the game and pronounced themselves cured: so we hear no more of their fits or their spirits, or Mrs. Joan's ghostly lovers fighting with cowl staves and breaking each other's heads out of jealousy and revenge: and the last record of the case is, that Sir Henry Cromwell left an annual sum of forty shillings to provide for a yearly sermon against witchcraft, to be preached at Huntingdon by a B.D. or D.D. member of Queen's College, Cambridge. How terrible to think that three human lives were sacrificed for such wild and wilful nonsense, and that sane and thoughtful and noble-minded people of this present day walk on the way towards the same faith! Better by far the most chill and desolate scepticism, which at least will light no Smithfield fires for any forms of creed or monstrous imaginings of superstition, than beliefs which can only be expressed and maintained by blood, and the culmination of which is in the suffering and destruction of all dissentients.

THE MAN OF HOPE AND THE DEVIL.[108]

A young lawyer, a Mr. Darrel, had a call to the ministry. He was made aware of this by the extraordinary sluggishness that came upon him when he turned to open a law book; so, as preaching puritanical sermons extempore was less toilsome and cost less study than learning the intricacies of the Codex Anglicanus, he became converted to extreme doctrines, and was principally regarded as a Man of Hope, skilful in casting out devils and marvellously apt at discovering witchcraft. His first essay at this work was in 1587 with Katherine Green, a young girl of seventeen, who had some hysterical affection which caused her to swell to an enormous size and led her to fancies and delusions, as, that she saw shapes and apparitions, and a young child without feet or legs looking at her from out a well. She also had fits, which she afterwards confessed were simulated in order to make her father-in-law, who was generally exceedingly severe with her, more kind and pliable: but Mr. Darrel said they were the fits of possession, and, as a proof, cast eight devils out of her; specially one sturdy devil, called Middlecub, which had been sent into her by Margaret Roper. Mr. Darrel at once seized Margaret Roper, accusing her of this Middlecub imp, and sending her off to the magistrate, Mr. Fouliamb; and in the meanwhile Katherine suffered herself to be repossessed, having been imprudent enough to talk with the devil in the likeness of a handsome young man who met her in the lanes, where he entertained her with propositions of marriage, and gave her some bread to eat. Mr. Fouliamb happened to be a man of sense, and discharged Margaret Roper, at the same time threatening to send Darrel to prison in her stead if he took

---

[108] Hutchinson's 'Historical Essay concerning Witchcraft.' Boulton's 'History of Magic.' Harsent's 'Discovery of the Fravdvlent Practises of J. Darrel.' 'A True Relation of the Strange and Grevovs Vexation by the Devil of 7 Persons in Lancashire, and William Somers of Nottingham.' By John Darrel. 1600.

on himself to calumniate honest folk without cause. This rebuff cooled the young lawyer parson's ardour a little; but in 1594 the Starkies of Lancashire announced themselves possessed, and Mr. Darrel must needs go down to vex the foul fiend that had gotten them. For he was so holy a man that the devils hated him mightily, being sorely vexed in his presence, and crying out, "Now he is gone; now he is gone; now blacke coate is gone," as soon as he quitted them, wearied with his wrestling. The story of the Starkies was this:—

Anne, aged nine, and John, of ten, were taken with "dumpish heavie countenances," and fearful startings of their bodies, loud shouting fits, and convulsions. The father went to Hartley, a known conjuror, who came to their aid with popish charms and certain herbs; and so stilled them for a year and a half. But when he "fained as thought he would haue gone into another countrey," the children fell ill again, and Mr. Starkie thought it best to secure the perpetual services of the conjuror by a fee of forty shillings yearly. But Hartley wanted more, and thereupon began a quarrel which ended in the Possession of the children, of three scholars living at the Starkies, of Margaret Byron, and lastly of Hartley himself. Now Hartley had a devil, and whomsoever he kissed he inoculated with this devil and breathed it into them. And as he was always kissing some one—John for love often, the little wenches in jest, to Margaret Hardman "promising a thraue of kisses," "wrestling with Johan Smyth, a maid, to kiss her"—he had given the devil in rich proportion all through the Starkies' house, and only Mr. Darrel could exorcise him. The possessed leaped about like goats, and crawled on all fours like beasts, and barked like dogs, and had communications from a white dove, and saw horned devils under the beds, and had visions of big black dogs with monstrous tails and bound with chains, and huge black cats and big mice that knocked them down at a blow, and left them speechless, cold, and dead. And then they took to "slossinge up their meat like greedy dogges or hogges," and they made the same noises as a broken-winded horse; and they howled and shrieked; and one of them, Jane Ashton the servant aged thirty, fell foul of Edmund Hartley for all his kisses and promises of marriage; and they "yelled and whupped;" and there was in very truth the devil to pay in that horrible house when Mr. More and Mr. Darrel went to exorcise the fiends and restore the possessed to their senses. After some days of prayer, and of fighting with the devil who would cry out when Mr. Darrel was preaching, "Bible bable, he will never have done prating, prittle prattle;" and "I must goe, I must away; I cannot tarrie; whither shall I goe? I am hot, I am too hot, I will not dye!" and such like, six of them were delivered, and visibly and bodily dispossessed. With one, Mary Byron, the devil came up from her stomach to her breast, then to her throat, when it gave her "a sore lug," whilst a mist dazzled her eyes. Then she felt it go out of her mouth, leaving behind it a sore throat and a filthy smell, and it was in the likeness of a crow's head, and it sat in a corner of the parlour in the dark; but suddenly flashing out all a fire it flew out of the window, and the whole place was in a blaze, according to her imagination. John Starkie lost his in the shape of a man with a humpback and very ill-favoured, who, when he had gone out wished much to re-enter, but Master John withstood him, and had the best of it. He was like a "foule ugly man with a white beard and a 'bulch' on his back." The same tale had little Ellin Holland and Anne Starkie to tell, all save the white beard. Elinor Hardman lost hers as an urchin, but presently returning through a little hole in the parlour, he offered her gold and silver in any quantity if she would let him enter again, and when she resisted he threatened to cast her into the fire and the pit, and to break her neck; all of which threats being unheeded by the little maid of ten, he left her again in his old form of "urchin." The next day, and the next, all these

249

devils came again, seeking to repossess the children. They came in various forms—as a black raven; a black boy, with his head bigger than his body; a black rough dog with a firebrand in his mouth; five white doves; a brave fellow like a wooer; two little whelps that played on the table, and ran into a dish of butter; an ape; a bear with fire in his mouth; a haystack—all, haystack as well as the rest, promising them bags of gold and silver if they might come into them again, but threatening to break their necks and their backs, and throw them into the pit and the fire, and out of the window, if denied. But Messrs. More and Darrel were instant in prayer, and successfully withstood them. The children were pronounced finally dispossessed: all save Jane Ashton, who went away to a popish family and became popish herself; wherefore the devil recovered her, says Mr. Darrel, and her last state was worse than her first. As for Edmund Hartley, he was hanged at Lancaster, chiefly through Mr. Darrel's exertions.

In 1596 Mr. Darrel had more work. Thomas Darling, "the Boy of Burton," had offended old Alice Goodridge; so Alice possessed him, and Mr. Darrel was sent for the undoing. His chief weapon in this case was a ranting tract called "The Enemie of Securitie," which the devil could not abide any how, and during the reading of which he would cry out—through the earthly medium of the Boy of Burton—"Radulphus, Belzebub can doe no good, his head is stricken off with a word."—"We cannot prevaile (against the church and Mr. Darrel), for they will not be holpen by witches. Brother Radulphus, we cannot prevaile; let us go to our mistress and torment her; I have had a draught of her blood to-day." "Againe—'There is a woman earnest at prayer, get her away.' 'Nay,' quoth John Alsop (a man that was present), with a loude voice, 'we cannot spare her.' Thus the Boy graced Mistress Wightman, his aunt. And againe, 'Brother Glassop (another devil), we cannot prevaile, his faith is soe strong. And they fast and pray, and a preacher prayeth as fast as they.'" And "I bayted my hooke often, and at last I catcht him. Heere I was before, and heere I am againe, and heere I must stay, though it be but for a short tyme. I leade them to drink, carouse, and quaffe. I make them to sweare. I have leave given mee to doe what I will for a time. What is wightier than a Kinge in his owne lande? A King I am, in whome I raigne, heere I am King for a time." With much more of the same kind. In the mean time old Alice Goodridge, who had wrought all this mischief, died in prison, while her devilish spirit or imp, Minnie, whom she had sent into the boy, racketed and rioted in his soul and body, and Mr. Darrel wrestled against him with prayer and "the Enemie of Securitie." He finally prevailed, and after Thomas Darling had been possessed and dispossessed and repossessed again, delivered him from Radulphus and Minnie and Glassop and Beelzebub, and so had leisure to turn to some one else when needed.

That some one else was soon found; for there was Will Somers, a lad living with Mr. Brakenbury at Ashby-de-la-Zouch during the time of Mr. Darrel's ministry there, who was now at Nottingham, and one of the most accomplished demoniacs of the day. Nothing would satisfy Will but that Mr. Darrel should be sent for to cast the devil out of him. He had known of his prowess with Katherine Wright, and the Starkies, and the Boy of Burton, and why should he not glorify God and the Puritans as well in Nottingham as in Lancashire? Accordingly, that gentleman was sent for on the 5th of November, 1597, and the farce began. Before Mr. Darrel even saw the lad he said he was possessed, and he said the same thing to himself—counterfeiting or illness being of course put out of court; and he described to the bystanders in what shape the devil would appear when driven out of the lad—for he would make himself visible to them if they had but faith and courage and patience to see the end, and if they would not be terrified when the boy "scriehed or cryed aloude in a strange and supernaturall manner; sometimes roaring fearfullye lyke a beare, and crying like a swyne." The shapes, then, in which he would go were these—"a Mouse, a Man with a Hunch-back higher than his Head, an ugly Man with a white Beard, a Crow's Head round, a great Breath, ugly like a Toad, an Urchin, &c." And he told them, also in the lad's hearing, of what other possessed persons had done: how they had cast themselves into fire or water, gnashed with their teeth, writhed with their necks, and drawn their mouths awry, foaming. Then he said that Will Somers was afflicted for the sins of Nottingham, and God had made even the devil a preacher to deter them from them; whereat Will acted by signs all the sins of Nottingham, and Mr. Darrel explained them to the people as he went on. With such a master as this, it was no difficult matter for the pupil to succeed. Two sermons were preached on his behalf. During Mr. Aldred's he lay still, excepting a little struggle now and then: this was to show that Mr. Aldred was not powerful as a Man of God. But when Mr. Darrel began, he roused himself up, and on his describing the fourteen signs of Possession one after the other, acted them all to the life as he told them off. "He tore; he foamed; he wallowed; his Face was drawn awry; his Eyes would stare and his Tongue hang out; he had a Swelling would seem to run from his Forehead down by his Ear and Throat, and through his Belly and Thighs, to the Calf of his Legs; he would speak with his Mouth scarce moving; and when they looked his Tongue would seem drawn down his Throat; he would try to cast himself into the Fire and Water; he would seem heavy that they could not lift him, and his Joints stiff that they could not bend them." And when Mr. Darrel further exhorted them all to stand firm, and they would see the glory of God in the dispossession, he cried and rended and laid as if dead, just in the order which the preacher desired. Then he rose up cured and exorcised; but Mr. Darrel told him he might be possessed again, and he must be very careful and watchful.

Of course he was possessed again. He had been too great a gainer by the first trial not to venture on a second. If he had been bought off his apprenticeship, had large presents of clothes, and kept in idleness at his father-in-law's, for a first trial, what might not fall from the skies on this second occasion? So Will began to talk wildly of a black dog that haunted him, offering him gold and ginger, and of the devil who came with six more shapes to torment him—namely, as a cock, a crane, a snake, an angel, a toad, a newt, a set of viols, and dancers, and that he stood before him "with a foure-forked cappe on his heade;" sometimes, too, making noises and motions like whelps or "kitlings." Fourteen persons were thrown into prison, accused of bewitching Master Will, of whom the most celebrated was Millicent Horslie, whom no human skill could have saved had not the impostor betrayed himself in time. For Will Somers had a revelation concerning her, which must be told in the words of his "confession," as reported by Harsnet:—"Maister Darrel told my father-in-law and others in my hearing, that he, the said Maister Darrel, Maister Aldred, and some others, were going to carrie Millicent Horsley (that present morning) to the said Maister Perkins, to be examined. Whereupon, I gessing by the time of Maister Darrel's departure, and by the distance of the way, and of the likelihood that she woulde deny herselfe to bee a witche, said to those that were present by mee in one of my fittes, about eleven of the clocke, that Millicent Horsley was in examining, and that she denyed herselfe to be a witch." This coincidence was too striking an instance of supernatural power to be overlooked. Mr. Darrel worked on it as one of the most marvellous proofs of the boy's undeniable possession, and Millicent Horsley lay in gaol, together with thirteen others, to satisfy the craft of one and the credulity of the other, and to prove the whole age sick, diseased, and enfeebled by superstition.

Will's sister, Mary Cowper, seeing how pleasant and profitable a thing it was to be bewitched, followed in her brother's steps, and cried out on Alice Freeman, a poor old creature who thought to escape by saying she was with child. The plea was not a very safe one, for Mr. Darrel told her if she was, it was by the devil, and she had better have held her tongue. But by this time the parish authorities got frightened, and interfered; sending Will off to the workhouse, where he still continued his fits and antics, until a rough fellow there, one John Shepheard, told him that if he "did not leave and rise up he would set such a pair of Knip-knaps upon him as should make him rue it"—when he gathered himself up and confessed his imposture. Mr. Darrel would have none of this recantation. He said he was more possessed than ever, and that it was the devil within him that made him to lie. So Will wrote the following letter, as a kind of quietus to his zealous friend:—

"Mr. Darrel, my hearty Commendations unto you. This is to desire you that you would let me be at quiet: For whereas you said that I was Possessed, I was not; and for those Tricks that I did before you came, was through Folks Speeches that came to me: And those that I did since, was through your Speeches, and others. For as you said I could not hear, I did hear all Things that were done in the House, and all Things that I did were counterfeit; And I pray you to let it pass; for the more you meddle in it, the more discredit it will be for you: And I pray God, and you, and all the World to forgive me."

Even this was not enough. Will was bribed over by the promise of a good place in a gentleman's house if he would be properly demoniac again; and consenting thereto, played again his old tricks; but the Lord Chief Justice, Sir Edmund Anderson, not believing a word of it all, encouraged him kindly to tell the truth, and not be afraid; so Will started up and was perfectly well, and for the greater satisfaction of the gentlefolks showed them how he worked.

And to prove how small was the value of evidence in those days, one Richard Mee—who was held to have deposed "That he had seen William Somers turn his Face directly backward, not moving his Body, and that his Eyes were as great as Beasts' Eyes, and that his Tongue would be thrust out of his Head to the bigness of a Calve's Tongue" when re-examined explained himself thus:—"My Meaning was that he turned his Face a good Way towards his Shoulder, and that his Eyes were something gogling; and by reason that it was Candle-light when I saw his Tongue thrust out, and by reason of my Conceit of the Strangeness of Somers's Troubles, it seemed somewhat bigger than, if Somers had been well, I should have thought it to have been." Again, a black dog which Will had cried out on as the devil, and which, by reason of his words had actually been taken for the devil with eyes glaring like fire, come back to repossess him, turned out to be nothing but a spurrier's dog crouching in the background of the darkening chamber. So, when carefully sifted, would the evidence of all such-like marvels prove to be merest chaff scattered on the ground; and yet, a century after, Mr. Richard Boulton is found repeating the story of Will Somers' possession as if it had never been disproved; and there are some even now living who would cite it as a case of proved spiritualism. Mr. Darrel was degraded from the ministry, and committed to close prison: rather harsh measures simply because he had more faith and a little less discretion than his neighbours.

GIFFARD'S ANECDOTES.[109]

George Giffard, "minister of God's word in Maldon," put forth a little book in 1603, containing a number of witch stories and anecdotes, without names, dates, or places, yet written in a manner and style evidently proving their reliability, and all seeming to have come within his own personal knowledge as believed in by others. One, whom he knew, under the assumed name of one of his characters was constantly troubled by a hare, which his conscience accused him was a witch "she stared at him so;" and sometimes an ugly weasel would run through his yard; and sometimes a foul big cat sit upon his barn, for which he had no manner of liking; and an old woman of the place, whom he had been as careful to please as if she had been his mother, still frowned upon him to his exceeding discomfort; and a hog which overnight had eaten his meat with his fellows, quite hearty and well, in the morning was stark dead; and five or six hens died too, in a manner no one could understand, save by the power of witchcraft. And once another of his friends went to a cunning man who lived twenty miles off, complaining of his farm-yard losses: so the cunning man took a glass, and bidding him look in it, showed him a certain suspected witch therein, telling him that she had three or four imps, "some call them puckrels," one of which was like a gray cat, another like a weasel, a third like a mouse. There was also another cunning person—a woman—to whom a father took a child that had long been lame and pained. The woman told the man he had an ill neighbour, and that the child was forespoken. "Marie, if he would go home and bring her some of the clothes which the child lay in all night, she would tell him certainely." The father went home and did as he was bid, when the wise woman informed him that the girl was

[109] 'A Dialogue concerning Witches and Witchcrafts.' 1603.

bewitched, counselled him what to do, and the "girle is well at this day, and a pretie quicke girle," says George Giffard, with a sneer at his neighbour's easy faith. Another had his wife much troubled; so he, too, went off to a wise woman, who told him that his wife was haunted by a fairy. As a counter-charm she was bidden to wear a part of St. John's Gospel ever about her, against which the fairies could not stand, so fled. Another good wife could not make her butter come: it was bewitched, and for a whole week obstinately disregarded the laws of butter nature: wherefore they heated a spit, red hot, and thrust it into the cream—and it came at once. The next morning the good wife met the suspected witch—"the old filth," she calls her with more emphasis than euphony. "Lord, how sowerly she looked upon me, and mumbled as she went! Ah, quoth she, you have an honest man to your husband. I hear how he doth use me!" The wife longed to scratch the witch, her stomach rose so against her, but she was afraid she would prove the stronger, for she was "a lustie old quean," and let her pass unmolested.

In a certain village a wealthy man was suddenly reduced to comparative poverty by extraordinary losses in his farm; he himself fell ill, and his child of seven years of age sickened and died. He sent to the same wise woman at R. H., who told him that he was bewitched, and moreover, that there were three witches and one wizard in the town where he lived. The forespoken farmer caused the one whom he most suspected to be seized and examined, who at last confessed, after making "much ado," and taking up the time of the worshipful justice to no good. She said that she had three imps, a cat Lightfoot, a toad Lunch, a weasel Makeshift. Lightfoot had been given to her sixteen years ago, by one Mother Barlie of W. in return for an oven cake; the toad and the weasel came of their own accord and offered their services gratuitously. The cat killed kine, the weasel killed horses, and the toad plagued men; so the poor old creature was sent to the county gaol, where she died before the assizes. Another woman, old Mother W. of Great T., had an imp like a weasel. "She was offended highly with one H. M.; home she went, and called forth her spirit, which lay in a pot of woole under her bed: she willed him to go plague the man: he inquired what she would give him, and he would kill H. M. She said she would give him a cocke, which she did, and he went, and the man fell sicke with a greate paine in his belly, languished and died; the witch was arraigned, condemned, and hanged, and did confesse all this."

Seven miles hence, at W. B., a man in good health suddenly fell sick, pined for half a year, and then died. His wife, suspecting evil doings, went to a cunning woman, who showed her in a glass the likeness of the witch who had destroyed him, wearing an old red cap with corners, such as women were used to wear. The old red-capped woman was taken, tried, soon brought to confess to the bewitching of the man, and executed. But before she died she told them all, how that she had a spirit in the likeness of a yellow dun cat, which came to her one night as she sat by the fire nursing angry thoughts against a neighbour with whom she had fallen out. She was frightened, she said, but the cat bid her not be afraid, for it had served an old dame, that was now dead, for five years down in Kent, and would serve her now, an she would. The woman took the cat at its word, and by it killed many a cow and hog of those who angered her: at last she sent it to this man, and the cat killed him. She was hanged, and the yellow dun imp was never more seen.

Mr. Giffard knew a church which had been robbed of its communion service: a wise man told the churchwardens what to do and the thief would surely ride in all haste to confess. As it proved. Another case was that of a child taken piteously ill. Under the cunning man's advice the father burnt its clothes, and while they were burning, the witch came running in, grievously pained. The child was well within two days. A butcher had a son, John, terribly afflicted with sores. Salves and plasters would not heal him; but when a cunning man showed him in a glass the form of the witch who had laid this harmful thing upon him, and they had cut off some of the boy's hair and burnt it, the old woman came to the house in all speed, crying, "John, John, scratch me!" So John scratched her till the blood came, and his sores all healed of themselves, without salve or plaster helping. A woman had blear eyes that were watery; a knave lodging at the house wrote a charm which she was always to wear about her neck, and never lose or look at. She wore her charm, and her eyes got quite well; but one day, prompted by Eve's sin, she opened the packet, and found a piece of paper on which was written, in the German tongue, "The devil plucke out thine eyes and fill their holes with dirt." Terrified at the unholy nature of her cure, the woman flung the charm away, and her eyes immediately became bleared and watery as before.[110] A woman suspected of witchcraft was taken in hand by a gentleman, who undertook to induce her to confess. She was very stiff about the matter, and denied all dealings with the devil in any way. Suddenly, at some distance from them, appeared a weasel or a lobster, looking straight at them. "Look!" said the gentleman, "yonder same is thy spirit!" "Oh, master," said she, "that is a vermine. There be many of them everywhere." But as they went towards it, the weasel or lobster vanished clean out of sight. "Surely," said the gentleman, "it is thy spirit." But still she denied, "and with that her mouth was drawn all awrie." When a little further pressed she allowed all, and the gentleman, being no justice, sent her home, exhorting her to go to a magistrate and ease her soul by confession. As she got home she was met by another witch who came violently

---

[110] This is an old story, found in all books on witchcraft.

enraged against her. "Ah, thou beast! what hast thou done? thou hast bewrayed us all!" she said. "What remedy now?" said she. "What remedy?" saith the other, "send thy spirit and touch him." At that moment the gentleman felt, as it were, a flash of fire about him; but he lifted his hat and prayed, and the spirit came back and said it could do him no hurt, because he had faith. So then they sent it against his child, and the child was taken ill with great pain and died. The witches confessed and were hanged. Another witch had her spirit hidden in the boll of a tree; and there she held long conversations with this ghastly Ariel, he answering in a hollow ghoustie voice, as might be expected. When any offended her, she would go to the tree and release her imp to do them harm. She had killed many hogs, horses, and the like by this spirit; but at last justice got hold of her with its mailed hand and killed her. Another friend of Giffard's, also under the disguise of one of his characters, was twice on a jury, when certain old women were charged with harming their neighbours' goods and lives. There was no proof in either case, and the old women protested their innocence passionately; but the jury brought them in guilty, which was perfectly logical and right according to their notions of the law of that God who suffers the devil to torment the sons of men, and to delude old women into the possession of unholy powers. What, indeed, could be done with them when, by a look or a word, they could afflict even unto death the most beautiful of God's creatures, and send the devil to inhabit the purest of souls? The mischief lay in the fundamental creed, not so much in the application of it, terrible and bloody as it was; and it is against this creed, that I would most earnestly insist. It must be remembered, too, that Giffard writes ironically, and brings together all these cases as evidence of the foolishness and wickedness of the faith.

THE POSSESSED MAID OF THAMES STREET.[111]

In 1603, Mary Glover, a merchant's daughter in Thames Street, gave herself out as bewitched, and said that Mother Jackson had done it. A little glimmering of reason made the physician Dr. Boncraft tell the Lord Chief Justice Anderson that Mother Jackson was wrongfully accused, and the girl was counterfeiting. So the Lord Chief Justice caused the Recorder of London, Sir John Crook, have her to him in his chambers in the Temple. The maid went with her mother and some neighbours, and in an hour's time came Mother Jackson, disguised like a country market woman, with a muffler hiding her face, an old hat, and a short cloak bespattered with mire. As soon as she entered the maid fell backward on the floor; "her Eyes drawn into her Head, her Tongue toward her Throat, her Mouth drawn up to her Ear, her Bodie became stiff and senseless, Her Lips being shut closs a plain and audible Voice came out from her Nostrils saying 'Hang her, hang her.'" The Recorder, willing to try her, called for a candle at which to light a sheet of paper, then held the burning paper to her hand till a blister came, rising and breaking and the water running down on the floor. But still the maid lay as if dead, with the Voice coming out of her Nostrils, saying, "Hang her, hang her." Not satisfied with the trial of burning, the Recorder got a long pin, which he made hot and thrust up her nostrils to see if she would "neese," wink, bend her brows, or stir her head; but still she lay as before, stiff, senseless, and as one dead. The minister, one Lewis Hughes, who tells this story which Sinclair quotes, told the Recorder that he had often prayed with the maid, and that when he concluded with the Lord's Prayer and came to "but deliver us from all evil," the maid would be tost and shaken as a mastiff might shake a cur. Then the Recorder

---

[111] George Sinclair's 'Satan's Invisible World Displayed.'

bade the witch say the Lord's Prayer, but she could not say it: she kept on all right until the clause "deliver us from evil," and this she skipped over; neither would she confess that Jesus Christ was our Lord in the Articles of the Christian Faith. When Mary was in her fits, if the witch but so much as laid her hand upon her she was tost and shaken fearfully. This the Recorder wished to verify: so he bade first one, then another, of the neighbours come forward and touch her; which they did; but she never stirred till Mother Jackson touched her, when she was shaken as before. Then the Recorder said, "Lord, have mercy upon the woman!" for he was now fully convinced; and sent poor old Mother Jackson off to Newgate. As soon as she was sent off the maid came to herself, the voice ceased out of her nostrils, and she went home with her mother. Three weeks or more after the witch was condemned, the maid had the same fits, strange and fearful to behold, and the Recorder told the minister, and all the ministers of London, "that we might be ashamed to see a Child of God in the Claws of the Devil without any hope of deliverance but by such means as God had appointed—Fasting and Prayer." Then five ministers, all good Christians and sound believers, assembled and prayed from morning to candle-light, when Mary suddenly started out of her chair—they crying "Jesus help, Jesus save!"—and came up to Lewis Hughes, in a state of wildness and dismay. As he stood behind her holding her by the arms, she lifted both herself and him off the ground, foaming at the mouth and struggling thus all over the chamber; and then her strength gave way, and she fell as if dead, her head hanging down and her limbs, which had been so stiff and frozen, now supple and limber. In a short time her eyes came back into their place and her tongue came out of her throat, and she looked round and said cheerfully, "Oh! he is come, he is come! The Comforter is come! the Comforter is come! I am delivered, I am delivered!" Her father hearing these words wept and said,

"These were her grandfather's words when he was at the stake, the fire crackling about him," for he died a martyr to the Reformed Faith in Queen Mary's time. Then she prayed and thanked God till her voice was weak, and so the company separated, and Mary went home. Afterwards she was put with Lewis Hughes for a year, lest Satan should assault her again, and Mr. John Swan wrote the most canting and nauseating book on her "case" that ever fanatic penned or the duped and the gulled believed. But poor old Mother Jackson was dead: and those who mourned for her, mourned in secret and silence and shame.

There was another case of possession, this same year—Thomas Harrison, the Boy of Norwich—chiefly remarkable for having procured such attention from the ecclesiastical authorities that seven persons were formally licensed to have private prayers and fasting for his deliverance. But the bishop and commissioners who had seen his fits thought him an impostor, so his case died out for want of public support.[112]

And now we have the master of kingcraft on the throne, with his mania against witches, his private vices, and public follies, treacherous, cruel, narrow-minded, and cowardly beyond anything that has ever disgraced the English throne before or since. And one of the first trials for witchcraft during his reign was that disgraceful affair in which Somerset and his wife, Foreman, Sir Thomas Overbury, and Mrs. Turner were all mixed up together.

---

[112] Hutchinson's 'Essay on Witchcraft.'

SWEET FATHER FOREMAN.

That Carr and Lady Essex should have an intrigue together was not so bad, but that Mrs. Turner should have recourse to charms and conjurations, "to inchant the Viscount's affection towards her," that "much time should be spent, many words of witchcraft, great cost in making pictures of wax, crosses of silver, and little babies for that use," that specially, there should be among the images of wax, one "very sumptuously apparrelled in silke and sattin, as alsoe another sitting in forme of a naked woman spreading and laying forth her haires in a glass," was terrible misdoing against both God and the king. The murder of Sir Thomas Overbury was venial; the intrigue between his favourite and another man's wife was venial too; his own vices were mere kindly flea-bites on his dignity; but charms and conjurations, and my Lady Essex calling that old wizard Foreman her "sweet father"—this was more than the British Solomon could well digest. So when he had got tired of Carr and wanted to be rid of him, he suddenly remembered sweet Father Foreman, disciple of Dr. Dee, and Mrs. Turner, inventor of yellow starch for ruffs and falling bands, and not only smote Somerset straight in the face for his own share, but sent a side shaft after him, through his "creatures." Well for himself was it that sweet Father Foreman was dead and buried deep; so there only remained Mrs. Turner and one or two inferior agents in the matter—just enough to keep the people amused, and satisfy the royal lust for witch blood. Somerset came to the block on another count, about as false as the rest; and Mrs. Turner swung from the gibbet in her yellow ruff on every plea but the right one, and for any sin but those of her real and actual life. After her death was found her black scarf full of white crosses: and the mould in which Father Foreman had cast his leaden images of women; and written charms spread out on fair white parchment; and, worst of all, a list of all the ladies who had gone to consult the sorcerer as to how they might gain the love of other lords than their own; which list the Lord Chief Justice would not read out in court because, said the gossips, his own wife's name was the first that caught his eye.

THE WITCHES OF NORTHAMPTONSHIRE.[113]

"Of poor parentage, and poor education," old Agnes Browne had but a sorry life of it in the little town of Gilsborough where she lived. She had one daughter, Joan Vaughan, or Varnham, "a maide, or at least unmarried," says the old black-letter book maliciously; "as gratious as the mother, and both of them as farre from grace as Heaven from hell;" which Joan was "so well brought up vnder her mother's elbow, that she hangd with her for company vnder her mother's nose." It seems that one day, Joan, being in the company of a certain Mistress Belcher, "a virtuous and godly Gentlewoman of the same towne of Gilsborough, whether of purpose to giue occasion of anger to the saide Mistris Belcher, or but to continue her vilde and ordinary custome of behauiour, committed something either in speech or gesture so vnfitting, and vnseeming the nature of womanhood" that Mistress Belcher's patience could bear with her no longer. She got up, beat Joan Vaughan, and "forced her to avoid the company." Joan went away muttering that she would be revenged; to which replied Mrs. Belcher stoutly, that she feared neither her nor her mother, and bade her do her worst. Then Joan went home to her mother, and both together devised such a punishment that Mrs. Belcher was griped and gnawed of her body, her mouth drawn all awry, and in such powerful fits that she could scarce be held, crying out incessantly in her fits,

---

[113] 'The Witches of Northamptonshire.'

Agnes Browne,   Arthur Bill,
} Witches.
Ioane Vaughan, Hellen Ienkinson,

Mary Barber.

Who were all executed at Northampton the 22 of Iuly last, 1612.
'London. Printed by Tho. Purfoot for Arthur Iohnson. 1612.' A rare and valuable little black-letter tract.

"Here comes Joane Vaughan, away with Joane Vaughan!"
till all the world knew that she was bewitched, and that old
Agnes Browne and her daughter had caused the trouble.
Mistress Belcher's brother, one Master Avery, hearing of
his sister's sickness and extremity, came to see her; and
when he saw her, was moved to such anguish and
indignation that he must needs go to the house of the
witches to hale them to his sister, that she might draw their
blood. But though he twice essayed, he was twice arrested
by some miraculous agency, spell-bound, and unable to
move hand or foot; he could not, by any possibility,
advance beyond a certain spot, whereby the witches were
safe for this time at least, "the devil, who was standing
sentinel," being stronger than he. Wherefore sorrowfully he
turned back, and went home to his own place. But these
"imps of the devil" had longer arms than he, and in a very
short time he was as grievously tormented as his sister, his
torments enduring until the witches were arrested and taken
to Northampton gaol. When there, nothing would satisfy
Mistress Belcher and her brother Master Avery but that
they should go to the prison and "scratch" the witches;
which they did, and both recovered of their pains
marvellously on the instant. "Howbeit they were no sooner
out of sight, but they fell againe into their old traunces, and
were more violently tormented than before; for when
Mischiefe is once a foote, she grows in short time so
headstrong, that she is hardly curbed." Mistress Belcher
and Master Avery returning home from Northampton in a
coach, after their godly exercise of drawing blood from
these two wretched women, saw suddenly a man and
woman riding both upon a black horse. At which Master
Avery cried out that either they or their horses should
presently miscarry; and he had no sooner spoken than both
their horses fell down dead. Wherefore, for all these crimes,
as well as for bewitching a young child to death, Agnes
Browne and her daughter Joan were adjudged guilty, and

hanged on that 22nd of July, protesting their innocence to the last. And then it came out that about a fortnight before her apprehension Agnes Browne, Katherine Gardiner, and Joan Lucas, "all birds of a winge," had been seen riding on a sow's back to a place called Ravenstrop, to see one Mother Rhoades, an old witch that dwelt there. But before they got there old Mother Rhoades had died, "and in her last cast cried out that there were three of her old friends comming to see her, but they came too late. Howbeit she would meet with them in another place within a month after. And thus much concerning Agnes Browne and her daughter Joane Vaughan," says the old black-letter book contemptuously.

The son of witches, Arthur Bill could not control his appointed fate. Suspected by the authorities, but without proof, he and his father and mother were swum for trial, tied cross bound and flung into the water, where they floated and did not sink. Arthur was accused of bewitching to her death one Martha Aspine, as also of having bewitched sundry cattle; and as the parents had a bad name, it was thought best to try them all. After this trial of the water, Arthur was afraid, says the black-letter book, lest his father should relent and betray him and them all; whereupon he sent for his mother, and both together bewitched a round ball into his father's throat, so that he could not speak a word. When the ball was got out, the father proved the principal witness against them. The poor mother, who seems to have been a loving, sensitive, downcast woman, fainted many times during this terrible period; "Many times complaining to her spirit," says the bitter, uncharitable, anonymous author, "that the power of the Law would bee stronger than the power of her art, and that shee saw no other likelihood but that shee should be hanged as her Sonne was like to bee: To whom her spirit answered, giuing this sorry comfort, that shee should not bee hanged, but to preuent that shee should cut her owne throatt. Shee, hearing this sentence and holding it definitive, in great agony and horror of minde and conscience fell a rauing, crying out that the irreuocable Iudgement of her death was giuen, and that shee was damned perpetually; cursing and banning the time wherein shee was borne, and the houre wherein shee was conceiued." A short time after "shee made good the Deuil's worde, and to preuent the Iustice of the Law, and to saue the hangman a labour, cut her owne throate." The poor boy was in great misery when he heard of his mother's death, and knew now that what despair had done for her, the tyranny of superstition would do for him; yet "he stood out stiffly for his innocence," and when found guilty, broke out into grievous cries, saying that he had now found the Law to have a power above Justice, for that it had condemned an Innocent. At the gallows he said the same thing, refusing to confess to Martha Aspine's murder, and "thus with a dissembling Tongue, and a corrupted conscience, hee ended his course in this world, with little hope or respect (as it seemed) of the world to come." What became of his three familiars, Grissil, Ball, and Jack, we are not informed, neither of what forms or functions they were, nor of what colours or dimensions.

Grievously did Mistress Moulsho offend Ellen Jenkinson, when she caused her to be searched for witchmarks, which of course were found; for Helen's character was notorious, and there is no smoke without a little fire. So Helen, in revenge, played Mistress Moulsho a trick that brought herself to the gallows. For "at that time Mistris Moulsho had a Bucke of clothes to be washt out. The next morning, the Mayd, when shee came to hang them forth to dry, spyed the Cloathes, but especially Mistris Moulsho's Smocke, to bee all bespotted with the pictures of Toades, Snakes, and other ougly Creatures, which making her agast, she went presently and told her mistris, who, looking on them, smild, saying nothing else but this: 'Here are fine

Hobgoblins indeede.' And being a Gentlewoman of a stout courage, went immediately to the house of the sayd Hellen Ienkinson, and with an angry countenance told her of this matter, threatening her that if her Linnen were not shortly cleered from those foule spots shee would scratch out both her eyes; and so not staying for any answere, went home and found her linnen as white as it was at first." Helen was soon after arraigned for the death of a child, by witchcraft, but this story of Mrs. Moulsho's clothes all bespotted with the figures of toads and snakes stood in the stead of any more rational evidence. When found guilty, the poor creature cried out, "Woe is me, I now cast away!" And when at the place of execution, she "made no other Confession but this. That shee was guiltlesse, and neuer shewed signe of Contrition for what was past, nor any sorrow at all, more than did accompany the feare of death. Thus ended this Woman her miserable life, after shee had lived many yeares poore, wretched, scorned, and forsaken of the world."

Of Mary Barber, the last of the sad crew hanged at Northampton on those bloody assizes, the author gives no special account, but plenty of abuse, mixed up with the strangely cruel and immoral morality of the day. He says that "as shee was of meane Parents, so was she monstrous and hideous both in her life and actions. Her education and barbarous Nature neuer promising to the world anything but what was rude, violent, and without any hope of proportion more than only in the square of uitiousnesse. For out of the oblyuion and blindnesse of her seduced senses, she gaue way to all the passionate and earthly faculties of the flesh, and followed all the Fantazmas Vanities and Chimeras of her polluted and vnreasonable delights, forsaking the Society of Grace, and growing enamored vpon all the euill that Malice or Frenzy could minister to her vicious desires and intendments." She was put in prison on the charge of bewitching a man to death, but "the prison (which makes men bee fellowes and chambermates with theeves and murtherers) the common guests of such dispised Innes, and should cause the Imprisoned Party (like a Christian Arithmetician) to number and cast vp the amount of his own Life, neuer put her in minde of the hatefull transgressions shee had committed, and to consider the filth and leprosie of her soule, and intreate heaven's mercy for the release thereof. Prison put her not in minde of her graue, nor the grates and lockes put her in remembrance of hell, which depriued her of the ioy of liberty, which shee saw others possesse. The iangling of irons did not put her in minde of the chaines wherewith shee should be bound in eternall torments, vnlesse heaven's mercy vnloosed them, nor of the howling terrors and gnashing of teeth which in hel euery soule shall receiue for the particular offences committed in this life, without vnfained and hearty contrition. Shee neuer remembered or thought shee must die, or trembled for feare of what should come to her after death. But as her use was alwaies knowne to be deuilish, so her death was at last found to be desperate. For shee (and the rest before named) being brought from the common gaole of Northampton to Northampton Castle, where the Assizes are vsually held, were seuerally arraigned and indited for the offences they had formerly committed, but to the inditement they pleaded not guilty. Putting therefore their causes to the triall of the Countrey, they were found guilty, and deserued death by the verdit of a credible Iury returned. So without any confession or contrition, like birds of a feather they all held and hangd together for company at Abington gallowes hard by Northampton the two and twentieth day of Iuly last past; Leauing behinde them in prison many others tainted with the same corruption, who without much mercy and repentance are likely to follow them in the same tract of Precedencie."

THE WITCHES OF LANCASHIRE.[114]

In Pendle Forest, a wild tract of land on the borders of Yorkshire, lived an old woman about the age of fourscore, who had been a witch for fifty years, and had brought up her own children, and instructed her grandchildren, to be witches. "She was a generall agent for the Deuill in all these partes;" her name was Elizabeth Southernes, usually called Mother Demdike; the date of her arraignment 1612. She was the first tried of this celebrated "coven," twenty of whom stood before Sir James Altham and Sir Edward Bromley, charged with all the crimes lying in sorcery, magic, and witchcraft. Old Mother Demdike died in prison before her trial, but on her being taken before the magistrate who convicted them all, Roger Nowell, Esq., she made such a confession as effectually insured her due share of execration, and hedged in the consciences of all who had assailed her from any possible pangs of self-reproach or doubt.

About fifty years ago, she said, she was returning home from begging, when, near a stone pit in the Pendle Forest, she met a spirit or devil in the shape of a boy, with one half of his coat brown and the other half black, who said to her, if she would give him her soul, she should have all that she might desire. After a little further talk, during which he told her that his name was Tibb, he vanished away, and she saw him no more for this time. For five or six years Mother Demdike never asked any kind of help or harm of Tibb, who always came to her at "daylight gate" (twilight); but one Sabbath morning, she having her little child on her knee, and being in a light slumber, Tibb came to her in the likeness of a brown dog, and forced himself on her knee, trying to get blood from under her left arm.

[114] 'The Wonderful Discoverie of Witches in the County of Lancaster.' By Thomas Potts. 1613. Thomas Wright's 'Narrative of Sorcery and Magic.' 1851.

Mother Demdike awoke sore troubled and amazed, and strove to say, "Jesus, save my child," but could not, neither could she say, "Jesus, save myself." In a short time the brown dog vanished away, and she was "almost starke madde for the space of eight weekes." She and Tibb had never done much harm, she said; not even to Richard Baldwin, for all that he had put them off his land, and taken her daughter's day's work at his mill without fee or reward, and when she, led by her grandchild Alison (for she was quite blind), went to ask for pay, gave them only hard words and insolence for their pains, saying, "he would burn the one, and hang the other," and bidding them begone for a couple of witches—and worse. She confessed though, after a little pressing, that at that moment Tibb called out to her, "Revenge thee of him!" to whom she answered, "Revenge thou either of him or his!" on which he vanished away, and she saw him no more. She would not say what was the vengeance done, or if any. But if she was silent, and not prone to confession, there were others, and those of her own blood, not so reticent. Elizabeth Device her daughter, and Alison and James and Jennet Device, her grandchildren, testified against her and each other in a wonderful manner, and filled up all the blanks in the most masterly and graphic style.

Alison said that her grandmother had seduced her to the service of the devil, by giving her a great black dog as her imp or spirit, with which dog she had lamed one John Law, a petit chapman or pedlar, as he was going through Colnefield with his pack at his back. Alison wanted to buy pins of him, but John Law refused to loose his pack or sell them to her; so Alison in a rage called for her black dog, to see if revenge could not do what fair words had failed in. When the black dog came he said, "What wouldst thou have me to do with yonder man?" To whom she answered, "What canst thou do at him?" and the dog answered again, "I can lame him." "Lame him," says Alison Device; and

273

before the pedlar went forty yards he fell lame. When questioned, he, on his side, said, that as he was going through Colnefield he met a big black dog with very fearful fiery eyes, great teeth, and a terrible countenance, which looked at him steadily then passed away; and immediately after he was bewitched into lameness and deformity. And this took place after having met Alison Device and refused to sell her any pins. Then Alison fell to weeping and praying, beseeching God and that worshipful company to pardon her sins. She said further that her grandmother had bewitched John Nutter's cow to death, and Richard Baldwin's woman-child on account of the quarrel before reported, saying that she would pray for Baldwin himself, "both still and loud," and that she was always after some matter of devilry and enchantment, if not for the bad of others then for the good of herself. For once, Alison got a piggin full of blue milk by begging, and when she came to look into it, she found a quarter of a pound of butter there, which was not there before, and which she verily believed old Mother Demdike had procured by her enchantments. Then Alison turned against the rival Hecate, Anne Whittle, *alias* Chattox, between whom and her family raged a deadly feud with Mother Demdike and her family; accusing her of having bewitched her father, John Device, to death, because he had neglected to pay her the yearly tax of an aghen dole (eight pounds) of meal, which he had covenanted to give her on consideration that she would not harm him. For they had been robbed, these poor people, of a quarter of a peck of cut oatmeal and linens worth some twenty shillings, and they had found a coif and band belonging to them on Anne Whittle's daughter; so John Device was afraid that old Chattox would do them some grievous injury by her sorceries if they cried out about it, therefore made that covenant for the aghen dole of meal, the non-payment of which for one year set Chattox free from her side of the bargain and cost John's life. She said, too, that Chattox had bewitched sundry persons and cattle, killing John Nutter's cow because he, John Nutter, had kicked over her canfull of milk, misliking her devilish way of placing two sticks across it; and slaying Anne Nutter because she laughed and mocked at her; slaying John Morris' child, too, by a picture of clay—with other misdeeds to be hereafter verified and substantiated. So Alison Device was hanged, weeping bitterly, and very penitent.

James Device, her brother, testified to meeting a brown dog coming from his grandmother's about a month ago, and to hearing a noise as of a number of children shrieking and crying, "near daylight gate." Another time he heard a foul yelling as of a multitude of cats, and soon after this there came into his bed a thing like a cat or a hare, and coloured black, which lay heavily on him for about an hour. He said that his sister Alison had bewitched Bullock's child, and that old Mother Chattox had dug up three skulls, and taken out eight teeth, four of which she kept for herself and gave four to Mother Demdike; and that Demdike had made a picture of clay of Anne Nutter, and had burned it, by which the said Anne had been bewitched to death. Also she had bewitched to death one Mitton, because he would not give her a penny; with other iniquities of the same sort. He said that his mother, Elizabeth Device, had a spirit like a brown dog called Ball, and that they all met at Malking Tower; all the witches of Pendle—and they were not a few—going out in their own shapes, and finding foals of different colours ready for their riding when they got out: Jennet Preston was the last: when they all vanished. He then confessed, for his own part, that his grandmother Demdike told him not to eat the communion bread one day when he went to church, but to give it to the first thing he met on the road on his way homewards. He did not obey her, but ate the bread as a good Christian should; and on the way he met with a thing like a hare which asked him for the bread; but he said he had not got it; whereupon the hare got very angry and threatened to tear him in pieces, but James "sained" himself, and the devil vanished. This, repeated in various forms, was about the pith of what James Device confessed, his confession not including any remarkable betrayal of himself, or admission of any practical and positive evil. His young sister Jennet, a little lassie of nine, supplied the deficiencies. She had evidently been suborned, says Wright, and gave evidence enough to have hanged half Lancashire. She said that James had sold himself to the devil, and that his spirit was a black dog called Dandy, by whom he had bewitched many people to death; and she confirmed what he had said of Jennet Preston's spirit, which was a white foal with a black spot in its forehead. And then she said that she had seen the witches' meetings, but had taken no part in them; and that on Good Friday they had all dined off a roasted wether which James had stolen from Christian Swyers; and that John Bulcocke turned the spit. She said that her mother Elizabeth had taught her two prayers, the one to get drink and the other to cure the bewitched. The one to get drink was a very short one, simply—"Crucifixus, hoc signum vitam eternam, Amen;" but this would bring good drink into the house in a very strange manner. The other, the prayer to cure the bewitched, was longer:—

"Vpon Good Friday, I will fast while I may,
Vntill I heare them knell,
Our Lord's owne Bell,
Lord in his messe
With his twelve Apostles good,
What hath he in his hand?
Ligh in[115] Leath[116]wand:

---

[115] "Ligh in," perhaps lykinge, lusty, or craske.
[116] "Leath," flexible.

What hath he in his other hand?
Heauen's doore key.
Open, open, Heauen doore keyes,
Steck, steck, hell doore.
Let Crizum[117] child
Go to it Mother mild.
 What is yonder that casts a light so farrandly?[118]
Mine owne deare Sone that's nail'd to the Tree,
He is nail'd sore by the heart and hand,
And holy harne Panne.[119]
Well is that man
That Fryday spell can,
His Childe to learne
A Crosse of Blewe, and another of Red,
As good Lord was to the Roode.
Gabriel laid him downe to sleepe
Vpon the grounde[120] of holy weepe;
Good Lord came walking by,
Sleep'st thou, wak'st thou, Gabriel?
No, Lord, I am sted with stick and stake,
That I can neither sleepe nor wake:
Rise vp, Gabriel, and goe with me,
The stick nor the stake shall neuer deere[121] thee,
Sweete Jesus our Lorde. Amen."

On such conclusive testimony as this, and for such fearful crimes, James Device was condemned for "as dangerous and malicious a witch as ever lived in these parts

---

[117] The chrism was the white cloth placed over the brow of a newly-baptized child in the Roman Catholic service. When children died within the month they were called chrisoms.

[118] "Farrandly," fair, handsome.

[119] "Harne panne," brain case, cranium.

[120] Gethsemane.

[121] "Deere," hurt.

of Lancashire, of his time, and spotted with as much Innocent bloud as euer any witch of his yeares." Poor lad!

"O Barbarous and inhumane Monster, beyond example; so farre from sensible vnderstanding of thy owne miserie as to bring thy owne naturall children into mischiefe and bondage, and thyselfe to be a witnesse vpone the gallowes, to see thy owne children, by thy deuillish instructions, hatcht vp in villanie and witchcraft, to suffer with thee, euen in the beginning of their time, a shamefull and untimely Death!" These are the words which Thomas Potts addresses to Elizabeth Device, widow of John the bewitched, daughter to old Demdike the "rankest hag that ever troubled daylight," and mother of Alison and James the confessing witches; mother, also, of young Jennet of nine, their accuser and hers, by whose testimony she was mainly condemned. Elizabeth was charged with having bewitched sundry people to death, by means and aid of her spirit, the brown dog Ball, spoken of by James; also she had gone to the Sabbath held at Malking Tower, where they had assembled to consult how they could get old Mother Demdike, their leader, out of prison, by killing her gaoler and blowing up the castle, and where they had beef and bacon and roasted mutton—the mutton that same wether of Christopher Swyers' of Barley, which James had stolen and killed; with other things as damnable and insignificant. So Elizabeth Device, "this odious witch, who was branded with a preposterous marke in Nature even from her Birth, which was her left Eye standing lower than the other, the one looking down the other looking up," was condemned to die because she was poor and ugly, and had a little lying jade for a daughter, who made up fine stories for the gentlefolks.

Anne Whittle, *alias* Chattox, was next in influence, power, and age to Mother Demdike, and she began her confession by saying that old Demdike had originally seduced her by giving her the devil in the shape and proportion of a man, who got her, body and soul, and sucked on her left ribs, and was called Fancie. Afterwards she had another spirit like a spotted bitch, called Tibbe, who gave them all to eat and to drink, and said they should have gold and silver as much as they wanted. But they never got the gold and silver at all, and what they ate and drank did not satisfy them. "This Anne Whittle, *alias* Chattox, was a very old withered, spent, decrepid creature, her Sight almost gone; A dangerous Witch of very long continuance; always opposite to old Demdike; For whom the one fauoured the other hated deadly: and how they curse and accuse one an other in their Examinations may appear. In her Witchcraft always more ready to doe mischiefe to men's goods than themselves; Her lippes ever chattering and talking; but no man knew what. She lived in the Forrest of Pendle amongst this wicked Company of dangerous Witches. Yet in her Examination and Confession she dealt always very plainely and truely; for vpon a speciall occasion, being oftentimes examined in open Court, she was neuer found to vary, but alwayes to agree in one and the selfe same thing. I place her in order next to that wicked Firebrand of mischiefe, old Demdike, because from these two sprung all the rest in order; and even the Children and Friendes of these two notorious Witches."

Nothing special or very graphic was elicited about old Chattox. She had certainly bewitched to death sundry of the neighbourhood, lately deceased; but then they all did that; and her devil, Fancie, came to her in various shapes— sometimes like a bear, gaping as though he would worry her, which was not a pleasant manner of fulfilling his contract—but generally as a man, in whom she took great delight. She confessed to a charm for blessing forespoken drink; which she had chanted for John Moore's wife, she said, whose beer had been spoilt by Mother Demdike or some of her crew:—

"Three Biters hast thou bitten,
The Hart, ill Eye, ill Tonge;
Three Bitter shall be thy boote,
Father, Sonne, and Holy Ghost,
a God's Name
Fiue Paternosters, fiue Auies,
and a Creede,
For worship of fiue woundes
of our Lord."

Of course there was no help or hope for old Chattox if she said such wicked things as these. The righteous justice of England must be satisfied, and Anne Whittle was hung—one of the twelve who sorrowed the sunlight in Lancaster on that bloody assize.

Her daughter, Ann Redfearne, was then taken, accused of making pictures of clay and other maleficent arts; and she, too, was hanged; and then well-born, well-bred, but unfortunate Alice Nutter—a gentlewoman of fortune living at Rough Lee, whose relatives were anxious for her death that they might come into some property, out of which she kept them while living, and between whom and Mr. Justice Nowell there was a long-standing grudge on the question of a boundary-line between their several properties—Alice Nutter, whom one would have thought far removed from any such possibility, was accused by young Jennet of complicity and companionship, and put upon her trial with but a faint chance of escape behind her. For Elizabeth Device swore that she had joined with her and old Demdike in bewitching the man Mitton, because of that twopence so fatally refused; and young Jennet swore that she was one of the party who went on many-coloured foals to the great witch meeting at Malking Tower; and so poor Alice Nutter, of Rough Lee, the well-born, well-bred gentlewoman, was hanged with the rest of that ragged crew; and her relations stood in her place, quite satisfied with their dexterity.

Then there was Katherine Hewitt, *alias* Mouldheels, accused by James Device, who seemed to think that if he had to be hanged for nothing he would be hanged in brave company, and, by sharing with as many as could be found, lessen the obloquy he could not escape; and John Bulcocke, who turned the spit, and Jane his mother, for the same crimes and on the same testimony; for the added crime, too, of helping in the bewitching of Master Leslie, about which nefarious deed other hands were also busy; and Margaret Pearson, delated by Chattox as entertaining a man spirit cloven-footed, with whom she went by a loophole into Dodson's stable, and sat all night, on his mare until it died. She was also accused by Jennet Booth, who went into her house and begged some milk for her child; Margaret good-naturedly gave her some, and boiled it in a pan, but all her reward was, that Jennet accused her of witchcraft, for there was, said she, a toad, or something very like a toad, at the bottom of the pan when the milk was boiled, which Margaret took up with a pair of tongs and carried out of the house. Of course the toad was an imp, and Jennet Booth was quite right to repay an act of neighbourly generosity by accusation and slander. Margaret got off with standing in the pillory in open market, at four market towns on four market days, bearing a paper on her head setting forth her offence written in great letters, about which there could be no mistake; after which she was to confess, and afterwards be taken to prison, where she was to lie for a year, and then be only released when good and responsible sureties would come forward to answer for her good behaviour.

And there was Isabel Roby, who bewitched Peter Chaddock for jilting her, and in the spirit pinched and buffeted Jane Williams, so that she fell sick with the impression of a thumb and four fingers on her thigh; and Jennet Preston, she who had the white foal spirit, and who was afterwards hung at York for the murder of Master Thomas Lister—for Master Thomas in his last illness had been for ever crying out that Jennet Preston was lying on him, and when she was brought to see the body it gushed out fresh blood on her, which settled all doubts, if haply there had been any. So the famous trial of the Pendle Witches came to an end; and of the twenty who were accused twelve were hanged while the rest escaped only for the present, many of them meeting with their doom a few years afterwards.

GRACE SOWERBUTS AND THE PRIESTS.[122]

At the same time and place, namely, "at the Assizes and Generall Gaole-delivery, holden at Lancaster, before Sir Edward Bromley," old Jennet Bierly, Ellen Bierly her daughter-in-law, and Jane Southworth, were accused by Grace Sowerbuts of bewitching her, so that her "bodie wasted and was consumed." Grace was fourteen years old—a very ripe time for bewitchment and possession—and her evidence ran that for some years past she had been fearfully tormented by these women, for that "they did violently draw her by the Haire of the Head, and layd her on the toppe of a Hay-mowe;" and that Jennet Bierly appeared to her, first under her own shape and form, then as a black dog, and that as she was going over a style "she picked her off," but did not hurt her much, for soon she was enabled to rouse herself up, and go on her way without any great damage. But often the women came to her as black dogs, tempting her to cast herself into the water, or dragging her into the hay-loft where they covered her with hay on her head and with straw on her body, they, the black dogs, lying on the top of the straw till they took away all sense and feeling and she knew not where she was; and oft they "carried her where they met black things like men that danced with them and did abuse their bodies, and they brought her to one Thomas Walsham's House in the Night, and there they killed his Child, by putting a Nail into the Navil, and after took it forth of the Grave, and did boil it, and eat some of it, and made Oyl of the bones; and such like horrid lies," says honest Webster, indignantly. But fortunately for the three accused, Grace Sowerbuts was a popish pet, and suspected of decided papistical leanings; and it was said that she was put up to all this by one Thomson, a popish priest, whose real name was

---

122 Potts's 'Discovery.' Webster's 'Displaying.'

Southworth, and who was a relation of old Sir John
Southworth the great popish lord of the district; to whom
also Jane, one of the accused, was a near relative, but a
hated enemy, as is often the case—Sir John having been
known to ride miles round to avoid passing by her house.
Jane Southworth was a Protestant and a convert, therefore
likely to receive the protection of public opinion in those
parts; likely, too, to be doubly hated by her relative, first for
herself, and secondly for her apostacy. So Grace
Sowerbuts, an excitable young maid with but a slender
regard to truth, was hit upon as the person best fitted to
carry confusion into the enemy's camp, and it was resolved
to prove her bewitched by the devilish arts of the two
Bierlys and the popish recusant. But Sir Edward Bromley,
who cared nothing for the protestations of the Pendle
witches, and hung every one of them with the most placid
belief that he was doing a just and righteous work, gave a
very different countenance to these Samesbury witches, all
of whom would have been strung up like dogs had not the
taint of papistry rested on Grace and her supporters.
Leading her quietly to a denial of all she had asserted, Sir
Edward got her to confess that she was an impostor, and
that every article of her accusation was a lie and a fallacy
from beginning to end. She had never known nor seen any
devils; she had never been cast upon the henroof nor upon
the hay-mow, but when she was found there she had gone
of her own accord, and had covered herself with hay and
straw to better prove the witches' despite against her; she
knew nothing of any child done to death by nails in its
body; and all that she had said about the bones, and the oil,
and the tender flesh roasted at the fire, was as false as the
rest. She had never been possessed, but had flung herself
into these fits by her own will and independent power; and
what she did in them was a mere trick, which she could
show their worships if they liked. In short, Grace
Sowerbuts was forced to play the losing game in as

masterly a manner as might be, and to own herself a cheat and an impostor while yet there was time for pardon. So the three Samesbury witches got off with a stern exhortation from the judge, who scarcely seemed to relish the release of even Protestant witches delated by papistical accusers.

MARY AND HER CATS.[123]

Mary Smith of Lynn, wife of Henry Smith, glover, was envious of her neighbours for their greater skill in making cheese: in the midst of her discontents, and while her mind, by its passion and evil thoughts, was in a fit condition for the devil to enter therein, Satan came to her as a black man, provoking her in a "lowe murmuring and hissing Voyce," to forsake God and follow him; to which she "condescended" in express terms. The devil then constantly appeared to her—sometimes as a mist; sometimes as a ball of fire, with dispersed spangles of black; but chiefly as a black man; and sometimes as a horned man, in which shape he came to her when in prison. Mary was a good hand at banning. She cursed John Orkton, and wished his fingers might rot off, and they did so; she cursed Elizabeth Hancock, whom she accused of stealing her hen, wishing that the bones might stick in her throat, calling her a "prowde linny, prowde flurts, and shaking the hand bade her go in, for she should repent it;" and incontinently Elizabeth Hancock was taken with a pinching at the heart, and sudden weakness of all her body, and fainting fits, and racking pains, and madness, and raving, so that she tore the hair off her head as she tossed about distracted. Her father went to a wise man, who showed him Mary Smith's face in a glass, and bade him make a cake according to certain directions, which then he was to lay, half on Bessie's head and half on her back, and which would infallibly cure her, as she was not ill but bewitched. The father did so, and the daughter mended. Soon after this she married one James Scot, who, having a mortal hatred against Mary Smith, killed her cat, and threatened that if his wife had any such fits as she had before they married, he would hang Mary

---

[123] A 'Treatise of Witchcraft.' By Alexander Roberts, B.D., and Preacher of God's word at King's Linne in Norfolk. 1616.

Smith without mercy. At this Mary clapped her hands, and cried "They had killed her cat!" and the next day Elizabeth had the old nipping round her heart. So James went to Mary and said he would most certainly take her before the magistrates, if she did not amend her ways and heal his wife at once. Fortunately for Mary the woman got better, and the evil day was staved off for a time. To Cecily Balye, the maid-servant next door, she sent her cat to sit upon her breast when she slept, in revenge at the maid's sweeping a little dust awry; and Cicely gave awful evidence how, through the thin partition which divided them, she used to see Mary Smith adoring her imp in a submissive manner—down on her knees, using strange gestures and uttering many murmuring and broken speeches; and if she had listened, and looked more attentively, she might have seen and heard more: "but she was with the present spectacle so affrighted, that she hurried away in much feare and distemper."

"The fourth endammaged by this Hagge," says Roberts, was one Edmund Newton. He was a cheesemonger, like herself, and she thought he got the best of the trade; so she, or her imp in her likeness, came to him as he was lying in bed, and "whisked about his face a wet cloath of very loathsome savour; after which he did see one clothed in russet, with a little bush beard, who told him he was sent to looke vpon his sore legge, and would heale it." When Newton rose to take a fairer look, he saw that the russet man with a little bush beard had cloven feet, so refused his offer of chirurgery. After this Mary was constantly sending her imps to him—a toad and crabs—which crawled about the house, "which was a shoppe planchered with boords, where his seruants (hee being a shoo maker) did worke;" and one of them took the toad and flung it into the fire, during which time the witch was grievously tormented. So nothing would serve Edmund Newton's turn but he must "scratch her;" yet when he

287

strove to do so his nails turned like feathers, and he had no power over her, not even to raise the skin so much as a nine weeks' old babe might have done. At another time a great water-dog ran over his bed—the chamber door being shut—and he fell lame in his hand, and did not recover the use of it again. And then the law interfered, and Mary Smith was brought before the magistrates to answer to the charge of witchcraft—by them committed to the assizes—found guilty by judge and jury—and hanged by the neck till she was dead, as a warning to the time and her own kind. This murder was done 1616.

RUTTERKIN.[124]

The Earl and Countess of Rutland had shown much kindness to the widow Joan Flower, and her two daughters Philip and Margaret. Joan and Philip were employed at the castle pretty constantly as charwomen, and Margaret was taken into the castle itself, "looking both to the poultrey abroad and the washhouse within doores," and evidently a great favourite with my Lady, who trusted her much. Their good fortune raised them up a host of enemies, as is always the case; and backbiters went with tales to the Lord and Lady, saying, "First, that Ioane Flower the Mother was a monstrous malicious woman, full of oathes, curses, and imprecations, irreligious, and, for any thing they saw by her, a plaine Atheist; besides of late days her very countenance was estranged, her eyes were fiery and hollow, her speech fell and enuious, her demeanour strange and exoticke, and her conuersation sequestered; so that the whole course of her life gaue great suspition that she was a notorious witch, yea some of her neighbours dared to affirme that she dealt with familiar Spirits, and terrified them all with curses and threatening of reuenge, if there were neuer so little cause of displeasure and vnkindnesse. Concerning Margaret, that she often resorted from the Castle to her Mother, bringing such Provision as they thought was vnbefitting for a seruant to purloyne, and coming at such unseasonable houres, that they could not but coniecture some mischeife between them, and that their extraordinary ryot and expences tended both to rob the Lady, and to maintaine certaine deboist and base company which frequented this Ioane Flower's house the mother, and especially her youngest Daughter. Concerning Philip that she was lewdly transported with the loue of one Th.

---

[124] Tract. Printed at London by G. Eld for I. Barnes, dwelling in the long Walke, neare Christ-Church. 1619.

Simpson, who presumed to say, that she had bewitched him: for he had no power to leaue, and was as he supposed maruellously altered both in minde and body, since her acquainted company: these complaints began many yeares before either their conuiction or publique apprehension: Notwithstanding such was the honour of this Earle and his Lady; such was the cunning of this monstrous woman in her obseruation towards them; such was the subtilty of the Diuell to bring his purposes to passe; such was the pleasure of God to make tryall of his seruants; and such was the effect of a damnable womans wit and malitious enuy, that all things were carried away in the smooth Channell of liking and good entertainment on euery side, untill the Earle by degrees conceiued some mislike against; and so peraduenture estranged himself from that familiarity and accustomed conferences he was wont to haue with her; untill one Peate offered her some wrong; against whom she complained, but found that my Lord did affect her clamours and malicious information, vntill one Mr. Vauasor abandoned her company, as either suspicious of her lewd life, or distasted with his oun misliking of such base and poore Creatures, whom nobody loued but the Earle's household; vntill the Countesse misconceiuing of her daughter Margaret and discovering some vndecencies both in her life and neglect of her businesse, discharged her from lying any more in the Castle, yet gave her 40$s.$, a bolster, and a mattresse of wooll; commanding her to go home vntill the slacknesse of her repayring to the Castle, as she was wont, did turne her loue and liking toward this honourable Earle and his family into hate and rancor; wherevpon despighted to bee so neglected, and exprobated by her neighbours for her Daughters casting out of doores, and other conceiued displeasures, she grew past all shame and womanhood, and many times cursed them all that were the cause of this discontentment, and made her so loathsome to her former familiar friends and beneficial acquaintance."

Things being come to this pass, it was not difficult to persuade the Earl and his Countess that, when their eldest son Henry, Lord Ross, sickened very strangely, and after a while died,—when their second son Francis was also tortured by a strange sickness—and the Lady Katherine their daughter was in danger of her life "through extreame maladies and vnusuall fits"—it was all done by Joan Flower's witchcraft, and that the quickest way out of their troubles was to arrest the widow and her two daughters and see what could be done with them, both by their own confessions and the neighbours' relations. They were arrested accordingly, and carried before the magistrates where witnesses were not awanting. The first evidence given was that of Philip Flower, sister to Margaret, and daughter of poor old Joan. On the 4th of February she confessed that her mother and sister "maliced" the Earl of Rutland, his countess, and their children, because they were put out of the Castle; wherefore her sister Margaret, by desire of her mother, got Lord Henry's right-hand glove which she found on the rushes in the nursery, and delivered it to Joan, who presently rubbed it on the back of her spirit Rutterkin, bidding him "height and goe and doe some hurt to Henry Lord Rosse," then put it into boiling water, pricking it many times with a knife, and burying it in the yard with a wish that Lord Henry might never thrive. Whereupon he fell sick and shortly after died. She also said that she often saw the spirit Rutterkin leap on her sister Margaret's shoulder and suck her neck, and that her mother had often cursed the earl and his lady, and boiled feathers and blood together, "vsing many Deuillish speeches and strange gestures." On the 22nd of the same month Margaret was examined, and she also gave no trouble. She confessed that truly she had got Lord Henry's glove, and that her mother had done with it in all particulars of stroking

Rutterkin's back, and putting it into boiling water, and pricking, and burying it, according to the words of Philip; also that some two or three years ago she had found a glove of the Lord Francis', which her mother rubbed on Rutterkin the cat and bade him go upward, and which, by her incantations and sorceries, caused a grievous illness to light on the little nobleman. And she got a piece of Lady Katherine's handkercher, which her mother put into hot water, "and then taking it out rubbed it on Rutterkin, bidding him 'flye and go;' whereupon Rutterkin whined and cryed 'Mew,'" and the mother said he had no power over Lady Katherine to hurt her. A few days later both sisters were examined again, when Philip confessed that she had a spirit which sucked her in the form of a white rat, and which she had entertained for the space of two or three years, on condition that it should cause Thomas Simpson to love her; and Margaret allowed that she had two spirits, one white, the other black-spotted, to whom she had given her soul, they covenanting to do all that she commanded them. Then she rambled off into a wild statement of how on the thirtieth of January last, she, being in Lincoln gaol, four devils appeared to her at eleven or twelve o'clock at night; the one stood at her bed's foot, and had a black head like an ape, and spake unto her; but what she could not well remember; at which she was very angry that he would not speak plainer and let her understand his meaning. She said that the other three were Rutterkin, Little Robin, and Spirit, "but shee never mistrusted them nor suspected herselfe till then." This closed the examinations of the two younger women: for poor old Joan had died on her way to gaol "with a horrible excruciation of soul and body," and so an end was come to of her. But if there was nothing more to be got out of the Flower family, their neighbours were not backward to help them with a bad word, when handy. Anne Baker, evidently mad, Joan Willimot, and Ellen Greene, were brought to say their say in the face of the country and before the county justices. Joan Willimott gave evidence that Joan Flower had oftentimes complained to her of the unfriendly conduct of my Lord of Rutland, in turning her daughter out of the house, adding that though she could not have her will of my Lord himself, she had spied his son and stricken him to the heart—stricken him with a white spirit, which yet could be cured if she so willed. Joan Willimott then "fyled" herself for a witch, saying that she had a spirit called Pretty, given to her by her master, William Berry of Langholme, in Rutlandshire, whom she had served three years. When he gave it to her, he bade her open her mouth and he would blow into her a Fairy which should do her good; and she did so; and he blew into her mouth, and presently after there came out of her mouth a spirit which stood upon the ground in the shape and form of a woman, and asked of her her soul—which Joan granted—being willed thereto by her master. She did not own to having ever hurt anyone, but said instead that she had helped divers who had been stricken and forespoken, and that the use she made of her spirit was to know how those did whom she had undertaken to mend. She said, too, that her spirit came to her last night, in the form of a woman mumbling something, but she could not understand what; and that she was not asleep, but was as waking as at this present. On another occasion she fyled two of her neighbours, saying how Cooke's wife had said that John Patchet might have had his child alive, if he had asked for it, insinuating that Cooke's wife had forespoken the said child, and that Patchet's wife had an evil thing within her, and she knew it by her girdle. Also that Gamaliel Greete, of Waltham, had a spirit like a white mouse put into him in his swearing, and that those on whom he looked with intent to hurt were hurt; and that he had a mark on his left arm, which had been cut away; and that her own spirit had told her all this. And that she, and Joan, and Margaret Flower, had met in Blackborrow hill, the week before Joan's apprehension; and that she had seen in Joan's house two spirits, the one like a rat, and the other like an owl, and that one of them had sucked under her left ear—as she thought; and that Joan Flower said her spirits had informed her she should be neither burnt nor hanged.

On this same day Ellen Green gave in her account, saying that some six years since Joan Willimott had come to her in the wolds, persuading her to forsake God and betake her to the devil, and she would give her two spirits: which this Examinate consented unto. Whereupon Joan called two spirits, one in the likeness of a "kittin," the other of a "moldiwarp," the first of which was called "pusse," and the second "hiffe hiffe;" and they leapt on her shoulder, and sucked her. And that she sent the kittin to a baker in the town who had offended her, but whose name she had forgotten, and bade it bewitch him to death; and the moldiwarp she despatched to Ann Dawse, for the same purpose and the same offence. And of other deaths by the like means did Ellen Green accuse herself; adding that Joan Willimott's spirit was in the form of a white dog, and that she had seen it suck her in Barley harvest last.

And then came mad Ann Baker, who started with informing her audience that there are four colours of planets, black, yellow, green, and blue, and that black is always death, and that she saw the blue planet strike William Fairbairn's son, but when William Fairbairn did beat her and break her head, his said son Thomas did mend. Yet she sent not the blue planet. She said that she saw a hand appear to her, and a voice in the air say, "Anne Baker, save thyself, for to-morrow thou and thy maister must be slain;" and that the next day, as she and her master were together in a cart, suddenly she saw a flash of fire, but when she said her prayers the fire went away, and then a crow came and pecked her clothes; whereat she said her prayers again, and bade the crow go to whom it was sent, "and the Crow went vnto her Maister and did beat him to death, and shee with her prayers recouered him to life: but he was sick a fortnight after and saith that if shee had not had more knowledge than her Maister, both he and shee and all the Cattell had beene slaine." The rest of her confessions turned upon the histories of the various deaths and bewitchments with which she was charged, and most of which she denied; saying, that she had merely lain Ann Stannidge's child on her skirt, but had done it no harm, and that when the mother had burnt the little one's hair and nail parings, and she, Ann Baker, had gone in to the house in great pain and suffering, she knew nothing whatever of this burning, but that she was sick and knew not whither she went. Of the Rutland case all she knew was, that when she came back from Northamptonshire, whither she had gone three years ago, two good wives had told her that my young Lord Henry was dead, and that there was a glove of the said Lord buried underground, and that "as his glove did rot and wast, so did the liver of the young Lord rot and wast;" and that her spirit was a good spirit and in the shape of a white dog. The tract does not inform us what was done with these three wretched women. The two Flowers were hanged, the old mother having died as I have said: but whether the untimely death of a sickly lad was revenged by more innocent blood than this remains unknown. The death-sacrifices of savages, the witches of Africa, and the Red Indian "Medicine-men," are not so very far removed from our own forefathers that we should quite ignore the likeness between them and the recent past at home.

THE BOY OF BILSTON.[125]

The war between Papists and Protestants still went on, and the favourite weapon with each was the old one of Possession, and its result—exorcism. The patient in the present case was William Perry, a youth of twelve, generally called the Boy of Bilston, whom Joan Cock bewitched for the better showing forth the glory of God and the Church, and to the hurt of her own soul and body. One day William Perry met old Joan as he returned from school, and forbore to give her good time of the day, as a well-bred youth should: whereat the old woman was angry, and called him "a foul thing," saying "that it had been better for him if he had saluted her." At which words the boy felt something prick him to his heart, and when he came home fell into fits of the most demoniac kind. The parents seeing his extremity went cap and knee to some Catholics in the neighbourhood, and they, after long solicitation, proceeded to the exorcising. They poured holy water and holy oil in goodly quantity upon him, and left supplies of both to be used in their absence. The devil was sore afflicted by the holy water and the holy oil, and made the boy cast up pins, and wool, and knotted thread, and rosemary leaves, and walnut leaves, and feathers, and "thrums." For there were three devils inside him, he said, and they had uncommon power. On Corpus Christi day he brought up eleven pins, and a knitting needle folded in divers folds; all after extreme fits and heavings; and then the spirit told him not to listen to the exorcising priest—which was a great compliment from the devil—and that the witch had said she would make an end of him. When told to pray for the witch, the boy and the devils were furious; but afterwards calmed down on the exorciser getting extra power; and then the boy prayed his prayer and grew better. Then he

---

[125] Wright and Hutchinson.

296

demanded that everything about him should be blessed, and that all his family should be Catholics; but when any Puritans came in, he said the devil assaulted him in the shape of a black bird. So it was a vastly pretty little case of witness and conversion, and the Catholics made the most of it. Joan must now be arrested; for the fits continued, and the young gentleman was not to be pacified with anything short of the witch's blood. When brought into his presence the boy had extreme fits, crying out: "'Now she comes, now my Tormentor comes!' writhing and tearing and twisting himself into such Shapes as bred at once Amazement and Pity in the Spectators:" so the old woman was sent to Stafford gaol, but, because this was a Popish matter, acquitted without long delay. Then the Bishop of Coventry and Lichfield, desirous of testing the matter, and unwilling that the Catholics should take any glory to themselves for their holy oils and their anointings which were said to have calmed the most "sounding fits," took William Perry home to the Castle, and there had him watched: and watched so well that certain dirty tricks not to be spoken of here were found out, and the physiological part of the "miracle" set at rest. But before this the Bishop tried the devils with Greek. For they could not abide the first verse of the first chapter of St. John, and always fell on the boy with fury when it was read; so, said the Bishop, whose wits sectarian hatred had sharpened—one bigotry driving out another—"Boy, it is either thou or the Devil that abhorrest those Words of the Gospel: and if it be the Devil (he being so ancient a Scholar, as of almost six Thousand Years' standing) knows, and understands all Languages; so that he cannot but know when I recite the same sentence out of the Greek Text: But if it be thyself then art thou an execrable Wretch, who plays the Devil's part; wherefore look to thyself, for now thou art to be put to Trial, and mark diligently, whether it be that same Scripture which shall be read." Then was read the twelfth verse of the first chapter, at which William, supposing it to be the abhorred first, fell into his customary fits; but when, immediately after, the first verse was read, he, supposing it was another, was not moved at all. By which means this part of the fraud was discovered also; and when, moving his eyes and staring about him wildly, he declared that he saw mice running round the bed, no one gave any credit to his words. When the whole thing was blown to the winds, and the Greek test had failed, and the dirty tricks had been found out, the boy made a pretended confession, which was evidently no more true than anything else had been. He said that one day as he was coming home, an old man called Thomas, with gray hair and a cradle of glasses on his shoulders, met him, and after asking him if he went to school and how he liked it, told him that he could teach him a few tricks which should prevent his going to school any more, and would instead lead all people to pity and lament him, holding him to be bewitched. But it was shrewdly suspected that the old man Thomas, with his gray hair and cradle of glass, was but a pleasant phantasy of the imagination; and that the real secret had lain with the Catholic priests, who, finding the boy apt and handy, thought they could make good capital out of him for their Church, and put him forth as a witness for its divine power and holy office, seeing that it could dispossess the demoniac and drive away evil spirits. Fortunately they reckoned without their host—the host of "reformed" bigotry and hatred: for we need not congratulate ourselves on any clearsightedness or common sense in the matter. Had the Boy of Bilston been a sound Protestant, he would have been held as indubitably Possessed by the Devil, and some poor wretch would have been found as a convenient sacrifice to the stupidity of that devil.

MR. FAIRFAX'S FOLLY.

The next year saw Mr. Fairfax of Knaresborough—Edward Fairfax, the scholar, the gentleman, the classic, our best translator of Tasso, graceful, learned, elegant Edward Fairfax—pursuing with incredible zeal six of his neighbours for supposed witchcraft on his children. The children had fits and were afflicted with imps, so Edward Fairfax thought his paternal duty consisted in getting the lives of six supposed witches, the hanging of whom would infallibly cure his children, and drive away the evil spirits possessing them. But fortunately for the accused the judge had more sense than Mr. Fairfax; and, though the women were sent back again for another assize, suffered them to escape with only the terror of death twice repeated. It is strange to find ourselves face to face with such stupid bigotry as this in a man so estimable and so refined as Fairfax.

THE COUNTESS.[126]

Lady Jennings and her young daughter Elizabeth, of thirteen, lived at Thistlewood in the year 1622. One day an old woman, coming no one knew whence, perhaps from the bowels of the earth, appeared suddenly before the girl, demanding a pin. The child was frightened, and had fits soon after—fits of the usual hysteric character, but quite sufficiently severe to alarm Lady Jennings. A doctor was sent for; but also, as well as the doctor, came a clever shrewd woman called Margaret Russill, or "Countess," a bit of a doctress in her way, perhaps a bit of a white witch too, who thought she could do the afflicted child some good, and had beside a love of putting her fingers into everybody's pie. At the end of one of her fits the child began to cry out wildly, then mentioned Margaret and three others as the persons who had bewitched her. And then she went on, incoherently, "These have bewitched all my mother's children—east, west, north, and south all these lie—all these are witches. Set up a great sprig of rosemary in the middle of the house—I have sent this child to speak, to show all these witches—Put Countess in prison, this child will be well—If she had been long ago, all together had been alive—Them she bewitched with a cat-stick—Till then I shall be in great pain— Till then, by fits, I shall be in great extremity—They died in great misery." No mother's heart could resist the appeal contained in these wild words; poor Countess was arrested, and taken before Mr. Slingsby, a magistrate. When there she said, though heaven knows what prompted her to tell such falsehoods, "Yesterday she went to Mrs. Dromondbye in Black-and-White Court, in the Old Baylye; and told her that the Lady Jennings had a daughter strangely sicke, whereuppon the said Dromondbye wished her to goe to inquire at Clerkenwell

---

[126] Wright, quoting Lord Londesborough's MSS.

for a minister's wiffe that cold helpe people that were sicke, but she must not aske for a witch or a cunning woman, but for one that is a phisition woman; and then this examinate found her and a woman sitting with her and told her in what case the child was, and shee said shee wold come this day, but shee ought her noe service, and said shee had bin there before and left receiptes there, but the child did not take them. And she said further that there was two children that her Lady Jennins had by this husband, that were bewitched and dead, for there was controversie betweene two howses, and that as long as they dwelt there, they cold not prosper, and that there shold be noe blessing in that howse by this man." When asked what was this "difference," she answered, "Between the house of God and the house of the world:" but when told that this was no answer, and that she must explain herself more clearly, she said that "she meant the apothecary Higgins and my Lady Jennings." "And shee further confessed that above a moneth agoe she went to Mrs. Saxey in Gunpouder Alley, who was forespoken herself, and that had a boke that cold helpe all those that were forespoken, and that shee wold come and shewe her the booke and help her under God. And further said to this examinate, that none but a seminary priest cold cure her." So here again we have the constantly recurring element of sectarianism, without which, indeed, we should be at a loss how to understand much that meets us. "Countess" was committed to Newgate, and the bewitched child cried out more and more against her, making new revelations with each fit, when the pitiful farce was brought to a close by the minister's wife, Mrs. Goodcole, who, when confronted with Countess, denied point blank the more important parts of her evidence. And then all this evil—this much ado about nothing—was found to have arisen from a private quarrel; and when Dr. Napier was sent for, he unbewitched the possessed child with some

very simple remedies, and the great balloon burst and fell
to the ground in hopeless collapse.

THE TWO VOICES.[127]

On the 13th of August, 1626, Edward Bull and Joan Greedie were indicted at Taunton for bewitching Edward Dinham. Dinham was a capital ventriloquist, and could speak in two different voices beside his own, as well as counterfeit fits and play the possessed to the life. One of his two feigned voices was pleasant and shrill, and belonged to a good spirit; the other was deadly and hollow, and belonged to an evil spirit. And when he spoke his lips did not move, and he lay as if in a trance, and both he and the voices said that he was bewitched, and all the people believed them. And the good voice asked who had bewitched him, to which the bad replied, "A woman in greene cloathes and a blacke hatt with long poll, and a man in gray srite, with blewe stockings." When asked where she was now, the bad spirit answered, "At her own house," while he was at a tavern in "Yeohull," Ireland. Then after some pressing the bad spirit said that the name of one was "Johan," of the other "Edward;" and after more pressing still, confessed to the surnames, "Greedie and Bull." So in consequence of this reliable report messengers were sent off to find old Joan, and when found arrest her. Then the good spirit, who played the part of a benevolent Pry, asked how these two became witches, to which the bad answered, "By descent." "But how by descent?" says the good spirit, anxious not to leave a lock unfastened or a problem unsolved. "From the grandmother to the mother, and from the mother to the children," says the bad. "But howe were they soe?" says Goody. "They were bound to us and we to them," answered the bad, with more words than explanation.

Good Spirit—"Lett me see the bond."

Bad Spirit—"Thou shalt not."

---

[127] Wright.

Good Spirit—"Lett me see it, and if I like it I will seale it alsoe."

Bad Spirit—"Thou shalt, if thou wilt not reveale the contentes thereof."

Good Spirit—"I will not."

At this point it was pretended that a spectral bond was passed from the bad to the good ghost; and then broke out the "sweet and shrill voice" of the ventriloquist with "Alas! oh, pittifull, pittifull, pittifull! What! eight seales? bloody seales! four dead and four alive; oh, miserable!" Then came in the man's natural voice, addressing the spirit: "Come, come, prithee tell me why did they bewitch me?" Bad Spirit— "Because thou didst call Johan Greedie witche." Man—"Why, is shee not a witche?" Bad Spirit—"Yes, but thou shouldst not have said so," which was a fine bit of worldly policy in the bad ghost. Good Spirit—"But why did Bull bewitche him?" Bad—"Because Greedie was not strong enough."

On this evidence further messengers were sent off for Edward Bull, but whether to Yeohull or not I cannot say. They were disappointed for the moment, for Bull had run away; and then, in a future interview, and to fill up the time until braver sport should be provided, the bad and the good spirits had a wrestle for Dinham's soul, which, judging from what evidence we have had left us, was not worth the struggle, and would be no great gain to either party. In the struggle the good spirit speaks Latin. "Laudes, laudes, laudes," says he, being well educated and not ashamed. But the bad was, as befitted his nature, churlish and ill-taught, and did not understand his opponent's talk, but translated it into "ladies," which made a laugh among them all. Then they struggled for the Prayer Book; but here again the bad was discomfited, and the man kept the talisman; after which the good spirit made "the sweetest musicke that ever was heard." When they set out to catch Bull again, they found him in bed; and now, when both the Possessors were safe, Dinham was freed and his voices dumb for ever. Perhaps he had caught cold. I do not know the fate of these poor wretches, but I should not think it doubtful.

In 1627 Mr. Rothnell exorcised an evil spirit out of one John Fox; but notwithstanding this John continued dumb for three years after; which was rather an unfortunate comment on the exorcism, but not at all likely to open the eyes of any one willing to be blind.

THE SECOND CURSE OF PENDLE.[128]

We have seen what Lancashire was in sixteen hundred and twelve: it was not much better twenty-one years later; for in 1633 we find that Pendle Forest was still of bad repute, and that traditions of old Demdike and her rival Mother Chattox yet floated round the Malkin Tower, and hid, spectre-like, in the rough and desert places of the barren waste. Who ever knew of evil example waiting for its followers? What Mothers Demdike and Chattox had done in their day, their children and grandchildren were ready to do after them. The world will never lose its old women, "toothless, blear-eyed, foul-tongued, malicious," for whom love died out and sin came in long years ago; and Edmund Robinson, son of Ned of Roughs, was one of those specially appointed by Providence to bring such evildoers to their reward.

Edmund, then about eleven years of age (how many of these sad stories come from children and young creatures!), lived with his father in Pendle Forest; lived poorly enough, but not without some kind of romance and interest; for on the 10th day of February, 1633, he made the following deposition:—

"Who upon oath informeth, being examined concerning the great meeting of the Witches of Pendle, saith that upon All Saints' Day last past, he, this Informer, being with one Henry Parker, a near-door neighbour to him in Wheatley-lane, desired the said Parker to give him leave to gather some Bulloes, which he did. In gathering whereof he saw two Grayhounds, viz., a black and a brown one, come running over the next field towards him, he verily thinking the one of them to be Mr. Nutter's, and the other to be Mr. Robinson's, the said Gentlemen then having such like. And saith, the said Grayhounds came to him, and

---

[128] Webster. Wright. Harleian MSS.

fawned on him, they having about their necks either of them a Collar, unto each of which was tied a String; which Collars (as this Informer affirmeth) did shine like Gold. And he thinking that some either of Mr. Nutters or Mr. Robinsons Family should have followed them; yet seeing no body to follow them, he took the same Grayhounds, thinking to course with them. And presently a Hare did rise very near before him. At the sight whereof he cried Loo, Loo, Loo: but the Doggs would not run. Whereupon he being very angry took them, and with the strings that were about their Collars, tied them to a little bush at the next hedge, and with a switch that he had in his hand he beat them. And in stead of the black Grayhound, one Dickensons Wife stood up, a Neighbour, whom this Informer knoweth. And in stead of the brown one a little Boy, whom this Informer knoweth not. At which sight this Informer, being afraid, endeavoured to run away; but being stayed by the Woman, (viz.) by Dickensons Wife, she put her hand into her pocket, and pulled forth a piece of Silver much like to a fair shilling, and offered to give him it to hold his tongue and not to tell; which he refused, saying, Nay, thou art a Witch. Whereupon she put her hand into her pocket again, and pulled out a thing like unto a Bridle that gingled, which she put on the little Boyes head; which said Boy stood up in the likeness of a white Horse, and in the brown Grayhounds stead. Then immediately Dickensons wife took this Informer before her upon the said Horse and carried him to a new house called Hoarstones, being about a quarter of a mile off. Whither when they were come, there were divers persons about the door, and he saw divers others riding on Horses of several colours towards the said House, who tied their Horses to a hedge near to the said House. Which persons went into the said House, to the number of three score or thereabouts, as this Informer thinketh, where they had a fire, and meat roasting in the said House, whereof a young Woman (whom this Informer knoweth not) gave him Flesh and Bread upon a Trencher, and Drink in a Glass, which after the first taste he refused, and would have no more, but said it was nought.

"And presently after, seeing divers of the said company going into a Barn near adjoining, he followed after them, and there he saw six of them kneeling, and pulling all six of them six several ropes, which were fastened or tied to the top of the Barn. Presently after which pulling, there came into this Informers sight flesh smoaking, butter in lumps, and milk as it were syleing (straining) from the said ropes. All which fell into basons which were placed under the said ropes. And after that these six had done, there came other six which did so likewise. And during all the time of their several pulling, they made such ugly faces as scared this Informer, so that he was glad to run out and steal homewards; who immediately finding they wanted one that was in their company, some of them ran after him near to a place in a Highway called Boggard-hole, where he, this Informer, met two Horsemen. At the sight whereof the said persons left following of him. But the foremost of those persons that followed him he knew to be one Loinds Wife; which said Wife, together with one Dickensons Wife, and one Jennet Davies, he hath seen since at several times in a Croft or Close adjoining to his Fathers house, which put him in great fear. And further this Informer saith, upon Thursday after New Years Day last past he saw the said Loinds Wife sitting upon a cross piece of wood being within the Chimney of his Fathers dwelling-house; and he, calling to her, said, Come down, thou Loynds Wife. And immediately the said Loynds Wife went up out of his sight. And further this Informer saith, that after he was come from the company aforesaid to his Fathers house, being towards evening, his Father bad him go and fetch home two kine to seal (tie up). And in the way, in a field called the Ellers, he chanced to hap upon a Boy, who began to quarrel with him, and they fought together, till the Informer had his ears and face made up very bloody by fighting, and looking down he saw the Boy had a cloven foot. At which sight, he being greatly affrighted, came away from him to seek the kine. And in the way he saw a light like to a Lanthorn, towards which he made haste, supposing it to be carried by some of Mr. Robinson's people; but when he came to the place he only found a Woman standing on a Bridge, whom, when he saw, he knew her to be Loinds Wife, and knowing her he turned back again; and immediately he met the aforesaid Boy, from whom he offered to run, which Boy gave him a blow on the back that made him to cry. And further this Informer saith, that when he was in the Barn, he saw three Women take six Pictures from off the beam, in which Pictures were many Thorns or such like things sticked in them, and that Loynds Wife took one of the Pictures down, but the other two Women that took down the rest he knoweth not. And being further asked what persons were at the aforesaid meeting, he nominated these persons following." Here follows a list of names of no interest to the modern reader. At the end of this deposition is one from the Father.

"Edmund Robinson of Pendle, Father of the aforesaid Edmund Robinson, Mason, informeth,

"That upon All Saints-day last he sent his Son the aforesaid Informer, to fetch home two kine to seal, and saith that his Son, staying longer than he thought he should have done, he went to seek him, and in seeking of him heard him cry pitifully, and found him so affrighted and distracted that he neither knew his Father nor did know where he was, and so continued very near a quarter of an hour before he came to himself. And he told this Informer his Father all the particular passages that are before declared in the said Robinson his Son's Information.

(Signed) "Richard Shuttleworth.
"John Starkey."

Who would dare to doubt such testimony as this? Here was another child of God grievously mishandled; and what might not be done to the servants of the devil who had so evilly intreated him? And was not Edmund Robinson evidently raised up and directed by God to be the scourge of all witches, and the great discoverer of their naughty pranks? So the lad was elevated to the post of witch-finder, and was taken about from church to church—accusing any who might strike his fancy or his fears, and sending them off to prison at the impulse of his childish will. Among other places he was brought to the parish church of Kildwick, where Webster was then curate. It was during the afternoon service, and the lad was put upon a stall to look the better about him, and discern the witches more clearly. After service Webster went to him and found him with "two very unlikely persons that did conduct him and manage the business:" the curate of Kildwick would have drawn him aside, but the men would not suffer this. Then said Webster, "'Good boy, tell me truly and in earnest, didst thou hear and see such strange things of the meeting of witches as is reported by many that thou dost relate, or did some person teach thee to say such things of thyself?' But the two men, not giving the boy leave to answer, did pluck him from me, and said he had been examined by two able Justices of the Peace, and they did never ask him such a question; to whom I replied, 'The persons accused had therefore the more wrong.'" So Webster got nothing by this, and the boy was not damaged nor his credit shaken. Very many persons were arrested on this young imp's accusations, beside those seventeen whom he had seen "syleing" butter and bacon from witch-ropes in the magic barn. And among the rest Jennet Device, (was she our old acquaintance of perjured memory?) who was charged with killing Isabelle, the wife of William Nutter; and Mary Spencer, who was in imminent danger for having "caused a pale or cellocke to come to her, full of water, fourteen yards up a hill from a well;" and Margaret Johnson, accused of killing Henry Heape, and wasting and impairing the body of Jennet Shackleton—but there was no proof against her, save certain witch marks, which, however, were indisputable, and on the finding of which she was soon brought to confess. She said that, seven or eight years since, she was in a mighty rage against life and the world in general, when there appeared to her the devil like a man, dressed all in black tied about with silk points, who offered her all she might wish or want in return for her soul; telling her that she might kill man or beast as she should desire, and take her revenge when she would; and that if she did but call "Mamillion" when she wanted him, he would come on the instant and do as he was bid. So "after a sollicitacion or two, she contracted and condicioned with the said devill or spiritt for her soul," and henceforth became one of the most notorious of the Lancashire witches. She confessed that she was at the great witch-meeting held at Harestones, in Pendle, on All Saints'-day last past, and again at another the Sunday after; and that all the witches rode there on horses, and went to consult on the killing of men and beasts; and that "there was one devill or spiritt that was more greate and grand devill than the rest, and yf anie witch desired to have such an one, they might have such an one to kill or hurt anie body." She said, too, which was a new idea on her part, that the sharp-boned witches were more powerful and malignant than those with "biggs" only; and then she wandered off, and accused certain of her neighbours, of whom one, "Pickhamer's wife, was the most greate, grand, and auncyent witch." Then she told her audience that if any witch desired to be carried to any place, a cat, or a dog, or a rod would convey them away; but not their bodies, only their souls in the likeness of their bodies. The judge was not quite satisfied with either Edmund Robinson's depositions or Margaret's confessions, and for all that the jury brought in a verdict of guilty, managed to get a reprieve, and to send up some of the accused to London. He managed also to interest the king, Charles I., who had not his father's craze on the subject; and Charles ordered the bishop to make a special examination of the case, and send in his report. By this time, too, Edmund and his father were separated, and the boy fully examined; when at last he confessed to the entire worthlessness and fraud of all he had said. He had been robbing an orchard of bullees (plums) more than a mile off the barn at the day and hour named; and, counselled by his father, had made up those wicked lies to screen himself. And then, finding the game profitable—for in a short time they made so good a thing by it that the father bought a couple of cows—he flew further a-field, and attacked every one within reach. Fortunately for his victims, the judge was a man of sense and independent judgment; so the judiciary records of England are stained with one crime the less, and the neighbours lost the excitement of an execution.

THE WITCH ON A PLANK.[129]

"Many are in a belief that this silly sex of women can by no means attaine to that so vile and damned a practise of Sorcery and Witchcraft, in regard of their illiteratenesse and want of learning, which many men have by great learning done;" nevertheless the Earl of Essex and his army, marching through Newberry, saw a feat done by a woman which not the most learned man of them all could have accomplished by natural means. Two soldiers were loitering behind the main body, gathering nuts, blackberries, and the like, when one climbed up a tree for sport, and the other followed him, jesting. From their vantage place, looking on the river, they there espied a "tall, lean, slender woman treading of the water with her feet with as much ease and firmnesse as if one should walk or trample on the earth." The soldier called to his companion, and he to the rest; and soon they all—captains, privates, and commanders alike—saw this marvellous lean woman, who now they perceived was standing on a thin plank, "which she pushed this way and that at her pleasure, making it a pastime to her, little perceiving who was on her tracks." Then she crossed the river, and the army after her; but there they lost her for a time, and when they found her all were too cowardly to seize her. At last one dare-devil went up and boldly caught her, demanding what she was. The poor wretch was dumb—perhaps with terror—and spoke nothing; so they dragged her before the commanders, "to whom, though she was mightily urged, she did reply as little." As they could bethink themselves of nothing better to do with her, they set her upright against a mud bank or wall, and two of the soldiers, at their captain's command,

---

[129] 'A most Certain Strange and true Discovery of a witch, being taken by some Parliamentary Forces as she was standing on a small planck-board and sayling on it over the River of Newberry. 1643.' Evidently a political matter, and perhaps with no substratum of truth in the story at all.

made ready and fired. "But with a deriding and loud laughter at them, she caught their bullets in her hands and chew'd them, which was a stronger testimony than her treading water that she was the same that their imagination thought her for to be." Then one of the men set his carbine against her breast and fired; but the bullet rebounded like a ball, and narrowly missed the face of the shooter, which "so enraged the Gentleman, that one drew out his sword and manfully run at her with all the force his strength had power to make, but it prevailed no more than did the shot, the woman though still speechlesse, yet in a most contemptible way of Scorn still laughing at them, which did the more exhaust their furie against her life; yet one amongst the rest had heard that piercing or drawing bloud from forth the veines that crosse the temples of the head, it would prevail against the strongest sorcery, and quell the force of Witchcraft, which was allowed for Triall: the woman, hearing this, knew then the Devill had left her, and her power was gone; wherefore she began alowd to cry and roare, tearing her haire, and making pitious moan, which in these words expressed were: And is it come to passe that I must dye indeed? Why then his Excellency the Earle of Essex shall be fortunate and win the field. After which no more words could be got from her; wherewith they immediately discharged a Pistoll underneath her eare, at which she straight sunk down and dyed, leaving her legacy of a detested carcasse to the wormes, her soul we ought not to iudge of, though the euills of her wicked life and death can scape no censure. Finis. This Book is not Printed according to order."

THE WITCH-FINDING OF HOPKINS.

And now the reign of Matthew Hopkins, of Mannington, gent., begins—that most infamous follower of an infamous trade—the witch-finder general of England. It was Hopkins who first reduced the practice of witch-finding to a science, and established rules as precise as any to be made for mathematics or logic. His method of proceeding was to "walk" a suspected witch between two inquisitors, who kept her from food and sleep, and incessantly walking, for four-and-twenty hours; or if she could not be thus walked she was cross-bound—her right toe fastened to her left thumb, and her left toe to her right thumb—care being taken to draw the cords as tightly as possible, and to keep her as uneasily, and in this state she was placed on a high stool or chair, kept without food or sleep for the prescribed four-and-twenty hours, and vigilantly watched. And Hopkins recommended that a hole be made in the door, through which her imps were sure to come to be fed, and that her watchers be careful to kill everything they saw—fly, spider, lice, mouse, what not; for none knew when and under what form her familiars might appear; and if by any chance they missed or could not kill them, then they might be sure that they were imps, and so another proof be indisputably established. If neither of these ways would do, then, still cross-bound, she was to be "swum." If she sank, she was drowned; if she floated—and by putting her carefully on the water she generally would float—then she was a witch, and to be taken out and hung. For water, being the sacred element used in baptism, thus manifestly refused to hold such an accursed thing as a witch within its bosom; so that, when she swam, it was a proof that this "sacred element" rejected her for the more potent keeping of the fire. This was the explanation which, it seemed to King James the First, was a rational and religious manner of accounting for a certain physical fact.

This, then, was the wise and liberal manner in which an impossible sin was discovered, and judgment executed, in those fatal years when Matthew Hopkins ruled the mind of England; yet years wherein Harvey was patiently at work on his grand physiological discovery, and when Wallis, and Wilkins, and Boyle were founding the Royal Society of liberal art and free discussion. It was only a piece of poetical justice that in the future he should be "swum" cross-bound in his own manner, and found to float according to the hydrostatics of witches. The shame and fear of this trial hastened the consumption to which he was hereditarily predisposed; and after this stringent test we hear no more of this vile impostor and impudent deceiver, this canting hypocrite, who cloaked his cruelty and covetousness under the garb of religion, and professed to be serving God and delivering man from the power of the devil when he was pandering to the worst passions of the time, and sacrificing to his own corrupt heart. The blood money, for which he sent so many hapless wretches to the gallows (he charged twenty shillings a town for his labours), though not an exceeding bribe, as he himself boasts, was money pleasantly earned and pleasantly spent; for what man would object to travel through a beautiful country, surrounded by friends, and carrying influence and importance wherever he went, and have all his expenses paid into the bargain?

In 1664[130] we find him at Yarmouth, accusing sixteen women in a batch, among whom was an old woman easily got to confess. She said she used to work for Mr. Moulton, a stocking merchant and alderman of the town; but one day, going for work, she found him from home, and his man refused to let her have any till his return, which would not be for a fortnight. She, being exasperated against the man, applied to the maid to let her have some knitting to do, but

---

[130] A collection of Modern Relations. 1693.

316

the maid gave her the like answer: upon which she went home sorely discontented with both. In the middle of the night some one knocked at the door: on her rising to open it she saw a tall black man, who told her that she should have as much work from him as she would, if she would write her name in his book. He then scratched her hand with a penknife, and filled the pen with her blood—guiding her hand while she made her mark. This done, he asked what he could do for her: but when she desired to have her revenge on Mr. Moulton's man, he told her he had no power over him, because he went constantly to church to hear Whitfield and Brinsley, and said his prayers morning and evening. The same of the maid; but there was a young child in the house more easy to be dealt with, for whom he would make an image of wax which then they must bury in the churchyard, and as the waxen image wasted and consumed, so would the child; which was done, and the child thrown into a languishing condition in consequence; so bad, indeed, that they all thought it was dying. But as soon as the witch confessed, the little one lifted up its head and laughed, and from that instant began to recover. The waxen image was found where she said she and the devil had buried it, and thus the whole of the charm was destroyed, and the child was saved; but the poor old crazy woman with her blackbird imp, and her fifteen compeers with their whole menagerie of imps, were hung at Yarmouth, amid the rejoicings of the multitude.

At Edmonsbury, that same year, another witch had a little black smooth imp dog, which she sent to play with the only child of some people she hated. At first the child refused to play with its questionable companion, but soon got used to its daily appearance, and lost all fear. So the dog-imp, watching its opportunity, got the boy one day to the water, when it dragged him underneath and drowned him. The witch was hanged: could they do less in such a clear case as this?

Another woman was hanged at Oxford for a story as wild as any to be found in Grimm or Mother Bunch. There were two sisters, left orphans but well provided for. The eldest, somewhat prodigal, married a man as bad or worse than herself, who spent her money and afterwards deserted her, leaving her with one child and in extreme poverty. The younger, being very serious and religious, waited for two or three years before she settled herself, then married a good, honest, sober farmer, with whom she lived well and prosperously; her gear increasing yearly, and herself the happy mother of a pretty child. Her sister was moved to envy to see all this prosperity and contentment, and in her passion made a compact with the devil, by which she became a witch for the purpose of killing her sister's child as the greatest despite she could do them. For this purpose she used to mount a bedstaff, which, by the uttering of certain magical words, carried her to her sister's room; but she could never harm the child, because it was so well protected by the prayers of its parents. Her own daughter, a little one of about seven, watched her mother in her antics with the bedstaff, and from watching took to imitating— going through the air one night after its dame, and in like fashion. However, it chanced that she was left behind in her uncle's house; so presently she fell a-crying, her powers being apparently limited to going, not including the magic words that insured the return. Her uncle and aunt, hearing a child cry where never a child should be, took a candle and discovered the whole matter. Next day the child was taken before the magistrate, to whom it told its tale, and the mother was apprehended. On the trial this little creature of seven years old was admitted as the chief evidence against her mother; and after they had made the poor woman mad among them, she confessed, and was hanged quite quietly. These were only two out of the hundreds whom that miserable man, Matthew Hopkins, gent., contrived to send to the gallows. Beaumont, in his Treatise on Spirits, mentions that "thirty-six were arraigned at the same time before Judge Coniers, An. 1645, and fourteen of them hanged, and an hundred more detained in several prisons in Suffolk and Essex." But the most celebrated and the saddest of all the trials in which Hopkins played a part was that of

THE MANNINGTREE WITCHES,

held before Sir Matthew Hale in 1645—Hopkins's great witch-year.

In a very scarce tract called 'A true and exact relation of the severall Informations, Examinations, and Confessions of the Late Witches Arraigned and Executed in the county of Essex, Published by Authoritie, and Printed by M. S. for Henry Overton and Benj. Allen, and are to be sold at their shops in Popes-head-alley, 1645,' is an account of these Manningtree witches. One John Rivet's wife, living in Manningtree, was taken sick and lame and with violent fits, and John swore before Sir Harbottel Grimston, one of the justices of the peace, that a cunning woman—wife of one Hovye at Hadleigh—told him that his wife was cursed by two women, near neighbours; of whom one was Elizabeth Clarke, *alias* Bedingfield. Elizabeth's mother, and others of her kinsfolk, had been hanged for witchcraft in the bygone years: so it ran in the blood, and it was not to be wondered at if it broke out afresh now. Sir Harbottel Grimston and Sir Thomas Bowes, the two Justices before whom this deposition was taken, then admitted the evidence of Matthew Hopkins of Manningtree, gentleman and witch-finder, who deposed to having watched Elizabeth Clarke last night, being the 24th of March, 1645, when he and one Master Sterne, who watched with him, saw some strange things which he would presently tell their worships of. Elizabeth told this deponent and his companion that if they would stay and do her no harm, she would call one of her imps, and play with it in her lap; which at first they refused, but afterwards consenting, there appeared to them "an Impe like to a Dog, which was white, with some sandy spots, and seemed to be very fat and plump, with very short legges, who forthwith vanished away." This was Jarmara. Then came Vinegar Tom, in the shape of a greyhound with very long legs; and then for a moment only came one for Master Sterne, a black imp which vanished instantly; then one like a polecat, only bigger.[131] Elizabeth now told them that she had five imps of her own, and two of Beldam West's, and that they sucked turn and turn about: now she was sucked by Beldam West's and now Beldam West by hers. She further said that Satan, whom she knew very much too well as "a proper Gentleman with a laced band, having the whole proportion of a Man," would never let her have any peace till she slew the hogs of Mr. Edwards of Manningtree, and Mr. Taylor's horse. When she had slain them Satan let her be quiet. Then of his own accord, Mr. Hopkins said that going from Mr. Edwards's house to his own, that night at nine or ten, he saw the greyhound which he had with him jump as if after a hare; and coming up hurriedly, there was a white thing like a "kitlyn," and his greyhound standing aloof from it; but by-and-by the white kitlyn came dancing round and about the greyhound, "and by all likelihood bit off a piece of the flesh of the shoulder of the greyhound; for the greyhound came shrieking and crying to this Informant, with a piece of fleshe torne from her shoulder." To crown all, coming into his own yard, Mr. Hopkins saw a thing like a black cat, only three times as big, sitting on the strawberry-bed

---

[131] Matthew's own account of them in a little tract called 'Certaine Queries Answered, which have been and are likely to be objected against Matthew Hopkins, in his way of finding out witches,' was slightly different.—1. Holt, like a white kitling.—2. Jarmara, a fat spaniel without any legs at all, which she said she kept fat, for he sucked good blood from her body.—3. Vinegar Tom, a long-legged greyhound with an head like an ox, a long tail and broad eyes, who, when Hopkins spoke to, and bade him go to the place provided for him and his angels, transformed himself into the shape of a child of foure years without a head, and gave half a dozen turns about the house and vanished at the door.—4. Sack-and-sugar, like a black rabbit; and 5. Newes, like a polecat. Also he said that no mortal could invent such names as Elemauzer, Pyewacket, Peck in the Crown, Griezel Greedigut, &c., which, however, one of our great word-masters, Charles Dickens, would find no difficulty in doing, and which certainly have no very infernal sound in them.

glaring at him; but when he went towards it, it leaped over the pale, ran right through the yard—his greyhound after it—then flung open a gate which was "underset with a paire of Tumbrell strings," and so vanished, leaving the greyhound in a state of extreme terror. Which, if there was any truth at all in these depositions, and they were not merely arbitrary lies, would make one suspect that Master Matthew Hopkins had been drinking, and knew a few of the phenomena of delirium tremens.

John Sterne, Matthew's slavey or attendant, then gave information. Watching with Matthew Hopkins, he asked Elizabeth Clarke if she were never afraid of her imps? to whom she made this notable answer, "What, doe you thinke I am afraid of my children?" His tale of imps was rather different to his patron's: they had consulted hurriedly, or John's memory was bad. The white imp was Hoult; Jarmara had red spots; Vinegar Tom was like a "dumbe Dogge;" and Sack-and-Sugar was a hard-working imp, which would tear Master John Sterne when it came. And it was well that Master Sterne was so quick, else this imp would have "soon skipped upon his face, and perchance had got into his throate, and then there would have been a feast of toades in this Informant's belly." Elizabeth had one imp, she said, for which she would fight up to her knees in blood before she would lose it; and when asked what the devil was like as a man, said he was a "proper man," a deal "properer" than Matthew Hopkins.

Other witnesses affirmed that if Elizabeth smacked with her mouth then a white cat-like imp, would come, and that they saw five more imps, named as above. And furthermore that she confessed that old Beldam, meaning Ann West—which was a very disrespectful way of speaking of her gossip—had killed Robert Oakes' wife and a clothier's child of Dedham, both of whom had died about a week since; and also that "the said old Beldam Weste had the wife of one William Cole of Mannintree in handling,

322

who deid not long since of a pining and languishing disease," and that she had raised the wind which sunk the hoy in which was Tom Turner's brother thirty months agone. She also said that Beldam West had taught her all she knew; for that one day as she was pitying her for her lameness—she had but one leg—and for her poverty, she told her how she might get imps and be rich, for that the imps would help her to a husband who would keep her ever after, so that she need not be put to such miserable shifts as gathering sticks for a living. Elizabeth Clarke then accused Elizabeth Gooding of being one of the tribe: and Robert Taylor came forward to give corroborative evidence against her. He said that nine weeks since, Elizabeth Gooding came to his shop for half a pound of cheese, on trust; that he denied it to her; whereupon she went away, "muttering and mumbling" to herself, and soon came back with the money. That very night his horse, which was in the stable, sound and in good condition, fell lame and in four days' time died of a strange disease, and Elizabeth Gooding was the cause thereof. Elizabeth Gooding "is a lewd woman, and to this Informant's knowledge, hath kept company with the said Elizabeth Clarke, Anne Leech, and Anne West, which Anne West hath been suspected for a Witch many years since, and suffered imprisonment for the same." Elizabeth Gooding contented herself with saying quietly that she was not guilty of any one particular charged upon her in the examination of the said Robert Taylor. Nevertheless she was executed at Chelmsford.

Richard Edwards said that twelve months since he was driving his cows near to the house of Anne Leech, widow, when they both fell down and died in two days; the next day his white cow fell down within a rod of the same place, and died in a week after. In August last his child was out at nurse at goodwife Wyles', who lived near Elizabeth Gooding and Elizabeth Clarke; which said child was taken very sick, with rolling of the eyes, strange fits, extending of the limbs, and in two days it died: and Elizabeth Gooding and Anne Leech were the cause of its death.

And now poor old Anne Leech was brought on the scene, to "confess," as so many wretched victims did. She said that she and Elizabeth Clarke and Elizabeth Gooding sent their imps to kill Mr. Edwards's black cow, and his white cow; she sent a grey imp, Elizabeth Clarke a black one, and Gooding a white; also that thirty years since she sent her grey imp to kill Mr. Bragge's two horses, because he had called her a naughty woman—and that the imps did their work without fear of failure. When these imps were abroad, she said, and after mischief, she had her health, but when they were unemployed and for ever hanging about her, she was sick. They often spoke to her in a hollow voice which she easily understood, and told her that she should never feel hell's torments: which it is very sure the poor old maniac never did. She and Gooding killed Mr. Edwards's child too; she with her white imp, and Elizabeth with her black one. She had her white imp about thirty years since, and a grey and a black as well, from "one Anne, the wife of Robert Pearce of Stoak in Suffolk, being her brother." Three years since she sent her grey imp to kill Elizabeth Kirk; and Elizabeth languished for about a year after and then died; the cause of her, Anne Leech's, malice being that she had asked of Elizabeth a coif, which she refused. The grey imp killed the daughter of Widow Rawlyns, because Widow Rawlyns had put her out of her farm; and she knew that Gooding had sent her imp to vex and torment Mary Taylor, because Mary refused her some beregood; but when she wanted to warn her, the devil would not let her. Lastly, she said, that about eight weeks ago she had met West and Gooding at Elizabeth Clarke's house "where there was a book read wherein she thinks there was no goodnesse."

So all these wretched creatures were hanged at Chelmsford, and the informants plumed themselves greatly on their evidence. But before their execution, poor Hellen Clark, wife of Thomas Clark, and daughter of Anne Leech, was "fyled." On the 4th of April, 1645, Richard Glascock gave information that he had heard a falling out between Hellen, and Mary wife of Edward Parsley, and that he "heard the said Hellen to say as the said Hellen passed by this Informant's door in the street, that Mary the daughter of the said Edward and Mary Parsley should rue for all, whereupon presently the said Mary, the daughter, fell sick and died within six weeks after." When Helen was arrested she made her confession glibly. She said that about six weeks since the devil came to her house in the likeness of a white dog by name Elimanzer, and that she fed him with milk porridge; that he spoke to her audibly, bidding her deny Christ and she should never want; which she did: but she did not kill Mary Parsley nevertheless. She was executed at Manningtree all the same as if she had spoken sober truth.

On the 23rd of the same month Prudence Hart came to the magistrates with an accusation. About eight weeks since, she said, being at church very well and healthful— some twenty weeks gone with child—she was suddenly taken with pains, and miscarried before she could be got home: and about two months since, being in bed, something fell upon her right side, but being dark she could not tell of what shape it was: but presently she was taken lame on that side, and with extraordinary pains and burning, and she believed that Anne West and Rebecca West, the daughter, were the cause of her pains. John Edes also swelled the count of accusations. He said that Rebecca had confessed to him that seven years since her mother incited her to intercourse with the devil, who had since appeared to her at divers times and in various shapes, but chiefly as a proper young man, desiring of her such things as proper young men are wont to desire of women; promising her that if she would yield to his wishes she

325

should have what she would, and especially should be avenged of her enemies; and that then Rebecca had demanded the death of Hart's son of Lawford, who, not long after, was taken sick and died. At which Rebecca had said "that shee conceived hee could do as God." And furthermore, that Rebecca said, while she lived at Rivenall her mother Anne came to her and said, "the Barley Corn was picked up," meaning one George Francis; and that shortly after George's father said his son was bewitched to death; to which Anne replied, "Be it unto him according to his faith." When Rebecca was called on the 21st of March, to answer to these charges, she confirmed all that John Edes had said, adding a few unimportant particulars which insured the execution of her mother in the August following; but in spite of her own confession she herself, though found guilty by the grand jury, was acquitted for life and death. Matthew Hopkins struck a few dashes of colour over the canvas, telling the judges that Rebecca had told him she was made a witch by her mother; and that when she met the four other goodies in Clarke's house, the devil, or their familiars, had come, now in the shape of a dog, then of two kittyns, then of two dogs—and that they first did homage to Elizabeth Clarke, skipping up into her lap and kissing her, and then to all the rest, kissing each one of them save Rebecca. Afterwards, when Satan came as a man, he gave her kisses enough: and not quite so innocently as the "kittyns and the dogges."

Susan Sparrow and Mary Greenliefe lived together. Each had a daughter thirteen or fourteen years old; and one night Susan Sparrow, being awake, heard Mary's child cry out, "Oh mother, now it comes, it comes! Oh helpe, mother, it hurts me, it hurts me!" So Susan said, "Goodwife Greenliefe, Goodwife Greenliefe, if your childe be asleep awaken it, for if anybody comes by and heare it make such moans (you having an ill name already), they will say you are suckling your Impes upon it." To which Mary replied that this was just what she was doing, and that she would "fee" with them (meaning her Imps), that one night they should suck her daughter, and one night Susan Sparrow's; which fell out as she said. For the very next night Susan's child cried out in the same manner as Mary's had done, and clasped her mother round the neck, much affrighted and shrieking pitifully. She complained of being pinched and nipped on her thigh; and in the morning there was a black and blue spot as broad and long as her hand. Susan Sparrow also said that the house where they lived was haunted by a leveret, which came and sat before the door; and knowing that Anthony Sharlock had a capital courser, she went and asked him to banish it for her. Whether the dog killed it or not she did not know; all that she did know was, that Goodman Merrill's dog coursed it but a short time before, but the leveret never stirred, and "just when the dog came at it he skipped over it, and turned about and stood still, and looked on it, and shortly after that dog languished and dyed. But whether this was an Impe in the shape of a Leveret, or had any relation to the said Mary, this Informant knows not, but does confesse shee wondered very much to see a Leveret, wilde by nature, to come so frequently and sit openly before the dore in such a familiar way." Mary was searched, and found marked with witch marks, but contented herself with quietly denying all knowledge of familiars, witchcraft, "bigges," and the like.

Mary Johnson was accused of having a familiar, in shape like a rat "without tayl or eares," which she used to carry about in her pocket, and set to rock the cradle. She kissed Elizabeth Otley's child, and gave it an apple, and the child sickened and died of fits; and Elizabeth herself had extraordinary pains, which left her when she had scuffled with Mary Johnson and gotten her blood. And she killed Annabell Durant's child by commending it as a pretty thing, stroking its face, and giving it a piece of bread and butter; and Annabell knew that she had been the death of the child, because, "setting up of broome in the outhouse after the little one had been taken, she saw the perfect representation of a shape just like Mary Johnson, and was struck with such a lamenesse in her Arms that she was not able to bow her arms, and so continued speechless all that day and night following. Mary came also as the noise of a Hornet, to the room where Annabell's husband lay sick, for he cried out, 'It comes, it comes! Now Goodwife Johnson's Impe is come! Now she hath my life!'" And immediately a great part of the wall fell down. So was not Mary Johnson an undoubted witch with all this testimony against her?

Anne Cooper was executed at Manningtree because she had three black imps, by name Wynow, Jeso, and Panu; because she gave her daughter Sarah a grey imp like a kite, and called Tomboy, telling her there was a cat for her to play with; because she cursed a colt and it broke its neck directly after; and because she sent one of her imps to kill little Mary Rous—which it did. Elizabeth Hare was condemned, but afterwards reprieved, for giving two imps to Mary Smith. The poor old woman "praying to God with her hands upward, that if she was guilty of any such thing, He would show some example on her, presently after she shaked and quivered, and fell to the ground backward, and tumbled up and down the ground, and hath continued sick ever since."

Old Margaret Moone had twelve imps, but her informants could only remember the names of "Jesus, Jockey, Sandy, Mrs. Elizabeth, and Collyn." Her imps killed cows and babes; spoiled brewings; broke horses' necks; bewitched "aples" so that the eaters thereof died; sent Rawbodd's wife such a plague of lice that they might have been swept off her clothes with a stick; and did other maleficent things, proper to imps and witches. When searched she was found to have "bigges" where the imps sucked; and confessed the same, saying that "if she might have some bread and beere she would call her said Impes;

which being given unto her, she put the bread into the beere and set it against a hole in the wall, and made a circle round about the pot, and then cried, Come Christ, come Christ, come Mounsier, come Mounsier." No imps appearing, she said her daughters had carried them off in a white bag, and demanded that the said daughters might be "searched," "for they were naught." They were searched, and were found witch-marked. Margaret denied all the charges against herself, but was condemned nevertheless; and only escaped the executioner's hands by dying on her way to the gallows.

Judith Moone helped her mother a step gallowsward by a rambling, pointless confession about some wood, and how her mother threatened her, and how something seemed to come about her legs that night; but when she searched she found nothing; so Judith Moone probably died because she did not know how to distinguish a false sensation from a true one.

Elizabeth Harvey, widow, Sarah Hating, wife, Marian Hocket, widow, were "searched:" the first two were marked, the last not, but yet was the worst witch of all, for she had made Elizabeth Harvey as bad as herself by bringing her three things the bigness of mouses, which she said were "pretty things," and to be made use of. As for Sarah Hating, she had sent Francis Stock's wife a snake, which the said wife espied lying on a shelf, and strove to kill with a spade, but the snake was too quick for her and vanished away; so Francis Stock's wife was taken sick, and within one week died. A daughter was taken ill immediately after her mother, and she also died, and then another child; all because Francis Stock had impressed Sarah Hating's husband for a soldier, and Sarah Hating was angered. Marian Hocket was told on by her own sister, Sarah Barton, who said that she had given her three imps, "Littleman, Prettyman, and Dainty." They were all executed, Sarah and Marian denying their guilt, but

Elizabeth Harvey sticking to her tale of the three mouses which Marian had brought her, and which sucked her.

Rose Hallybread bewitched Robert Turner's servant so that he crowed like a cock, barked like a dog; groaned beyond the ordinary course of nature, and, though but a youth, struggled with such strength that four or five men could not hold him. Says Rose, fifteen or sixteen years ago, Goodwife Hagtree brought an imp to her house which she nourished on oatmeal, and suckled according to the manner of witches, for the space of a year and a half—when she lost it; then Joyce Boanes brought her another, as a small grey bird, which she carried to Thomas Toakley's house in St. Osyth, putting it into a cranny of the door, so that his son should die, as he did—crying out all the time that Rose Hallybread had killed him. She then accused Susan Cocks and Margaret Landish, and died in prison, cheating the hangman.

Old Joyce Boanes now took up the tale. She had two imps like mouses she said, and they killed the lambs at the farm-house called Cocket-wick, and one of these imps called "Rug" she took to Rose Hallybread, that they might torment Turner's servant. Wherefore her imp made him bark like a dog; Rose Hallybread's "inforced him to sing sundry tunes in his great extremity of paines;" Susan Cock's compelled him to crow like a cock; and Margaret Landish's made him groan. Poor old Joyce Boanes was hanged in return for her drivelling ravings.

So was Susan Cock; who confirmed all that had gone before, adding only that the night her mother died she gave her two imps, one like a mouse "Susan," the other yellow and like a cat "Besse," with which she did sundry acts of spite and damage. Wherefore Susan was put out of the way of further harm. Margaret Landish knew not much about the matter, but was executed nevertheless, for having bewitched Thomas Hart's child—incited thereto by the girl's pointing at her and crying "There goes Pegg the witch!" upon which Peg turned back and clapped her hands in a threatening manner, saying "she should smart for it," and that very night the child fell sick in a raving manner, and died within three weeks after; often in its fits crying out that "Pegg the witch was by the bedside making strange mouths at her."

Rebecca Jones owned to knowing the devil as a handsome young man, who pricked her wrist and made her his in soul and body. This was about four or five and twenty years ago, when living with John Bishop as his servant. About three months since too, going to St. Osyth to sell her master's butter, she met a man in a ragged suit and with such great eyes that she was afraid of him, and he gave her three things like "moules," having four feet apiece but no tails, and black, which he told her to nurse carefully and feed on milk. Their names were Margaret, Anie, and Susan, and they killed cows and sheep and hogs, and revenged her on her enemies. So Rebecca was hanged as befitted.

Johan Cooper, widow, had three imps, two like mouses and one like a frog; their names were "Prickeare, Robyn, and Frog," and they killed men and beasts. Wherefore she too was hanged like the rest.

Anne Cate had four, given her by her mother twenty years ago, "James, Prickeare, Robyn, and Sparrow:" the first three like mouses, and the fourth like a sparrow; and they did evil and mischief and killed all whom she would. She was hanged too.

At the end of the tract is a very curious bit of evidence, given by an honest man of Manningtree, one Goff, a glover, concerning old Anne West, then on her trial. He said that one moonlight morning, about four o'clock, as he was passing Anne West's house, the door being open, he looked in and saw three or four little things like black rabbits which came skipping towards him. He struck at them, but missed; when, by better luck, he caught one in his

331

hand and tried to wring its head off; but "as he wrung and stretched the neck of it, it came out betweene his hands like a lock of wooll," so he went to drown it at a spring not far off. But still as he went he could not hinder himself from falling down, so that at last he was obliged to creep on his hands and knees, till he came to the water, when he held the imp for a long space underneath, till he conceived it was drowned, but, "letting goe his hand, it sprang out of the water up into the aire, and so vanished away." Coming back to Anne West's, he found her standing at her door in terrible undress, and to his complaint of why did she send her imps to molest him? she answered "that they were not sent out to trouble him, but as Scouts upon another designe."

But one of the most painful murders of the Hopkins Session was that of old Mr. Lewis,[132] the "Reading Parson" of Franlingham; a fine old man of good character, but generally regarded as a Malignant, because he preferred to read Queen Elizabeth's Homilies instead of composing nasal discourses of his own, of the kind so dear to the Puritan party: wherefore the authorities and Matthew Hopkins—who was a devout Puritan—had their eyes upon him, and were not disposed to be lenient. He was swum in Hopkins's manner, cross-bound; set on a table cross-legged; kept several nights without sleep, and twenty-four hours without food; run backwards and forwards in the room, two men holding him, until he was out of breath; "pricked" and searched for marks; after all which barbarity it is not surprising to find that the poor old Reading Parson of eighty-five "confessed." Yes, he had made a compact with the devil and sealed it with his blood; and he had two imps that sucked him, one of which, the yellow dun imp, was always urging him to do some mischief, but the other was more amiable. Accordingly, to please the yellow dun

---

[132] Baxter, Hutchinson, &c.

he had one day sent it to sink an Ipswich ship, which he spied out in the offing: a commission which the imp executed with zeal and precision before the eyes of a whole beach full of spectators. This Ipswich ship was one of many that rode safely enough in the calm sea, but the imp troubled the waters immediately about her, and down she went like a stone, as all present could testify. Asked if he had not grieved to make so many—they were fourteen—widows in a few moments he said "No, he was glad to have pleased his imp." This confession and various witch "bigges" found on him were held proofs conclusive; and Mr. Lewis was condemned to be hanged; his eighty years, and his gown, protecting him nowise. As soon as he was a little refreshed he denied all the ravings he had been induced to utter, read the burial service for himself with cheerfulness and courage, and met his death calmly and composedly; perhaps not sorry to resign into God's keeping a life which Matthew Hopkins and the Puritans were rendering intolerable.

A Penitent Woman[133] of the same time confessed that when her mother lay sick a thing like a mole ran into bed to her. She, the Penitent Woman, started, but her mother told her not to fear, but to take the mole and keep it, saying, "Keep this in a pot by the fire, and thou shalt never want." The daughter did as she was bid, and made the mole comfortable in its pot. And after she had done this, a seemingly poor boy came in and asked leave to warm himself by the fire. When he went away she found some money under the stool whereon he had sat. This happened many times, and so her mother's promise and her imp brought the poor penitent romancer Barmecidal good luck. It could not have been much, for Hopkins, or at least his friend and comrade John Sterne, says in the examination of Joan Ruccalver, of Powstead, Suffolk, that "six shillings

---

[133] Baxter.

was the largest amount he had ever known given by an imp to its dame."

That all this seemed right and rational in the eyes of sane men is one of the most marvellous things connected with the delusion: that well-educated Englishmen should send such a wretch as Matthew Hopkins with legal authorisation to prick witches, associating with him Mr. Calamy "to see that there was no fraud:" that they should arraign miserable old women by scores, and hang them by dozens: and that Baxter should gravely argue for the validity of ghosts and spectres on the plea that "various Creatures must have a various Situation, Reception, and Operation: the Fishes must not dwell in our cities nor be acquainted with our affairs"—strikes me chiefly with amazement at the marvellous imbecility of superstition. It is well for the leaders of sects to bid us cast down our reason before blind faith; for, assuredly, our reason, which is the greatest gift of God, pleads loudly against the follies of belief and the vital absurdities into which religionists fall when unchecked by common sense. It was only the "Atheists" and "Sadducees," as they were called, who at last managed to put a stop to this hideous delusion: all the pious believers upheld the holy need of searching for witches, and of not suffering them to live wherever they might be found. All sects and denominations of Christians joined in this, and found a meeting-place of brotherly love and concord beneath the witches' gallows. And though one's soul revolts most at the so-called "Reformed Party," because of the greater unctuousness of their piety, and their mighty professions, yet they were all equally guilty, one with the other; all equally steeped to the lips in insanest superstition. The temper of the times has so far changed now that men and women are no longer hung because they have mesmeric powers, or because hysterical and epileptic patients utter wild ravings: but the thing remains the same; there is the same amount of superstition still afloat, if somewhat altered in its direction; and modern Spiritualism, which has come to supersede Witchcraft, is, when it is true at all and not mere legerdemain, as little understood and as falsely catalogued as was ever the art of magic and sorcery.

THE HUNTINGDON IMPS.

In another very scarce tract by "J. D." (John Davenport) "present at the trial," we come to a strange and mournful group of judicial murders that took place in Huntingdon, 1646. First, there was Elizabeth Weed, of Great Catworth, who confessed that twenty-one years ago, as she was saying her prayers, three spirits came suddenly to her, one of which was like a man or youth, and the other two like puppies, of which one was white and the other black. The young man asked her if she would renounce God and Christ: to which she assented, her faith being weak; and then the devil promised that she should do all the mischief she would, if she would covenant to give him her soul at the end of twenty-one years. She assented to this too; and sealed the bargain with her blood. He drew the blood from under her left arm, and "a great lump of flesh did rise there, and has increased ever since;" and the devil scribbled with her blood, and the covenant was signed and sealed. The name of her white imp, like a puppy, was "Lilly," of the black "Priscille;" and the office of the white was to hurt man, woman, and child, but of the black to hurt cattle. The man spirit's function was that of her husband, in which relation she lived with him to her great satisfaction. Lilly killed Mr. Henry Bedell's child, and Priscille sundry cattle; but she had not had much good of the bargain, for the twenty-one years were to be out next Low Sunday, when her soul would be required of her and the devil would take her away; and she desired to be rid of the burden of her life before then. The judges acquiesced in her desire: which a little good food and careful watching would have proved to them was but the phantasy of disease; and the hangman had her body, though no devil took her soul, and her sufferings and her sins vexed the universe no more.

John Winnick's confession is one of the most graphic and extraordinary of any in the tract. I give it word for word as I found it.

"The examination of John Winnick, of Molseworth in the said County, Labourer, taken upon the 11th day of Aprill, 1646, before Robert Bernard, Esquire, one of His Majesties Justices of the Peace for this County. Hee saith, that about 29 yeares since, the 29th yeare ending about Midsommer last past, he being a Batchellour, lived at Thropston with one Buteman, who then kept the Inne at the George, and withall kept Husbandry: this Examinate being a servant to him in his Husbandry, did then loose a purse with 7s. in it, for which he suspected one in the Family. He saith that on a Friday being in the barne, making hay-bottles for his horses about noon, swearing, cursing, raging, and wishing to himselfe that some wise body (or Wizzard) would helpe him to his purse and money again: there appeared unto him a Spirit, blacke and shaggy, and having pawes like a Beare, but in bulk not fully so big as a Coney. The Spirit asked him what he ailed to be so sorrowfull, this Examinate answered that he had lost a purse and money, and knew not how to come by it again. The Spirit replied, if you will forsake God and Christ and fall down and worship me for your God, I will help you to your purse and money again. This Examinate said he would, and thereupon fell down upon his knees and held up his hands. Then the Spirit said, to-morrow about this time of the day, you shall find your purse upon the floor where you are now making bottles, I will send it to you, and will also come my selfe. Whereupon this Examinate told the Spirit he would meete him there, and receive it, and worship him. Whereupon at the time prefixed, this Examinate went unto the place, and found his purse upon the floore, and tooke it up, and looking afterwards into it, he found there all the money that was formerly lost: but before he had looked into it, the same Spirit appears unto him and said, there is your purse and your money in it: and then this Examinate fell downe upon his knees and said, My Lord and God I thanke you. The said Spirit at that time brought with him two other Spirits for shape, bignesse, and colour, the one like a white Cat, the other like a grey Coney; and while this Examinate was upon his knees, the Beare Spirit spake to him, saying, you must worship these two Spirits as you worship me, and take them for your Gods also: then this Examinate directed his bodie towards them, and called them his Lords and Gods. Then the Beare Spirit told him that when he dyed he must have his soule, whereunto this Examinate yielded. Hee told him then also that they must suck of his body, to which this Examinate also yielded; but they did not sucke at that time. The Beare Spirit promised him that he should never want victuals. The Cat Spirit that it would hurt Cattel when he would desire it. And the Coney-like Spirit that it would hurt men when he desired. The Bear Spirit told him that it must have some of his blood wherewith to seale the Covenant, whereunto this Examinate yielded, and then the beare Spirit leapt upon his shoulder, and prickt him on the head, and from thence tooke blood; and after thus doing, the said three spirits vanisht away. The next day about noone, the said Spirits came to him while hee was in the field, and told him they were come to suck of his body, to which he yielded, and they suckt his body at the places where the marks are found, and from that time to this, they have come constantly to him once every 24 hours, sometimes by day, and most commonly by night. And being demanded what mischiefe he caused any of the said spirits to do, he answered never any, onely hee sent his beare Spirit to provoke the maid-servant of Mr. Say of Molmesworth, to steale victualls for him out of her Master's house, which she did, and this Examinate received the same.

The marke of
John Winnicke
Rob. Bernard.

He was hanged, 1646.

Eight years before this—namely, in 1638—Frances Moore had a black puppy imp of Margaret Simson of Great Catworth, which she called Pretty, and whose office was to harm cattle. Then Goodwife Weed gave her a thing like a white cat, called Tissy, saying, if she would deny God and affirm the same by her blood, to whomsoever she sent this cat, and cursed, would die. So she cursed William Foster, who, sixteen years ago would have hanged two of her children because they offered to take a piece of bread; and he died: but she could not remember what the cat imp did to him. Poor old creature! such naïve little bits of truth and scientific direction come out in the midst of all the wildness and raving of the "examined!"—such little quiet bits of unconscious common sense, to redeem the whole account from the mere maunderings of lunacy! Frances Moore did not remember what her imp did to William Foster, yet she went on to say that she got tired of having them about her, and killed them both a year since; but they haunted her still, and when she was apprehended crept up her clothes and tortured her so that she could not speak.

Elizabeth Chandler, widow, had something that came to her in a "puffing and roaring manner," and that now hurt her sorely. She denied that she ever spoiled Goodwife Darnell's furmety, but Goodwife Darnell, by causing her to be ducked, she did heartily desire to be revenged on. She had been troubled with these roaring things for a quarter of a year, and had two imps besides, one called "Beelzebub," and the other "Trullibub." This she denied when asked, while sane and awake, saying that "Beelzebub was a logg of wood and Trullibub a stick." But the neighbours testified against her, so her denial went for naught.

Ellen Shepheard had four iron-grey rat imps that sucked her; and Anne Desborough had two—mouses—Tib and Jone, one brown and the other white. She had been told to forsake God and Christ, and that she would then have her will on men and cattle; as she did, and got her mouse imps in consequence.

Jane Wallis saw a man in black clothes, about six weeks since, as she was making her bed. She bid him civilly good morning, and asked him his name. He told her it was "Blackeman," and, in turn, asked her if she was poor. Yes, she said "she was." Then he would send her two imps said he, Grissel and Greedigut, that should do anything for her she would. At this moment, Jane, looking up, saw he had ugly feet, and was fearful; still more fearful when he became at one moment bigger and at another less, and then suddenly vanished. Grissel and Greedigut came in the shape of "dogges, with great brisles of hogges hair upon their backs." They said they came from Blackeman to do whatever she might command: and sometimes all three of them—the two dogs and the man—brought her two or three shillings at a time; and once they robbed a man and pulled him from his horse.

On September 25, 1645,[134] Joan Walliford confessed before the major and other jurates, "that the divell, about seven yeares agoe did appeare to her in the shape of a little dog, and bid her to forsake God and leane to him; who replied, that she was loath to forsake him." Still, she wished to be revenged on Thomas Letherland and Mary Woodrufe, now his wife; and as "Bunne," the devil, promised she should not lack, and did actually send her money, she knew not whence—sometimes a shilling and sometimes eightpence, "never more"—devil-worship did not seem such a bad trade after all. She further said that her retainer, Bunne, once carried Thomas Gardler out of a window; and

---

[134] Tract.

that twenty years ago she promised her soul to the devil, and that he wrote the covenant between them in her blood, promising to be her servant for that space of time, which time was now almost expired; that Jane Hot, Elizabeth Harris, and Joan Argoll, were her fellows; that Elizabeth Harris curst the boat of one John Woodcott, "and so it came to passe;" that Goodwife Argoll, curst Mr. Major and John Mannington, and so it came to pass in these cases too; and that Bunne had come to her twice since in prison, and sucked her "in the forme of a muce." So poor Joan Walliford was hanged, and at the place of execution exhorted all good people to take warning by her, and not to suffer themselves to be deceived by the divell, neither for love of money, malice, or anything else, as she had done, but to sticke fast to God; for if she had not first forsaken God, God would not have forsaken her.

Joan Cariden, widow, said that about three quarters of a year since, "as she was in the bed about twelve or one of the clocke in the night, there lay a 'rugged soft thing' upon her bosome which was very soft, and she thrust it off with her hand; and she saith that when she had thrust it away she thought God forsooke her, and she could never pray so well since as she could before; and further saith that shee verily thinks it was alive." On a second examination she said that the divell came to her in the shape of a "black rugged Dog in the night time, and crept into the bed to her, and spake to her in a mumbling tongue." Two days after she made further revelations of how "within these two daies," she had gone to Goodwife Pantery's house, where were other good wives, and where the divell sat at the upper end of the table.

Jane Hot said that a thing like a "hedg-hog" had usually visited her for these twenty years. It sucked her in her sleep, and pained her, so that she awoke: and lay on her breast, when she would strike it off. It was as soft as a cat. On coming into the gaol she was very urgent on the others to confess, but stood out sturdily for her own innocence;

saying, "that she would lay twenty shillings that if she was swum she would sink." She was swum and she floated; whereat a gentleman asked her "how it was possible that she could be so impudent as not to confesse herselfe?" to whom she answered, "That the Divell went with her all the way, and told her that she should sinke; but when she was in the Water he sat upon a Crosse beame, and laughed at her." "*These three were executed on Munday last*," says the tract in emphatic italics.

It now came to the turn of Elizabeth Harris. She said that nineteen years ago the devil came to her in the form of a muse (mouse) and told her she should be revenged. And she was revenged on all who offended her; on Goodman Chilman, who said she had stolen a pigge, and who therefore she wished might die—and her Impe destroyed him; on Goodman Woodcot, in whose High (hoy?) her son had been drowned, when "she wished that God might be her revenger, which was her watchword to the Divell"—and the hoy was cast away, as she conceived, in consequence of her wish. And did not Joan Williford's imp tell her that "though the Boate went chearfully oute it should not come so chearfully home?" She said further that sundry good wives, named, had "ill tongues;" and that she had made a covenant with the devil, written in the blood which she had scratched with her nails from out her breast.

Alexander Sussums of Melford, Sussex, said he had things which drew his marks, and that he could not help being a witch, for all his kindred were naught—his mother and aunt hanged, his grandmother burnt, and ten others questioned and hanged. At Faversham about this time, three witches were hanged, one of whom had an imp-dog, Bun; and on the 9th of September[135] Jane Lakeland was burnt at Ipswich for having bewitched to death her husband, and Mrs. Jennings' maid, who once refused her a needle and

---

[135] 'The Laws against Witches.' Published by Authority, 1645.

dunned her for a shilling. Jane Lakeland had contracted with the devil twenty years ago. He came to her when between sleeping and waking, speaking to her in a hollow voice, and offering her her will if she would covenant with him. To which she, assenting, he then stroke his claw into her hand and with her blood wrote out the covenant. She had bewitched men and women and cows and corn, and sunk ships, and played all the devilries of her art, but remained ever unsuspected, holding the character of a pious woman, and going regularly to church and sacrament. She had three imps—two little dogs and a mole—and Hopkins burnt her as the best way of settling the question of her sanity or disease.

It would have been well for all these poor people if their respective judges—Sir Matthew Hale included—had had only as much liberality and common sense as Mr. Gaule, the minister of Stoughton in Huntingdonshire; for though Gaule was no wise minded to give up his belief either in the devil or in witches, he utterly repudiated Matthew Hopkins and his tribe and his ways, and condemned his whole manner of proceeding, from first to last. He preached against him, and when he heard a rumour of his visiting Stoughton he strongly opposed him, whereupon Matthew wrote this insolent letter, which Mr. Gaule printed as a kind of preface to his book of "Select Cases," put out soon after.

"My Service to your Worship presented. I have this Day received a letter, &c., to come to a Town called Great Stoughton, to search for evil disposed Persons, called Witches (though I heare your Minister is farre against us through Ignorance:) I intend to come the sooner to heare his singular Judgement in the Behalfe of such Parties; I have known a Minister in Suffolk preach as much against this Discovery in a Pulpit, and forced to recant it, (by the Committee) in the same place. I much marvaile such evil Members should have any (much more any of the Clergy) who should dayly preach Terrour to convince such Offenders, stand up to take their Parts, against such as are Complainants for the King and Sufferers themselves, with their Families and Estates. I intend to give your Towne a visite suddenly. I am to come to Kimbolton this Week, and it shall be tenne to one, but I will come to your Town first, but I would certainly know afore, whether your Town affords many Sticklers for such Cattell, or willing to give and afford as good Welcome and Entertainment, as other where I have beene, else I shall wave your Shire, (not as yet beginning in any Part of it myself) and betake me to such Places, where I doe, and may persist without Controle, but with Thanks and Recompense. So I humbly take my leave and rest, Your Servant to be Commanded,

"Matthew Hopkins."

I have not been able to find what was the result of this letter, but I do not suppose that Hopkins, who was a great coward like all tyrants, cared to brave even the small danger of one minister's opposition, not knowing how many "sticklers for such cattle" might be at his back. In his Apology, or "Certaine Queries Answered, which have been and are likely to be objected against Matthew Hopkins, in his way of finding out Witches," he says that "he never went to any towne or place, but they rode, writ, or sent often for him, and were (for ought he knew) glad of him;" and if this was true, Mr. Gaule most likely was rid of him at Great Stoughton, and one rood of English land left undefiled. Besides, his hands were full elsewhere; for when we think that at Bury St. Edmunds eighteen persons were hanged on one day alone, and a hundred and twenty more left lying in prison, all through his instrumentality, we must imagine that he had enough to do in places where he was caressed and desired, not to forbear troubling those where he was abhorred and might run some danger.

MR. CLARK'S EXAMPLES.

A few other men, too, were about as sane as Mr. Gaule
on this maddest of all mad subjects. Mr. Clark, a minister—
and the ministers were generally the worst—had a
marvellous allowance of common sense, remembering the
times. A certain parishioner of his cried out that she was
grievously beset by a neighbour who came in the spirit, that
is, as an apparition, to teaze and torment her. Mr. Clark, the
minister, knew the accused woman, and believed in her
innocency; but it happened one day, by one of those
curious coincidences which, by-the-bye, are so often
exaggerated into far more significance than they deserve,
that the suspected woman while milking her cow was
struck by it on the forehead, and naturally fell a-bleeding.
At that moment, or said to be at that moment, her "spectre"
appeared to the afflicted person, and she, pointing out the
place where it stood, desired some of those who were with
her to strike at it. They did so, and she said they fetched
blood. Hereupon a posse of them went to the supposed
witch, and found her with her forehead bleeding, just as the
afflicted had said. There was no question now of doubt, and
they rushed off to Mr. Clark to tell them what they had
seen, and demand that she be put to the proof. Mr. Clark
went to the woman and asked what had made her forehead
bleed? She told him, a blow from her cow's horn;
"whereby he was satisfy'd that it was a Design of Satan to
render an innocent person suspected." Another instance of
the same kind of thing happened at Cambridge. A man
believed that a certain widow sent her imps, as cats, to
bewitch and torment him. One night as he lay in bed one of
these imps came within reach, and he struck it on the back:
when it vanished away, as was to be expected. The next
day the man sent to inquire of his old enemy, and found
that she had a sore back; at which he rejoiced exceedingly,
having now in his hands the clew which would guide him

to revenge and her to justice and the scaffold. But Mr. Day, her surgeon, stopped his triumph before it was ripe, and cut the clew before it had spun out; telling him that the sore back was nothing but a boil, which had gathered, headed, and healed, like any other boil, and that it could have had no connexion whatever with the blow which he had so valiantly given the cat-imp when in bed. So this bit of cruelty was put a stop to, and the poor old creature, with a boil on her back, slept her last sleep unhastened by the hangman. Another wretched being who had been kept without sleep or food for twenty-four hours, pricked, tried, and tortured into a state of temporary imbecility, at last confessed to her imp Nan; but a gentleman in the neighbourhood, very indignant at the folly and barbarity of the whole thing, rescued the poor victim, and made her eat some meat and go to sleep. When she woke up she said she knew nothing of what she had confessed, but that she had a pullet which she sometimes called Nan, and which of a surety was no imp, but an honest little hen that had to lay good eggs some day, and be eaten at table when her work was done.

THE NEWCASTLE PRICKERS.

Hopkins was not the only one of his trade in England, for Ralph Gardner, in his "England's Grievance Discovered" (1655), speaks of two prickers, Thomas Shovel and Cuthbert Nicholson, who, in 1649 and 1650, were sent by the Newcastle magistrates into Scotland, there to confer with a very able man in that line, and bring him back to Newcastle. They were to have twenty shillings, but the Scotchman three pounds, per head of all they could convict, and a free passage there and back. When these wretches got to any town—for they tried all the chief market towns of the district—the crier used to go round with his bell, desiring "all people that would bring in any complaint against any woman for a witch, they should be sent for and tryed by the person appointed." As many as thirty women were brought at once into the Newcastle town-hall, stript, pricked, and twenty-seven set aside as guilty. This said witch-finder told Lieut.-Colonel Hobson that "he knew women, whether they were witches or no, by their looks; and when the said person was searching of a personable and good-like woman, the said Colonel replyed and said, Surely this woman is none, and need not be tried; but the Scotchman said she was, for all the Town said she was, and therefore he would try her: and presently, in sight of all the people, laid her body naked to the Waste, with her cloaths over her head, by which Fright and Shame all her bloud contracted into one part of her body, and then he ran a Pin into her Thigh, and then suddenly let her Coats fall, and then demanded whether she had nothing of his in her body, but did not bleed, but she, being amazed, replied little, and then he put his hand up her coats and pulled out the pin and set her aside as a guilty person and child of the Devil, and fell to try others, whom he made guilty. Lieut.-Colonel Hobson, perceiving the alteration of the foresaid woman by her blood settling in her right parts, caused that woman to be brought again, and her cloaths pulled up to her Thigh, and required the Scot to run the pin in the same place, and then it gushed out of blood, and the said Scot cleared her, and said she was not a child of the Devil."

If this Scotch witch-finder had not been stopped he would have found half the women in the north country witches; at last Henry Ogle got hold of him, and "required Bond of him to answer the Sessions;" but he got away to Scotland, and so escaped for the time. Fifteen women lay in prison, charged by him, and were executed—all protesting their innocence; and "one of them, by name Margaret Brown, beseeched God that some remarkable sign might be seen at the time of their execution, to evidence their innocency; and as soon as ever she was turned off the Ladder her blood gushed out upon the people to the admiration of the beholders." Which touching little history we must relegate to the realms of fable and delusion, like others just as sad and supernatural. This precious wretch (was it John Kincaid?) was hung in Scotland, when the magistrates and people had got tired of him and his cruelty, and at "the gallows he confessed that he had been the death of two hundred and twenty men and women in England and Scotland, simply for the sake of the twenty shillings a head blood-money." Truly it was time for brave Ralph Gardner to write his bold and scorching "England's Grievance Discovered," when such monstrous crimes as these might be done without even the colour of a monstrous law.

In "Sykes's Local Records" mention is made of a curious little entry in the parish books of Gateshead, near Newcastle: "Paid as M^{ris} Watson's when the Justices call to examine witches, 3^s 4^d; for a graue for a witch, 6^d; for trying the witches, £1. 5." This was in 1649, in which year Jean Martin, "the myller's wyfe of Chattim," was executed for a witch, and the authorities of Berwick sent for the witch-finder to come and try witches there, promising that no violence should be done him by the townspeople. In the parish register of Hart, under the date of July 28, 1582, the office of Master Chancellor against Allison Lawe, of Hart, was brought into requisition. Allison was "a notourious sorcerer and enchanter," but was pulled up in the midst of her evil career, and sentenced to a milder punishment than she would have had a century later. Notorious witch and enchanter as she was, all she had to suffer was open penance once in the market-place at Durham, with a paper on her head setting forth her offences, once in Hart church, and once in Norton church; but what was the award to Janet Bainbridge and Jannet Allinson, of Stockton, "for asking counsell of witches, and resorting to Allison Lawe for the cure of the sicke," we are not told. The madness which possessed all men's minds in the next century had not then begun to rage: the storm that was to burst over the world was then giving forth only its warning mutterings, and it was reserved for a later age, with all its progress in art and science and freedom of thought and religious knowledge, to lay the coping-stone to the most monstrous temple of iniquity which fear has ever raised to ignorance. It is a humiliating thought; humiliating, too, the milder phases of this same fury which have so often possessed society; but it must be remembered that, though each wave of the tide recedes, each succeeding wave dashes farther over the reach, and the long lines of sea-wrack mark the point of progress as well as the point of declension.

THE WITCH IN THE BRAKE.[136]

At Droitwich, in Worcestershire, a boy, looking for his mother's cow, saw a bush in a brake move as if something was there. Thinking it to be his mother's cow he went to the place, but found no cow, only an old woman who cried "Ooh!" and so frightened the lad that he could not speak intelligibly. But no one knew what he meant by his strange mouthings and mutterings, until one day, seeing the old woman eating porridge before Sir Edward Barret's door, he rushed up to her, and flung her porridge in her face, and otherwise behaved violently and ill. The neighbours, thinking there was something in it, apprehended her as a witch, and took her to the Checker Prison. At night, the mother of the boy, hearing a great noise overhead, ran up stairs and found her son with the leg of a form in his hand, fighting furiously with something in the window; but what it was she could not see. He then put on his clothes and ran to the prison, midway recovering his speech. When he got there he found that the gaoler had kept the witch without food or sleep till she would say the Lord's Prayer and "God bless the boy:" which pious exercise she had completed at the very moment when his speech was restored. When the boy complained to the gaoler of his negligence in letting her out to hurt and annoy him, the gaoler answered that he had kept her very safe. "Nay," says the boy, "for she came and sat in my chamber window, and grinned at me; whereupon I took up a form and banged her:" the gaoler looked and they found the marks. She was a Lancashire woman, who, when Duke Hamilton was defeated, and there was a scarcity in those parts, "wandred abroad to get victuals." She was hanged, poor half-starved vagrant!

---

[136] 'Collection of Modern Relations.'

THE TEWKESBURY WITCH
THAT SUCKED THE SOW.

About the same time a Tewkesbury man had a sow and a litter of pigs: the sow with abundance of milk, but the pigs lean and miserable. He concluded that something which had no right to it came and robbed his piglings of their milk; so he watched; and sure enough a "black four-footed Creature like a Pole-Cat" came and beat away the pigs and sucked the sow; but the farmer got a pitchfork and ran it into the thigh of the pole-cat, which struggled so mightily that, though it was nailed to the ground, it got away and made off. When he asked some neighbours, standing near, what they had seen, they said they had only seen a wench go by, with blood falling from her as she went. They caught the wench and searched her, and, sure enough, found her wounded as the man said he had wounded the thing sucking his sow. She was apprehended, tried, and hanged, because she made herself into a creature like a black pole-cat, and went and sucked the farmers' sows. "These two Relations, I received from a Person of Quality, of good Ability and of unquestionable Credit, who was present at both the Tryals, and wrote them in his Presence, and afterwards read them to him; and he assured me they were very true in all the Particulars, as they were given in Evidence," says the author of the "Collection of Modern Relations" complacently.

THE DEVIL'S DELUSION.[137]

That same year, in the month of July, a man and woman, John Palmer and Elizabeth Knott, were hanged at St. Albans for curing folks of disease without the leave and license of the authorities, and by the aid of the devil. John made some curious revelations. He said, first of all, that Marsh of Dunstable was the head of the whole college of witches, and that he could do more than all the rest. Then he went on to say that he, John Palmer, had held a blood covenant with the devil for sixty years, and that he bore his brand; also that he had two imps, "George," a dog, and "Jezabell," a woman, who did what he would. He had seduced to himself and his arts Elizabeth Knott, his kinswoman; and both together they made a clay picture of goodwife Pearls of Norton, which they put under some embers, and as the picture consumed away, so did goodwife Pearls—miserably and fatally. This was out of revenge for hanging a lock on his door because he did not pay his rent. Then he sent "George" to kill Cleaver's horses; and Elizabeth killed John Laman's cow by sending her imp, which was a cat. The cat had promised that she should have all she wanted, save money; but poor Elizabeth Knott did not add that puss had promised to give them a halter and the gallows at the end of their revenge: which would have been the only truth in the whole relation. She killed Laman's cow, she said, because she had been teazed for money due to him, or rather to his wife. When she was swum, her cat imp came up to her and sucked upon her breast; so she said, poor raving creature: but when she was taken out of the water she never saw it more. Palmer also confessed that once he lay as a toad in the way of a young man he hated, to get himself hurt. The young man kicked the toad, and Palmer had a sore shin; but he bewitched the

---

137 'The Devil's Delusion.' 1649.

youth, so that he languished for years in woe and torment. Then is given the list of all the people bedevilled and bewitched by these two persons, and the account is signed, "Yours, Misodaimon." Misodaimon would have done better if he could have called himself Philalethes.

THE WITCH OF WAPPING.

In April, 1652, Joan Peterson, the witch of Wapping, was hanged at Tyburn in just retribution of her sins. Joan had long had an ugly name in that mean house of hers on the small island near Shadwell; for she was known to heal the sick in a manner more suggestive than satisfactory, and she had a black beast that used to suck her: which every one knew was the art and function of an imp. That this was true of her who could doubt, for a man said he had seen it, and it took even less direct testimony than this to prove a woman a witch. Let the sceptical read the "Country Justice" to see what subtle threads were strong enough for a witch-halter! One evening a neighbour woman was watching by the cradle of a child who was strangely distempered. In jumped a black cat, coming no one knew whence, and stopped her cradling. This woman, and another watching with her, flung the fire-fork at the cat, when it vanished as quickly as it had come. In an hour's time it came again from the other side: one of the women raised her foot and kicked it; and immediately her foot and leg swelled, and were very sore and painful. Then, terrified, they called the master of the house, told him that they could not watch in a place so beset with evil spirits, and left him and the child to get on as they could. On their way home they lighted on a baker, who told them that he had just met a big black cat which had affrighted him so that his hair stood all on end; and when the women told their tale, he said "on his conscience he thought it was Mother Peterson, for he had met her going towards the island a little while before." When on his oath, under examination, this valiant baker declared that he had never been afraid of any cat before in his life; and to a further question answered, "No, he had never seen such a cat before, and he hoped in God he should never see the like again." But what connection old Joan Peterson was assumed to have with this mysterious black cat remains a mystery to this day: it was none to the judge and jury, who condemned her to be hanged with safe and tranquil minds.

THE GEOLOGICAL BEWITCHMENT.[138]

In April, 1652, Mary Ellins, aged nine years, daughter of Edward Ellins, of Evesham in the county of Worcester, was playing in the fields with some neighbours' children. They were gathering cowslips in a pretty innocent way, in which it would have been well if they had been contented to remain; but on passing by a ditch they saw crouching therein one Catherine Huxley, an old woman of no very good repute, generally supposed to be a witch of the worst kind, and quick at casting an evil eye when offended. The children seeing her, took up stones to throw at her, calling her "witch" and other opprobrious names; whereat old Catherine cursed them, and especially Mary Ellins, who made herself conspicuous as the chief tormentor. Her curses had the desired effect. Mary went home, bewitched, and who but Catherine had done it? For ever from that day she had strange and troublesome passages with stones, so that it seemed as if the child had fed upon stones, and nothing but stones, of all kinds of geological formation. Scores of people went to see them: they were handled, and looked at, and reasoned about, and discussed, and yet so many as ever might come away, more still remained behind, and the supply was never failing. When Mary's extraordinary power of elaborating flint and granite and boulder and pebble in her young body had become troublesome and expensive, and the parents wanted to get rid of the whole concern, they undertook the prosecution of old Catherine, and *on this evidence alone, that she had cursed their daughter, and that their daughter had since then had extraordinary discharges of stones*, the old woman was condemned and executed—hung up as a public show at Worcester in the bonny summer months of 1652. As soon as she was hanged Mary had instant and complete

---

[138] Baxter.

relief; and hid no more pebbles in her pockets to delude good, credulous, prayerful Mr. Baxter into the profound belief that she was bewitched.

THE BURNING BEWITCHMENT.[139]

Brightling of Sussex, too, where now we have our sea-side London, was under a cloud, with the devil in actual human form possessing the place and haunting good folk out of their proper wits; for Joseph Cruttenden's house was bewitched, and they were sore holden how to restore the spirit of grace within it, and exorcise the spirit of evil. Joseph Cruttenden had a young servant girl, to whom one day came an old woman, unknown, saying to her that sad calamities were coming on her master's family by-and-bye, but that she was not to speak of them to any one; for he and his dame should be haunted, and their house fired and bewitched. She was to be particularly careful not to give warning of this to any, for if she did, the devil would tear her in pieces. The girl kept her own counsel; of course she did; there would have been no sport else: and that very night the troubles began. As Joseph and his wife lay in bed, dirt and dust and rubbish of all kinds were thrown at them, so that there was no way of escaping the handfuls of filth flung fast and furiously, and all the doors and windows shook as with a storm, though the air was still outside. On another night the house was set on fire in many places at once, flashing out like gunpowder; and as fast as one corner was extinguished another began; for they had no sooner trodden out the ashes and gone to another part, than they flamed up afresh, and they had all their work to do over again. Some said that a thing like a black bull was seen tumbling about in the flames; but Mr. Baxter halts at this, and declines to endorse it. At another time the furniture was all flung about, and a wooden "tut" came flying through the air, and a horseshoe struck the man on the breast, and there was no peace night or day for the black bull, the fire, and all the other things besetting. And then the man confessed

---

[139] Baxter's 'Certainty of the World of Spirits.'

that he had been a thief long time agone, whereby Satan had this extraordinary power over him; and the girl, despising the threat of the devil's tearing her to pieces, confessed to her mistress what the old woman had said. So the country was searched for an old woman answering the maid's description, and a poor old wretch was pitched upon as being most like. She was sent for and examined— watched for twenty-four hours; but nothing seems to have come of it this time. The girl "thought" she was "like" the same woman as had spoken to her, yet declined to swear positively. But the old woman had a bad name. She had been suspected as a witch before, "and been had to Maidstone to clear herself," which it seems she had done, for she got off, and had been living near Brightling ever since. She had a narrow escape now, for the country people were much excited against her, and naturally did not wish the presence of one who could haunt their houses with fire and dirt, and a big black bull tumbling about at his will. Had the maid had one grain less of conscience, this nameless wretch would have closed her earthly career a few years too soon; as it was she got off, and "lived miserably about Burwast ever since." It was a small sign of grace in that young jade that she would not swear away the life of an innocent woman to conceal her own childish tricks. It was not often that the accusing witnesses showed even this scant mercy to their victims, for the excitement of the game seemed to be in the largest amount of cruelty that could be perpetrated within the rules.

THE STRINGY MEAT.[140]

"Kent, the first Christian, last conquered, and one of the most flourishing and fruitful Provinces of England, is the Scene, and the beautiful Town of Maidstone, the Stage, whereon this Tragicall Story was publicly acted at Maidstone Assizes, last past."

In this Christian province and most beautiful country, Anne Ashby, Anne Martyn, Mary Browne, Mildred Wright, and Anne Wilson, all of Cranbrooke, and Mary Reade, of Lenham, were brought before Sir Peter Warburton, charged with "the Execrable and Diabolicall crime of Witchcraft." Anne Ashby, "who was the chiefe Actresse, and who had the greatest part in this Tragedy," and Anne Martyn were "confessing" witches; but their confessions did not amount to much, compared with the more highly spiced accounts of other witches. That they had both known the devil as a man, and in dishonesty and sin, was of course one of the chief items of their confession, as it was of most witches; but Anne Ashby further informed the Bench that the devil had given them each a piece of flesh, which, whensoever they should touch, would give them their desires; and that this piece of flesh was hid somewhere among the grass. As was proved: for upon search it was found. Of a sinewy substance and scorched was this redoubtable talisman, for it was both seen and felt by this Observator, E. G., and reserved for public view at the sign of the Swan in Maidstone. Anne Ashby had an imp too, called "Rug," which sometimes came out

---

[140] A Prodigious and Tragicall History of the Arraignment, Tryall, Confession, and Condemnation of six Witches at Maidstone, in Kent, at the Assizes held there in July, Fryday 30, this present year 1652. Before the Right Honourable Peter Warburton, one of the Justices of the Common Pleas. Collected from the Observations of E. G. Gent, a learned Person, present at their Conviction and Condemnation, and digested by H. F. Gent.' London: Printed for Richard Harper in Smithfield, 1652.

of her mouth like a mouse, and was of so malicious and venificall a nature that a certain groom belonging to Colonel Humfrey's regiment, for sport, said, "Come Rug into my mouth," and the said groom was dead in a fortnight after: "as it is reported," adds E. G. with saving grace. Anne was hysterical, poor soul: and "in view of this Observation, fell into an extasie before the Bench, and swell'd into a monstrous and vast bigness, screeching and crying out dolefully." When she recovered they asked her if she had been possessed by the devil at that time, to which she made answer "that she did not know that, but that her Spirit Rug had come out of her mouth like a mouse." After they were "cast" and judgment had been pronounced against them she and Anne Martyn pleaded that they were with child: but, being pressed on this point, they confessed that it was by no man of honest flesh and blood, but by the devil, their customary spouse. The plea was not suffered to stand. For proof against the rest, all that is recorded by E. G. is, that when pricked neither Mary Browne, nor Anne Wilson, nor yet Mildred Wright felt pain, or lost blood; and that Mary Read had a visible teat under her tongue which she did show to this Observator as well as to many others. But they were all hanged, at the common place of execution; though some there were who wished that they might be burnt instead, for burning had such virtue, that it prevented the blood of a witch "becomming hereditary to her Progeny in the same evill, which by hanging is not." The hangers, however, carried the day, and the blood of the progeny was left to take its chance of hereditary evil. It was supposed that these six witches, to whom were added five other persons, had bewitched nine children, one man, and one woman, lost five hundred pounds' worth of cattle, and wrecked much corn at sea.

THE LOST WIFE.[141]

That same month and year saw a strange matter of witchcraft at Warwick. "In Warwick Town one Mrs. Katherine Atkins, a Mercer's Wife, standing at her Door on Saturday night, the 24 July 1652. A certain unknown Woman came to her and sayd, Mistris, pray give me two-pence, she answered, two-pences are not so plentifull, and that she would give her no Mony. Pray Mistress, sayd she, then give me that Pin, so she took the Pin off her sleeve and gave her, for which she was very thankfull, and was going away. Mistress Atkins seeing her so thankfull for a Pin, called her again, and told her if she would stay, she would fetch some victuals for her, or give her some thread, or something out of the shop. She answered, she would have nothing else, and bid a pox of her victuals, and swore (by God) saying, You shall be an hundred miles off within this week, when you shall want two-pence as much as I, and so she went grumbling away.

"Hereupon the sayd Mistress Atkins was much troubled in mind, and did advise with some Friends what were best to be done in such a case, but receiving no resolution from any one what to do, she attended the Event what might befall within such a time, and upon the 29 of July she exprest to a kinsman, Mr. Nicholas Bikar, that she was much troubled about the forsayd businesse, but hoped the time was so much expired, that it would come to nothing.

"But the sayd Thursday night, betwixt the hours of 8 and 9, She, going into the Shop, and returning thence in the Entry adjoyning to the sayd Shop, she was immediately gone, by what means and whither we do not know, nor can we hear of upon enquiry made to this present.

---

[141] A true Relation of one Mrs. Atkins, a Mercer's Wife in Warwick, who was strangely carried away from her house in July last, and hath not since been heard of.

"The desire of her Husband and Friends is of all the Inhabitants of this Nation, That if they hear of any such Party in such a lost condition as is before expressed, That there may be speedy Notice given thereof to her Husband in Warwick, and that all convenient Provisions, both of Horse and Mony may be made for the conveying of her to the place aforesayd, and such as shall take pains, or be at expences herein shall be sufficiently recompenced for the same, with many thanks.

"It's likewise desired that Ministers in London, and elsewhere, when the notice of these presents shall come, would be pleased to present her sad condition to God in their severall Congregations. The truth hereof we testifie, whose names are subscribed.

Richard Vennour.

John Halleford. { Hen. Butler, Ministers of Warwick.

Joseph Fisher, Minister.

DR. LAMB AND HIS DARLING.[142]

Dr. Lamb, Buckingham's domestic physician in times past, and his maid Anne Bodenham, both met with a tragical fate, though not in the same year, for Dr. Lamb was brutally murdered for a conjuror and wizard by a mob in 1640, while Anne Bodenham was not executed until 1653. That Lamb was a terrible necromancer is testified by Richard Baxter, in his 'World of Spirits,' a book "written for the conviction of Sadducees and Infidels," but which now would convince none but the weak or half crazed of anything beyond Richard Baxter's own exceeding credulity and want of critical faculty. His story of Dr. Lamb's necromancy is so curious, it had better be given verbatim, for to translate would be to ruin it.

"Dr. Lamb, who was killed by the Mob for a Conjuror about 1640, met one Morning Sir Miles Sands and Mr. Barbor in the Street, and invited them to go and drink their Mornings Draught at his House: Discoursing about his Art, he told them that if they would hold their Tongues, and their Hands from medling with any thing, he would shew them some Sport. So falling to his Practice in the middle of the Room springs up a Tree; sone after appeared three little Fellows, with Axes on their Shoulders, and Baskets in their Hands, who presently fell to work, cut down the Tree, and carried all away. But Mr. Barbor observing one Chip to fall on his Velvet Coat, he slips it into his Pocket, That Night when he and his Family were in Bed, and asleep, all the Doors and Windows in the House opened and clattered, so as to awaken and affright them all. His Wife said, *Husband, you told me you was at Dr. Lamb's this Day, and I fear you medled with something.* He replied, *I put a Chip into my Pocket. I pray you,* said she, *fling it out, or we shall have*

---

[142] Dr. George More's 'Antidote to Atheism.' Dr. Lamb's 'Darling.' By James Bower. 1653.

no Quiet. He did so, and all the Windows and Doors were presently shut, and all quiet, so they went to sleep."

With such powers of conjuration and sorcery as these, it is not surprising if Dr. Lamb's character tainted that of Anne Bodenham his maid; for the very fact of their living together under the same roof was inimical enough to Anne's reputation. We hear nothing of her for some years, beyond that she lived near New Sarum, was married to one Edward Bodenham, "clothyer," and that she was eighty years of age at the time of her trial. So at least says Edmund Bower, in his "Doctor Lamb revived." But her getting into trouble at all proves that she had long lived under the suspicion of commonly practising witchcraft and sorcery; for Anne Styles, the accuser, had been backwards and forwards to her on her own account scores of times, and thought nothing of it; neither was it considered wonderful when Mr. Mason, son-in-law of Richard Goddard, Anne Styles's master, sent her to Anne Bodenham to learn now their lawsuit would turn. Bodenham, who had a knack of "foretelling things to come, and helping men to their stolen goods, and other such like feats," expressed no surprise, but at once began her conjurations. "She took her staff, and there drew it about the house, making a kinde of a Circle, and then took a book, and carrying it over the Circle with her hands, and taking a green glasse, did lay it upon the book, and placed in the Circle an earthern Pan of Coals, wherein she threw something, which burning caused a very noisome stink, and told the Maid she should not be afraid of what she should then see, for now they would come (they are the words she used), and so calling Belzebub, Tormentor, Satan, and Lucifer appear, there suddenly arose a very high wind, which made the house shake, and presently the back door of the house flying open, there came five Spirits, as the Maid supposed, in the likenesse of ragged Boyes, some bigger than others, and ran about the House, where she had drawn the staff: and the witch threw down upon the ground crums of bread, which the Spirits picked up, and leapt over the Pan of Coals oftentimes, which she set in the midst of the Circle, and a Dog and a Cat of the witches danced with them; and after some time the witch looked again in her book, and threw some great white Seeds upon the ground, which the said Spirits picked up, and so in a short time the wind was laid and the witch going forth at the back door the Spirits vanished." After which Anne told the girl that Mr. Mason should demand fifteen hundred pounds, and one hundred and fifty pounds per annum of Mr. Goddard, and if it was denied he was to take the law and prosecute. For all which Anne Bodenham received the sum of three shillings: little enough too, considering the charges she must have been at for noisome roots and magic lanthorns, not to speak of the chance of being haled off to prison whenever the maid Anne Styles might choose to accuse her.

Another time Anne Styles was sent to her by Mrs. Goddard, to find where was hidden the poison which she said her two young step-daughters were designing to give her, but which Anne Styles herself had bought, as she said, by the witch's request. This Anne Bodenham denied. The witch took her stick as before, going through the same forms of conjuration; when on her adjuring "Belzebub, Tormentor, Lucifer, Satan," to appear, there came out of the mist first a little boy, who then turned into a snake, and then into "a shagged dog with great eyes, which went about in the Circle." And after she had burnt her noisome herbs again, and looked in her Magic book—her Book of Charms as she called it—she took a glass and showed in that "Mistress Sarah Goddard's Chamber, the colour of the Curtains, and the bed turned up the wrong way, and under that part of the bed where the Bolster laye she shewed the poison in a white paper." It was no discredit to maid or witch that this poisoning matter was found a mere suspicion and delusion, and that the young ladies never designed to poison their mother-in-law; though she, on the other hand, sent to Bodenham for charms and poisons against them. This time Anne got vervain and dill, which the little ragged boys (spectres, or spirits, or imps) gathered for her, in return for which she threw them bread which they ate, dancing about, then vanished on their mistress reading in her book. The witch gave the maid the leaves powdered, and dried—one packet of each—while, in a third packet, she put the parings of her nails; all of which the maid was to give to her mistress. The powder was to be put into Mistresses Sarah and Anne Goddard's drink or broth, to give them hideous indigestion rather too coarsely expressed for modern reading; the leaves were to rub about the rim of the pot, to make their teeth fall out of their heads; and the paring of the nails to make them drunk and mad. But Mrs. Goddard only laughed when she got these charms, and said "they were brave things:" she did not use them, luckily for her; though the young ladies would not have been much the worse, save for the white poison before mentioned.

Anne Bodenham had taken a great fancy to this servant girl, and wanted her to live with her, telling her that she would teach her all she knew, and enable her to do as she did; asking her, too, whether she would go to London high or low: for if high she should be carried through the air and be there in two hours, if low she should be taken at Sutton's town end, and before, "unless she had help." When she thus sought to seduce the girl, Anne Styles asked what she could do, whereupon Bodenham incontinently appeared in the form of a great black cat, and lay along by the chimney; but the girl being much frightened, she appeared in her own shape again, and tempted her no more. But first, before she would let her go, she made her swear to seal with her body and blood a vow that she would never discover what she had seen; so she took her forefinger and pricked it, and filled a pen with the blood, and made her write in a book, one of the imps—like "great boys with long shagged black hair," this time—having his hand or claw on the witch's, while Anne Styles wrote. And when she had done writing, the witch said "Amen," and the maid said "Amen," and the spirits said "Amen" each: and the spirit gave the witch a bit of silver for the maid, which he first bit. The maid's hand touched his, and she found that his was cold. Then Bodenham stuck two pins in her head-dress, which she bid her keep, and be gone; saying, "I will vex the Gentlewoman well enough, as I did the man in Clarington Park; which I made walk about with a bundle of Pales on his back all night in a pond of water, and could not lay them down till the next morning." The piece of silver, and the hole in her forefinger, the maid showed the judge and jury in the trial; and both were held to be conclusive evidence against Dr. Lamb's unfortunate "Darling." How far Anne Styles may be believed is not difficult to determine; for as to the conjurations about poisoning Mrs. Goddard, it came out that she, the maid, had gone to the apothecary's for an ounce of arsenic; and then set abroad the report that the two young ladies had bought it for the purpose of poisoning their step-mother. As the young ladies were not disposed to sit down quietly under this suspicion, they had the report sifted to the bottom, and Anne Styles fled in fear; which was the meaning of the witch's demanding how she would like to go to London—high or low—by witch's art, or justice's power. Mr. Chandler, Mr. Goddard's son-in-law, pursued her, and overtook her at Sutton-town end; when, to save herself from the unpleasant consequences of her various misdeeds, beginning with stealing a silver spoon and ending with buying arsenic, she made this "confession," which was safety to her but death to old Anne. Anne earnestly and passionately denied every word the girl said: whereupon Anne Styles, to give greater colour to her story, fell into fits, so strong that six men could not hold her. She was drawn up high into the air—so at least runs the report—her feet as high as the spectators' breasts; and she had scuffles with a black man with no head, who came and tumbled her about, as a little boy deposed. The little boy was sleeping in the same room with her, and he said that the black spirit came to her, and wanted her soul, but the maid answered her soul was none of hers to give; that he had got her blood already, but should never have her soul; and after a tumbling and throwing of her about rarely, he vanished away. At another time the witch was brought to the maid suddenly, when she instantly closed her eyes and fell back in so deep a sleep that they could not by any means awaken her; but so soon as the witch had gone, she woke up of herself, and was quite well. Anne Bodenham was condemned to die, and there was no help for her; but when sentence was passed, Anne Styles fell to bitter weeping and wailing, lamenting her own wickedness, and willing that the witch should be reprieved, if possible to the law. This was taken as a sign of her sweet and loving Christian spirit of forgiveness; we, who read such signs more clearly by the light of a better knowledge, know that it meant simply the weak pity of a selfish conscience, grieving for its sin, yet afraid to retract and make amends. Beside all this evidence, and its lies, Anne Bodenham had a tame toad which she wore in a green bag round her neck; and she had a great deal of natural clairvoyance and mesmeric power; and she was evidently a highly superstitious woman, who believed in her own powers, and was not unwilling to aid them by a little extra supernaturalism and good mechanical tricks. But she would confess to no witchcraft; knew nothing of a Red Book half written over in blood, which red book with its bloody writing contained a catalogue of those who had sold themselves to the devil; though she acknowledged that she had a Book of Charms, much as a servant maid of to-day might have a Book of Dreams: and that she could say the Creed backwards as well as forwards; and that she sometimes prayed to the planet Jupiter. The time-honoured belief in astrology and the power of the planets might well linger in the brain of an old country woman, who had a smattering of knowledge far beyond her station, and who had dabbled in mechanics and the art of conjuring; who could not, moreover, understand her own sensitive condition; and who had the alternative, as one of the witnesses said, of passing for a witch or a woman of God. The judge and jury had a very distinct idea as to which category she ought to be placed in; and fully believed what James Bower reports, that she could turn herself into a "mastive Dog, a black Lyon, a white Bear, a Woolf, a Monkey, a Horse, a Bull, and a Calf." Such a woman as this had no business here on this solid earth, so she was hanged at Salisbury, 1653, dying very hard and completely crazed. Before the hour came she wrote a letter to her husband desiring him never to live in his own house again; and she asked the woman who was to "shroud" her, to root up all her garden herbs and flowers when she should be dead; and she clamoured for a knife to stick into her heart; and she wanted to die drunk, calling for beer on her way to execution, and giving her gaolers much trouble to hold her in at all; and she would have no psalm sung, and no prayer read, and would forgive none of them, but cursed them all fiercely as she stood on the rungs of the ladder despairing and defying. So miserably she died, poor old wretch! and Anne Styles never looked up again into the fair face of heaven without the stain of blood across her hand, and the brand of Cain on her brow.

THE SPRIGHTLY LAD OF SOMERSETSHIRE.[143]

One certain Sunday afternoon, in November 1657, Richard Jones, "a sprightly youth of twelve," living at Shepton Mallet, in Somersetshire, being left at home alone, and looking abroad as sprightly youth will, saw an old woman of the place, by name Jane Brooks, look in at the window. He went to the door to see what she wanted, when she asked him to give her a piece of "close bread," and she would give him an apple. He did so, and she thanked him, stroked him down the right side, shook him by the hand, and bade him good night. When the father and our coz. Gibson came back, they found the sprightly youth ill, and complaining of pain in the right side. He continued in the same state through the night, and on the following day became much worse, falling into fits of speechlessness, &c., immediately after having roasted and eaten the apple which Jane Brooks had given him. He then told the father that an old woman of the place, name unknown but person remembered, had stroked his right side, and thus had caused his illness; whereupon his father decided that all the women of Shepton Mallet should come to see him, and that in case he was in his fit, and not able to speak when the true witch came, he should give a "jogg," which would be sufficiently expressive. All the women of Shepton Mallet were brought in by turns; but the boy remained quiet until Jane Brooks appeared, when he fell into a fit, and was for some time unable to see or speak. Recovering himself, "he gave his father the Item," and drew towards Jane. She was standing behind her two sisters, but the boy singled her out and put his hand upon her; which the father seeing, he flew on the poor creature, scratched her face "above her breath," and drew blood. After this rather rough manner of exorcism, Master Richard Jones cried out that he was well,

---

[143] Glanvil's 'Saducismus Triumphatus.'

and condescended to remain well for seven or eight days. But at the end of this time, Alice Coward, sister to Jane, happening to meet him and to say, "How do you do, my Honey?" he fell ill again, and "cried out" on them without intermission. One Sunday he was in his fits, his father and cousin Gibson with him as usual, when he suddenly exclaimed that he "saw Jane Brooks there"—pointing to the wall. Cousin Gibson at once struck a knife into the spot; whereupon the sprightly youth cried, "O father, couz Gibson hath cut Jane Brooks's hand, and 'tis Bloody." The father and Gibson on this went to the constable, "a discreet Person," and telling him what had happened, took him with them to Jane's house, where they found her sitting on a stool, with one hand over the other. After a few questions they drew her hand away, and found that which was underneath all bloody; which appearance she explained away as well as she could, by saying that it was scratched with a great pin. This kind of thing going on for some time, the pitiful plot grew ripe for execution, and on the 8th of December Jane Brooks and her sister, Alice Coward, were taken to Castle Cary to be examined by the justices, Mr. Hunt and Mr. Cary. Here Richard performed all the usual tricks of the bewitched, lying speechless and motionless while the suspected women were in the room; springing up into tetanic fits if they laid their hands upon him, or so much as looked towards him; bringing on himself, by his own will, convulsive fits and catalepsy, and many of the more violent symptoms of hysteria, and insisting that the two women came constantly to see him—as apparitions— "their Hands cold, their Eyes staring, and their Lips and Cheeks looking pale." "In this manner on a Thursday about Noon, the Boy being newly laid in his Bed, Jane Brooks and Alice Coward appeared to him, and told him that what they had begun they could not perform. But if he would say no more of it, they would give him Money, and so put a Twopence into his Pocket. After which they took him out of his Bed and laid him on the ground and vanished, and the Boy was found by those that came next into the Room lying on the Floor as if he had been dead." This twopence had odd properties. When put upon the fire and made hot, the boy fell ill; when taken out and cooled, he was all right again. The trick was tried in the presence of many, and was found to answer admirably. Between the 8th of December and the 17th of February, he practised another variation of the same air. "Divers persons at sundry times" heard a croaking, as of a toad, proceed from the boy, and though they held a candle to his face they could not discern any movement of tongue, teeth, or lips. And this croaking as of a toad repeated incessantly, "Jane Brooks, Alice Coward, Jane Brooks, Alice Coward." On the 25th of February he performed his greatest feat of all; or was reported to have done so—which did quite as well in those days; for Richard Isles's wife said she saw him raised up from the ground, mounting gradually higher and higher till he was carried full thirty yards over the garden wall, when, falling at last at one Jordan's door, he was there found as if dead. Coming to himself, he declared that Jane Brooks had taken him by the arm, and carried him up, as Isles's wife had seen; which fact was told and believed in as a fearful instance of her malicious and wicked sorcery against the sprightly youth. At another time, as many as nine people at once saw him hanging from a beam, his hands placed flat against the wood, and his whole body raised two or three feet from the ground. He continued to play these extraordinary tricks from the 15th of November to the 10th of March; when, being much wasted and worn, it was deemed advisable to save his life if yet there might be time. Jane Brooks was sent to gaol, condemned, and hanged at Charde assizes, March 26th, 1658; and Richard Jones, having no longer any inducement to act the possessed, consented to remain with his feet on the ground and his head in the air, according to the laws of nature and Newton, and took no more fits, real or simulated, to extort compassion or obtain revenge.

THE WITCHES OF THE RESTORATION.

The poor witches were always seeing troublous times. At about the time of the Lord Protector's death one was hanged in Norwich and several in Cornwall. In 1659 two suffered at Lancaster, for crimes which I cannot discover; while in 1660, on the 14th of May, the Restoration had its victims in the persons of a widow, her two daughters, and a man, who were carried to Worcester gaol on the double charge of witchcraft and high treason. For the eldest daughter had been heard to say that if they had not been taken the king would never have come to England: which was enough to frighten all the court into fits. And when they were taken, and tried, and condemned, she said further that "though he now doth come, yet he shall not live long but shall die as ill a death as they" adding that had they not been taken "they would have made corn like pepper:" that is, they would have blighted it. As there were many other charges against them, they were swum: when they floated like ducks—or witches; and then they were searched: when the man was found to have five "bigges," two of the women three, but the eldest daughter only one. When first searched, none of these marks were visible on any of the women, whereat the inquisitors were advised to put them flat on their backs and keep their mouths open, until they should appear; which advice was taken, with the happiest and most palpable results.

THE WITCH-FINDER FOUND

Sometimes knavery defeated itself, though unhappily not often, as in the case of the famous witch-finder Mother Baker[144] and the young maid Stuppeny, of New Romsey in Kent. The young maid Stuppeny was sick, and as sickness in those days never meant the natural consequence of filthy habits, filthy food, and filthy habitations, but was by the supernatural devilry of witches and wizards, the parents concluded that their young maid must be bewitched, so set off to old Mother Baker to learn who was the guilty person. Old Mother Baker asked whom they suspected? and they mentioned a near neighbour of theirs—particulars not given. "Yes," says the hag, "it is she, and she has made a heart of wax, which she daily pricks with pins and knitting-needles, and which is now concealed in the house, for the destruction of the young maid your daughter." So the parents Stuppeny searched their house, but found no heart of wax; whereupon old Mother Baker, with big pockets to her sides, said she herself must search. And she did search, and turned out the charm from the very spot where she said it was. But certain prying neighbours, whose eyes were sharp and wits clear, had watched old Baker and her pockets; and as she laid the image in a corner that had been most diligently searched and looked into, her cheat was discovered, and the anonymous wretch living next door escaped, while Mother Baker suffered the penalties awarded in Scot's time to cozenage and deceit with intent to defraud or do ill.

---

[144] Reginald Scot.

DOLL BILBY AND HER COMPEER.[145]

Burton Agnes, in the county of York, was troubled; for Faith Corbet, the young daughter of Henry Corbet, was taken violently ill, and Alice Huson and Doll Bilby had bewitched her. Good Mrs. Corbet—beyond her age in generous unbelief—refused to entertain her daughter's suspicions; indeed she had chidden her some years ago for calling old Alice a witch, for she had a liking to the poor widow, and kept her about the house, looking after her young turkeys, &c., and was kind and liberal to her, and sought to make her wasting life pass as easily as might be. But Miss Faith hated the old woman, and cried out against her as a witch; and when she lost her gloves, swore that Alice had taken them to play cantrips with, and that she should never be well again. Then she began to fall into fits, when she would be so terribly tormented that it took two or three to hold her; and she would screech and cry out vehemently, and bite and scratch anything she could lay hold of, all the while exclaiming, "Ah, Alice, old witch, have I gotten thee!" And sometimes she would lie down, all drawn together in a round, and be speechless and half swooning for days together; and then she would be wildly merry, and as full of antics as a monkey. Physicians were consulted, but none came near to her disorder; and though her father carried her about hither and thither, for change of air, nothing would cure her, she said, so long as Alice Huson and Doll Bilby remained at liberty. Still the father and mother held out, until, one day, before a whole concourse of people come to look at her in her fits, she cried out, "Oh Faithless and incredulous People! shall I never be believed till it be past Time? For I am as near Death as possibly may be, and when they have got my Life you will repent when it is past Time." On hearing this the

---

[145] 'Collection of Modern Relations.'

father went to the minister of Burton Agnes, Mr. Wellfet, and he, Sir Fr. Boynton—a justice of the peace—and Mr. Corbet himself at last dragged the old woman Huson into Faith's chamber. At which Miss Faith gave a great screech, but presently called for toast and beer; then for cordials; and having taken a somewhat large quantity of both, she got up, dressed herself, and came down stairs. This, too, after she had been so weak that she could not turn herself in bed: which proved that Mother Huson had some extraordinary influence over the girl—an influence more potent than holy said the bystanders. This happy state did not continue. Faith said she should never be well while the two women were at liberty; and so it proved; for when they were at last arrested, and held in strict security and durance, the young lady pronounced herself healed, and gave no one any more trouble. Then Alice Huson was got to make confession to Mr. Wellfet, the minister, and thus sealed her own doom, and saved the prosecution the pain of conviction.

She said that for three years she had had intercourse with the devil, who, one day as she was on the moor, appeared to her in the form of a black man riding on horseback. He told her she should never want if she would follow his ways and give herself up to him: which Alice promised to do. Then he sealed the bargain by giving her five shillings; at another time he gave her seven; and often—indeed six or seven times—repeating his gifts to the like munificent extent. He was like a black man with cloven feet, riding on a black horse, and Alice fell down and worshipped him, as she had covenanted. And she had hurt Faith Corbet by her evil spirit, for she did, in her apprehension, ride her; and when Mr. Wellfet examined her once before, the devil stood by, and gave her answers; and she was under the Corbets' window as a cat when Mrs. Corbet said she was—for even her kindly faith was shaken at last; and Doll Bilby had a hand in all this evil too; for

Doll wanted to kill Faith outright, but old Alice interposed, thinking they had done enough harm already. She confessed to killing Dick Warmers "by my wicked heart and wicked eyes;" and to having lent Lancelot Harrison eight shillings of the ten which the devil had given her at Baxter's door, a fortnight ago, "about twilight or daygate;" and she had a bigge, or witch mark, where the devil sucked from supper-time till after cockcrowing, twitching at her heart as if it was drawn with pincers the while; and she meant to practise witchcraft four years ago, when she begged old clothes of Mrs. Corbet, and the children refused her; and the devil told her not to tell of Doll Bilby. And to all this raving Timothy Wellfet, minister of Burton Agnes, set his name, and so hanged Alice Huson and Doll Bilby at the next York assizes: after which Miss Faith Corbet was for ever rid of her fits and fancies.

THE ASTRAL SPIRIT'S ASSAULT.

Can we wonder at anything which it might please those servants of the devil, the witches, to do, when even a spirit—a disembodied ghost—a mere appearance—a spectre—an apparition—could audibly box a lad's ears before a whole room full of spectators, and at last box them so soundly as to break his neck, and kill him? Baxter's "World of Spirits" gives this story as happening to a barber's apprentice in Cambridge, in the year 1662. The spectre who killed the boy was in the garb and appearance of a gentlewoman; and at about the same hour, as near as they could guess, when it boxed the boy's ears and broke his neck at Cambridge, while the father was sitting at dinner with the boy's master at Ely, "the appearance of a Gentlewoman comes in, looking very angrily, taking a Turn or two, disappeared." It seems that the spectre had that night been endeavouring to persuade the boy to leave his apprenticeship and return home to Ely, where she and he were very free and had long been wont to disport together, even while company was in the room, and while the father, a minister named Franklin, was sitting there. After some treaty the boy resolutely said he would not go home, whereupon the spirit gave him a sounding box on the ear, which made him very ill; but he rose as usual when the morning came, though unfit for work or even play. When the master heard the story, he rode over to Ely to see Mr. Franklin, and confer with him respecting the uncomfortable and inconvenient desires of the spirit; and in the forenoon of the day, the boy sitting by the kitchen fire, his mistress being by, suddenly cried out, "O, mistress, look: there's the gentlewoman!" The mistress looked, but saw nothing, yet soon after heard a noise as of a great box on the ears, and turning round saw the boy bending down his neck: and presently he died. This is the story gravely told by Baxter, in the fullest faith that all was as he narrated, and that there was no natural explanation possible to a circumstance which derived its only importance from its supernaturalism.

Another spirit, a few years later—in 1667—took to haunting a man's house at Kinton, six miles from Worcester; and boxed his ears as he sat by the fire over against the maid. At which the man cried out, and went away to his son's in the town, not caring to continue where a ghost could make itself equal to a living body with bones and muscles, and give him undeniable proofs of the same. A minister of the place, Charles Hatt, went to the house to exorcise the ghost by prayer, and had not been there long before "there was a great noise in the said room, of groaning, or rather gruntling, like a Hog, and then a lowd Shriek." Mr. Charles Hatt prayed on; and after the spectre had done its best to frighten him with noises, but finding that the louder it gruntled the louder he prayed, it died away, and the man was troubled no more to the day of his death, which happened about two years after.

If this was a book on spirits instead of on witchcraft many stories from Baxter could be given bearing on the question; but, fascinating as they are, they are somewhat foreign to my design; so I must pass them by, and go on to the more material, and more guilty, records of the witchcraft superstition. All the mere spectre or ghost stories are both tame and innocent compared to the witch delusions. At least they caused no bloodshed; and if they broke hearts it was not through shame and despair and ruin.

JULIAN'S TOADS.[146]

At the Taunton assizes, in 1663, Julian Cox, about seventy years old, was indicted before Judge Archer for practising her arts of witchcraft upon a "young Maid, whereby her Body languished, and was impaired of Health." And first were taken proofs of her witchcraft. One witness, a huntsman, swore that one day, as he was hunting not far from Julian's house, he started a hare, which the dogs ran very close till it came to a bush; when, going round to the other side to keep it from the dogs, he perceived Julian Cox grovelling on the ground, panting and out of breath. She was the hare, and had had just time enough to say the magic stave which changed her back to woman's form again, ere the dogs had caught her. Another man swore that one day, passing her house as "she was taking a Pipe of Tobacco upon the Threshold of the Door," she invited him to come in and join her; which he did; when presently she cried out, "Neighbour, look what a pretty thing there is!" and there was "a monstrous great Toad betwixt his Legs, staring him in the Face." He tried to hit it, but could not, whereupon Julian told him to desist striking it and it would do him no hurt; but he was frightened, and went off to his family, telling them that he had seen one of Julian Cox her devils. Yet even when he was at home this same toad appeared again betwixt his legs, and though he took it out, and cut it in several pieces, still, when he returned to his pipe, there was the toad. He tried to burn it, but could not; then to beat it with a switch, but the toad ran about the room to escape him; presently it gave a cry and vanished, and he was never after troubled with it. A third witness swore that one day, when milking, Julian Cox passed by the yard where he was, and "stooping down scored upon the ground for some small time, during

---

[146] Glanvil.

which time his Cattle ran Mad, and some of them ran their Heads against the Trees, and most of them died speedily." Concluding by which signs that they were bewitched, he cut off their ears to burn them, and, while they were on the fire, Julian Cox came in a great heat and rage, crying out that they abused her without cause; but, going slily up to the fire, she took off the ears, and then was quiet. By the laws of witchcraft it was she who was burning, not the beasts' ears. A fourth, as veracious as the former, swore to having seen her "fly into her own Chamber-window in her full proportion;" all of which testimony gave weight and substance to the maid's charge.

The maid was servant at a certain house, where Julian came one day to ask for alms; but the maid gave her a cross answer, and said she should have none; so Julian told the maid she should repent her incivility before night. And she did; for she was taken with convulsions, and cried out to the people of the house to save her from Julian, for she saw her following her. In the night she became worse, saying that she saw Julian Cox and the black man by her bedside, and that they tempted her to drink, but "she defy'd the Devil's Drenches." The next night, expecting the same kind of conflict, she took up a knife and laid it at the head of her bed. In the middle of the night came the spiritual Julian and the black man, as before, so the maid took the knife, and stabbed at Julian, whom she said she had wounded in the leg. The people, riding out to see, found Julian in her own house with a fresh wound on her leg, and blood was also on the maid's bed. The next day Julian appeared to the maid and forced her to eat pins. Her apparition was on the house wall; and "all the Day the Maid was observ'd to convey her Hand to the House wall, and from the Wall to her Mouth, and she seem'd by the motion of her Mouth as if she did eat something." So towards night, still crying out on Julian, she was undressed, and all over her body were seen great swellings and bunches in which were huge pins—as many

383

as thirty or more—which she said Julian Cox, when in the house wall, had forced her to eat. Was not all this enough to hang a dozen Julian Coxes? Judge Archer thought so; especially when was added to this testimony Julian's own enforced confession, of how she had been often tempted by the devil to become a witch, but would never consent; yet how one evening, walking about a mile from her house, she met three persons riding on broom-staves, borne up about a yard and a half from the ground, two of whom she knew—a witch and a wizard, hanged for witchcraft several years ago—but the third, a black man, she did not then know. He however tempted her to give up her soul, which she did by pricking her finger and signing her name with her blood. So that, by her own showing, as well as by the unimpeachable testimony of reputable witnesses, she was a witch and one coming under the provisions of the Awful Verse. And further, as she could not repeat the Lord's Prayer, but stumbled over the clause "And lead us not into Temptation," which she made into "And lead us into temptation," or "And lead us not into no temptation," but could in no manner repeat correctly, the judge and jury had but one conclusion to come to, which was that she be hanged four days after her trial. But some of the less blind and besotted spoke harsh words of Judge Archer for his zeal and precipitancy, and openly declared poor Julian's innocence when advocacy could do her strangled corpse no good.

THE YOUGHAL WITCH.

About this time, too, or rather two years before old Julian Cox had been seen flying in at her window in full proportion, one Florence Newton, of Youghal, was overhauled for her misdeeds towards Mary Longdon. Mary was John Pyne's servant, and deposed that one day Florence came to where she lived and asked her for a bit of beef out of the powdering tub, to which Mary would not consent (these witnessing servants were always so moral and honest!), saying she had no right to give away her master's beef. The witch, being angry, muttered, "Thou had'st as good have given it me," and went away grumbling. A few days after, meeting with Mary going to the water with a pail of cloth on her head, she came full against her, and violently kissed her, and said, "Mary, I pray thee let thee and I be friends, for I bear thee no ill will, and I pray thee do thou bear me none." Mary does not give her reply, but says that she went home, and in a few days after "saw a Woman with a Vail over her Face stand by her bedside, and one standing by her like a little old Man in silk Cloaths, and that this Man, whom she took to be a Spirit, drew the Vail from off the Woman's Face, and then she knew it to be Goody Newton; and that the Spirit spake to the Deponent, and would have had her promise him to follow his Advice, and she should have all things after her own Heart; to which she says she answered 'That she would have nothing to say to him, for her Trust was in the Lord.'" After this Mary Longdon was taken very ill, vomiting pins and needles and horse-nails and stubbs and wool and straw, while small stones followed her about the room, and from place to place, striking her sharply on her head and shoulders and arms, then vanishing away. She was also strangely put upon by beds, and other such assailants. Sometimes she was forcibly carried from one bed to another; sometimes taken to the top of the house, or laid on a board betwixt two sollar beams, or put into a chest, or laid under a parcel of wool, or betwixt two feather beds, or (in the day time) between the bed and the mat in her master's room. All of these pranks done by Florence Newton's Astral Spirit, by which Mary maid was bewitched. Florence Newton also bewitched to his death David Jones, who had constituted himself one of her watchers while she was in "bolts" in prison. David took great pains to teach her the Lord's Prayer, but Florence, being a witch, could not repeat it correctly; at last she called out to him, "David! David! come hither; I can say the Lord's Prayer now." Not that she could, for when she came to the clause "Forgive us our Trespasses," she skipped over it, or boggled at it, or got round it in some way or other that was not holy; then seizing David's hand between the bars of the grate she kissed it thankfully; and thus and there possessed him, so that he died fourteen days after of that strange languishing disease known to all the world as a bewitchment.

THE WITCHES OF STYLES'S KNOT[147]

Elizabeth Hill, aged thirteen, had strange fits. She was much convulsed and contorted; she writhed, foamed, and could with difficulty be held or mastered; she had moreover swellings and holes in her flesh, which were made she said by thorns, and whence the bystanders averred they saw the child hook out thorns. Even the clergyman of the parish, William Parsons rector of Stoke Trister, added his testimony to the rest: and on the 26th of January, 1664, in an examination taken before Robert Hunt, vouched for the truth of the fits, and the swellings, and the black thorns in the midst of the swellings; but he did not add to this testimony the further assertion that it was Elizabeth Styles who had bewitched the child, though she herself "cried out" on her, and said that she tormented her in her fits. Elizabeth Styles was further accused of causing Richard Hill's horse to sit down and paw with his fore feet when attempted to be crossed, and of having bewitched Agnes Vining by means of a rosy-cheeked apple, which was no sooner eaten than it caused a grievous pricking in Agnes' thigh, who forthwith languished and died, "her hip rotted, and one of her eyes swelled out." These are signs of a worse bewitchment than poor old Mother Styles's rosy-cheeked apple—signs of the deadly sorcery of scrofula induced by the poverty, dirt, bad food and worse lodging of the times; for the effects of which many a poor wretch lost her life who yet had done no more harm than the nursling at the breast. Robert Hunt the Justice, and one of our fine old English gentlemen, did not take this materialistic view of the matter. When told of Agnes Vining's illness and manner of disease, and seeing Elizabeth Styles looking appalled and concerned, he said to her: "You have been an old sinner, you deserve little mercy." To which the poor soul answered, humbly, "I have

---

[147] Glanvil.

asked God for it." She then said that the devil had seduced her, and so began her confession on the 26th of January—three days after the first accusation by the Hills. She said that about ten years ago the devil appeared to her as a handsome man changing afterwards to the shape of a black dog; "that he promised her money, and that she should live gallantly, and have the Pleasures of the World for twelve years," if only she would sign a certain bond with her blood, give him her soul, obey his laws, and let him suck her blood. To all of which she consented after four solicitations, whereupon he pricked her finger—the mark thereof to be seen at this time—and she, with her own blood signed the paper with an O, when the devil gave her sixpence and vanished with the bond. Since then he appeared to her constantly, under the forms of a man, a cat, a dog, or a "fly like a millar" (a large white moth), as which last he usually sucked her poll about four in the morning; and hurt her terribly in doing so. She also said that when she wanted him to do anything for her, she called him by the name of "Robin," adding, "O Satan give me my purpose!" which he never failed to do. It was he who stuck the thorns into Elizabeth Hill; but then she implicated three other women, Alice Duke, Ann Bishop, and Mary Penny, saying that they too had stuck thorns into an enchanted picture meant for Elizabeth Hill, one night when they had all met the devil on the common, he, as a man in black clothes with a little band, first anointing its forehead with oil, saying, "I baptize thee with this oyl." After which they had a supper of wine, cakes, and roast meat, all brought by the man in black, and they ate and drank and danced and were merry. This they did always, whenever they would destroy any one obnoxious; and so had a merry time of it upon the whole. When they wanted to go to their meetings "they would anoint their wrists and foreheads with an oyl the spirit brings them, which smells raw," after which they were carried off, saying: "Thout, tout, a tout, tout, throughout and about:" on their return changing the stave to "Rentum Tormentum," which was the shibboleth to bring them back. But before they left they used to make obeisance to the man in black, who usually played to their dancing, saying, "A Boy! merry meet, merry part;" on which he vanished, and the conclave was broken up. She then told the "several grave and orthodox divines" who assisted Robert Hunt to take her examination, that Alice Duke's familiar was a cat, and Ann Bishop's a rat. Her own was a millar; concerning which Nicholas Lambert made some strange revelations. He said that as he and two others, hired to watch Elizabeth Styles in prison, were sitting near her as she crouched by the fire—he, Nicholas Lambert, reading in "The Practise of Piety"—about three in the morning they saw a "glistering bright fly," about an inch in length, come from her head and pitch on the chimney: then instantly vanish. In less than a quarter of an hour after, in came two other flies and seemed to strike at his hand, but which dodged him cleverly when he struck at them with his book. At this, Styles's countenance became very black and ghastly, and the fire also changed its colour; so the watchers, conceiving that her familiar was about her, and seeing also her hair shake very strangely, went to examine her poll, when out flew a great millar, which pitched on a table board and then vanished away. Her poll was red like raw beef, but presently regained its natural colour. Upon which Elizabeth confessed that it was her familiar, and that she had felt it tickle her poll. She was condemned, after having inculpated thirteen other persons, but "prevented execution by dying in gaol, a little before the expiring of the term her confederate dæmon had set for her enjoyment of Diabolical Pleasures."

Alice Duke, "another witch of Styles's Knot," a widow living in Wincaunton, county of Somerset, was then apprehended and examined. She seems to have given no trouble, but to have come frankly to the point, and to have admitted whatever they liked to demand. She said that, eleven or twelve years ago, Ann Bishop persuaded her to go one night to the churchyard, and "being come thither to go backward round the church, which they did three times." In their first round they met a man in black clothes who accompanied them: in their second a thing like a great black toad, which leaped up against Duke's apron: in the third, "somewhat in the shape of a rat" which vanished away. After which they both went home, but before they went the man in black said something softly to Ann Bishop, yet what it was Alice did not hear. Soon after this she signed herself away in the same manner and for the same purposes as Elizabeth Styles had done; and the devil gave her sixpence as he had given Styles, and vanished away with the fatal paper. She confirmed all that Styles had said concerning the meetings on the common, the enchanted pictures and the greenish oil, the devil, the wine, and cakes, and music; she gave information, though, of many more such pictures which were to doom the unfortunate likenesses to death; and she said farther that Ann Bishop was the devil's favourite, and that she sat next him, and wore "a green Apron, a French Waistcoat, and a red Petticoat." She gave the same phrase that Elizabeth Styles had given, as the magic password which took them to and from the devil's meetings; and she confessed that her familiar came to her each night, about seven o'clock, "in the shape of a little Cat of a dunnish colour, which is as smooth as a Want, and when she is suck'd she is in a kind of Trance." She had hurt several people; specially Thomas Hanway's daughter by giving her a pewter dish for a "good handsel" in the time of her lying in. This pewter dish was of such a malicious and venefical nature that when Thomas Hanway's daughter used it to heat some deer suet and rose water for her breasts, she was put to extreme pain; which pain she had not when she heated the same deer suet and the same rose water in a common spoon. So, suspecting harm in the dish, she put it into the fire, "which then presently vanished, and nothing of it was afterwards to be found." Alice Duke also said that she called the devil "Robin," and demanded of him aid and help in her undertakings. Like Styles and many others, she said that when the devil vanished he left an ill smell behind him; which is explained as, "Those ascititious Particles he held together in his visible vehicle, being loosened at his vanishing, and so offending the Nostrils by their floating and diffusing themselves in the open air."

ROBIN AND HIS SERVANTS[148]

Somersetshire was sorely afflicted at this time. On the 2nd of March still in the year of grace, 1664, Christian Green, aged about thirty-three, and wife of Robert Green of Brewham, was taken before Robert Hunt, Esq., to be examined and induced to confess. She did confess, without torture as it would appear; at all events without more than the ordinary torture of "pricking" and sleeplessness always applied to witches. She said that about a year and a half ago, she being in great poverty, was induced by one Catherine Green (her husband's sister?) to give her body and soul to the devil on condition that he would give her clothes, victuals, and money, as she might desire. She was to keep his secrets, and suffer him to suck her once in the twenty-four hours; to which at last she consented, the devil giving her fourpence-halfpenny as earnest money wherewith to buy bread in Brewham. Since this time he came to her ever at five o'clock in the morning, much in the likeness of a hedgehog bending, and sucked her left breast: a painful process, though she was generally in a kind of trance at the time. Christian Green gave no new particulars relative to the devil and his works. He was always as a man in black clothes; and he charmed pictures to the undoing of those for whom they were designed; and when he vanished he left an ill smell behind him; and he spake them very low when they arrived; and they did three horses to death by saying simply, "A Murrain on them Horses to death;" and they bewitched unlikely sinners by mere word or look: all of which processes we have read of twenty times before. Nor was there much more to be got out of "the villainous Feats of that rampant hag Margaret Agar," of Brewham, tried also in 1664, whom poor hysterical Christian Green had delated, for she did nothing

---

148 Glanvil.

beyond curse her enemies and those who offended her, whereupon they died "as if stabbed with daggers," or were "consumed and pined away;" some with one disease, some with another; but all dying without reprieve because of her curse. She also, in company with many others, was proved to have met "a little man in black clothes," whom they called "Robin," and to whom they all made obeisance, the little man putting his hand to his head, saying, "How do ye?" speaking low, but big. And they made "pictures" of wax into which the little black man stuck thorns, one in the crown, another in the breast, and a third in the side, which then Margaret would fling down saying, "This is Cornish's figure with a murrain to it," and Elizabeth Cornish would languish and die; or "This is Bess Hill's;" or any other person's whom it was desired to "forespeak" and destroy; who of course were forespoken and destroyed from that hour. Margaret Agar was a "rampant hag" indeed in one sense, being evidently an ill-conditioned old woman, quick at a curse, and passionately eager to avenge herself, but her magical arts appear to have been of the lowest possible order, and pale and lifeless compared with the more highly-coloured doings of others. Anything, however, was sufficient for the worshipful Master Robert Hunt and his fellow justices, and curses did as well as the rest; so poor old Margaret Agar was taken to the tree whereon grew the fatal fruit of death, to meditate there on Christian charity and the wise compassionateness of men, before learning by what steps the weary soul passes from earth to immortality. She was probably no great loss to the community, but her death placed her among the martyrs to superstition, and left her for ever as an object of historic pity.

SIR MATTHEW HALE'S JUDGMENT.[149]

At Bury St. Edmonds, in the county of Suffolk, a remarkable "Tryal of witches" was held on the tenth day of March, 1664, before Sir Matthew Hale, Lord Chief Baron of the Court of Exchequer. Rose Cullender and Amy Duny, both widows and both of Leystoff, were indicted for bewitching Elizabeth and Ann Durent, Jane Bocking, Susan Chandler, William Durent, and Elizabeth and Deborah Pacy. William Durent, being an infant, was sworn by grace of his mother Dorothy, and she deposed that some little time ago, having occasion to go from home, she desired Amy, who was her neighbour, to look after her child, but expressly forbade her to suckle it in her absence. When asked by the court why she gave this caution to an old woman far past the age of performing such an office, Dorothy answered that Amy had long had the character of a witch who might suckle the devil himself or any of his imps; and that moreover old women were apt to give the breast to a crying child, to please it during its mother's absence; a habit that made the children ill. But it seems that Amy disobeyed her, for when she came home the old woman told her that she had given the breast to her infant, which made Dorothy very cross, and a high quarrel ensued. And that very night her child was taken with "strange fits of swounding," and was held in such a terrible manner that she expected to lose it every moment. Not knowing what to do or where to get it relief, she went to a certain Doctor Jacob, well known through the country for skill in helping children that were bewitched, and this Dr. Jacob advised her to hang up the child's blanket in the chimney corner all the day, and to put the child into it at night, and not be afraid at anything she might see, but to throw it at once into the fire. Dorothy did as she was bid, and when she took the

[149] Tract; Published 1682.

blanket from the chimney-corner, down fell a great toad, "which ran up and down the hearth, and she having a young youth only with her in the House, desired him to catch the Toad and throw it into the Fire; which the youth did accordingly, and held it there with the Tongs; and as soon as it was in the Fire it made a great and horrible noise, and after a space there was a flashing in the Fire like Gunpowder, making a noise like the discharge of a Pistol, and thereupon the Toad was no more seen nor heard." But Amy Duny sat by her fireside all smirched and scorched, and in revenge bewitched the little daughter Elizabeth to death, and further afflicted Dorothy herself with a lameness in both her legs, so that she was forced to go upon crutches. About which the strangest thing was, that though she had gone on them for three years now, no sooner was Amy Duny condemned than she cast them away and went home without them, "to the great admiration of all persons." This was the first count completed.

The second was made by Samuel Pacy, "a Merchant of Leystoff aforesaid (a Man who carried himself with so much soberness during the Tryal, from whom proceeded no words either of Passion or Malice, though his Children were so greatly Afflicted)," on behalf of his daughters, Elizabeth and Deborah; the one aged about eleven, the other nine. Elizabeth had fits. She remained as one wholly senseless or in a deep sleep, the only sign of life being that, as she lay on cushions in the court, her stomach was raised to a great height on the drawing of her breath. After she had remained there for some time she came somewhat to herself, and then "laid her Head on the Bar of the Court with a Cushion under it, and her hand and her Apron upon that;" when Amy Duny was brought privately to touch her. She had no sooner done so than the child, although not seeing her, suddenly leaped up and caught her by the hand and face, and scratched her till the blood came: after which she was easier. Samuel deposed that his younger daughter,

Deborah, was suddenly taken with a lameness in her legs, which continued from the 10th to the 17th of October; when the day, being fair and sunshiny, she desired to be carried to the east part of the house, and then set upon a bank which looks towards the sea. While sitting there, came Amy Duny to buy some herrings; but being denied she went away grumbling, and on the instant "the Child was taken with the most violent Fits, feeling most extream Pain in her Stomach, like the pricking of Pins, and shreeking out in a most dreadful manner, like unto a Whelp, and not like unto a sensible Creature." The doctor, not understanding this disorder, and Amy Duny being under ill fame for a witch, Samuel Pacy caused her to be set in the stocks, as the most powerful remedy he knew of for his child's disorder. Being in the stocks, a neighbour told her that she was suspected of being the cause of Mr. Pacy's trouble: whereupon Amy answered, "Mr. Pacy keeps a great stir about his Child; let him stay until he has done as much by his Children as I have by mine." And being further examined what she had done to her children, she answered, "That she had been fain to open her Child's Mouth with a Tap to give it victuals." When, therefore, Elizabeth, the elder girl, fell ill within two days after this, and could by no means be made to open her mouth without a good-sized tap being put into it, the thing was certain, and might no longer be gainsayed. And when they both vomited crooked pins, and as many as forty broad-headed nails, and were deprived of sight and hearing, and cried out perpetually against Amy Duny and Rose Cullender, and could not be got to say the names "Jesus," "Lord," or "Christ," but when they came to "Satan" or "Devil," would clap their fingers on the book (the New Testament), crying out, "This bites, but makes me speak right well," what sane person could doubt the truth? Other strange things beside happened to them. They used to see creatures of the appearance of mice run up and down the house, and one of them "suddainly snapt one with the Tongs, and threw it into the Fire, and it screeched out like a Rat." At another time a thing like a bee flew into Deborah's face, and would have got into her mouth, had she not gone shrieking into the house; when, with much apparent pain and effort, she brought up a twopenny nail with a broad head, which she said the bee had forced into her mouth. Again, another time, Elizabeth cried out that she saw a mouse under the table, which she caught up in her apron and flung into the fire. Deponent, her aunt, confessed that she saw nothing in the child's hand, nevertheless the fire flashed as if gunpowder had been flung in; also "at another time, the said Child being speechless, but otherwise of perfect understanding, ran round about the House, holding her Apron, crying 'Hush, hush,' as if there had been Poultry in the House; but this Deponent could perceive nothing; but at last she saw the Child stoop as if she had catch't at something, and put it into her Apron, and afterwards made as if she had thrown it into the Fire; but this Deponent could not discover any thing; but the Child afterwards being restored to her speech, she, this Deponent, demanded of her what she saw at the time she used such a posture? who answered, That she saw a Duck."

Others deposed to the same kind of things: as Edmund Durent, father to the girl Ann, whom Rose Cullender had bewitched—also because denied the right of buying herrings; and Diana Bocking, mother to Jane likewise afflicted with crooked pins and tenpenny nails; and Mary Chandler, mother of Susan, who was stricken blind and dumb, and had the plague of pins upon her too, and who cried out "in a miserable manner, 'Burn her, burn her,'" which were all the words she could speak, and which meant that poor old Rose was to be burnt that Susan Chandler might be dispossessed. And there was Dr. Brown, of Norwich, a person of great knowledge, who gave it as his deliberate opinion that the girls were bewitched, every one of them, and that "the Devil in such cases did work upon the Bodies of Men and Women upon a Natural Foundation, (that is) to stir up and excite such Humours superabounding in their Bodies to a great Excess, whereby he did in an Extraordinary Manner Afflict them with such Distempers as their Bodies were most subject to, as particularly appeared in these Children; for he considered that these swooning Fits were Natural, and nothing else but that they call the Mother, but only heightened to a great excess by the subtilty of the Devil co-operating with the Malice of these which we term Witches, at whose instance he doth these Villanies." Such an argument as this was then held quite as pertinent and irresistible as would now be the evidence of the microscope and the test of chemical experiment. It is refreshing, in the midst of all this wild nonsense, to find that some gentlemen—Lord Cornwallis, Sir Edmund Bacon, and Mr. Serjeant Keeling, who had been directed by the Lord Chief Justice to make an experiment with these girls—openly protested against the whole thing, affirming it to be an imposture from first to last; and that when the children covered up their heads in their aprons, and shrieked and writhed when Rose Cullender or Amy Duny touched them, they did it in full possession of their senses, and perfectly understanding what they were about. For when they tried them with other women whom they made believe were the two, cried out on, and took care that their eyes were held, so that they should not see, the children shrieked and howled, and went off into their fits all the same; which double experiment satisfied the gentlemen of the fraudulent character of it all. But this little nucleus of rationality was not strong enough to disperse the thick darkness gathered round the minds of all present—gathered round the mind of even Sir Thomas Brown and the "good" Sir Matthew Hale; and when one witness had deposed that his cart had stuck fast between some posts, and that the haymakers could not unload the

398

hay until the next morning, because Rose Cullender had threatened him; and another that his pigs and cattle died in a most extraordinary manner, and he himself swarmed with vermin which he could not get rid of, because he also had been threatened by her; and a third that she had lost her geese because Amy Duny had said she should; and that a chimney had fallen down because Amy Duny had said it would—when all these things had been sworn to and proved, then the minds of the judge and jury admitted of no further doubt. Amy Duny and Rose Cullender were brought in guilty, and hanged at Cambridge on Monday, March 17, confessing nothing.

"The next morning the children came with their Parents to the Lodgings of the Lord Chief Justice, and were in as good Health as ever they were in their lives, being restored within half an hour after the witches were convicted." A fact then sufficiently conclusive, but which now is the strongest proof that could be offered of the wicked deception of the whole matter.

THE WAITING-MAID AND THE PIN.[150]

In 1665 Elizabeth Brooker, servant to Mrs. Hieron, of Honiton, in Devonshire, waiting at table one Lord's day, suddenly felt a pricking as of a pin in her thigh, and, on looking, found indeed a pin there, but inside her skin, drawing no blood nor breaking the skin, and thrust in so far that she could scarce feel the head of it with her finger. By Tuesday it had worked so far inwards that she could no longer feel it at all; and the day after she went to Mr. Anthony Smith, a surgeon of great repute, who was obliged to have recourse to incisions and cataplasms, and all the appliances of the surgery, in order to extract this obstinate and malevolent pin. For it was a bewitched pin; and either Agnes Richardson, who had been angry with Elizabeth "about miscarriage in an errand that she sent her on," or an unknown woman who had lately been near her, was suspected of the crime of sticking it into her. Mrs. Hieron was a widow, and kept a draper's shop in Honiton, and Elizabeth Brooker, her servant, sold small wares in a stall before her mistress's door. On market day, which was Saturday, came a certain woman and asked Elizabeth for a pin. She took one from her sleeve readily enough; but the woman was dissatisfied, and demanded one of a bigger sort hung up in a paper to sell. The maid said they were not hers to give; they were her mistress's: if she would ask her mistress for one, and get her leave to have it, she, Elizabeth, would then give her one willingly. This woman went away in a great fume, saying "she should hear farther from her, and that she would wish e'er long she had given the pin as desired." The next day a pin was thrust into her thigh as she was waiting at table, and no Christian person could doubt whence it came or why it was sent. Mr. Anthony Smith, the "Chirurgeon of great Reputation," who

---

[150] Baxter's 'World of Spirits.'

could not extract a pin without a fortnight's illness supervening, wrote a detailed account of the whole matter; but whether the unknown woman was traced and found, or whether Agnes Richardson got any mishandling for the suspicion cast on her, or whether, again, the trick passed off without result, and no one was the worse because a maid-servant chose to run a pin into her thigh, I can find no record to inform me. As not much harm was done, perhaps the devil was let off easy this time, and the hags, his mistresses, suffered to extend their trade a little longer.

JANE STRETTON AND THE CUNNING WOMAN.[151]

Jane Stretton and her parents lived at Ware in the year 1669, Jane being then a young maid of about twenty, generally out at service. It chanced that Thomas, her father, lost a Bible, and must needs go to a cunning man to ask where it was, and who had it—a thing which, as a good Christian, he should have been ashamed of: to which the cunning man replied darkly, "he could tell him if he would." Whereupon Stretton, not in the least grateful for such a doubtful reply, broke out with, "Then thou must be either a witch or a devil, seeing thou canst neither read nor write." This was all that passed, and it seems but scant substance for a deadly quarrel; but a few days afterwards this cunning man's wife went slily to Stretton's, and asked daughter Jane for a pot of drink. This was to establish direct communication. "Innocency dreads no danger: the child will play with the Bee for his gaudy Coat, and mistrusts not his sting," says this flowery tract; but soon after Jane had thus committed herself to transfers and communication with the witch, the "devil, who is a sly thief, and though he keeps his servants poor, yet indues them, with a plentifull stock of malice, revenge, and dissimulation," suffered this bad woman, or this cunning man, to afflict Jane, but not so grievously as they were suffered to do hereafter. In about a week's time the cunning man's wife went and desired a pin of her, which Jane, granting, became suddenly beset with fits, most terrible to behold. "But her misery ends not here: the squib is not run out to the end of the rope. When the Devil has an inch given to him he will take an ell;" so poor Jane was not only troubled with fits, but must needs have her mouth stopped so that she ate nothing for weeks and months, and was forced to live like a chameleon, on air.

---

[151] 'Hartfordshire Wonder; or, Strange News from Ware.' London. Printed for John Clark, at the Bible and Harp, in West-Smith-Field, near the Hospital Gate. 1669.

Besides this, she was made to perpetually vomit flax and hair and thread-ends and crooked pins; while blue, white, and red flames came in the intervals out of her mouth, and her body was continually slashed and cut with a knife, and imps in the shape of frogs, and toads, and mice, and the like, for ever haunted her; and the wise man's wife was the cause of all. Then the neighbours took some of the foam which Jane had always hanging round her mouth, and burnt it for a counter charm, and to hurt the besetting witch; and chancing to light on the woman, they told her they would take her to the maid to be scratched. To which she made answer, "That if they had not come she could not have stayed any longer from her:" so great was the potency of the burnt foam. For nine months did this girl befool her world, and then—the cunning man and his wife being probably put to death—she managed to get well of all her ailments, and to find meat and milk more sustaining diet than crooked pins, hair, or wool; though, indeed, the meat and milk had never been wanting in the dark hours undiscovered, for Jane had taken care to live as usual when the night had blinded prying eyes, and there was no one to count off the tale of slices cut and devoured.

Fortunately for the sanity of society, every one did not believe these monstrous stories. Webster's book, published about this time, was one of those brave few which openly discredited the truth of the witch stories afloat in the world, and made as great a sensation, or even greater, than the grand old work of Reginald Scot. Like him, Webster doubted the truth of the witch of Endor's enchantments, which the upholders of the faith rested on as the very keystone of their position. The witch herself he calls "a cozening quean," "a crafty subtile quean," "an idolatrous, wicked, and couzening witch:" for they understood the value of forcible language in those days: Saul is "a drowned puppet"—to Glanvil's intense wrath at this rude mishandling of a "noble prince;" Samuel but "a confederate knave," or "but a lying phantasie;" in the conjurations the witch, "casting herself into a feigned Trance, lay grovelling upon the Earth with her face downwards, and so changing her voice did mutter, and murmur, and peep, and chirp, like a bird coming forth of the shell;" with other knockdown assertions of common sense not afraid, by which the curate of Kildwick demolished the whole argument of supernaturalism, and left the poor witch of Endor and Saul himself not an inch of ground to stand on. So with all the other stories that came into his hands; so with the special points of faith, peculiar to the creed of witchcraft, such as communion and covenant with the devil, transportation through the air on sticks, straws, or bedstaves; transformation into the shapes of cat, dog, wolf, raven, &c.; intercourse with imps and familiars; witches' sabbaths; charms; conjurations; weeping the prescribed three tears with the left eye only, or not weeping at all; swimming on the surface of the water, because of the Christian character of that element, which refused to admit a devil-devoted soul within its bosom; apparitions, or spectres of witches troubling the afflicted—souls quitting their bodies, but taking with them the spiritual substance even of woven garments; with the whole course of lies and delusions belonging to the subject, from the devil's baptism to the imps' bigges. All this seemed but so much delusion to plain John Webster, with his unidealising common sense and kindly heart; yet a delusion so fraught with sin and danger as to make it a Christian man's first duty to combat and destroy it. Wherefore was he most barbarously and evilly entreated by Glanvil in his "Saducismus Triumphatus"— the answer to the "Displaying of Supposed Witchcraft"— and a mighty pretty quarrel, full of the choicest amenities, was the result. But as Glanvil had error and credulity, and Webster reason and right judgment on his side, it mattered little who was assumed to have the best of it for the moment. Time and education gradually settled the question, and buried it for a time out of sight; yet it has sprung up anew of late, and now needs settling again.

THE BIDEFORD TROUBLES.[152]

In the July of 1682, Temperance Lloyd, of Bideford, or "Bytheford," was accused of bewitching Mrs. Grace Thomas. Temperance, being a little crazy, had cried one day on meeting Mrs. Grace, who had been for long months but a poor, "dunt," feckless body; and when asked why she wept had made answer, "For joy to see her who had been so ill, walk abroad again without disaster." But that very same night Mrs. Grace was taken with fresh pains, "sticking and pricking Pains, as if Pins and Awls had been thrust into her Body, from the Crown of her Head to the Soles of her Feet, and she lay as if she had been upon a rack;" and none but Temperance Lloyd the cause thereof, despite all her hypocritical tears. And did not Elizabeth Eastcheap see her knee, which looked as if it had been pricked in nine places with a thorn? And when Temperance was asked if she had any clay or wax wherewith to torment Mrs. Grace, did she not confess to a bit of leather which she had pricked nine times, and which was as full of venom and sorcery as any wax or clay in the world? Besides, it came out afterwards, that she had gone to Thomas Eastcheap's shop in the form of a gray or "braget cat," and thence taken out a "puppit or picture, commonly called a child's baby," which she stuck full of pins, whereby to prick Grace to death. When asked in what part of the house the said puppet or picture was hidden, she refused to tell, saying the devil would tear her in pieces if she confessed. Anne Wakely, too, the neighbour who went to nurse poor Grace, had her word to say; for one morning—it was on a bonny day in June—she saw "something in the shape of a magpye come at the chamber window;" and when Temperance was questioned as to what she knew of this fluttering thing, she made answer that it was the Black Man in the shape of a

---

[152] Boulton's 'Compleat History of Magick.'

bird which she had sent to trouble poor rheumatic pain-racked Grace. For Temperance was not stiff. She was easily brought to confess how she had given herself over to the service of a black man, who made her do all manner of hurt to her neighbours—made her pinch Grace Thomas, and bewitch William Herbert to his death twelve years ago, and destroy Anne Fellows three years since—for both of which crimes she had been arraigned and questioned at the time, but had managed to get clear. Now, however, she confessed that she had been guilty of them. The dread and evil fame and poverty under which she had lived so long had done their appointed work on her poor old brain; and she was ready to confess to anything which it was desired she should allow. Yes, she had bewitched the eyes of Jane Dalbin, but so secretly that no one had suspected her: and she had destroyed one woman by kissing her, holding her so tight that she squeezed her to death—the blood gushing out of her mouth and nose: and she hunted with the devil, he going before her in the shape of a hound; "doubtless he hunted for souls," says a very odd tract which gives this additional trait of diabolical management and the economy of time. Being asked of what stature was her black man, she said "he was above the Length of her Arm; and that his Eyes were very big; and that he hopped, or leaped in the way before her;" but when asked if she had made any contract with him she said "No; neither had she gone through the keyhole when she went to harm Grace Thomas, but through the door, the devil leading her, and both invisible; and that she had been made to pinch and torment Grace; and that the devil beat her about the head grievously because she would not kill her." She had never bewitched any ships or boats, nor done a child to death; for the child who stole her apple died of the small-pox, and she was guiltless of its decease; nor had she ever ridden over an arm of the sea on a cow—"No, master, never; it was she," meaning another delated witch, Susanna Edwards, who did this. The worst thing she had ever done was to Grace Thomas, and then the devil made her do it, beating her about the head and back in shape and form, "black like a bullock." Temperance Lloyd was executed; and died penitent and crazy.

Mary Trembles was another delated witch. She bewitched Agnes Whitefield with all manner of pains; and Grace Barnes deposed to pricks and pains like awls and pins thrust into her, which evil Mary Trembles and Susanna Edwards had done together; for they were comrades and cronies, and would go hand-in-hand about the world, invisible to all save themselves and their master the devil. It was Susanna Edwards who had seduced Mary and got her to accept the service of the devil, who came to her as a lion; at which she was much frightened, though not hurt; and made her bewitch Grace Barnes, because said Grace would give her no meat. She was also executed, very penitent and quite resigned.

Susanna Edwards was active and powerful in forespeaking. She sent pains to Dorcas Coleman—tormenting pains, and very grievous—so that Dr. George Bear could do her no good, but openly proclaimed her beyond his power for that she was bewitched; and she held Anthony Jones pretty hardly, as Joane his wife deposed. For when Susan was apprehended, Anthony "observing her to gripe and twinkle her Hands upon her own Body, said to her, 'Thou Devil, thou art now tormenting some Person or other.'" Upon which the said Susanna was displeased with him, and said, "Well enough I will fit thee." And fit him she did, for on his making one of the rabble that dragged her before the magistrates, Susanna turned round and looked at him, "so that he cried out, 'I am now bewitched with this Devil, wife,' meaning Susanna Edwards, and presently leaped and capered like a madman, and fell a-shaking, quivering, and foaming, and for the space of half an Hour like a dying or dead Man." Susan knew the devil as a gentleman dressed in black clothes, and also as a little boy; but could not be induced to confess to any of the more striking monstrosities beyond what might have well belonged to an ordinary case of hallucination. She was executed as the other two; but we are not told if Grace Thomas, or Dorcas Coleman, or Grace Barnes, or Anthony Jones recovered their health now that the witches were dead, or if hysteria and rheumatism and neuralgia and scrofula were found more troublesome enemies to conquer than three crazy old women. It would be curious as well as interesting to know the condition of the honestly deceived and actually diseased after the death of the possessing witch. In those instances where crutches were thrown away, and fits suddenly brought to a close, the instant the law had laid its gripe on the neck of the unfortunate accused, we have no choice but to refer the whole proceedings to imposture quickened by enmity or the desire of notoriety; but there were cases where a strange and sudden disease did really appear as bewitchment to the afflicted, and of these one would be glad to know the after mental condition when the obsessing witch was killed, yet the obsessing sickness unconquered. Did experience ever open their eyes or shake their faith? or did they die in their belief that the stake and the gallows were the finest remedies known for disordered functions or organic mischief? No one of the time was sufficiently accurate, or sufficiently unprejudiced, to be able to give us reliable information, and thus we have lost a most valuable indication of the absolute power exercised by the mind over the body.

SIR JOHN HOLT'S JUDGMENTS.[153]

Mr. May Hill, minister of Beckington, in Somersetshire (near Frome), had a servant, one Mary Hill, whom Satan and the malice of his servants had grievously bewitched. Mr. Baxter had brought to him a bag of iron, nails, and brass which the girl had vomited, and he kept some of them to show his friends. "Nails about three or four inches long, doubled, crooked at the end, and pieces of old Brass doubled, about an Inch broad and two Inches long, with crooked edges," all of which Mary had brought up, together with about two hundred crooked pins. Elizabeth Carrier was first committed on the charge of having bewitched her; but a fortnight after, Mary, whom this sacrifice had temporarily appeased, went back to her old ways, and began to vomit nails and pieces of nails, brass, and handles of spoons, and so continued to do for six months and more; all the while crying out against Margery Coombes and Ann More, who, she said, appeared to her and tormented her. These two poor creatures were immediately apprehended and committed to the county gaol; but Margery died as soon as she was imprisoned: and when my Lord Chief Justice Holt came to try old Ann, he said there was not sufficient evidence against her, so directed the jury to acquit her. But the maid was worse than ever after this acquittal, and took to vomiting pieces of glass, and several pieces of bread and butter besmeared with a poisonous matter, adjudged to be white mercury, and a great board nail, and, in short, Mr. May Hill and the neighbours did not know what she might not throw up at last, her mouth was so capacious, and the space against her gums so flexible. But as it was observed that she never vomited these things save in the morning, and that in the afternoon she was quiet; and when, upon inquiry, it was

---

[153] Baxter, Hutchinson.

found that she always slept with her mouth wide open, and slept so soundly, that she could not be awakened by pulling, or jogging, or calling; then Mr. Hill commanded that some one should sit up with her, and keep her mouth rigidly and pertinaciously shut. And when they did this she vomited nothing, for the witches had not been able to convey their trash into her mouth. This experiment was satisfactorily tried for thirteen nights; but as soon as she was left to sleep by herself, and with her mouth open, the wicked witches were sure to come to her and force all kinds of trash into it. But at last she wearied of her work; and, Sir John Holt not holding out much inducement to ill-tempered young women to declare themselves possessed because they had a disagreeable neighbour or two, she owned herself quite cured, and no more was heard of her fits or her nails.

Poor old Widow Chambers,[154] of Upaston, in Suffolk, "a diligent, industrious, poor woman," was accused of witchcraft, upon what grounds does not appear. "After she had been walk'd betwixt two," and, we may naturally suppose, pressed and plied with questions, she became confused and overwrought, and began to confess a great many things of herself. She said that she had killed both her husband and Lady Blois, though the last had died a fair and evident death, "without any Hurt from that poor Woman:" and then some, to make trial of her wits, asked her if she had not killed such and such persons then living? to which old Widow Chambers maundered out yes, she had killed them sure enough. She was committed to Beccles Gaol, even after this; but died before her trial, happily for her.

This was in 1693. The following year was a busy one for the witch-finders, but fortunate for such of the witches as came before Lord Chief Justice Holt, a man of clear, well-balanced mind, evidently not given to superstitious

---

[154] Dr. Hutchinson.

beliefs, or to much veneration for the Black Art. Mother Munnings, of Hartis, in Suffolk, was one of those brought before him at Bury St. Edmunds. She came with a bad character enough, accused of bewitching men to their death, spoiling brewings and churnings, and hurting cattle and corn—of being, in fact, a terrible pest to the whole neighbourhood. She killed Thomas Pannel her landlord, who had offended her by a rather summary method of ejectment, namely, taking her door off the hinges, since he could not get her out of his house any other way. Mother Munnings was angry: who would not have been? "Go thy way," she cried to him passionately; "thy Nose shall lie upward in the Churchyard before Saturday next." This was enough. Thomas Pannel sickened on Monday and died on Tuesday, and was buried within the week according to her word. That this was true was attested by a certain witness, a doctor, who said also that Mother Munnings "was a dangerous woman: she could touch the Line of Life." Mother Munnings had an imp, a thing like a polecat; and a man swore that one night, coming from the alehouse—a rather important circumstance—he saw her lift out of her basket two imps, a black one and a white; and it was well known that Sarah Wager was taken both dumb and lame after a quarrel with her, and was in that condition even at the time of trial. But in the face of all these tremendous accusations the Lord Chief Justice Holt directed the jury to bring her in Not Guilty, and poor old Mother Munnings lived in peace and quietness for about two years longer, doing no harm to anybody, and when dying declaring her innocence. Dr. Hutchinson gives a very rational, but somewhat quaint, explanation of two of the charges against her. On the death of her landlord, he says, that he, Thomas Pannel, "was a consumptive spent Man, and the Words not exactly as they swore them, and the whole Thing 17 years before;" and as to the imps—"the White Imp is believed to have been a Lock of Wool taken out of her Basket to spin;

and its Shadow, it is supposed, was the Black one." Not an impossibility with an ignorant country clown, reeling home half drunk from the alehouse, and disposed to make a miracle out of the plainest matter before him seen through a witch's window.

At the Ipswich assizes of that same year the Lord Chief Justice had to hold the sword of judgment unsheathed between Margaret Elnore and her accusers. Margaret belonged to a family of witches, her grandmother and her aunt having been both hanged for that rational offence; and now, when Mrs. Rudge had been for three years in a languishing condition—ever since her husband had refused to take Elnore for his tenant—what so likely as that she was bewitched, and that the enraged witch and relative of witches had done it? Besides, women who had quarrelled with Margaret had found themselves suddenly covered with vermin, not at all due to their own uncleanly habits, but to the diabolical power of old Elnore, who would send lice or locusts, disease or death, just as it suited her. For she had eight or nine imps, and she was plainly branded with the witch marks. Lord Chief Justice Holt pooh-poohed the imps and the vermin, and directed again a verdict of Not Guilty. So Margaret Elnore was suffered to live out the natural term of her life, and Mrs. Rudge recovered her health for a certain time; but—some years after Margaret was peaceably laid in her grave—"fell again into the same Kind of Pains (supposed from the Salt Humour), and died of the same Distemper."

The next year Mary Guy was tried at Launceston for bewitching Philadelphia Row, who swore to her apparition perpetually troubling her, and who had the uncomfortable habit of vomiting pins, straws, and feathers. But the Lord Chief Justice turned a deaf ear to Philadelphia Row also, and Mary Guy was acquitted. So was Elizabeth Horner, who, in 1696, was brought before him at Exeter, charged with having bewitched three children belonging to William

Bovet, whereof one was dead: "another had her Legs twisted, and yet from her Hands and Knees she would spring Five Foot high." The children brought up crooked pins, and were grievously bitten, and pinched, and pricked, and bruised—the marks of all this ill usage appearing plainly on the flesh; and they swore that Bess Horner's head would go off her shoulders and walk quietly into their stomachs: and the mother deposed "that one of them walked up a smooth plastered Wall, till her Feet were nine Foot high, her Head standing off from it." This she did five or six times, laughing and saying that Bess Horner held her up. Old Bess had a kind of wart or excrescence on her shoulder, which William Bovet's children said was her witch-mark, and where her imp—a toad—sucked; but the Lord Chief Justice shook his head, and Bess Horner was let to live on in her own way, taking off her head at will, and sending it into children's bodies, and nourishing a devil in shape of a toad on her shoulder—the law and judgment not interposing. The Lord Chief Justice had very many cases of witchcraft brought before him—about eleven places in all being supposed to be so infected—but he brought in every one "not guilty."

One of the most celebrated cases tried by him was that of Richard Hathaway, who came before him at the Guildford Assize of 1701 with a pitiful tale of possession and bewitchment, all owing to Sarah Morduck, of Southwark, in which parish he too was living as apprentice to Thomas Wellyn, blacksmith. Richard had fits and convulsions, in all probability real enough, for he was sent to the hospital, where he lay for seven weeks in a pitiable condition, sometimes bent double, and at all times strangely and fearfully contorted. This began in September, 1690,[155] he said, when the first appearances of being bewitched manifested themselves. For then he vomited crooked pins

---

[155] That date seems wrong: ought it not to be 1699?

in great numbers, and lumps of tin, and loose nails, and nut-shells, and stones; and he foamed at the mouth; and bowed himself into an arch; and lay as if dead; and barked like a dog; and burnt as if with fire; and in the midst of all signed that Sarah Morduck had bewitched him, and that he should never be well till he had "scratched" her. So she was brought to him to be scratched; after which he ate and drank and had his sight and was perfectly well for six weeks together. Then he fell ill again, and must needs scratch her for this attack; and this time with more unction, for Sarah "was assaulted in her own House, and grievously abused; her Hair and Face torn; she was kicked, thrown to the Ground, stamped on, and threatened to be put into a Horse Pond, to be tried by Swimming, and very hardly escaped with her Life." To avoid being absolutely murdered, she left Southwark and went into London; but still was not safe, for she was constantly being followed in the streets, and was often in danger of being pulled to pieces by a mob which credited all that Richard Hathaway said and did. In 1701 she was taken before one Sir Thomas Lane, who ordered her to be stript and searched, and let Hathaway loose again on her to scratch her. After which he was well as before; and then Sarah Morduck was committed, and prayers were offered up in the churches for Hathaway, and collections made for him in the congregations, and six or seven pounds at a time got for him, besides various other sums, to bear his charges at the Assizes, and indemnify him for the evil the witch had inflicted. At the Assizes (Guildford, July, 1701) Sarah Morduck was brought out of prison to be tried for her life by the Lord Chief Justice: with the usual result in his trials of witches: she was released, but Hathaway took her place, and was committed to the Marshalsea as a cheat and impostor, lying, for the first part of the time, well and hearty, but afterwards falling into his fits again as if bewitched. He was then experimented with; given another woman to scratch, under the idea that it was Sarah; whom he scratched quite contentedly, and as well after he had done so. When he found out his mistake he was blind and dumb again. But now, it being specially desired to know the truth, when he brought up his crooked pins, his hands were kept carefully out of his pockets, which then were searched, and found plentifully supplied; and all the strange noises which had been heard to issue out of his bed were discovered to have been made by his own feet scratching the bedposts; and his miraculous fasting was proved a cheat, for Mrs. Kensy's maid, who had got into his confidence by a stratagem, brought him meat and drink privately, and Mr. Kensy and his friends peeping through a private hole saw him eat it quite composedly. So one by one his pretences were destroyed, and he was openly convicted of cozening and imposture. The Lord Chief Justice thought this a more cognizable crime than witchcraft, and condemned Richard Hathaway to be imprisoned for a year, and to stand in the pillory thrice during the period. Thus he was made a warning to all hysterical youths and maidens who took to possession as a good trade, and who liked the prayers of the faithful, and the money of the credulous, and the luxury of ill-treating any one specially spited, and the attentions of the gentry, and the pity of the commonalty, and all manner of petting and cossiting better than coarse hard fare and the scanty pleasures wrung from horny-handed labour. This Lord Chief Justice, Sir John Holt, may be taken as one of the greatest, if of the less noisy and notorious, benefactors of England known; setting himself so firmly as he did against this cruel and debasing superstition, and so manfully upholding the claims of humanity and common sense against all the "possibilities" of idealism, and the wild errings of credulity. From his time the witch madness sensibly declined, and folks woke gradually to the possession of their ordinary faculties.

THE SURREY DEMONIAC.[156]

"What, Satan! is this the Dancing that Richard gave himself to thee for? Can'st thou Dance no better? Ransack the old Records of all past Times and Places in thy Memory: Can'st thou not there find out some better way of Trampling? Pump thine Invention dry: Cannot that universal Seed-plot of subtile Wiles and Stratagems spring up one new Method of Cutting Capers? Is this the top of Skill and Pride, to shuffle Feet, and brandish Knees thus, and to trip like a Doe, and skip like a Squirrel? And wherein differs thy Leapings from the Hoppings of a Frog, or Bouncings of a Goat, or Friskings of a Dog, or Gesticulations of a Monkey? And cannot a Palsy shake such a loose Leg as that? Dost thou not twirl like a Calf that hath the Turn, and twitch up thy Houghs just like a Spring-hault Tit?" This was one of the conversations, or rather exhortations, which the dissenting ministers had with the devil inhabiting Richard Dugdale—he who was called by some the Surrey demoniac,[157] by others the impostor, as faith or reason was the stronger. Richard drew largely upon the faith of his generation, largely even for the credulous generation flourishing in the year of our Lord 1695: for Richard the "possessed" vomited gold, silver, and brass rings, hair buttons, blue stones like flints, and once a big stone bloody at the edges; and he was transformed sometimes to the manner of a horse, when he would gallop round the barn on all fours, quite as quickly as any cob ever foaled, and whinny like a cob, and eat provender like a cob; and sometimes he was like a dog, "harring" and snarling and growling and barking so like a mastiff, that once a dog, a real mastiff and no counterfeit, set upon him, and would have given him rather an undesirable taste of canine

---

[156] Boulton's 'Compleat History of Magick.' Dr. Hutchinson's 'Historical Essay.'

[157] Surrey in Lancashire.

fraternity had he not been prevented. Then he would be heavy or light in the same fit—now so heavy that six men could not lift him, now so light that he did not weigh six pounds: "sometimes light as a Feather-Boulster, but before he came out heavier than a Load of Corn," says a husbandman; "as light as a Chip, and as heavy as a horse," says a carpenter: and he had fits of leaping, as fast as a man could count; and he would dance on his toes and his knees, with marvellous agility—dance more quickly than ordinary men, not possessed, could do on their honest feet; then he would lie as if dead; or he would gape and snatch with his mouth, catching at flies; and he had noises in his mouth and breast, as if a family of young whelps were lapping, snarling, or sucking in his inside; and he rolled up his tongue into a lump and turned his eyes inward; and talked gibberish, which some one said was Latin; and played with rushes as if they had been dice and bowls. "And when he had thrown the 'Jack,' he said, 'I must now throw my Gill;' then running a good way, as if he had been running after a bowl, swearing, 'Run, Run, Flee, Flee, Hold a Biass;' and sometimes he catched up rushes, as if they had been bowls, swearing, 'Sirrah, stand out of the Way, or I'll knock out your Brains,' adding, 'I never was a Bowler, But don't Gentlemen do thus?'" which is scarcely evidence to us that he was possessed, or in any abnormal condition whatsoever. Neither was his habit of swearing and cursing, "so that he would have affrighted ordinary men," any very distinct sign of supernaturalism; nor yet his insolence in saying to Mr. Carrington, who had adjured the devil in him mightily, "Thou shalt be Porter of Hell-Gates, Thou'st have Brewis and Toad Broath." Any bold-faced lad of eighteen might have said the same under cover of what he chose to call a fit. And as for the strange swelling, as big as a turkey's egg, which ran like a mouse about his body, whatever in that account was naturally impossible was either trick on his part, or self-deception on the part of those who gave their testimony. Besides, they were all inclined to believe. Why, John Fletcher, who slept one night with Richard, and felt something come up towards his knees, creeping higher and higher till it got to his heart—something about the bigness of a little cat or dog, which when he thought to catch "slipped through his hands like a Snig"—even that most unterrifying occurrence was transformed into a demoniacal visitant, and the thing that slipped through John Fletcher's hands like a snig was no other than Richard Dugdale's devil come to pay him a midnight visit. Then Richard laid stones like hens' eggs, and in the manner of hens; and he flung them to incredible distances when newly laid, and they felt warm as milk; and he showed a slight amount of power in the matter of clairvoyance; but, oh faithless, feeble devil! when Drs. Chew and Crabtree got hold of him, and bled him well, and gave him physic, the devil, who hates blue pill and black draught worse than holy water, flew away, and what all the prayers and fastings and exhortations of the ministry could not do, the lancet and a good dose of calomel and aloes effected without trouble. And then Richard Dugdale confessed that he had never been possessed, but only ill, in consequence of a fight he had had with a man at a rush-bearing at Whalley, while he, Master Richard, was in drink. The next day he was heavy and troubled in his mind, and drank a quantity of cold water while in the hay field making hay; but being advised to go up to the hall and get a drink of something more nourishing, he took the advice, and went into the house, where the cook maid gave him some drink; and then he went into his own room and lay down. While thus on the bed the chamber door seemed to him to open of itself, and there came a thick smoke or mist, which on vanishing left him in extreme fear and horror; then appeared one Hindle, a fellow servant, with his hair cropped close to his ears, and he lay very heavy on his breast, but soon turned himself into the likeness of a naked child, which he caught by the knee; but the child became a "filmet" (foumart, pole-cat?), and went away with a shrill shriek. After this he raved, and was delirious; but when Dr. Chew physicked him, and Dr. Crabtree bled him, and Dr. Chew physicked him again, he had no more "fits," no more "obsessions" or "possessions," was no longer the demoniac of Surrey, half maniac, half impostor, but went quietly back to ordinary life, and the whole tribe of exorcising ministers were for once discomfited. It was a singular mercy to his friends and acquaintances that Master Richard did not take it into his head to delate any of them as witches, for assuredly he might have hanged half Lancashire on the strength of the whelps inside his body, and his galloping on all fours like a horse. He would not have been the first to shed innocent blood for the sake of keeping up a notoriety which, originally begun in very ordinary and natural disease, was afterwards continued in deception, fraud, and lies.

THE GROCER'S YOUNG MAN.[158]

A few years after (1704) Sarah Griffiths lay suspected for a witch, and a bad one, for all the children in her neighbourhood were afflicted with strange distempers, and had visions of cats and the like, so that no one coveted poor Sarah's company, and many removed because of her. Her guilt was discovered at last by a jolly young grocer's lad, who was one day weighing her out some soap, but the scales would not hang right, whereat he laughed and cried out they were bewitched. Sarah Griffiths did not understand joking. She got very angry, and ran out of the shop threatening revenge; and the next night all the goods in the shop were turned topsy-turvy, and the day after the jolly young fellow was troubled with a strange disease—but by prayer released. Meeting her by chance some time after, as he and some friends were walking up to New River Head, they resolved to swim her. They tossed her in, and she swam like a cork. They kept her there for some time, but at last she got out, and struck the young man on the arm, telling him he should pay dearly for what he had done. He looked at his arm and found it black as a coal, with the exact mark of her hand and fingers on it. He went home much tormented, vomiting old nails, pins, and the like, afflicted with fits and strange contortions, and for ever calling out against Mother Griffiths as he lay sickening and disabled. And then his arm gangrened and rotted off: whereby he died. Mother Griffith was taken by the constable, who, on her attempting to escape, knocked her down. She was secured more firmly, taken before the judge, and committed to Bridewell, whence—though I find no sequel to this strange little page—there is very little doubt that she was haled forth at the assizes only to be convicted and hanged.

---

[158] A Tract of one leaf in a collection of trials.

We are coming now (1712) to the last authentic trial for witchcraft where the accused was condemned to death for an impossible crime by a jury of sane, decent, respectable Englishmen. Jane Wenham was this latest offshoot of the old tree of judicial bigotry; not the latest fruit, but the last instance of the law and judgment. There is a report current in most witch books of a case at a later period—but I can find no *authentic* account of it—that, in 1716, of a Mrs. Hicks and her little daughter of nine, hanged at Huntingdon for selling their souls to the devil, bewitching their neighbours to death and their crops to ruin, and, as a climax to all, taking off their stockings to raise a storm. It may well be so, but I have not met with it in any reliable shape, so meanwhile we must accept Jane Wenham as the last officially condemned.

THE WITCH OF WALKERNE.[159]

Jane Wenham was the witch of Walkerne, a little village in the north of Hertford. She had long lived under ill fame, and her neighbours were resolved to get rid of her at the earliest opportunity. That opportunity presented itself in the person of John Chapman's man, one Matthew Gilson, whom Jane sent into a daft state by asking him for a pennyworth of straw, which he refused to give her. The old woman went away, muttering and complaining, whereupon Matthew, impelled by he knew not what impulse, ran out of the barn for a distance of three miles, asking as he went for pennyworths of straw. Not getting any, he went on to some dirt heaps, and gathered up straw from them, which he put in his shirt and brought home. A witness testified that he had seen Gilson come back with his shirt stuffed full of straw, that he moved along quickly, and walked straight through the water, instead of passing over the bridge like any other decent man. For this odd behaviour of his servant, John Chapman, who had all along suspected Jane of more cunning than was good for him or her— called her a witch the next time he saw her; and Jane took him before the magistrate, Sir Herbert Chauncey, to answer to the charge of defamation. But the magistrate recommended them to go to Mr. Gardiner the minister, and a great believer in witchcraft, and get their matter settled without more trouble or vexation. Mr. Gardiner was too zealous to be just. He scolded poor old Jane roundly, and advised her to live more peaceably with her neighbours—which was just what she wanted to do—and gave as his award that Chapman do pay the fine of one shilling. While this bit of one-sided justice was going on, Anne Thorne, Mr. Gardiner's servant, was sitting by the fire with a dislocated knee. Jane, not able to compass her wicked will on

---

[159] Various Tracts—and 'Thomas Wright's Narrative.'

Chapman, and angry that Mr. Gardiner had spoken so harshly to her, turned her malice on the girl, and bewitched her, so that as soon as they all left the kitchen Anne felt a strange "Roaming in her Head, and she thought she must of Necessity run somewhere." In spite then of her dislocated knee, she started off and ran up the close, and away over a five-barred gate "as nimbly as a greyhound," along the highway and up a hill. And there she met two of John Chapman's men, who wanted her to go home with them; and one took her hand; but she was forced away from them, speechless, and not of her own volition, and so was driven on, on, towards Cromer, where the great sea would have either stopped or received her. But when she came to Hockney Lane, she met there a "little Old Woman muffled up in a Riding-Hood," who asked her whither she was going. "To Cromer," says Anne, "for sticks to make me a fire." "There be no sticks at Cromer," says the little old woman in the riding hood: "here be sticks enow; go to that oak tree and pluck them there." Which Anne did, laying them on the ground as they were gathered. Then the old woman bade her pull off her gown and apron, and wrap the sticks in them; asking her if she had ne'er a pin about her; but finding that she had not, she gave her a large crooked pin, with which she bade her pin her bundle, then vanished away. So Anne Thorne ran home half naked, with her bundle of leaves and sticks in her hand, and sat down in the kitchen, crying out "I am ruined and undone!"

When Mrs. Gardiner had opened the bundle, and seen all the twigs and leaves, she said they would burn the witch, and not wait long about it; so they flung the twigs and leaves into the fire; and while they were burning in came Jane Wenham, asking for Anne's mother, for she had, she said, a message to her, how that she was to go and wash next day at Ardley Bury, Sir Herbert Chauncey's place: which on inquiry turned out to be a falsehood: consequently Jane Wenham was set down doubly as a witch, the charm of burning her in the sticks having proved so effectual. John Chapman and his men then told their tale. Mr. Gardiner was not slow in fanning the flame into a fire, and poor old Jane was examined, searched for marks but none found, and committed to gaol, there to wait her trial at the next assizes. She earnestly entreated not to go to prison; protested her innocence, and appealed to Mrs. Gardiner to help her, woman-like, and not to swear against her; offering to submit to be swum—anything they would—so that she might be kept free of jail. But Sir Herbert Chauncey was just manly and rational enough not to allow of this test, though the Vicar of Ardeley tried her with the Lord's Prayer, which she could not repeat: and terrified and tortured her into a kind of confession, wherein she implicated three other women, who were immediately put under arrest, though they came to no harm in the end. When she was brought to trial, sixteen witnesses, including three clergymen, were standing there ready to testify against her, how that she had bewitched this one's cattle, and that one's sheep; and taken all the power from this one's body, and all the good from that one's gear; and slaughtered this child, and that man, by her evil eye and her curses; and in fact how that she had done all the mischief that had happened in the neighbourhood for years past. And there was Matthew Gilson, who had been sent mad, and forced to wander about the country with his shirt stuffed full of straw like a scarecrow; and Anne Thorne, who had had fits ever since her marvellous journey with the dislocated knee; and another Anne, very nearly as hardly holden as the first; and others beside, whom her malice had rendered sick and lame, and unfit for decent life: moreover, two veracious witnesses deposed positively to her taking the form of a cat when she would, and to hearing her converse with the devil when under the form of a cat, he also as a cat; together with Anne Thorne's distinct accusation that she was beset with cats—tormented exceedingly—and that all the cats had the face and the voice of Jane Wenham.

The lawyers, who believed little in the devil and less in witchcraft, refused to draw up the indictment on any other charge save that of "conversing familiarly with the devil in the form of a cat." But in spite of Mr. Bragge's earnest appeals against such profanation, and the ridicule which it threw over the whole matter, the jury found the poor old creature guilty, and the judge passed sentence of death against her. The evidence was too strong. Even one of the Mr. Chaunceys deposed that a cat came knocking at his door, and that he killed it—when it vanished away, for it was no other than one of Jane Wenham's imps; and all Mr. Gardiner's house went mad, some in one way and some in another: and credible witnesses deposed that they had seen pins come jumping through the air into Anne Thorne's mouth, and when George Chapman clapped his hand before her mouth to prevent them skipping in, he felt one stick against his hand, as sharp as might be; and every night Anne's pincushion was left full, and every morning found empty, and who but Jane could have conveyed them all from the pincushion into her mouth, where they were to be found all crooked and bent? But though the jury could not resist the tremendous weight of all this evidence, and the judge could not resist the jury, he managed to get a reprieve which left the people time to cool and reflect, and then he got a pardon for her—quietly and kindly done. And Colonel Plummer, of Gilston, took her under his protection, and gave her a small cottage near his house, where she lived, poor soul, in peace and safety for the end of her days, doing harm to no one and feared by none. As for Anne Thorne, the doctor, who had ordered her, as part of his remedy, to wash her hands and face twice a day in fair water, and who, as another part, had her watched and sat with by a "lusty young fellow" who asked nothing better, managed matters so well, that in a short time Anne and her brisk bachelor were married; and from that time we hear no more of her vomiting crooked pins, or being tormented with visions of cats wearing Jane Wenham's face, and speaking with Jane Wenham's voice. But though all the rest got well off with their frights and follies, no public compensation was given to poor old Jane for the brutal attacks of the mob upon her, for the hauling and maiming and scratching and tearing, by which they proved to their own satisfaction that she was a witch, and deserved only the treatment accorded to witches.

OUR LATEST.

But if the last officially condemned, Jane was not the last actually destroyed, for a curious MS. letter to be found in the British Museum "From Mr. Manning, Dissenting Teacher, at Halstead, in Essex, to John Morley, Esq., Halstead," gives us a strange garbled account of a reputed sacrifice; and the sadder and more brutal story of Ruth Osborne follows a few years after.

"Halstead, August 2, 1732.

"Sir—The narrative which I gave you in relation to witchcraft, and which you are pleased to lay your commands upon me to repeat, is as follows:—There was one Master Collett, a smith by trade, of Haveningham, in the county of Suffolk, who, as 'twas customary with him, assisting the maide to churne, and not being able (as the phrase is) to make the butter come, threw a hot iron into the churn, under the notion of witchcraft in the case, upon which a poore labourer, then employed in carrying of dung in the yard, cried out in a terrible manner, 'They have killed me, they have killed me;' still keeping his hand upon his back, intimating where the pain was, and died upon the spot. [160]

"Mr. Collett, with the rest of the servants then present, took off the poor man's clothes, and found to their great surprise, the mark of the iron that was heated and thrown into the churn, deeply impressed upon his back. This account I had from Mr. Collett's own mouth, who being a man of unblemished character, I verily believe to be matter of fact.

"I am, Sir, your obliged humble Servant,
"Sam. Manning."

---

[160] Thomas Wright.

The only falsehood, probably, in the history is the manner of the poor fellow's death, for either he was foully murdered on a wild suspicion of being concerned in the witching of a dirty milk vessel, or he died suddenly of some ordinary organic complaint, and the circumstances of the horse-shoe and the scarred back were purely imaginary. But again in 1751 was witch blood actually poured out on English soil, and the cry of the innocent murdered sent up to heaven in vain for mercy. At Tring, in Hertfordshire, lived an old man, one Osborne, and his wife; poor as witches always were; old—past seventy both of them—and obliged to beg from door to door for what, if the popular superstition was true, the devil had given them power to possess at any moment for themselves. But this was a point of view no one ever took. In the rebellion of '45, just six years ago, old Mother Osborne had gone to one Butterfield, a dairyman living at Gubblecot, to beg for buttermilk. Butterfield was a churlish fellow, and told her roughly that he had not enough for his hogs, still less for her. Says old Mother Osborne, grumbling, "The Pretender will soon have thee and thy hogs too." Now the Pretender and the devil were in league together, according to the belief of many, and old Mother Osborne might just as well have told the dairyman at once that he was going to the devil, or that she would send her imps to bewitch him; for soon Butterfield's calves became distempered, and soon his cows died, and his affairs went so far to the bad that he left his dairy and took a public house, in hopes that the imps which could bewitch the one might be powerless against the other. But he reckoned without his host, for in 1751 he himself was bewitched; he had fits—bad fits—and sent for a white witch all the way from Northamptonshire to tell him what ailed him. The white witch told him he was bewitched, and bade six men, with staves and pitchforks hanging round their necks as counter charms for their own safety, watch his house night and day. Doubtless they discovered all they were set there to seek.

Suddenly there appeared a notice that certain and various witches were to be ducked at Longmarston the 22nd day of April. A crowd assembled at Tring to watch the sport; and but one thought went through that crowd— the Osbornes were to be the ducked witches, and the sport they would have would be rare. The parish officers had taken the old couple into the workhouse for safety, but the mob broke through the gates, and crushed down the doors, and searched the whole place through, from end to end, even to the salt box, "lest the witch should have made herself little," and have hidden in the corners. But they could not find her, not even there; so, in a rage, they broke the windows, smashed the furniture, and then heaped up straw high against the house, threatening to burn it down, and every living soul within it, if the Osbornes were not given up them. The master was frightened; he had never faced such a scene before, and his nerve forsook him—not unreasonably. He brought the old people from their hiding place, and gave them up to that wild, tossing, furious mob. In a moment they were stripped stark naked, then cross- bound in the prescribed manner, wrapped loosely in a sheet, and dragged two miles along the road to a small pond or river, where with many a curse and many a kick they were thrown in, to prove whether they were witches or not. A chimney sweeper, called Colley, was the most active of the crew. Seeing that Mother Osborne did not sink, he waded into the water and turned her over with his stick. She slipped out of the sheet, and thus lay exposed, naked, and half choked with mud, before the brutal crowd, who saw nothing pitiful, and nothing shameful, in her state. After a time they dragged her out, flung her on the bank, and kicked and beat her till she died. Her husband died also, but not on the spot. The man who had arranged this rare diversion then went round among the crowd collecting money in return for his amusement. But government took the matter up. A coroner's inquest was held, and a verdict of wilful murder returned against Colley, the chimney sweep, who, much to his own surprise and the indignation of the people—many ranking him as a martyr—was hanged by the neck till he was dead, for the murder of the witch of Tring, poor old Ruth Osborne. The act against witchcraft, under colour and favour of which all the judicial murders had been done, had been repealed a few years before, namely, in 1736, and Colley's comrades bewailed piteously the degenerate times that were at hand, when a witch was no longer held fit sport for the public, but was protected and defended like ordinary folk, and let to live on to work her wicked will unchecked.

But the snake is scotched, not killed. So far are we in advance of the men of the ruder past, inasmuch as our superstitions, though quite as silly, are less cruel than theirs, and hurt no one but ourselves. Yet still we have our wizards and witches lurking round area gates and prowling through the lanes and yards of the remoter country districts; still we have our necromancers, who call up the dead from their graves to talk to us more trivial nonsense than ever they talked while living, and who reconcile us with earth and humanity by showing us how infinitely inferior are heaven and spirituality; still we have the unknown mapped out in clear lines sharp and firm; and still the impossible is asserted as existing, and men are ready to give their lives in attestation of what contravenes every law of reason and of nature; still we are not content to watch and wait and collect and fathom before deciding, but for every new group of facts or appearances must at once draw up a code of laws and reasons, and prove, to a mathematical certainty, the properties of a chimera, and the divine life and beauty—of a lie. Even the mere vulgar belief in witchcraft remains among the lower classes; as witness the old gentleman who died at Polstead not so long ago, and who, when a boy, had seen a witch swum in Polstead Ponds, "and she went over the water like a cork;" who had also watched another witch feeding her three imps like blackbirds; and who only wanted five pounds to have seen all the witches in the parish dance on a knoll together: as witness also the strange letter of the magistrate, in the 'Times' of April 7, 1857; and the stranger trial at Stafford, concerning the bewitched condition of the Charlesworths, small farmers living at Rugely, which trial is to be found in the 'Times' of March 28, 1857; the case reported by the clergyman of East Thorpe, Essex, who had actually to mount guard against the door of an old Trot accused of witchcraft; while the instances of silly servant maids, and fortune tellers whose hands are to be crossed with silver, and the stars propitiated with cast off dresses and broken meat, are as numerous as ever. And, indeed, so long as conviction without examination, and belief without proof, pass as the righteous operations of faith, so long will superstition and credulity reign supreme over the mind, and the functions of critical reason be abandoned and foresworn. And as it seems to me that credulity is even a less desirable frame of mind than scepticism, I have set forth this collection of witch stories as landmarks of the excesses to which a blind belief may hurry and impel humanity, and perhaps as some slight aids to that much misused common sense which the holders of impossible theories generally consider "enthusiastic," and of "a nobler life" to tread under foot, and loftily ignore.

www.ingramcontent.com/pod-product-compliance
Lightning Source LLC
Chambersburg PA
CBHW060808030726
47503CB00002B/386